OF CORPSE

OF CORPSE
Death and Humor in Folklore and Popular Culture

Edited by

PETER NARVÁEZ

UTAH STATE UNIVERSITY PRESS
Logan, Utah
2003

Cover design by Nancy Banks.
Manufactured in Canada.

An earlier version of Ellis's essay "Making a Big Apple Crumble" was published in the online journal *New Directions in Folklore,* 6 June 2002 (www.temple.edu/isllc/newfolk/index.html). Used by permission.
An earlier version of Harlow's essay "Creating Situations" was published in the *Journal of American Folklore* 110 (1997:140–168). Used by permission.
An earlier version of Kugelmass's essay "Wishes Come True" was published in the *Journal of American Folklore* 104 (1991:443–465). Used by permission.
An earlier version of Narváez's essay "Tricks and Fun" was published in *Western Folklore* 53 (1994:263–293). Used by permission.
A version of Roth's essay can be found as part of a larger essay in *Shakedown Street: The Art of Deadheads,* forthcoming from the University Press of Mississippi. Used by permission.

Library of Congress Cataloging-in-Publication Data

Of corpse : death and humor in folklore and popular culture / edited by
Peter Narváez.
p. cm.
Includes bibliographical references and index.
ISBN 0-87421-559-5 (pbk.)
1. Death—Folklore. 2. Death—Humor. I. Narváez, Peter.
GR455.O43 2003
398.27—dc21

2003004641

CONTENTS

Acknowledgments vii

Introduction: The Death-Humor Paradox 1
Peter Narváez

PART ONE: *Disaster Jokes*

1 Jokes That Follow Mass-Mediated Disasters in a Global Electronic Age 15
Christie Davies

2 Making a Big Apple Crumble: The Role of Humor in Constructing a Global Response to Disaster 35
Bill Ellis

PART TWO: *Rites of Passage*

3 Creating Situations: Practical Jokes and the Revival of the Dead in Irish Tradition 83
Ilana Harlow

4 Tricks and Fun: Subversive Pleasures at Newfoundland Wakes 113
Peter Narváez

5 "Pardon Me for Not Standing": Modern American Graveyard Humor 140
Richard E. Meyer

PART THREE: *Festivals*

6 Wishes Come True: Designing the Greenwich Village Halloween Parade 171
Jack Kugelmass

7 Making Merry with Death: Iconic Humor in Mexico's Day of the Dead 198
Kristin Congdon

8 *Calaveras:* Literary Humor in Mexico's Day of the Dead 221
Stanley Brandes

9 Exit Laughing: Death and Laughter in Los Angeles and Port-au-Prince 239
Donald J. Cosentino

PART FOUR: *Popular Culture*

10 Dancing Skeletons: The Subversion of Death Among Deadheads 263
LuAnne K. Roth

11 Traditional Narrative, Popular Aesthetics, *Weekend at Bernie's*, and Vernacular Cinema 294
Mikel Koven

Notes 311

References 335

Contributors 352

Index 354

ACKNOWLEDGMENTS

I would like to voice my appreciation to some of the people who have made this book possible. First and foremost, I would like to thank the contributors for their continuing interest and patience. Michael Spooner, Director, Utah State University Press, has been supportive throughout the project and has provided invaluable advice at critical moments. Special gratitude goes to Ilana Harlow, Lara Maynard, and Holly Everett for their extensive editorial input at various stages of the work. All my colleagues, as well as many of my students, in the Department of Folklore, Memorial University of Newfoundland, have discussed the topic of this book with me over the years; I have learned much from your wisdom. Sharon Cochrane and Cindy Turpin, from the staff of the department, supplied important communications assistance. Finally, I want to express my heartfelt appreciation to Holly, my wife, for her discerning eye, keen wit, consideration and love.

INTRODUCTION
The Death-Humor Paradox

PETER NARVÁEZ

In October 2002, after soliciting and critiquing over 40,000 jokes from seventy countries, Richard Wiseman (University of Hertfordshire), in collaboration with the British Association for the Advancement of Science, proclaimed the "world's funniest joke," a narrative submitted by Gurpal Gosall (Manchester, UK):

> A couple of New Jersey hunters are out in the woods when one of them falls to the ground. He doesn't seem to be breathing, his eyes are rolled back in his head. The other guy whips out his cell phone and calls the emergency services. He gasps to the operator: "My friend is dead! What can I do?" The operator, in a calm soothing voice says: "Just take it easy. I can help. First, let's make sure he's dead." There is a silence, then a shot is heard. The guy's voice comes back on the line. He says: "OK, now what?"
>
> www.laughlab.co.uk/winner.html: October 3, 2002

As the essays in this volume reveal, the fact that the winning joke features a theme of death is hardly surprising, nor are its mechanisms of humor. Laughter, humor theory suggests, is a socially constructed form of communication (Carrell 1997; Fine 1997a, 1997b; Norrick 1993) that expresses pleasure (Morreall 1983, 38-59). Moreover, as Thomas Hobbes (1588-1679) argued in 1650 with his famous descriptive, "sudden glory" (see Bergler 1956, 4-6; Gruner 1978, 29-30; Holland 1982, 44-47), laughter is often prompted by a sudden perception of incongruity (Alden et al 2000; Forabosco 1992; Koestler 1964; Morreall 1989; Oring 1992, 1-15, 1995a), that makes us feel superior to others. From Sigmund Freud's point of view, the aggressive pleasure of tendentious humor is a transformative, defensive process that can provide relief for repressed energies (inhibitions, thoughts, feelings) (Freud 1960 [1905]:181-236; also see Portous 1988). In conflating humor and death, the previous joke suddenly juxtaposes a serious matter, concern for the health of a collapsed hunting companion, with an absurd, murderous action—shooting him.

We are surprised by this incongruity and we laugh. More specifically, however, the depiction of the hunter protagonist as a fool, for his thoughtless misinterpretation of procedural advice from an operator, develops social distance between "us," the group comprised of the sophisticated narrator and laughing audience, and the inferior character in the joke. Derision is furthered by the protagonist's association with New Jersey, for this identification reifies a negative trait (stupidity) of a widespread country bumpkin "Jersey" stereotype, particularly relished by New Yorkers. Thus, in commenting on this joke, *New York Times* columnist Pamela LiCalzi O'Connell quipped, "it appears there is one element that universally adds to a joke's appeal: mention New Jersey" (2002). Whether the laughter of persons bearing such politically incorrect thoughts releases repressed energies is debatable, but familiarity with how the stereotype has been expressed in the past through humor, means that the "cognitive shift" (see Latta 1999) involved in the anticipation of foolish behavior from jocular New Jersey personae, greatly depends on *memories of past emotional experience,* a common characteristic of laughter affirmed in recent humor theory research (see Cetola 1988).

Given the importance of the past for our recognition of the comic, it follows that some "traditions," i.e., creative re-enactments through time, dispose us to ludic responses. The studies in this anthology, which takes its title from childhood wordplay, examine specific traditions of text (jokes, poetry, epitaphs, iconography, film drama) and social context (rites, festivals) that shape and generate laughter and drollery. Uniquely, however, these essays explore the remarkable paradox exhibited in the above joke—the convergence of death and humor.

THE DEATH-HUMOR PARADOX

My research into this paradox has centered on the "merry wake" in Newfoundland (see essay in this volume). Initially, however, my interest in the subject was triggered by encounters with similar instances of death-humor mixes in Newfoundland vernacular song (Narváez 1995). Having one of the world's great fisheries, numerous Newfoundland traditional songs concern disasters at sea ("The *Southern Cross,*" "The Loss of the *Jubal Cain,*" "The *Greenland* Disaster"). Folksong scholar Kenneth S. Goldstein persuasively argued that the lyrics of many such songs contain meanings of "religious fatalism" (Goldstein 1985). The last lines of "The Schooner *Huberry*" as sung by ballad singer Dorman Ralph typify this sentiment.

It is a sad occurrence but it happens every year,
The sea takes to the cemetery the lives of one's most dear,
They will be buried throughout our land in summer, spring and fall,
And how that they got cast away it's a mystery to us all.
No more to watch on a stormy deep and expecting them to come;
They got the call both one and all, for God has called them home.
(Ralph 1999)

Yet, as I have found, not all Newfoundland songs concerning the death of community members treat the subject so seriously. One example that unexpectedly juxtaposes the solemn and the frivolous is the Newfoundland elegiac song, "The Fisher Who Died in his Bed." Collected in 1961 by musicologist Kenneth Peacock from singer Patrick Rossiter of Fermeuse, the song exhibits a moving, mournful minor melody with lyrics that presumably pay tribute to a deceased friend. As similar items of occupational folklore which extol the skills of worker heroes, the first three stanzas generally praise fisher Jim Jones for his craftsmanship, speed, strength, physical endurance, and courage while on the job—the pursuit of fish (cod).

Old Jim Jones the fisher, the trapper, the trawler,
Jim Jones the fish-killin' banker [the Grand Banks] is dead.
No fisherman surely never stepped in a dory [small fishing craft]
Like Jim Jones the fisher who died in his bed.
Was there any old fellow tied sods or made bobbers
And set out his trawls in the dark it is said?
No fisherman ever braved such stormy weather
Like Jim Jones the trawler who died in his bed.
Jim Jones he would surely go out in a dory
And set out his traps all weighed down with lead.
No fisher from side on hauled traps with such tide on
As Jim Jones the trapper who died in his bed.

While wonderfully specific with regard to fishing equipment (uses of cod traps, trawl lines, sods and bobbers [as floats], lead weights), the sentiments of these verses are in keeping with heroic eulogies, for they focus on Jones's extraordinary efforts. The fourth stanza continues in this vein, but describes more mundane occupational operations, praising the protagonist for his ability to sort his fish trap catches by ridding them of unwanted species, such as dogfish, a necessary, but perfunctory task.

In the foggiest of weather he'd set out the leader [leading net to cod trap],
But who in the devil this side of the Head [place name]
Could haul up such codfish or pick out the dogfish
Like old skipper Jones who died in his bed.

The fifth and sixth verses similarly cite Jones's workaday dealings with gutting fish, saving valuable cod livers (for oil) and salting fish. But the flow of such positive sentiments about routine occupational techniques is suddenly shattered when the singer becomes humorously critical of the deceased, shifting his focus to Jones's avarice, wryly depicting him as a "glutton" for eating excessive amounts of cods' heads (cheeks) and as a common dog ("crackie") for consuming large amounts chewing tobacco.

There was never such a salter this side of the water
There was never such a glutton for eating cods' heads.
There never was a crackie who could chaw tobaccy
Like old skipper Jones who died in his bed.
Was there any old fisher or any old fellow
Cut throats or split fish or tear off the head?
For I'm darned if I ever saw one who'd pick liver
So fast as our skipper who died in his bed.

In final humorous aspersions, the last stanzas portray Skipper Jim Jones as a unique captain who aroused anxieties in others when he sailed the Atlantic (made them "frantic") and who, unlike heroic worker role models who gasp their last breath while engaged in colossal occupational effort (e.g. "John Henry"), peacefully "died in his bunk."

Is there any old fellow this side of the harbour
Sailed out of the harbour or tacked round the Head?
It would make you all frantic to sail the Atlantic
With old Skipper Jones who died in his bed.
His fishing days ended, his traps are unmended,
His trawls are all rotten, his fishing boat sunk,
And his days as a rover are finished and over,
Old Skipper Jim Jones who died in his bunk.
(Fowke 1984; Peacock 1965 I, 127–128; my explanatory brackets)

Thus, even though he is honored, the deceased Skipper Jones becomes the butt of humorous raillery which falls solidly into what Edward Ives long ago observed as the "satirical song tradition" of the Northeast (Ives 1962).

This example from Newfoundland song stems from long-established fishery traditions, but its blending of the serious and the ludic is most contemporary. Paradoxical juxtapositions of death and humor in today's world are on the rise, and an understanding of traditional combinations of this nature may assist us in coping with present realities. As our understandings of space and society have altered through communication technologies that offer global perspectives, the universal enigma of death looms as never before. Real and fictive visions of war, genocide, murder, natural catastrophes, disease and simply the biological process of aging, regularly appear at the flick of a remote control, all constantly reminding us of the fragility of our mortality. For many, therefore, death strikes both virtually, via electronic communications, and actually, as they experience the social reality of death amongst family, friends and acquaintances. Whether such experiences are immediate or virtual, individuals today may grieve (mild to intense) in response to a wide variety of death events. Bereaving persons may conventionally turn to traditions of institutionalized religion for the solace that their encompassing metanarratives offer, comfort based on doctrines which promise immortality, such as that offered in "The Schooner *Huberry*." However, they may also turn to more paradoxical traditions, such as the satirical song tradition represented by "The Fisher Who Died in his Bed" or the other vernacular traditions studied in this book, all of which offer humorous avenues for understanding and coping with death in less cosmological and more egalitarian ways.

FOLKLORISTICS AND DEATH

This work joins a growing number of folklore studies that focus on private and public traditions of death (Barrera 1991; Bennett and Rowbottom 1998; Brady 1988; Butler 1982; Cooper and Sciorra 1994; Everett 2002; Griffith 1992; Kvideland 1980; Meyer 1993; Pocius 2001; Santino 1994, 2001; Zeitlin and Harlow 2001). The majority of these works have dealt with serious sides of bereavement. Folklorists studying humor, however, have sometimes examined themes of death and the dead, especially as part of "sick," "cruel" and disastrous event joke cyles (see Nilsen 1993, 78-84; Gruner 1997, 41-73). Some of the best known of these studies are the psychological analyses of Alan Dundes (1987, 3-38). His treatment of "The Dead Baby Joke Cycle" of the 1960s and 1970s interpreted such jests as products of the rapid social changes that took place in American culture during the period. The cycle provided, therefore, "a means for adolescents ... to relieve their anxiety about impending parenthood" and remain a child, through the fantasy of "avoiding or disposing of unwanted babies" (13-14). In an examination of "Auschwitz jokes," Dundes scrutinized a cycle of anti-Semitic jests told in post World War II Germany. Quite unlike "gallows humor" (Obrdlik 1942; Hertzler 1970, 134-135; Goldstein and McGhee 1972, 104-105), humorous bravado expressed by condemned persons, these orally circulated hate jokes have been generated by oppressors. His analysis emphasizes the psychological function of catharsis for the bearers of such traditions. Tellers, he argues, have assuaged guilt feelings for the horrors of genocide "through an insidious form of projection," wherein "Jews are depicted as masochists; they enjoy being victimized" (35-37). As Dundes sadly observes, "prejudice, stereotyping, gross inhumanity, and even ethnic genocide do not seem to be on the wane" (38).

Unlike the contributions of Dundes, the essays in this volume provide ethnographic rather than symbolic expositions. Some of the forms examined in joke cycles, like those treated by Dundes, express extreme ethnocentrism, particularly the responses to the terrorist attacks on New York's World Trade Center. The majority, however, do not, and in many ways are testimonies to the resilience of the human spirit. In face of death, life's most solemn mystery, people frequently play and laugh. As the authors show, the juxtaposition of death and humor arises in many circumstances—occasions of direct bereaving for the passing of a known loved one; contexts of local, regional, national and global mourning for deceased persons known about but not known personally; encounters with the dead in material, carnivalesque, spiritual and symbolic forms; and finally in the contexts of fictive entertainments. Most of these events reflect traditional, small group, face-to-face human communications (folklore) both in content and enactment. As well, technologically mediated communications evidence similar messages globally, in virtual, rhetorical communities.

In their sociocultural contexts, the humorous responses to death described in this collection cover the full gamut of the ludic, from mild mirth (death iconography) to outright hilarity (jokes, pranks). Traditional manifestations of death dealt with include: *death as cosmological design*—an otherworld of magico-religious significance, reified through ritual; *death as divine or semi-divine being(s)* possessing extraordinary magico-religious powers; *death as restless soul*, sometimes trapped in a liminal area; *death as a sociable cadaver* who interacts with the living; and *death as space and time*—sites of death and calendar events concerning death and its history, often related to specific structures and spaces, as well as places of tragedy and interment.

THE ESSAYS

The essays in this book have been divided into four sections based on folkloric genres (jokes, rites of passage, festivals) and the culture of popular entertainments (music events, dramatic film comedy). Contributors to the first section on "Disaster Jokes" treat the most widespread contemporary examples of the death-humor paradox. In his initial essay on jokes which follow mediated disasters, sociologist Christie Davies argues that until the 1960s, when the medium of television triumphed, there were no "set piece jokes about particular disastrous events or the deaths of celebrities." Far from viewing the popular jests that followed as "sick," Davies' examination of joke cycles concerning celebrities and disasters convincingly interprets them as having been spawned through the mediating reportage of television, which given its emotional manipulation and its mosaic presentation of juxtaposing the serious and the ridiculous, truth and fantasy (e.g., disaster vis-à-vis trivial advertisements or game shows), provided appropriate contexts of incongruity and paradox for humorous response.[1] From such a reading, the creation and proliferation of contemporary disaster jokes, through oral and Internet means, may be understood as "resistance to a hegemony of feeling" and "one of the most modern and most democratic forms of folklore."

Bill Ellis's important essay on the role of humor in the construction of a global response to the tragic events of September 11, 2001 delineates the appearances of verbal and graphic World Trade Center (WTC) jests from a variety of sources, but primarily from the Internet through the author's monitoring of message boards. As he notes, this particular method allowed him to examine "the emergence of WTC jokes in unprecedented detail." Thus Ellis is able to describe "risible moments," i.e., points "at which making and passing on jokes provokes laughter and provides social rewards that outweigh the social risks of being thought sick or insensitive," as well as waves of popularity for specific forms of WTC humor in national and international contexts. His findings stress the distinctness of North American and British expressions and note the paucity of sentiments that might reflect a unified global community.

In his remarkably insightful work *An Essay on Laughter* (1907), James Sully discerned that a social occasion highly conducive to laughter was one "in which an unusual degree of solemnity is forced upon us" (79). Perhaps nothing could be more incongruous, and therefore potentially funny (despite taboos), than living persons socializing with and/or physically manipulating the dead in the midst of solemn religious ritual. Yet this is exactly what is described in the next section, "Rites of Passage," in articles by Harlow and Narváez on the rite known as the "Irish wake" or the "merry wake" (also see Abrahams 1982; Glasgow 1997, 136- 137). Harlow's research on Irish wakes details a variety of ludic activities which once flourished before official religious intervention. Focusing on practical jokes involving corpse manipulation, she finds that wake humor of this kind reflects a more general tendency in Irish tradition that is still maintained today, the "provocative ludic impulse," exhibited in activities in which protagonists "create situations" through verbal dueling ("slagging," "blaggarding") and verbal deception ("winding people up," "codding").[2]

My own essay centers on both the Newfoundland context of the merry wake as a cultural scene of courtship amongst youth, as well as the wake amusements themselves—the games, jokes, and songs that were popular at such events in Newfoundland's recent past. In face of measures taken by official religious authorities to curb the revelry of such occasions, the counter-hegemonic tactics developed by participants to maintain wake activities (e.g., hiding the corpse) may be viewed as popular subversive attempts to maintain egalitarian, local traditions.

In contrast to the collective activities of wakes, the verbal and graphic texts of American graveyard humor analyzed by Richard Meyer accent the expressions of unique individuals in reponse to a last rite of passage—interment.[3] A valuable overview of a complex subject, which has generated its own popular culture of spurious epitaph books, Meyer observes that historically, gravemarker commemoration has voiced "communal rather than personal perspectives and values," but that "since the 1960s commemoration has moved toward its individualized, personalized opposite." Thus contemporary American gravemarker texts incorporate idiosyncratic, recreational, occupational and popular culture elements in melanges that retrospectively celebrate activities of life "not death, the hereafter, or abstract metaphysical principles." Within this populist context, however, humor is linked to strong personalities who could "find a laugh even in death."

As R.D.V. Glasgow has written, overcoming death often means celebrating something that "cannot be genuinely separated from life," i.e., engaging in activities that "acknowledge that life and death are mutually interdependent, two sides of the same mortal coin" (136). The studies in the third section examine social leveling through celebratory laughter at festivals and calendar customs associated with death. All four articles cite syncretistic, cultural blending linked to Christian calendar holidays—All Hallows Eve ("Halloween," October 31), All Saints Day (November 1), All Souls Day (November 2), and additionally in the case of Haiti, Carnival (celebrations before Lent). In the first essay, Jack Kugelmass considers a localized Halloween tradition that has become one of New York City's major festival events—the Greenwich Village Halloween parade. As he explains, contemporary Halloween festivities blend Christian and Celtic (*Samhain*) elements that intertwine "notions of death, rebirth and celebration." However, the syncretistic roots of this North American festival are not the reasons for its popularity in Greenwich Village. Rather, it is the frame that Halloween provides for licentious behavior that attracts parade participants, whose masquerades and bizarre antics celebrate "a Bohemian, artistic, and frequently, gay way of life." The frequent uses of death masks (amongst many others, often displaying themes of playful sexuality) in this annual community validation of non-normative lifestyles, has been particularly significant in the context of the AIDS pandemic (also see Tannen and Morris 1989). Emphasizing the complex motivations for such events, however, Kugelmass suggests that the individualism exhibited in unique parade costumes and behaviors reflects the privatization of late capitalism, an expansion of the sexual self, and "an implicit rejection of the collective self prescribed within the Judeo-Christian tradition."

The essays by Kristin Congdon and Stanley Brandes focus on humorous *calaveras* (literally skulls, skeletons), traditions of Mexico's *Día de los Muertos* (Day of the Dead). The *calaveras* traditions researched by Congdon—customs (dancing with smiling cardboard skeletons, eating skulls made of sugar), the popular political art of José Guadalupe Posada (1852-1913), and the papier-mâché objects of the Linares family—all provide skeletal representations whereby the poor symbolically strip the wealthy of their sartorial elegance and pomposity to celebrate, as she notes, "the democratic spirit of death." Brandes's close examination of Day of the Dead literary *calaveras*, a parallel journalistic form stemming from the mid-nineteenth century, shows how these mock epitaphs constitute an anti-authoritarian satirical tradition which continues to scathingly critique Mexico's power elite (politicians, police, clergy). As Brandes relates, the death symbolism of this poetry "situates these public figures on the level of the common man."

In a similar vein, Donald J. Cosentino's personal ethnographic account, entitled "Death and Laughter in Los Angeles and Port-au-Prince" highlights the role of the Haitian family of playful, erotic death spirits known as *Gedes* during Carnival 1991. A particularly momentous time because of the democratic defeat (December 1990) of the despotic Duvalier regime by John-Bertrand Aristide, power reversal was dramatized by counter-hegemonic *Gedes* who as "bums, louts, and outlaws" were "all the more popular for their bad manners." Consentino observes that the equitable ideological implications of *Gede* antics have long been clear: "as state authority has refined its mechanisms of oppression, so too has Gede sharpened his flip-off."

Egalitarian chords are also struck in the last section, which features essays on death and humor in popular music and film. The first by LuAnne Roth on The Grateful Dead (a.k.a. "The Dead"), shows how the folkloric name and ludic iconography of this rock band nurtured participatory, cultural scenes of collective merriment. Similar to collective uses of *calaveras*, Deadhead subculture has embraced and parodied death ("I'd rather be Dead," "Born again Deadhead"). As Roth notes, an iconography of grinning skeletons has transformed death imagery "into a celebration of life manifested in music, dance and community."

After providing a fascinating survey of traditional "corpocentric" elements (motifs, tale types, legends involving corpses) in contemporary film, Mikel Koven's concluding essay deals with the popular aesthetics of "vernacular cinema," i.e., "films which demonstrate high resonance with an audience." For his case study, he inspects *Weekend at Bernie's*, a film employing the humorous manipulation of a corpse, which was universally dismissed by critics but supported at the box office. In considering this "dissonance between reviewers and audiences," Koven applies his adaptation of Walter Ong's "psychodynamics" theory of orality (formulaic repetition, crudeness in characterization, agonistic tone) and finds that *Bernie's* addresses today's "neo-orality" (1982). Ultimately, however, he contends that the film's success depended on its combination of oral address with traditional elements which have "stood the test of time." As a humorous idea, Koven maintains, "problematic corpse disposal still has currency today."

DEATH IN THE MULTICULTURAL MATRIX

While death may be viewed as a biological state that prompts psychophysiological responses from the living, such as weeping, hysteria (see

Morreall 1983, 57), and the uncontrolled laughter of bereaving persons (*fou rire*), what we perceive and communicate about death, that is, our ideas and attitudes toward that state, and their resultant behavioral and material manifestations, are cultural constructs. Such a construct is portrayed by Philip Ariès in his brilliant historical treatise, *The Hour of Our Death.* This influential work chronologically traces Western attitudes toward death, from an early orientation (500 to 1100 AD), wherein death was accepted as a part of life ("tame death"), to the invisibility of death in the twentieth century orientation of "death denied." His argument is convincing, meticulously documented and undoubtedly true. Yet it is an over-simplified picture by virtue of its emphasis on normative elite thought. While he admits the existence of "vestiges" (Ariès 1981, xv) of previous attitudes concerning death at any given time, his account exhibits a trajectory that does not deviate from its course in interpreting the documentation of dominant groups (clerics, lords, mercantile interests, corporate entities), to the neglect of working-class and marginalized voices. The essays in this volume provide a foil for Ariés' argument of "death denied" in our contemporary world, for they reveal a rich tapestry of varying views toward death, in these cases reflecting humor, that have simultaneously evolved in twentieth and twenty-first century multicultural environments. In the West and on its margins, alternative streams of thought concerning death continue to sustain themselves in great variety while co-existing with dominating currents, one of which Ariès describes so well.

En toto, these essays provide a wide variety of interpretations for complex expressive forms that link death and humor. Such forms may be understood as provocative socializing agents, celebrations of life, counter-hegemonic means of resistance, customs that facilitate courtship, or neo-oral statements. But a point of commonality with regard to their social functions is that whether it is in the context of a graveyard, wake, festival, joking session, or movie theatre, all of these expressions appear to unite groups through their own aesthetics of laughter. By disengaging themselves, i.e. letting down their guard together within play frames of humor, people collectively communicate in ways normatively judged as unsavory, affirming their own meanings, both in the face of official culture and death itself. Whether it alleviates the pain of loss, lessens fear of the unknown, or celebrates life in face of demise, the commingling of humor and death in informal and ritualistic circumstances appears to be a human universal, a technique for communicating and dealing with the enigma of our precarious mortality.

PART ONE

Disaster Jokes

1

JOKES THAT FOLLOW MASS-MEDIATED DISASTERS IN A GLOBAL ELECTRONIC AGE

Christie Davies

During the last forty years or so, "disasters"—such as a famine, an earthquake, the crashing of a plane, train, or spaceship, a multiple murder, or the sudden death of a celebrity—have tended to receive extensive, vivid, tear-jerking television coverage, often rapidly followed by a cycle of gruesome jokes. The jokes begin within hours or even minutes of the disaster's melodramatic presentation on television, rapidly increase in number, peak a couple of months later, and then new jokes cease to be created, bringing the cycle not to an end but to a plateau. The jokes no longer circulate as something new and exciting, but remain present in people's memories, notebooks, and computers. Here are some British and American favorites of the 1980s; they are examples of one of the most modern and most democratic forms of folklore, a truly people's joke, a joke of, by, and for the people that bypasses all official modes of transmission:

Regarding the death of Jessica Savitch, an American television personality:

> Why did Jessica Savitch drown?
> She was an anchorwoman.
> (Bronner 1985, 75)

Regarding the ferry disaster in 1987, when the *The Herald of Free Enterprise* sank outside Zeebrugge, with the loss of 193 lives:

> Why is *The Herald of Free Enterprise* like French contraception?
> Roll on, roll off, and the place is full of dead seamen.
> (In oral circulation in Britain in the late 1980s)

Regarding an explosion and fire on the oil-rig *Piper Alpha* in 1988, in which 166 workers were burnt to death:

Where do *Piper Alpha* workers go on holiday?
Burnham-on-Sea.

What's got four legs and goes woof?
Piper Alpha.
(In oral circulation in Britain in the late1980s)

It is, perhaps, significant that fifteen years later it is necessary to explain these jokes to the reader, even though they were major television stories at the time. They were tragedies for the individuals who died and for their families, but for others they were events that will not figure in a general history of the twentieth century. They will likely figure only in television documentaries, partly because television is self-referential and self-obsessed, and partly because pictures are a higher priority for the producers than the scholarship of their historical advisers. The Treaty of Versailles is thus reduced in television documentaries to an old (and therefore speeded up) black-and-white film of Lloyd George, Clémenceau, and Wilson trotting out of a building, raising their top hats to the crowd, and replacing them with unnatural celerity. It is a trivial and, incidentally, comic picture that no producer of "good," i.e., fatuous, television can resist. Likewise, the only convenient way for the author to check the details of the disasters that produced successive joke cycles in Britain in the late 1980s was to consult the Internet.[1] Most individuals do not remember the dates or scale of these disasters, or even what they were.

THE ABSENCE OF DISASTER JOKES IN THE PAST

It is important to note that jokes of this kind certainly did not exist in substantial numbers, and indeed probably did not exist at all, before the rise of television. "Sick" humor existed, but it did not crystallize in this particular form, as may be seen from a brief look at the history of such humor. There was no shortage of sick humor in the past (Davies 1990; Dundes 1987, 3–7; Gruner 1997, 41–53; Wilde 1979), including humor about death and destruction, but there are no set piece jokes about particular disastrous events or the deaths of celebrities. Before television, the human potential for telling such jokes was clearly already there, but the appropriate stimulus was absent.

Many sick and cynical humorous items, notably songs (Murdoch 1990; Palmer 1990; *Oh What a Lovely War* 1967) emerged from the worst disaster experienced by English-speaking peoples in the twentieth century, the First World War, but not set piece disaster jokes. It might well be wondered why men confronted with death, on a scale and with a directness unknown to their comfortable descendants watching televised disasters, should have enjoyed such humor, but that is not the question asked here. Rather, what is striking is that there are no sick riddle jokes left over from the First World War to circulate among soldiers and civilians alike; no jokes to grow old as the joke tellers who grow old might yet remember them. Jokes could have been told but they were not, nor did those who learned of distant disasters from the press or radio invent such jokes in either wartime or peacetime in the nineteenth and early twentieth centuries. There are no *contemporary* jokes about the Tay Bridge Disaster, the assassination of President Lincoln, the blowing up of the U.S. battleship *Maine* in Havana, the strangling of the exotic dancer Isadora Duncan when her trailing scarf got caught in the wheels of her car, or the mass murders by John Reginald Halliday Christie. Not even the eating of the Reverend Harold Davidson, the rector of Stiffkey in Norfolk, England, by a lion in a Skegness, England, amusement park in 1937 (Paris 1999, 65) produced a cycle of jokes. The idea of a Christian being eaten by a lion clearly amused the British public of the 1930s, as may be seen from the popularity of the comic monologue *The Lion and Albert* (Edgar 1932). Yet no jokes were invented about the scandalous rector who, after being defrocked for gross sexual irregularities, ended his life in a lion's den. Today, a televised news report on the ex-rector's career would produce scores of jokes from inventive viewers, but in 1937 there was no television, and there were no jokes.

The few jokes in circulation today that do dwell on long past disasters, such as the sinking of the *Titanic*, were, so far as we can tell, invented long after the events to which they refer. In the case of the *Titanic*, the jokes emerged mainly after the visually spectacular film of the late 1990s.

THE EARLIEST SICK JOKES

The first appearance of sick jokes with a short, quick, modern format occurred in the 1940s with variants of the little moron jokes, and in the cruel jokes of the 1950s (Gruner 1997, 54; Sutton-Smith 1960). Among these jokes are some that refer to *past* well-published disasters:

> Happy Father's Day, Mr. Lindbergh.
> (Sutton-Smith 1960, 21)

> Other than that, Mrs. Lincoln, how did you like the play?
> (Sutton-Smith 1960, 21)

Brian Sutton-Smith (1960, 12; see also Gruner 1997, 54) was able to collect 155 "cruel jokes" in the autumn of 1958 alone, which he divided into subsets with names such as cruel jokes, gruesomes, grimsels, sick jokes, and the comedy of horror:

> But Warden, I like Joe.
> Shut up and pull the switch.
> (Sutton-Smith 1960, 14)

> I'm going to take you out of the parade, if you don't stop dragging your cross.
> (Sutton-Smith 1960, 20)

However, the jokes still did *not* refer to *current* events. Indeed, they were generally non-specific. Most of them were one-liners, in contrast to the riddle jokes with a complex and sophisticated link between question and answer, (as distinct from unresolved nonsense riddles) of the kind that emerged in the 1960s, grew in the 1970s and 1980s, and boomed in the 1990s and into the new millennium. By the beginning of the 1960s, though, all the key elements were in place, namely major cycles of sick jokes, told mainly but not exclusively by young people, and the beginning of the production on a large scale of question-and-answer riddle jokes, notably those about ethnic minorities:

> How do you get a Polack out of a swimming pool?
> Throw in a bar of soap.
> (In oral circulation in America in the early 1960s)

The emergence of such jokes in America by the early 1960s indicates the growth of a mocking sense of humor, especially among the young, which violated the American pieties of the late 1950s. These included the belief in the equality, assimilation, and Americanization of immigrants, respect for religion (crucifixion jokes are not anti-clerical, but about the very core events, narratives, and faith of Christianity), and obsessive cleanliness. The humor also defied the appropriate sense of gravity and concern to be adopted towards death and disaster. These jokes of the late 1950s and early 1960s occurred during a period of confident modernity, and of faith in progress and science and in economic growth through the beneficent oligopolistic competition of big business, which were producing endless product improvements and wealth. The emergence of such jokes at this time completely refutes the explanations for the emergence of these jokes, put forward in terms of the much more recent emergence of a supposed period of post-modernity and its associated doubts (Paton, Powell, and Wagg 1996, 7; Ellis 1996, 226). Indeed, the much earlier emergence of such jokes further undermines the usual understanding of post-modernity as a distinctively *fin de siècle* phenomenon. The timing of the origins of the jokes demonstrates once again that there is no such thing as post-modernity (Davies 1999), and it is ironic that a generation ever more trapped in an iron cage of modernity should think that they have escaped into post-modernity. That said, we live in an unreflective, non-reflexive age (Davies and Neal 1998).

KENNEDY AND THE FIRST DEAD CELEBRITY JOKES OF AN ELECTRONIC AGE

All that was missing in the jokes of this time was any specific references to current events. This element only emerged and fell into place in the 1960s, with the total triumph of television as the medium that provided a new kind of disaster reporting, in which the audience cannot avoid the intrusive pressure of dominating pictures combined with insistent moralistic commentary about how they ought to feel. You are watching Big Brother, and he is talking to you.

This was the crucial new factor that precipitated the new sick disaster jokes based on current events. We can see it emerge through the evolution of jokes about the death of President Kennedy. Before his death, there were already jokes about his Roman Catholicism and the decisive effect that it might have on his politics (a very controversial issue at the time), and the form of the jokes was well-established. With Kennedy's assassination, and the first ever tear-jerking television coverage of the death of a celebrity, came the first cycle of dead celebrity disaster jokes. Possibly it had a precursor in the one-liner joke about the assassination of Lincoln from the 1950s cited earlier, but Kennedy's assassination provided the first joke cycle about a contemporary disaster, and coincided with the growth and dominance of television coverage of a particular style and type. First the political jokes about Kennedy's religion:

> Have you heard the Kennedy jokes? Well, he (JFK) was asking everyone to save their old bowling balls—he was going to make a rosary for the statue of liberty.
>
> (UCBFA[2] Anglo-American file. Jokes II-2, F3, P6 U9 K4. Collected by Michael Denas 1965, circulating in 1961)

Did you hear that President Kennedy is going to reinstate Roosevelt's "fire-side chats" program? It's going to be called "coast to coast with the Holy Ghost."

(UCBFA Anglo-American file. Jokes II-2, F3, P6 U9 K4. Collected by Marcia Rasumoff)

Then came the assassination:

Question: What did Johnson say to Mrs. Kennedy?
Answer: I guess John needed that trip to Dallas like a hole in the head!

(UCBFA Anglo-American file. Jokes II-2, F3, P6 U9 K4. Collected by Jane Rudofsky. In circulation in Los Angeles in 1962 a few days after the assassination)

What did John-John get for his fifth birthday?
A Jack-in-a-box.

(UCBFA Anglo-American file. Jokes II-2, F3, P6 U9 K4. Collected by Denise Adelman)

The latter joke was collected by a woman who heard it "shortly after President Kennedy's death" and felt "rather sick and disgusted with whomever it was that told it to me." She adds that JFK's son John-John's fifth birthday fell on the day of his father's funeral.

What's Jackie Kennedy's new name now?
Jackie Idlewild.

(UCBFA Anglo-American file. Jokes II-2, F3, P6 U9 K4. Collected by Susan Knopow, 1965)

The joke reverses the tendency to arbitrarily rename all manner of things 'Kennedy' after JFK's assassination, such as Idlewild Airport, and suggests that Jackie to-be-Onassis was now wild and idle.

These jokes set a pattern for the later Kennedy jokes about disaster—the assassination of Robert Kennedy, the slaughter of Mary Jo Kopechne through the drunk driving, negligence, and cowardice of Edward Kennedy, and the loss of John Kennedy, Jr. (the "John-John" of the jokes) while flying his own plane. Each wave of jokes was numerically larger, and the best of the jokes cleverer than in the preceding cycle. Disaster jokes were now on an ascending curve, and were partly driven by the ever-increasing pervasiveness of television and partly by the rise of the "anti-risk society," in which early death had become rare due to improved nutrition, public health, and medical treatment. Occasional loss of young life through violence or accident was now seen as the ultimate tragedy (Davies and Neal 1998, 43–44).

In the jokes about Edward Kennedy, we can also see a precursor of the later and equally media-driven jokes about President Clinton. In the case of America's "Father Ted," public shock and horror were mixed with private laughter:

What did Edward Kennedy say to his secretary when she told him confidentially, "I've got a problem?"
He said, "We'll cross that bridge when we come to it."

(UCBFA Anglo-American file. Jokes II-2, F3, P6 U9 K4.
Collected by Richard Peters, 1970)

Kennedy drove off a bridge at Chappaquiddick and his aide, Mary Jo Kopechne, was tragically drowned. The joke plays quite unfairly with the notion that either she or some subsequent secretary might have been pregnant, and that this was his way of dealing with such a problem.

THE GLOBALIZATION OF THE DISASTER JOKE

The television jokes discussed thus far have been concerned with events occurring in and reported in the country where the jokes were told. However, the *global* television reporting of distant disasters has led to jokes that place these events within a framework of *local* trivia.

The following phrase was habitually used when a bar was due to close for the night in Britain, but it acquired a double meaning at the time of the Armenian earthquake:

What does a pub landlord say at the end of the evening in Armenia?
All right, you lot, closing time. Haven't you got homes to go to?

(In oral circulation in Britain in the 1980s)

Regarding the Mexico City earthquake of 1985:

What did they rename the Hilton Hotel in Mexico City?
The International House of Pancakes.

(UCBFA Anglo-American file II-2 T6, D5 Topical Disasters
Miscellaneous. Collected by Andrea Collette, 1986)

Regarding the assassination of Ghandi:

Why doesn't India have Halloween anymore?
Cause they ain't got no Gandhi.

(UCBFA Anglo-American file, Jokes II-2, F3, P6, N6 Famous political
Non U.S. Collected by Lewis Rosman)

Successive waves of recycled jokes about African famines also circulated on both sides of the Atlantic—the Biafran, Ethiopian, Eritrean, and Somali famine jokes (Christopher 1984–5; Gruner 1997, 57–8):

How do you get an Ethiopian into a phone box?
Throw a tin of baked beans in.
(In oral circulation in Britain 1980s)

What's black, round and covered in cobwebs?
An Ethiopian's asshole.
(Christopher 1984–85, 39)

What's new about the McDonald's restaurant in Ethiopia?
It features a crawl-up window.
(Christopher 1984–85, 40)

What did Poland send to Ethiopia for famine relief?
4000 pounds of after-dinner mints.
(Christopher 1984–85, 41)

What do Yoko Ono and Ethiopians have in common?
They both live off dead beetles.
(Christopher 1984–85, 41)

These were perhaps the first famines to be shown directly on television. The horrific pictures, with a strong emphasis on starving children, were accompanied by a rhetoric that implied that viewers should not only feel shocked and upset, but guilty, even though there was no connection between them and the racist and ideology-driven warring African governments who were responsible for causing the famines. Show business personalities now ran highly publicized fund-raising events that cashed in on the television pictures. Significantly, no one thought to make a major television news story out of that, or to put on a show to raise money to ameliorate the steady high death rate of children and adults alike from malnutrition or diarrhea caused by dirty drinking water in very poor countries. Nor were there jokes on this subject.

Many young people were clearly responding to being lectured about their moral responsibilities by inventing jokes that mocked their media mentors. Such a response is very common. In Israel *after* teaching about the Holocaust became *compulsory* in secondary schools, there was a wave of sick jokes on this subject (Zajdman 1995), something that had never happened in Israel before. There is no point in searching for "deeper" (i.e., inaccessible and untestable) reasons for these responses, or speculating about coping mechanisms or systems of meaning. Young people resist secular preaching, and that is all that need be said. It is for this reason that secular moral crusades to alter their behavior tend to fail.

TELEVISION AS THE CAUSE OF DISASTER JOKES

The explosion of the *Challenger* space shuttle on live television in 1986 set off what was probably the first of a series of joke cycles about accidents. A leading humor scholar, Elliott Oring, soon noticed the significance of the incorporation into the *Challenger* jokes of references to commercial products and phrases from television advertising (1987, 1992). Oring wrote:

> A number of the shuttle jokes (as well as other disaster jokes) increasingly employ the names of familiar and amiable commercial products from television advertising: Coke, Seven-Up, Tango, Head and Shoulders, Ocean Spray, Bud Light. "What were the last words said on the *Challenger*? I want a light. . . . No, no a Bud Light." In this joke an incongruous image is created of the *Challenger* destruction being caused by someone mistaking an order for beer as a request for an explosion. The incongruity is appropriate because incendiaries were indeed part and parcel of Budweiser Light beer commercials in the mid-1980s. . . . Like the *Challenger* newscasts themselves, they were so omnipresent that it was almost inevitable that they would be employed in parody. . . . But the juxtaposition of commercial products with images of disaster seems a particularly appropriate commentary on the television medium and images it presents to viewers at home. Television news programs regularly conjoin images and stories about death, disease and destruction with images of commercial products. Virtually every television report of a news disaster is preceded and followed by a commercial message (or each and every message is preceded and followed by the report of a disaster). Thus the concatenation of brand name products and images of disaster achieved in the jokes is really no more incongruous than that achieved several times each evening by national and local news programs. (1992, 38–9)

Q. What's the favourite drink at NASA?
A. Seven-Up with a splash.
(Oring 1992, 32)

Q. How did they know Christa McAuliffe had dandruff?
A. Her head and shoulders were washed up on the beach.
(Oring 1992, 32)

Q. What was Christa McAuliffe's favourite drink?
A. Ocean Spray.

(Oring 1992, 33)

Christa McAuliffe was a civilian schoolteacher travelling as a *publicity passenger* on the space shuttle to show how safe it was. It exploded in full view of those watching the launch on live television, scattering the inmates as molecules over the shore and sea at Cape Canaveral.

To Oring's *Challenger* examples we can add:

Why did Indira Gandhi change her deodorant?
Because her right guard was killing her.

(UCBFA Anglo-American Jokes II- Political Non U.S. Collected by Christina Bartolucci in California in 1984, two days after Mrs. Gandhi was shot by her Sikh bodyguard)

Biafran housewives every day open a tin of beans and say, "One each."

(In oral circulation in Britain among young people in the late 1960s. Sung to the author by Dr. Anne Curry, distinguished singer and military historian, over a cafeteria lunch in 1999)

The latter joke is a play on the words of the television advertising jingle: "Millions of housewives everyday open a tin of beans and say 'Beanz Meanz Heinz.'" Baked beans are, as the advertisement implies, an instant convenience food for the young and are, as it happens, a source of flatulence and hence comedy. Heinz meanz fartz.

Elliot Oring's insights and observations can be extended to form a general theory of how television reporting of disasters such as the Biafran famine, the *Challenger* space shuttle, the sinking of *The Herald of Free Enterprise,* the *Piper Alpha* fire, Chernobyl, and the deaths of celebrities generates sick disaster jokes through new forms of paradox and incongruity. Before television, these forms of paradox and incongruity were not nearly as strong a part of people's "mediated" experiences, and distant shocking events could not and did not give rise to cycles of sick disaster jokes.

The first incongruity is that television is a rubbish sandwich. The announcement of sad and shocking disasters alternates not merely with advertisements, but with programs that are by any standard banal and trivial, such as low I.Q. quiz shows, costume dramas from England which are far more costume than drama, American sanitized thuggery for cheap excitement, and saponaceous operas. Television is a world of free circuses and advertisements for white sliced cardboard bread, in which trivia are used to sell trivia and appearance takes precedence over analysis. In consequence, messages about disaster arrive in an incongruous package. It is as if an official letter telling a family that one of their members in the armed forces had been killed in action were to arrive in a glitzy envelope with smiley face stickers, accompanied by advertisements for soap powder and chocolate bars. Whilst it is true that newspapers potentially have the same problem when they run a disaster story on the front page, a trip down naked mammary lane on page three, and sports in the back section, these are arranged in a known and segregated spatial pattern. There are no cartoons on the obituary page, and the reader who is upset by a disaster reported in the news section can postpone reading, or even consign to the bin, other potentially incongruous parts of the paper. A television viewer, by contrast, is hit by a bizarre mixture of messages in an almost random temporal pattern decided in advance by other people, to which only minimal changes are made when a disaster hits the news. Controllers might pull a comedy about trains or aircraft if there has been a bad crash, but in a normal evening's solid viewing or channel switching, incongruity is unavoidable. The incongruity of things seen is greater than that of things read or heard, and more likely to give rise to jokes. When disaster strikes, the dead donkey does not get dropped, but merely occurs later on the television news.

There is a second source of incongruity in television: the frequent and deliberate blurring of boundaries between fact and fiction, or between reality and fantasy, in television programs. There is the fakery of the drama documentary, those mendacious films purporting to represent real events; the fly-on-the-wall program from which anything that would bore, offend, or frighten the average fly has been deleted; and the reconstructions of distant history that boast of accuracy but from which fleas, facial blemishes, and ordure-filled streets have been eliminated. These may deceive and entrance many viewers, but they reduce others to cynical amusement. This cynical amusement is then extended to television news reports, whose only claim to truth is that they are showing you the pictures. When the pictures are accompanied by insistent moralizing, instructing the viewer on how to respond to them, it is no wonder that disaster jokes become not only possible, but also popular.

Finally, there is the incongruity between the viewer's situation, seated safely and comfortably at home in a clean, well-lit place, eating a more-than-adequate TV dinner, and the pictures of death by starvation or by accident with which they are being confronted. Television tries to deceive people into thinking they are being witnesses, when they are merely seeing pictures—selected, edited pictures at that. The broadcasters then exhort the viewers to respond to these distant events *as if* the disaster had directly impinged on them, their families, and communities, and harmed people they know directly and are attached to as particular individuals (Davies and Neal 2001). As Smyth shrewdly noted in relation to the *Challenger* disaster:

> The general public was made to feel as if they were there as witnesses and participants. To not feel shocked by this event would be unusual, yet at what point and for what reasons might one say "enough of this" and repeat or perhaps just laugh at jokes about this event? . . . How well do people really know these media figures and how long do they feel obliged to mourn for them? For the most part there is no real familiarity with them as persons, only the one-sided exposure to images absorbed by sitting in front of a television set. The shuttle crew members had never been woven into the fabric of most people's lives. They were not persons, only media personalities. (1986, 255–56)

The same point may be made in regard to the death by disaster of ordinary members of the public. Other than their particular loved ones, who have suffered very real personal bereavement, who else in the twenty-first century cares about the victims of *Piper Alpha, The Herald of Free Enterprise,* or the Clapham rail crash, or knows any of their names? The incidents were *tragic in and of themselves,* but television turned them into ephemeral media disasters and thus a fit subject for jokes. Television created the conditions for the jokes to be invented, but, of course, the jokes were never broadcast on television (Davies 1996). Before the Internet, the jokes could only be found in archives or in books of jokes labeled "gross," "tasteless," or "offensive," and often edited by unknown persons with female pseudonyms (Alvin 1983a, 1983b, 1984; Knott 1982, 1983a, 1983b, 1984; Thickett 1983a, 1983b).

Disaster Jokes as Resistance to a Hegemony of Feeling: A Comparative Analysis

The driving force behind the popularity of disaster jokes is the emotional hegemony enjoyed by those controlling television, who feel able to tell viewers what to feel in the same sense that authoritarian governments, such as those of the former socialist countries of Eastern Europe, told their subjects what to think. In consequence, the same kinds of jokes emerge in opposition to an illegitimate monopoly—political jokes under socialism (Davies 1989, 1998b) and disaster jokes in the West. I am *not,* of course, saying that Western viewers hate the controllers of television, much of the content of which is market-driven and consumer-led, so that viewers get the lowest common denominator of what they want—a sort of K-Mart of images. But it was also the case that *many* citizens under the old East European socialist regimes who were supporters, beneficiaries, or even privileged members of these regimes enjoyed anti-socialist political jokes (Deriabin and Gibney 1960, 173–5). Likewise, in National Socialist Germany, political jokes of an ostensibly anti-Nazi kind sometimes revealed insider knowledge of what was going on within the Nazi hierarchy (Gamm 1963, 23). Political jokes are sometimes not so much an index of political opposition as a way of playing with the forbidden, of taking time off from the official line. Individuals in authoritarian societies may well tell these jokes regardless of their political views, just as in democratic societies they may tell disaster jokes regardless of their emotional responses to disaster. Many true believers and true mourners may exclude themselves, but this leaves a wide spectrum of responders. There can be an evasion of and resistance to hegemony even from those who do not seek to undermine or even challenge its legitimacy. It is unfortunately probable that most Germans and Austrians supported the Third Reich, even if they sought an escape through jokes from being perpetually told that they *must.*

Likewise, disaster jokes are an evasion of compulsory rhetoric, rather than mere callousness. Viewers are often responsive to and genuinely upset by television disaster coverage, and indeed engage in and collaborate with it. Smyth commented in his analysis of the *Challenger* jokes: ''When something disastrous happens to a media figure, however, people spread the news and begin to grieve as if they had lost someone with whom they intimately shared their lives'' (1986, 256). The public may even help to drive the media pressure (O'Hear 1998), as when they created a mountain of flowers, messages, and sad redundant teddy bears outside the Princess of Wales' home in Kensington, England. Such spontaneity even occurred among the faithful in Soviet Russia, some of whom could speak quite genuinely of having been moved by a vivid vision of the long dead Lenin who spoke to them, comforted them, and advised them: the opiate of the *apparatchiks.*

The crucial point, however, is that the old regimes of Eastern Europe, like the Western mass media, made such feelings and thoughts *compulsory,* and the jokes emerged in *resistance* to this, regardless of where the joke-tellers' own sympathies lay. This phenomenon underpins many types of jokes. Joking consists of playing with the forbidden, whether the 'forbidden' is political, racial, sexual, or gruesome: it is the social fact that is common to them all. In the case of disaster jokes it is unlikely that the joke-tellers relish the reality of the disasters, and equally unlikely that the jokes were their way of coping with grief. We have no reliable way of finding out what their deeper feelings were, and even if we did, these would be of no use in explaining the other types of joke cited above. "Resistance to hegemony" and "playing with the forbidden," by contrast, are general concepts that can be employed to construct hypotheses about many types of jokes.

EAST EUROPEAN POLITICIZED DISASTER JOKES UNDER SOCIALISM

Indeed, jokes exist that display these characteristics in more than one direction at a time, as with the East European jokes that followed the Chernobyl nuclear disaster. The nuclear catastrophe in the Ukraine provided disaster jokes in many countries in the West (Kürti 1988f.; Milspaw 1981), but in Eastern Europe the jokes also became part of a much larger genre of political jokes (Kürti 1988).

> What's the new shopping craze?
> To save money, people are buying Kiev bread instead of fluorescent light bulbs.
> (331)

> What did the workers celebrate at the May Day Parade in Budapest?
> The radiant friendship between Hungary and the Soviet Union.
> (331)

> How was the May Day Parade in Kiev organized?
> In rows. In the first row were the party activists, in the second were all the youth communist activists, in the third all the union activists, and finally all the radioactivists.
> (333)

A similar fusion of disaster joke and political joke may be seen in an East German joke of the 1980s about the killing by East German border guards of those who tried to escape to the West over the Berlin Wall.

> When does a good border guard fire the warning shot?
> At the end of the second clip of ammunition.
> (Stein 1989, 93)

In the East European case, the jokes probably did generally coincide with resistance to political oppression (Davies 1998a, 1998b); the East European socialist regimes did after all collapse with remarkable speed in the wake of the jokes. However, their key characteristic was not resistance to the regimes as such, but to a hegemonic discourse; the jokes evaded the only form of discourse that was officially permitted. They were funny even to those who accepted the legitimacy of that discourse.

It is the same lack of pluralism in regard to media-mediated disasters that results in cycles of disaster jokes. The disaster jokes are not striking against the victims, nor even against the reporting of disasters as such, but against monopoly; if the disaster jokes are a form of aggression, it is a strange and diffuse kind of aggression, and to conflate it with other forms of aggression is misleading.

THE INTERNET AND THE PROLIFERATION OF DISASTER JOKES

The greatest *growth in the numbers* of disaster jokes came towards the end of the twentieth century, with the availability of cheaper, easier, and more accessible and universal forms of electronic dissemination. Cheaper long distance and international phone calls, and an expanding volume of such calls (for instance, between commodity and financial dealers), allowed a more rapid exchange of jokes between individuals. The phone was soon supplemented by e-mail, which enabled large numbers of geographically scattered individuals to convey jokes to a large network of associates in a single dispatch, particularly through the use of mailing lists. Each recipient may, in turn, become the apex of a further pyramid of distribution. Finally, in the 1990s, numerous web pages were created such that anyone who wanted to consult a set of files of disaster jokes indexed by subject could do so, and they could also add to the collection by e-mail. In consequence, disaster jokes proliferated. The *Challenger* space shuttle disaster generated fewer than fifty recorded jokes at the time of its explosion in 1986, even though it produced more jokes in America, and even in Britain, than any previous disaster, and inspired the leading academic studies of disaster jokes (Oring 1992, 1987; Simons 1986; Smyth 1986). The Internet was not at that time important as a means of joke dissemination. Disaster jokes were overwhelmingly still transmitted orally, either in face-to-face situations or by phone. By contrast, when Diana, Princess of Wales, died in a motor accident in 1998, more than three hundred jokes were invented and collected—six times as many as in the case of the *Challenger* explosion, the previously most successful joke-generating disaster. Diana jokes were banned from the mass media, and no joke book publisher has yet dared to bring out a collection of them.[3]

The key to this growth in the numbers, and also in the international popularity, of disaster jokes has been the Internet. Already, in 1998 itself, there were at least five web sites in English devoted exclusively to Diana jokes, including sites in the Netherlands and Australia. Diana jokes were even found on the web site *Blagues Lourdes* in French.[4] It may be that the Internet simply makes the jokes appear more numerous by enabling these otherwise scattered and forbidden items to be assembled in one place, but it seems more likely that the use of e-mail and web sites has a snowball effect, since the existence of an accessible core of jokes stimulates further jokes through imitation, modification, inspiration, emulation, and legitimation.

The jokes about the death of Diana demonstrate very clearly the antithesis between television and the Internet. Television is a form of centralized and homogenized mass production, from which anything that offends the management, the sponsors, or any significant section of the audience to whom they choose to defer, is excluded. The Internet is decentralized, international, and diverse. Setting up a web site is inexpensive, and censorship is ineffective, though growing. Individuals or small groups with relatively modest resources can send, collect, display, exchange, and read jokes or any other material they choose, including items banned by other media. You can search out what you want when you want it. The square-deal surfers are not dominated by a sequence or pattern of contents controlled by a small group of powerful, narrow-minded broadcasters combining huge resources with politically correct values. The official pieties of the broadcasters can be evaded and defied via the Internet. Television is hegemonic, the Internet libertarian. Jokes as anonymous creations fit into the anonymous Internet very well indeed.

THE INTERNET AND THE FURTHER GLOBALIZATION OF DISASTER JOKES

The Internet is not a cause of disaster jokes in the way that television is; it is merely a facilitator of their dissemination and storage that supplements their oral circulation. It has, however, helped to make the jokes even more global. It is particularly striking how the Internet has facilitated and globalized the circulation of disaster jokes referring to local incidents, jokes that otherwise would not have been as widely publicized, and, indeed, would have had little meaning outside their country of origin. The Deathsucks.com web site in the United States has a "Dead Celebrity Jokes Graveyard" which is activated by clicking on the appropriate tombstone. It even has a collection of jokes concerning the late British crimefighter Jill Dando, prefaced with the comment,

> Looks like another Brit has Bit the Dust! First Rod Hull now Jill Dando. I guess there is something to the saying that the English are all 'a bit of a homebody'. For those of you ignorant Americans (like me), Jill Dando was a popular correspondent who hosted a show called "Crimewatch UK" (kind of like "America's Most Wanted"). Jill was shot at her doorstep as she was leaving for work, most likely because of her crime-fighting reputation.
> (www.deathsucks.com/jokes/jilldando/html)

Forty-five jokes then follow. Some are clearly recycled from previous disasters, but most are local to Britain, some of them obviously so:

> What does [*sic*] Jill Dando and George Best have in common?
> They both ended their careers at Fulham.
> (www.Deathsucks.com/jokes/jilldando/html)

George Best was a famous international soccer player from Ulster who, in middle age, played for the Fulham team in London; the late Jill Dando lived in Fulham.

> What does [*sic*] Jill and the milkman have in common?
> They both leave four pints on the doorstep.
> (www.Deathsucks.com/jokes/jilldando/html)

The jokes were presumably in oral circulation in Britain and sent to America in response to the Celebrity Caretaker's request to "Contribute your jokes to this page, e-mail the caretaker@deathsucks.com with your tasteless Jill Dando jokes or vent your politically correct outrage against our blasphemy." Anyone in the world with access to the Internet can now read these jokes, but outside Britain Jill Dando jokes are largely a pure art form. They are jokes felt to be funny because they are playing with *someone else's forbidden notions*, albeit ones that are generically similar to those that are the basis of more familiar local disaster jokes. The very idea that North Americans at home, who do not and cannot watch this kind of British television, are in any sense involved with the jokes is absurd. If the jokes have a victim, it is not Jill Dando but those provoked into "outrage against our blasphemy," whether the blasphemy is one of content or merely one of form. Anyone's televised disaster now seems to be good for a joke; the jokes have gone global and are now *two* electronic stages removed from reality. By contrast, in the past Americans and Canadians would have had little access to and would have made no contribution to the British disaster joke cycles of the late 1980s cited earlier in this essay, which were purely local in their origins and appeal. The overall pattern of change due to both television and the Internet is summed up in the table below.

	Televised Disaster News	*Disaster Jokes*
Television (Stage 1)	national news	local jokes
Television (Stage 2)	global news (as well as local)	local jokes
Early Internet	global TV news	global jokes
Mature Internet	local TV news (as well as global)	global jokes

CONCLUSION

By the use of the comparative and historical method (Davies 1998a, 1998b, 2002) it is possible to demonstrate that disaster jokes were the product of the rise to dominance of new forms of electronic communication in the last decades of the twentieth century. They were and are caused by television, and their invention and dissemination has been greatly facilitated by the growing use of the Internet. Jokes of this kind were unknown, or at least very rare, prior to television becoming a dominant source of news and cheap entertainment in the 1960s. The jokes are the spontaneous inventions of ordinary people, set off by the incongruous way in which television conveys the news of a disaster or the death of a celebrity to its viewers, an incongruity far less apparent in other media.

Disaster jokes are common in democratic countries dominated by television, but political jokes are relatively rare, and only thrive in authoritarian countries where there is a hegemonic control over political discourse, notably under the former socialist regimes in Eastern Europe. From this we may see that both types of jokes are a form of resistance to compulsory political correctness. The controllers of television attempt to impose an emotional hegemony on viewers that restricts the ways in which they can openly speak about disasters, and the jokes defy this monopoly. Disaster jokes, like jokes about sex or race or, in some societies, religion or politics, are a way of playing with the forbidden for the sake of amusement.

Jokes about televised disasters have little in common with the humor used by those who directly experience danger and death by being involved in a real disaster (Abe and Ritz 1996), or in their everyday lives such as soldiers or high-ironworkers constructing tall buildings (Haas 1977). The making of jokes within small groups of men faced by danger and death may help to maintain morale and solidarity, and to train members in the ways of the group (Haas 1977; Obrdlik 1942). But jokes about current events reported on television have no such social functions; they are for amusement only. It is pointless to speculate as to whether they are a means of coping with a shocking report of sudden death, a means of extracting humor from a shared piece of grim knowledge, or an expression of Hobbesian triumph that it happened to somebody else (Gruner 1997, 41, 60). We do not know, and it would be very difficult to find out, which, if any, of these is the case, given the wide varieties of individuals telling or listening to such jokes, and the differences in the context and tone in which they are told. A large genre of jokes, such as the current-event disaster jokes discussed here, that is made up of many joke cycles is a social fact that can only be explained in terms of other social facts.

The rapid reporting of events on the other side of the globe is a nineteenth century electronic phenomenon that stems from the invention and spread of the telegraph (radio is merely wireless) and the subsequent growth of newspapers for the newly semi-literate. There is nothing new about globalization (Davies and Trivizas 1999). However, television, for the first time, had the capacity to thrust vivid pictures of distant disasters into people's homes and meeting places, and to set them joking about events on the other side of the world. Americans could now invent jokes about the assassination of Mrs. Gandhi, Chernobyl, and famine in Ethiopia, and the British about the *Challenger* space shuttle or an earthquake in Armenia. Disaster jokes have gone global.

As a result of the provision of the Internet and its rapidly increasing use, there has been a further degree of encouragement for and globalization of disaster jokes. The Internet is an electronic facilitator. It enables jokes to be exchanged and disseminated by e-mail, and to be accumulated on web sites in large numbers, which no doubt also stimulates the invention of disaster jokes and of death-of-a-celebrity jokes by providing templates for, encouraging emulation among, and granting legitimacy to disaster joke-tellers. The Internet is also a globalizing force, in that it enables the pooling of jokes from many countries in response to a globally reported, televised disaster, such as the death of Diana, Princess of Wales, that called in jokes from three continents and at least four European countries. This allowed a truly sharing event in which nation joked unto nation in a spirit of international cooperation. Television, far from creating a global village, destroyed local communities and institutions, leaving behind a mass of atomized and alienated individuals, but the Internet is now enabling them to recreate virtual substitutes for the world they have lost. Now globalization has gone a stage further, with webspinners in one country setting up sites to act as a storage place and a mail box for local disaster jokes from other countries, concerning disasters that would not have received much television coverage or had much impact abroad. The Internet thus goes beyond television, and also circumvents television; it is a free, decentralized electronic medium in an otherwise controlled and restricted electronic age. Whether this freedom to joke will continue is doubtful. Already there is pressure on servers in many English-speaking and European countries from pressure groups[5] to remove collections of jokes to which they object.

2

MAKING A BIG APPLE CRUMBLE

The Role of Humor in Constructing a Global Response to Disaster

BILL ELLIS

On the morning of September 11, 2001, terrorists associated with Osama bin Laden's al-Qaida, a fundamentalist Islamic political movement, hijacked four American jetliners. Two were crashed into the twin towers of New York's World Trade Center, causing them to collapse with catastrophic loss of life. A third was crashed into the Pentagon, costing an additional 189 lives, while passengers on a fourth evidently attacked the hijackers, causing the plane to crash in a rural area in western Pennsylvania with the loss of all 44 persons aboard. Much of the drama was played out live on national television, including the crash of the second plane into the South Tower at 9:03 AM and both towers' collapse, at 10:05 and 10:30 AM respectively.

The tragedy sent shock waves through American culture not felt since the equally public tragedy of the explosion of the space shuttle *Challenger* in 1986. To be sure, the September 11 terrorist attacks were preceded by other anxiety-producing terrorist events. The 1985 *Achille Lauro* hijacking and the 1988 terrorist bombing of Pan Am 103 over Lockerbie, Scotland had inspired previous cycles of disaster humor. However, neither the first terrorist bombing at the World Trade Center in 1993 nor the Oklahoma City bombing in 1995 had the international impact of the new attacks. Tony Fox, a spokesman for the cable network Comedy Central, recalled that the Oklahoma City bombing did cause a brief suspension of humor, but satirists soon turned their attention to other newsworthy events. "This seems so consuming, it's just different" from other national disasters, he told a reporter (Marcus 2001).

Folk culture played a central role in the process of allowing common citizens to react to the anxieties raised by these horrific events. Sylvia Grider (2001) has documented the spontaneous shrines created within hours to commemorate the dead. Patriotic displays became commonplace and remained in place alongside traditional decorations for Halloween and Christmas. Other, equally important reactions took the form of verbal and computer-generated art. Statements of solidarity and patriotic resolve, in the form of testimonies, poems, and images circulated widely. On a less formal level, rumors and legends concerning the terrorists and the events were generated and spread quickly. And, in a well-anticipated stage of this process, disaster humor was created, both immediately after the event and regularly over the next six weeks. This body of emergent humor, which I (and others) termed "World Trade Center (WTC) Humor," provides a large and revealing body of folklore to examine how Americans dealt with the psychological challenge the terrorist acts posed.

This study will look closely at the emergence of WTC humor as a phenomenon, documented in previously unobtainable detail, partially facilitated by the Internet's ability to link the nation and the world as one simultaneously present community.[1] This new sense of community challenges our previous assumption that folklore is the property of small, localized groups. When groups regularly communicate across geographical boundaries, what traditional factors of folklore remain the same, and what factors now constitute "contemporary" folklore in every sense of the word?

In an earlier essay, "A Model for Collecting and Interpreting World Trade Center Disaster Jokes" (2001; subsequently referred to as "Model"), I argued that such humor marks an important part of a community's response to tragedy. Disaster jokes do not simply appear singly, but emerge as a cycle out of a phenomenon with a recognizable structure. It follows predictable patterns: for instance, a "latent period" immediately after the disaster during which joking is suppressed, nominally out of respect for those grieving. When jokes appear, they express stages of coping with the aftermath of the event, so the earliest jokes in the *Challenger* cycle focused on scapegoats, while later jokes moved toward closure by "domesticating" the key images of the disaster. My model predicted that the WTC jokes would follow a similar pattern:

1. This cycle will emerge, in a series of waves, after a period of latency.
2. One or more of the common WTC jokes will reference the dominant visual images of the tragedy.
3. The WTC jokes will recycle elements from previous cycles.
4. The dominant mode of distributing WTC jokes will be e-mail.

This study will also examine the extent to which these predictions were fulfilled and suggest reasons why in some cases the actual cycle proved different from the one I anticipated.

Humor, even if it does not directly comment on tragic events, is often perceived as painful for those affected. Even those directly affected by a disaster, such as the emergency rescue workers surveyed by Moran and Massam (1997), find themselves caught in an awkward bind, needing black humor to cope with the horror of events but not being able to justify their actions to others. Thus much of the immediate humor might never be recorded, and indeed, participants find it difficult to remember details after the shock of the event is over. It is therefore difficult to know exactly what kinds of humor emergency workers at Ground Zero circulated orally among themselves during the days after the event. We do know that it existed; a New York City comedy writer who visited Ground Zero on September 19 recorded this example of black humor:

> I was talking to these two firemen. One was about 28. The other was about 40. The younger fireman told me that after the south tower collapsed he and his partner were running toward the north tower to get people out. His buddy got hit by the body of a person who had jumped. He had to get him medical attention; he ended up dying. Thirty seconds later, the north tower collapsed. Had this fireman's buddy not gotten hit, both of them would have died.
>
> There was a pause in the story, and that's when the older fireman turned to him and said, "Is this going to be a long story?" I thought to myself these guys have certainly earned the right to joke (Ferrante 2002, 28).

Clearly some workers needed such black humor to cope with the horrors with which they had to deal. But the larger public affected by the disaster were still expressing violent anger when such forms of joking became public, as we shall see. But in the case of a "media disaster" such as the September 11 events, the graphic details of death and destruction are shared with a mass audience, who must then improvise ways of coping with them in a way seen as socially acceptable.

Once the threat of the disaster is no longer imminent, the role of folklore turns to assigning blame, internally and externally, and to "naming" the most threatening elements of past events, and humor inevitably takes a role in these processes. However, a significant number of citizens at large must reach closure before jokes become strategically successful. That is, so long as the primary response to a joke is to see it as socially inappropriate, neither the person telling the joke nor those who hear it will be encouraged to pass it on. As the response becomes more mixed, with more people signaling that they find a joke funny, then the rewards of passing it on begin to outweigh the risks, and more people will be willing to forward such humor. In the past, this shift has taken place rather suddenly; jokes appear in an intense but short-lived cycle that signals Americans' readiness to gain control over the most dissonant images in the disaster and so reach closure in their grieving process.

The role played by the Internet in circulating and creating such cycle jokes, I anticipated, would be important. Although the web of persons directly and indirectly affected by this disaster was unquestionably large, still it was not omnipresent, so joking could take place almost at once with little social risk of hurting someone directly involved in the catastrophe. The distancing effect of the Internet likewise enables persons to propose and circulate jokes anonymously, and with little risk of social retaliation.

However, folkloristics has not to date exploited Internet-circulated lore or dealt directly with its potential. Communities who constitute themselves virtually, as Simon Bronner (2002) has said, "form around multiple, overlapping interests that go well beyond the formations of race, ethnicity, class, and gender." Media disasters, I noted in "Model," are instantaneously global, and WTC humor might reflect this "community of the world," just as material circulating immediately after the terrorist strikes reflected worldwide concern and support for Americans. It was therefore essential to observe how the Internet has impacted the folk process, and in so doing recognize its value as a resource for studying phenomena like the emergence and spread of contemporary legends and disaster humor.

I asked fellow folklorists to be ready to receive, gather, and transmit WTC jokes to me as they came to their attention. As a result, I received collections of Internet-collected humor from a number of colleagues.[2] Thanks to a tip from Alan E. Mays, I followed these leads using the newly upgraded Google.com Groups metasearch. This feature gives folklorists access to some 700 million archived messages on Usenet message boards, including many posted in the immediate wake of the disaster, allowing us to follow spontaneous conversations among participants of these message boards[3] and see both how jokes emerge and what social responses they provide. Also, since the search engine allows one to sort results by date, it was possible to trace the history of many items, giving hints as to the culture and subculture from which they arose and allowing us to determine when they peaked in popularity. As a result, we can now examine the emergence of WTC jokes in unprecedented detail. Overall, seeing WTC humor as a phenomenon, not as a miscellaneous collection of texts, produces a much clearer image of how humor functioned to construct a social response to disaster that allowed participants to move toward closure and "business as usual."

FOLK HUMOR AND THE INTERNET

Folklorists have responded in varying ways to the global culture created in the past decade through the Internet. Linda Dégh, for instance, has minimized the importance of traditional-seeming material circulated by e-mail or through websites, noting that they do not stem from a genuine live, face-to-face folklore communication (2001, 114-15). Further, because it is based on technology, it represents a social force seen as destructive of folk culture, if we define this concept in terms of "face-to-face interaction, close settlement, orality, and generational ties" (Bronner 2002). By contrast, John Dorst (1990) and Bruce Lionel Mason (1996) have argued strongly for considering the computer-mediated networks as an "active folkloric space," in which the lack of traditional boundaries gives users the opportunity to create a rich variety of new traditional forms. Mason argues for considering such conduits as a *virtual* space analogous to the sense of locality that folklorists normally emphasize. In fact, Internet users frequently use such a metaphor, and their interaction is governed by a set of social rules usually called "netiquette." Often such rules are implied rather than stated, just as face-to-face interaction reflects implicit social rules of communication.

Alan Dundes and Carl A. Pagter argue that the increased use of personal computers has indeed brought "a new generation of folklore" into being. Particularly in the realm of workplace humor, they observed, individuals increasingly have used e-mail and fax to circulate jokes of the sort previously passed on in the form of typed or photocopied texts. This position is supported by Dorst, who notes that the decentralized nature of computer networks allows individuals to appropriate structures originally owned by a dominant culture and to use them to express criticism of these hegemonic forces (1990, 187). The ubiquity of computers that, as Dundes and Pagter note, "have the technical capacity to generate graphic materials which previously could not be composed outside of professional print shops" (1996, xiv) has accelerated the "anti-hegemonic impulses" that Dorst says underlie many computer-mediated traditions. With computer communication becoming part of the daily routine for all generations, we can expect such increasingly sophisticated technology to take an increasingly important role in the transmission of folk culture.

But such a development, Dorst admits, demands that the scholar reconsider many of the stereotypes with which one has previously approached the field. Just as the World Wide Web has made global publication of information immediately within the realm of every individual willing to master its strategy, so computer-mediated communications have made the formal distinctions between official and informal communication more and more difficult to discern. In fact, Dorst suggests, such a blurring of folk and mainstream is central to the development of topical jokes, which as a genre appropriates mass media imagery in order to challenge official definitions of reality. In this way, such a joke cycle "reproduces or mimics the distinctive operations of the reigning hegemony" even as it parodies it (1990, 185-86),

Since this was the first international media disaster in which the Internet played a role in generating and circulating humor, it provides us with a chance to see how the increasingly global nature of information conduits has changed the literal form of humor genres. The scope of the data base used in this paper is broad beyond easy description, and it is revealing to see how broadly WTC humor cut across it. A sampling of a hundred postings of the first humorous item to become widely popular ("George W. Bush's Speech," to be discussed below) showed that it did come up, as one would expect, on several message boards focused on humor. Nine of its appearances were on boards such as *alt.comedy*, *alt.tasteless.jokes*, and *rec.humor.*[4] But the item appeared just as frequently on boards focusing on serious aspects of the terrorist attacks as well, such as *alt.current-events.wtc-explosion*, *alt.religion.islam*, and *rec.aviation.military.*[5]

Most surprisingly, the speech appeared even more often on a broad spectrum of forums devoted to virtually the whole range of interests. At least thirty eight of its appearances were on message boards devoted to topics having nothing directly to do with humor or terrorism. Participants' interests ranged from fundamentalist Christianity (*alt.christnet*), to sports (*alt.sports.hockey.nhl.ny-islanders*), to American soap operas (*alt.tv.days-of-our-lives*), to coping with chronic diseases (*alt.support.multsclerosis*). This sampling does reference topics typical of a young, computer-focused population (such as *alt.games.delta-force* [a popular computer game] and *rec.music.phish* [an alternative rock band]). But it also includes many other interests typical of older, more conservative subcultures (e.g., *rec.autos.sport.nascar* [American stock car racing], and *alt.fairs.renaissance*). A significant number of these dealt with international cultures not directly involved in the conflict, including Eastern Orthodox

Christianity, Cuba, and Czechoslovakia.[6] Thus WTC jokes affected a population much broader than conduits narrowly focused on participants' interest in topical jokes as such.

This breadth also makes reactions to ethnic stereotypes more complex: when one can be sure that the Other is not listening, there is no check to the extent to which one can marginalize Outsiders. But now there are no automatic Outsiders, given the increasing ability of non-Americans and ethnic minorities to access the Net. Old "camel-rider" and "rag-head" stereotypes from Desert Storm (and presumably from the earlier Iranian Hostage Crisis) arose from high-context, hermetic conduits. Yet such stereotypes still circulate, for new reasons. In some cases the relative anonymity and isolation that the Internet provides may encourage some persons to circulate such material, even though it may offend, because those offended have no easy way to retaliate against the perpetrator. In others, though, as we shall see, the use of such stereotypes may be ironic, a way of adopting an ignorant persona that in itself is intended as the butt of humor.

To be sure, message boards are only one part of the complex set of conduits over which WTC jokes sped; however, they provide a convenient sampling of dynamics that occur in personal e-mail and other forms of transmission. The availability of archived message boards allows us to document the multi-wave properties of a joke cycle, for they immediately provide verbatim texts in the context of more complicated virtual conversation, which can be reproduced along with the exact dates and times of each posting. They permit us, therefore, to pinpoint what we might call *the risible moment* in the aftermath of a given disaster: that is, the point at which making and passing on jokes provokes laughter and provides social rewards that outweigh the social risks of being thought sick or insensitive. Previous folklore research has been limited to collecting and documenting *successful* jokes, and only after they had emerged and come to folklorists' attention. But an Internet-enhanced collection now allows us a time machine, as it were, where we can observe what happens in the period *before* the risible moment, when attempts at humor are *unsuccessful*.

In addition, folkloristic observations tend to focus on the most *frequently forwarded ecotype* of a joke. But the availability of contemporary message board conversations allows us, with luck, to trace these jokes back to a period in which they were still being formed in conversation. In many cases, I found that extremely successful items of humor arose well before the risible moment, and in a form visibly different from the ecotype that became familiar during its peak popularity. Thus the purpose of this essay is both to test a series of hypotheses made about disaster humor and also to suggest the possibilities of Internet-enabled research into ephemeral folklore of all kinds.

Indeed, WTC humor emerged in a series of waves, and overviewing materials from many English-speaking contexts allows us to see how American-based and foreign-based disaster humor varied. We will look first at the material during the "latent period," the time when in the wake of the attacks humor was considered inappropriate. Then we will look closely at three overlapping waves, two American, one British, that illustrate the varying stages of adjustment to the tragedy and the social tensions it caused. Finally we will look at humor that behaved in a less emergent way and remained popular even after the crisis appeared over in most observers' eyes. This includes the single genuinely international WTC joke, one that arose in the Antipodes but proved equally successful in both Great Britain and in America.

1. THE LATENT PERIOD (SEPTEMBER 11-17, 2001)

Informants have often commented that jokes about disastrous events sprang up almost immediately after the event, although folklorists have found it difficult to document these until they emerged as a cycle. Internet-mediated message boards, therefore, prove to be an unexpectedly valuable data base for folklorists, because they record these early attempts at humor in permanent, searchable form, along with the contemporary reactions that they provoke. Further, the reactions to these failed jokes allow us to infer the social factors that temporarily suppress humor, as well as those looking ahead to a time when humor will function therapeutically.

Examination of the attempts made to post jokes during the seven days including and following the terrorist attacks confirms the prediction that public attempts at humor would be severely sanctioned. In virtually every case, the first reaction to the attempted joke was rage, usually expressed in highly aggressive language, always obscene and usually incorporating threats of violence. An interesting and unexpected observation, however, is that such reactions were often countered by others who defended the use of humor, often explicitly citing previous cycles of disaster humor as precedents.

In a report on the therapeutic potentials of humor, *Healingwell.com* reporter Adam Marcus observed a similar bind during the week immediately following the September 11 attacks. Television humorists such as David Letterman and Jay Leno spontaneously suspended live broadcasts, and while the Comedy Channel remained on the air through this period, the network screened only re-runs, carefully chosen as not to refer openly to disasters or to imply criticism of President Bush. When Leno and his NBC colleague Conan O'Brian resumed live shows on September 18, their comic monologues were replaced with heartfelt, personal narratives of shock and support for the nation's plight.

Marcus also consulted Chicago-area psychologist Ed Dunkelblau, who had just held a series of debriefing sessions to help groups develop ways to cope with the emotions provoked by the attacks. Dunkelblau noted that examples of "public humor" had been very scarce, but in private, among intimate groups of family and friends he had seen more attempts to make jokes (Marcus 2001). Nevertheless, even among trusted circles, many people found themselves deeply ambivalent about humor. One semi-anonymous New-Yorker who recorded his reactions, like many others, in a daily online journal, commented on this paradox as early as September 13, two days after the attacks:

> I spent the day going "Oh my God, I hope Jen is okay" and "Oh my God, I hope Dave is okay," and for once in my life my emotions weren't so concerned with the general populous as it was with two of my best friends in the whole world. I can laugh about stupid teenagers in trenchcoats blasting away at chicks with metal fishies on their car without regret,[7] or make jokes about Aaliyah not being able to "pick herself up and try again"[8] and not feel bad about it, because they have no relevance to my life. I can't go back and edit my mind and say "oh, you're evil for thinking that" because I'm not . . . the only way I've ever been able to deal with something on a scale like that has been to make bad jokes about it, and hope that my friends know that they're just bad jokes. I can't remember having malicious intent in my whole life, but I can't keep myself from making stupid jokes and I hate myself for it (Whatever-Dude 2001).

Interestingly, "Whatever-Dude" alludes to two previous media disasters that had inspired black humor, and recognizes that black humor is not evil but a normal way in which he and others have dealt with such tragedies. Significantly, this observer cannot explain why jokes were so necessary at this stage: he only knows that he feels compelled to make them, even though he himself recognizes the jokes as "stupid."

This observer does not record the actual "bad jokes" he made, but a number of message boards that specialize in humor, particularly *alt.humor* and *alt.tasteless.jokes,* give us a taste of what these semi-improvised "stupid" jokes were like. Such messages boards provided a regular "play space" for participants and so were logical "safe haven" for such jokes to be recorded. In fact, one item was posted on *alt.humor* barely two hours after the towers collapsed:

> What does World Trade Centre Stand for
> - Welcome to Canada
> - World Terrorist Convention
> - What ? Trade Centre
>
> (September 11, 2001 09:59:29 PST[9])

However, so intense was the shock of the attacks that even such message boards proved not to be safe havens after all. The reaction to this post was polarized, with a number of persons responding, within seconds, with angry, violent, and obscene attacks on the contributor:

> You sick fuck
>
> (September 11, 2001 10:00:20 PST)

> Why dont you shut your ignorant fucking mouth. If thousands of innocent people in your country died, and you cracked jokes, I hope somebody would have the common decency to take a block of solid metal and crack your fucking skull open.
>
> Ignorant, callous shithead.
>
> (September 11, 2001 10:10:06 PST)

It is clear that even in a space reserved for irreverent joking and tolerant of humor in general, participants simply were not yet in "play mode." A similar dynamic prevailed in *alt.tasteless.jokes* the next day, when a British member offered an improvised joke in a thread titled "New New York Joke."

> What are New Yorkers least favourite flavour of crisp/chips at the moment?
> . . . . . . Plain !
>
> (September 12, 2001 08:08:18 PST)

Like the previous example, this too provoked an angry, obscene response. Later on in the thread of responses, a reader had to ask to have the joke explained, a clear sign that even if the participants were by this time willing to consider humor, this item was simply too esoteric to be funny. The joke relied too heavily on British slang and foodways to translate well globally, a factor that we will see affecting even the more successful jokes that emerged later in the United Kingdom.

On September 17, the end of the latency period, a "list of proposed WTC jokes" was distributed to *alt.tasteless.jokes* and to other similar lists. This included 45 items plus a "top ten" list of "good things about the WTC Attack."[10] The appearance of this list on a message board devoted to "tasteless jokes" was hardly surprising. Indeed, the idea of a "canonical" list of WTC jokes supports John Dorst's idea that such a genre essentially consists of a *cycle,* not a group of individual jokes that happen to appear during the same period. Even if the list is not strictly "infinite," the fact that the viewer is presented with a large number of possibly funny jokes to choose from essentially validates the market economy that the terrorist attacks threatened (1990, 185). What is interesting, then, is that this list provoked so little comment and that so few of the items made the transition from lists to private circulation by e-mail.

Many of the items on the list were obviously recycled jokes from previous disaster cycles, notably the *Challenger* jokes:

> What color were the pilots eyes?
> Blue. One blew this way the other blew that way.[11]
>
> Where do Americans go on vacation?
> All over Manhattan.[12]

Others attempted to find ironic coincidences in the event:

> What's the area code of the World Trade Center?
> 220 (two to zero)
>
> The FBI has just identified the man who trained the hijackers:
> Dale Earnhardt.[13]

Still, the list had minimal impact, suggesting two things. First, it appeared during an unusually intense latency period, in which most Americans were not yet prepared to engage in the satire and cleverness of traditional cycle jokes. Second, by recycling older patterns, this list failed to express the most widely held emotions of Americans, and so they did not address the need to find humorous patterns strong enough to encompass this shock.

In the week following the attacks, the most popular items circulating on the Internet were other forms of narrative that affirmed patriotism or commented on the event with no humorous intent, including statements of sympathy, particularly from non-Americans, personal narratives about involvement in the attacks, and a persistent level of rumors attempting to assign guilt for the events. All of these narrative responses functioned to express shock and find meaning in the event. The nascent forms of humor too served this function, but they were not as widely accepted or appreciated. One observer's comment makes this clear.

> Someone made a joke today, and I didn't laugh (What's the difference between Christmas and Afganistan . . . Christmas will be there next year) nor found it remotely funny. Some people have very short memories.
>
> (*pgh.opinion*: September 14, 2001 20:28:54 PST)

In fact, as we will see, this item became one of the standards in the most widely circulated list of "Osama jokes," but these did not break into circulation until early October and did not become widespread in circulation until nearly a month after this observation. Most of the jokes told during the latent period were seen, like this one, as simply not *funny*. A vocabulary and a grammar had yet to emerge that would create a "play mode" that would allow such jokes to spread. For this reason, experimental joking during the latent period largely remained in the high-context, self-aware humor conduits such as *alt.tasteless.jokes*.

2. THE FIRST AMERICAN WAVE (SEPTEMBER 18-25, 2001)

As predicted, this first wave of humor was angry, expressing itself in an obscenity laced vocabulary of sexual aggressiveness, suggesting that one of the reasons that the terrorist attacks produced anxiety was that it was seen by many as a symbolic attack on the nation's genitals. Alan Dundes (1997) has noted important similarities between the folk speech used as part of male-specific games such as football and similar images used to describe the objectives of war, i.e., to penetrate enemy territory and commit acts intended to effeminize one's opponents. The September 11 event had already provoked rhetoric that was angry, hyperpatriotic, and obscene. The common verbal response to the experimental humor of the latent period was often sexually obscene as well as angry. Such vocabulary would allow Americans, particularly American males, to affirm their sexual identity and project the shame of the symbolic castration of New York City onto those considered responsible.

The first level of jokes to break the latency barrier were primarily visual in nature. While clearly related in content and style to folk cartoons documented by Dundes and Pagter (1992), they represent a new level of sophistication, using graphic programs like Microsoft Photo Editor to manipulate images and save them in a jpg or gif format suitable for posting on websites or attaching to e-mail messages. In dealing with the earliest generation of folk cartoons, Dundes and Pagter comment that the use of office photocopy machines ought to have stifled the creative incentive of the individuals who distributed them, "and that a given cartoon would be copied again and again with little or no change" (145). In contrast to what they found in the 1970s, the most popular items in this sample circulated in several variant forms. For want of a common term, I will call these new forms of folk art "cybercartoons."

The very first of these WTC cybercartoons was posted on a personal website within twenty-four hours of the event and publicized, interestingly, by a message board having nothing to do with interest in topical humor:

rec.music.makers.percussion: September 11, 2001 20:44:25 PST

The idea soon provoked a variant cybercartoon that used the "milk carton" even more explicitly:

"War Gallery" 2001: September 22

Both items clearly reference the enormous media publicity given the missing child problem in the last decade (Conrad 1998; Preston 1999). The humor of these cartoons relies on the dissonance between the tug of sympathy created by the child's picture on the milk carton and the emerging thirst for revenge against the presumed mastermind of the attacks. Hence while the child, if found, would be removed from peril and restored to his or her family, bin Laden, if found, could expect sudden death. Certainly this cybercartoon spoke to such emotions of anger, and it circulated through conduits far removed from young, irreverent computer-ready groups. A participant in the *alt.military.retired* message board, for instance, reported on September 17, "Outside my office cubicle at work I have a big American Flag hanging on the wall. I put on the next wall, at a respectful distance from the flag, [this] picture of Osama Bin Laden [i.e., "Have you seen me?"]."

Another quickly emerging cybercartoon was being actively circulated and discussed by the second evening after the disaster:

rec.humor: September 13, 2001 00:54:25 PDT;
alt.tasteless.jokes: September 13, 2001 00:55:26 PST[14]

The graphic, a modified image of Manhattan Island, shows the rebuilt WTC complex forming the familiar obscene gesture usually interpreted as "Up Yours," an offer to pedicate the offending person. The captions call the viewers' attention to the meaning of this gesture: the main caption notes that the new design "incorporates a gesture and spirit familiar to all New Yorkers," while a smaller caption adds, "To those who believe they can hold us down—you know where to go." This cybercartoon was successful enough that it was mentioned in a September 17 news account that lamented the lack of any other humorous responses to the event (Marcus 2001). And it appears to have inspired one of the first attempts at humor on the David Letterman show. One of his writers recalled:

> New York was in crisis and at that point [September 18] still needed healing and reassurance, rather than edgy comedy. So Dave would do a joke like this: "There's a guy who stands in front of the Ed Sullivan Theater [where the Letterman Show is taped], and every morning on my way to work, he gives me the finger. Well, today, he gave me the finger and a hug" (Ferrante 2002, 28).

The image is doubly significant: most obviously it is a traditional male aggressive response which, as Alan Dundes has noted, is central to American institutions such as football. Secondarily, it shows that the actual attack was associated in many American minds with an attempt to castrate the United States symbolically by destroying buildings that represented an architectural phallus. Thus using "the finger" as a joke simultaneously turns the aggressive threat back against the terrorists and reassures their victims by promising that the "gesture and spirit familiar to all New Yorkers" will live on. Such items offer the viewer, in Letterman's terms, "the finger and a hug." As the link to this item began to circulate more widely in the second week past the attacks, it inspired a number of imitations, one frankly pornographic in which the face of bin Laden has been superimposed on the figure of a naked male, bending over, while the Empire State Building in the form of a giant phallus is about to pedicate him.

Meanwhile, the tie-in with male sports imagery had inspired a verbal item, which verged on humor, to circulate. Clearly the work of an American, it first appeared September 15 on a message board hosted in Denmark.[15] On the following day a participant named "Rufus" posted it on *alt.med.ems*. The item clearly defined the terrorist strike, and the planned response, as a male- oriented competitive game:

> Dear Osama Bin Laden, Yasser Arafat, and Sadam Hussein, etc.
>
> We are pleased to announce that we unequivocally accept your challenge to an old-fashioned game of whoop-ass.[16] Now that we understand the rule that there are no rules, we look forward to playing by them for the first time.
>
> Since this game is a winner-take-all, we unfortunately are unable to invite you to join us at the victory celebration. But rest assured that we will toast you—LITERALLY. ...
>
> (*alt.med.ems*: September 16, 200110:32:48 PST)

This item was later expanded into a much fuller piece, presenting the coming war with bin Laden in terms of an all-star baseball match. The complete "Old Fashioned Game of Whoop-Ass" was a virtual encyclopedia of patriotic symbols, listing the American military branches as the major players, giving "Father, Son, and Holy Ghost" as team owners, and providing no less than four patriotic anthems to begin the "game."

Although the comparison of war to baseball verged on humor, "Whoop-Ass" seems to have been interpreted as patriotic rather than funny. As Dundes has shown, many sports such as football replace male aggressiveness with symbolic acts of violence. This piece, like the cybercartoon that appeared soon after entitled, "Ugliest Damned Piñata I ever saw ..." which depicted George W. Bush about to hit Osama bin Laden in the head with a baseball bat in front of a group of Little Leaguers (*e-mail*: September 23, 2001), simply reinsert the literal act of violence into the sports-play milieu. Hence such items were part of a broader outpouring of non-humorous but extreme patriotism, which in turn created yet another rhetoric for burlesque humor.

In providing models for this rhetoric of hyperpatriotism, two items were especially influential: one was a transcription of "America, the Good Neighbor," a staunchly pro-American radio editorial originally delivered on June 5, 1973, by Canadian radio commentator Gordon Sinclair.[17] Another was a parody of Dr. Seuss's well-known children's poem "How the Grinch Stole Christmas" (1957). Often titled "The Binch Who Stole Airplanes," this piece, portraying Osama bin Laden in terms of Dr. Seuss's Grinch, was written by Christian humorist Rob Suggs (2002).[18] Dated "September 13," it first appeared on a Usenet message board on September 14, then circulated explosively on September 19-20. Suggs's poem pointedly avoided extreme language, as well as the more extreme xenophobia seen in many messages at this time. But it included what many readers took to be an implicit ethnic slur on Arabic peoples:

> The Binch hated U.S! The whole U.S. way! Now don't ask me why, for nobody can say, It could be his turban was screwed on too tight. Or the sun from the desert had beaten too bright.

Suggs strongly denies intending even an implicit ethnic slur in this passage, which follows Dr. Seuss's original closely, substituting only "turban" for the original's "shoes" at this point. He later commented that he simply saw humorous rhyming possibilities for "turban," adding, "Osama does in fact wear a turban and it seems a stretch to proclaim that simply referring to it, in parallel to Seuss, constitutes an ethnic slur" (personal communication, June 23, 2002).

The rhetoric of these items combined hyperpatriotic sentiments with violent language that we have seen used in response to the first attempts at humor. This produced verbal items that were the equivalent of the "Up Yours" visual jokes. The most influential of these was an item attributed to a Mitchell R. Robb (otherwise unknown) and usually titled "If I Were President George W. Bush's Speech Writer" (hereafter referred to as "George W. Bush's Speech"). This item was a burlesque speech, one of a number of popular obscene items claiming to be a public address or official letter but which is actually an opportunity to assail the reader with outrageous sexual and/or scatological language. Such parody speeches have been documented as far back as the early 16th century, and a notorious example, supposedly inspired by a proposal to change the official pronunciation "Arkansas" to rhyme with "Kansas," was widely circulated in the early 20th century (Randolph 1976, 103-105). More immediately, a burlesque letter, purporting to have been sent by President George Bush Sr. to Saddam Hussein, was popular during the Desert Storm conflict. After a polite opening, the letter assaulted Saddam (and readers) with a series of obscenities, saying "get the fuck out of Kuwait, you rag head son of a camel humping bitch, before I turn loose my Air Force and make a multi-national parking lot out of your piece of camel shit country, and then send in the fuckin' Army and Marines to paint the fuckin' lines on it."[19]

Like this item, "George W. Bush's Speech" begins with plausibly polite political statements about the need to put aside differences and assuring the country's safety. Then it turns abruptly to the terrorists and assaults them with obscenity: "Are you fucking kidding me? Are the turbans on your heads wrapped too tight? Have you gone too long without a bath? Do you not know who you are fucking with?" The turban remark, of course, suggests that the author of this piece had seen the opening of Suggs's "Binch" parody, and its continuation also recalls Sinclair's chauvinistic survey of America's achievements, although in a way that is intended to be politically incorrect:

> Have you forgotten history? What happened to the last people that started fucking around with us? Remember the little yellow bastards over in Japan? We slapped them all over the Pacific and roasted about 2 million of them in their own back yard. That's what we in America call a big ass barbecue.

As a way of affirming American's patriotism and resolve, the burlesque concludes with a promise to avenge the terrorist attacks through violent military actions:

> Trust us, Afghanistan will end up a giant kitty litter box. Go ahead and try to hide, Bin Laden. There's not a hole deep enough or a mountain high enough that's going to keep your camel riding asses safe. We will bomb every inch of the country that harbors him, his camps and any place that looks and even smells like he was there.

This piece first appeared on message boards on September 14, the same day as the Sinclair speech was being posted on hundreds of message boards and also the same day that the "Binch" parody appeared. However, it did not spread until a few days later, peaking in popularity on September 20-21, coinciding with a highly anticipated speech on the nation's response to terrorism that Bush in fact did deliver to Congress on September 20. Thus its peak popularity fell a little after the "Binch" parody's peak circulation. The ethnic slurs in the piece provoked criticism from some readers, but significantly it was also the first WTC humorous piece to penetrate a wide spectrum of message boards beyond those focused on discussion of topical jokes. It also was the first item to inspire virtual praise and laughter.

When one participant challenged the appropriateness of racist humor, the person who had posted the speech responded, "i am not going to flame you because we all have opinions on the situation. i work in NYC and saw the entire attack unfold. i am not making any humorous jokes on the attacks, just the wrath of the USA against bin Laden and his buddies" (*rec.music.phish;* September 17, 2001 13:26:48 PST). A few minutes later, another participant on the same list commented, simply, "some people are humourless" (September 17, 2001 13:48:08 PST). Similarly, after the posting of the item on another list caused an exchange of "flaming" or caustic insults, a reader remarked, "<shrugs> Made me laugh" (*alt.music.dave-matthews;* September 18, 2001 04:45:53 PST).

The virtual <shrug> is significant, in that it marks a movement out of a latent period, when the appropriateness of humor needed to be defended, and into a risible moment, when humor is self-evidently valued and the *lack* of humor now is seen as deviant. And even though the person forwarding the item may have intended it quite literally as a statement of loyal American principles, many who read it construed it as humorous. This suggests that its popularity might not necessarily chart the literal popularity of the xenophobic and militaristic sentiments it expresses. Rather, as a number of postings indicate, the piece could be seen as a satire on the emptiness of the prevailing political rhetoric. Much disaster humor expresses anger and frustration specifically against the media, where carefully manicured official platitudes contrast dissonantly with the images of death and destruction that inspire them (Oring 1987; Davies 1999b).

By implication, the burlesque says, President Bush *should* be saying something of the sort, and in so doing he would have tapped into the actual rhetoric being used by many Americans to express their anger at the events. In any case, the item was seen as funny by many readers, and it was influential in creating a vocabulary for Americans' WTC jokes. In particular, the way in which the burlesque alludes to the nuclear attacks on Hiroshima and Nagasaki creates a "patriotic" image of a fireball that destroys an urban landscape and kills thousands of people, in a dynamic predicted by my model. Previous disaster humor, that is, referenced the dominant visual images of the tragedy, and the fireball caused by the second plane's impact, followed by the towers' ultimate collapse, became focal points of media coverage. Therefore, it is predictable that the first popular items would likewise focus on these images.

In fact, the earliest short joke found commonly circulating in the United States (first posted simultaneously with the items described above) referenced exactly the same image:

> Subject: Weather forecast for Kabul
> Cloudy, windy, 5,000,000 degrees farenheit.
>
> (*alt.humor:* September 14, 2001)

This joke was, as predicted, a recycled item from the Desert Storm cycle of 1991[20]:

> And now the long-range weather forecast for Baghdad, 8000 degrees and cloudy.
>
> (*eunet.jokes:* January 25, 1991)

A few days later, this was making the rounds again, slightly elaborated:

> Afghanistan Weather Report
>
> The weather in Afghanistan tomorrow is expected to be sunny in the morning with increasing mushroom clouds in the afternoon.
>
> The temperature looks to be a moderate 2000 degrees with cool winds upwards of around 700 miles per hour.
>
> (*rec.humor:* September 18, 2001)

And by September 23, this joke had been translated into graphic joke form, adapting an actual Weather Channel page reporting conditions in Kabul:

> Afghanistan weather forecast. [Tomorrow's predicted high—3000 degrees: image of a mushroom cloud.]
>
> (*e-mail*)

Such items were part of a more general cycle of visual jokes that began appearing on websites and circulating on e-mail around September 17. Many of these simply castigated bin Laden or predicted his imminent death in revenge for the attacks.[21] These included:

Osama's Head. [Statue of Liberty holds up bloody head of bin Laden, like that of an executed criminal.]

(*alt.tasteless.jokes*: September 18, 2001 01:35:45)

Osama MasterCard. "Ammunition $12 / New rifle $384 / Airline travel to Afghanistan $1349 / Clear line of fire *Priceless*." [Parody of MasterCard ad; recycled Columbine massacre joke.[22]]

(*e-mail*: September 23, 2001)

Like "George W. Bush's Speech," these items express fantasy desires to exterminate the alleged mastermind of the 9/11 attacks, but in ways parallel to previous visual jokes circulated during the 1991 Desert Storm military intervention. Somewhat grimmer are the following items:

If You Can Read This ... You're Fucked [Stenciled on the bottom of a B-2 bomber]

("War Gallery" 2001: September 18)

Osama window. [A missile is about to come through the glass.]

(*eunet.jokes*: September 19, 2001 09:55:00 GMT)

Can Osama Come Out and Play? [An airbase field covered with Stealth bombers]

("War Gallery" 2001: September 21)

These three essentially turn elements of the actual horror into similar horrific threats, defused by being projected onto the scapegoat Osama bin Laden. As we will see, such images became more popular in cybercartoons as time went on.

In "Model," I predicted that the WTC cycle would emerge after a latent period of 17-22 days. In actuality, the latent period was much briefer: from the evidence of e-mail and message boards, we see that it lasted at best seven days, and some jokes that later proved successful appeared on message boards within hours of the Towers' collapse. In particular, cybercartoons appeared to avoid many of the social factors that inhibit joking, probably because their form and mode of transmission on websites allowed them to be created and displayed anonymously. However, early verbal jokes appeared in limited, high-context conduits such as message boards devoted to topical humor, and they did not begin to spread until a broader-based risible moment was attained about a week after the event. This moment was marked both by the proliferation of humorous items on message boards not specifically focused on either humor or aspects of the terrorist attacks, as well as by the return of media broadcasts of live humor

However, this first wave of humor did not bring the cycle to closure. Even though it was more broadly based than the first experiments at humor, still it circulated so privately that even at the end of September some humor experts were still claiming a dearth of humor. As late as September 26, for instance, a *USA Today* reporter observed that, from her perspective, little widespread humor appeared to have generated (Kornblum 2001). There are perhaps two reasons that this wave went unobserved. First, the complex burlesque text of "George W. Bush's Speech" and the cybercartoons are more obviously anonymous than most verbal jokes. They refer back to genres familiar from photocopy-lore, in which the obviously much-reproduced copies that circulate insulate the individual passing them on from the responsibility of having been the first to produce them. Second, in the case of the visual jokes, the need to click onto an attached file or a link to a website makes the viewer implicitly consent to view them, thus protecting the sender from being flamed by someone who would otherwise claim to have been unwillingly forced to see such jokes.

Overall, the success of this first wave of humor relied on its ability to incorporate the violence and obscenity of many American's reactions into traditional structures. The extreme obscenity of "George W. Bush's Speech," however, limited its appeal, and it would be several days before a humorous item emerged that appealed to a still wider base of Americans. Meanwhile, however, the militaristic content of such items led to further attempts to recycle older Desert Storm material and eventually created a rhetoric for still more successful American WTC jokes emerging later.

3. THE BRITISH WAVE (SEPTEMBER 19-30, 2001)

Meanwhile, Britons were distanced geographically and culturally from the direct challenge represented by the terrorist attacks, and were thus able to reach the risible moment more quickly than Americans. The first successful British disaster jokes appeared on message boards on September 18, about the same time as the First American Wave. By the following day we see a fairly typical disaster joke cycle developing on British message boards such as *uk.misc* under the title "Re: Very sick":

1F. What's the difference between the World Trade Center and a wonderbra?
A wonderbra can hold two jumbos.
Still, I've a feeling the *REAL* WTC jokes will be coming along soon . . .
(September 19, 2001 [time not noted])

2M. Try this one on for size
Q. Why is the USA the country where miracles come true?
A. Because it's the only country with a four-sided Pentagon.

Any more?
(September 19, 2001 06:49:02 PST)

3M. daily telegraph to lead patriotic crusade against battersea dogs home . . . announces intention to bomb the hell out of those afghans . . .
(September 19, 2001 10:08:13 PST)

It is significant that these jokes rarely spread to the United States. There may be several reasons for the separation between the American and British waves. First, viewers in Great Britain were genuinely horrified and concerned by the events transpiring in the United States, which were disseminated there in the form of visual footage of carnage and destruction. However, such images did not have the same symbolic impact because they did not strike at the image of Great Britain's invulnerability. In fact, having been made the victim of many terrorist acts at the hands of the Irish Republican Army, Britons may have been better prepared to put the September 11 attacks into perspective. Thus they were able to reach psychological closure while Americans' internal wounds still felt fresh.

However, saying that Britons reached closure more quickly does not explain why British jokes did not readily spread to the United States at a later date. There may be two reasons for this. First, British jokes, like topical jokes generally, tended to use iconic references to brand names and television shows that were part of the media scene in the UK. Like the failed "least favourite flavour of crisps" joke discussed above, the cultural references would need to be explained to Americans, and a joke that requires explanation simply does not make its point well enough to spread. Second, British jokes often demonize Others, particularly the Irish, in a way that does not translate well to America. While Irish stereotypical characters do show up in American jokes, there is no cultural rivalry to support applying such humor to the World Trade Center disaster. Likewise, without the shared history of IRA bomb attacks, demonizing the Irish has no obvious point for Americans. Thus while ethnic stereotypes of Muslims appeared quickly in American WTC jokes, the same Outsider role was played in British jokes by the Irish.

From September 20 through October, WTC jokes appeared freely on British-based message boards and circulated privately by e-mail. The two most commonly found items, "Killing the Afghans" and "Big Apple Crumble," emerged about a week after the disaster and were most popular during the period September 21-28. The most commonly found joke, titled here "Killing the Afghans," first appeared on September 18 and enjoyed a long period of circulation, apparently peaking in popularity on September 28. The most common ecotype of this joke reflected traditional Irish stereotypes and turned the scenario into an "incompetent imitation" of the American militaristic response. Such a joke may have been successful because it could be read as implying criticism of the proposed war, but deflected this criticism onto an ethnic Other closer at hand.

> Gerry Adams today announced that he and the IRA were fully behind any military strikes in response to the WTC tragedy. To cement this vow, IRA SAS have today raided Battersee Dogs Home and executed 15 Afghans!!
>
> (*alt.tasteless.jokes* September 20, 2001 14:58:13 PST)

This argument is supported by the way in which this item was over time increasingly found combined with another, which we could term "Bed Linen." This joke, whether found separately or together with "Killing the Afghans," nearly always referenced anti-Irish ethnic humor:

> Apparently the Irish army has surrounded a department store in Dublin.
> They are acting on a tip-off that Bed Linen is on the second floor.
>
> (*alt.society.nottingham* September 26, 2001 09:30:09 PST)

And the ethnic slant of these items was found also in a number of other regularly found jokes, one of the most explicit being "Hijacking the Blimp":

> In a copycat attack, The IRA has highjacked the Goodyear blimp and bounced off Canary Wharf.
> Whaddyamean you've heard it?
>
> (*uk.misc:* September 21, 2001 11:24:21 PST)

> Did you hear that the IRA have hijacked the Goodyear Blimp ? So far they have crashed it into Big Ben five times . . . .
>
> (*alt.tasteless.jokes:* September 21, 2001 11:53:41 PST)

This again implies an "incompetent imitation" motif with a serious undertone most explicitly expressed in the "Canary Wharf" version. On February 9, 1996, the IRA had in fact detonated a huge bomb in a garage near Canary Wharf tower, a 50-story landmark of London's financial district that was Great Britain's closest analogue to the World Trade Center. Over a hundred persons were injured and property damage was extensive. The most commonly found form focused on the image of a strike on Westminster's Big Ben, an even more visible icon of British political power. These jokes are not really about the World Trade Center disaster, although they make use of it as an icon to initiate humor. Rather, they allude back to the British experiences with terrorism, and while the jokes make use of standard anti-Irish stereotypes, they also imply any follow-up attacks by the present threat to Britons—the Irish Republican Army—will be as incompetent and/or harmless as bouncing a hot-air balloon off British landmarks. More significant are the jokes that by implication criticize the military objectives of the allies. The invasion of Afghanistan, being planned and defended in extreme, jingoistic terms during this same period, is made to seem ridiculous, even as cruel as killing homeless dogs. Indeed, some versions make Americans an even less competent opponent of terrorism than the Irish:

> ********** NEWSFLASH *********
>
> US Delta force have stormed Battersea Dogs home and have killed all the Afghans.
> 15 of the 20 man team where [*sic*] also killed in friendly fire during this action
>
> (*uk.current-events.us-bombing:* September 20, 2001 12:53:51 PST)

The implication of this version is that military action in response to the WTC disaster will accomplish nothing constructive and may in fact be self-destructive.

Yet while "Killing the Afghans" appears to have been the most widespread of the British WTC jokes, another, which I term "Big Apple Crumble," most often shows up as a "signature" joke. That is, it was used to initiate the swapping of items in a way similar to the way "NASA – Need Another Seven Astronauts" often began a series of *Challenger* jokes. It also seems to have been the riskiest of the jokes, judging from the way in which those who posted it gave advance warnings of its offensiveness. It circulated in two forms, the first alluding to the irony that in 2000, KFC (originally the American chain Kentucky Fried Chicken) had added the "Tower Burger" and "Apple Crumble" to their menu in Great Britain.

> KFC have a new meal deal . . .
> 2 Flaming Towers
> 4 Hot Wings
> and
> A Big Apple Crumble
>
> (*alt.terrorism.world-trade-center* September 21, 2001 09:28:22 PST)

> Osama Bin Laden walks into a KFC and orders two flaming towers and a big apple crumble. George Dubya Bush walks into a KFC and says, "I don't know what I want, but I'm gonna murder the bastard".
>
> (Glass 2001 October 18, 2001)

However, this version was largely replaced by the one in which Osama bin Laden appears on a cookery show:

> I've just heard my first World Trade Centre joke.
> Osama bin Laden announced today that he will give up terrorism to become a TV chef. For his first programme he'll be showing us how to make a Big Apple Crumble.
>
> (*alt.babylon5.uk* September 30, 2001 11:56:42 PST)

Certainly it is a brief but complex joke, holding in tension two images. One is that of the notorious terrorist appearing on a cooking show. The other, more powerful image, is a reminder of one of the tragedy's most replayed images, in which the towers, representing the status and achievement of New York City, the Big Apple, crumble to debris before the TV viewer's horrified eyes. At the same time, the joke grudgingly implies admiration for Osama bin Laden, who, like the expert chefs who appear on cookery shows, are successful both at their trade and their ability to use the media to "show us how to make a Big Apple Crumble."

Perhaps this made "Big Apple Crumble" the most truthful and the most daring of the British disaster jokes, and also the least likely to spread to the United States. In fact, of the British Wave, none became popular in America. Of course, British English ("apple crumble") and popular culture icons (Tower Burgers) were major barriers. Less obvious are the reasons for not accepting "Killing the Afghans" but the implied anti-militarism in the first was not in line with the jingoistic hyperbole that constituted the dominant rhetoric of the First American

Wave. "Hijacking the blimp," while understandable to Americans, was essentially a put-down of a group that was an ethnic Other to Britons but just another nationality to Americans. In any case, no risible atmosphere developed in the US that would make it possible to circulate these kinds of disaster jokes, and instead a rather different set of American jokes, short and long, developed.

Further, we note that all recorded jokes showed considerable variation both in style and content. What this feature signifies is not clear from the data available here; perhaps British Internet users for some reason are more apt to recompose joke texts before sending them on to others. More likely, in Great Britain WTC jokes were shared orally before they were recorded on message boards, indicating that in Great Britain *the primary conduit of these jokes was oral transmission.* By contrast, American joke sessions rely on lengthy texts (like "George W. Bush's Speech") or lists of jokes that vary relatively little in style and content, indicating that, *for Americans the Internet was the primary means of sharing humor.*

Thus the American and British Waves were essentially distinct, even though each was presumably equally available to both cultures through the Internet. No "global humor," during this period, actually emerged. This unexpected finding is one that deserves more careful study to see if it remains valid with other bodies of humorous material, and, if so, what it signifies about the difference between the role of the Internet in the two cultures.

4. THE SECOND AMERICAN WAVE (SEPTEMBER 27-OCTOBER 20, 2001)

A *USA Today* article published on September 26 indicated that even at this point humor involved strategic risks for Americans trying to engage in it. Highly visible humor websites such as *The Onion* and *Modern Humorist* had essentially closed down in the wake of the tragedy, and, the report noted, only now were they beginning to test the waters for acceptable humor. "At the center is this unspeakable tragedy, and there's really not much humor can do relating to it," Michael Colton, editor of *Modern Humorist,* was quoted as saying (Kornblum 2001).

Despite this reporter's comment that disaster jokes were only then beginning to "trickle in," humor had been present in the United States almost immediately after the event, and two widespread and successful waves of humor had in fact already emerged, one in the US, one in Great Britain. However, neither wave was as visible as the more general nationwide emergence of humor that occurred, as predicted in "Model," around October 1. In part, this emergence was made up of two phenomena. One was a widening of the First Wave, driven by the nation's move toward active military conflict in Afghanistan, and the other was a distinct and novel Second Wave of jokes that challenged the militarism of the earlier wave.

Military action in Afghanistan began with allied air attacks on October 7 and widened into ground combat on October 19. The widening of the First Wave jokes represented a support for military action in reprisal for the World Trade Center strikes and seemingly represented a move away from jokes dealing directly with the disaster. True, many of the most successful jokes, as before, included horrific images of planes creating fireballs of death that might implicitly reference the "gross" aspects of the terrorist attacks. I had expected the larger cycle, like that seen in the *Challenger* cycle, to focus specifically on such "gross" elements. However, the development of the Afghani conflict during October continued to create tensions in the United States long after the impact of the media disaster had been brought to closure in this country and in Great Britain.

These prolonged tensions brought into being a distinct Second Wave whose theme was finding a more inclusive and pacifist vocabulary to try to signal closure to the crisis and a return to normalcy. Continued official attention to the threat of additional terrorist attacks quickly saturated the public and by mid-October such fire-drills clearly were provoking resentment. The allied forces' failure to capture or verify the death of Osama bin Laden by Halloween (or indeed by Christmas) likewise prevented Americans from reaching full closure on these tensions. Thus the development of the cycle also proved more complex and long-lived than expected. The Second Wave of American humor, that is, appealed to a broader faction of the American population, including women and liberals.

By October 5, a "List of Osama Jokes" was both appearing on websites and circulating by private e-mail. Most of these jokes were, like "Afghani Weather Forecast," obviously recycled from anti-Iraqi items popular during and even before the Desert Storm conflict:

> Q: How do you clear a afganistan bingo hall?
> A: Yell b-52 as loud as you can.
>
> Q: What does osama bin laden and General Custer have in common?
> A: They both want to know where those Tomahawks are coming from!

Q: What is the Taliban's national bird?
A: Duck

However, many of the jokes also reference, by implication, the firestorm and rubble created by the original terrorist attacks. Hence jokes like the following inevitably suggest not just the coming revenge on bin Laden and the Taliban, but also the firestorm and catastrophic building collapse that incited the military action:

Q: What do Bin Laden and Hiroshima have in common?
A: Nothing, yet.

Q: How is Bin Laden like Fred Flintstone?
A: Both may look out their windows and see Rubble.

This trend toward "revenge" scenarios that in fact replay key details from the Towers' collapse is also seen in the visual jokes that became most popular at this time. We have noted that some of the visual jokes showed aircraft, the weapon used by the terrorists, ominously redirected against stereotypical Middle Eastern scapegoats. Two new examples emerging during this period were:

The Chase. [A jet fighter is chasing an Arab on a flying carpet.]
("Osama bin Laden Pictures" 2002: October 15.)

Driving in Kabul. [A military helicopter appears in a side-view mirror, above the warning "Objects are closer than they appear."]
(*e-mail*: October 18)

But while most of the jokes in the first wave simply expressed the threat of airplanes, the cybercartoons that first appeared during the second made this humorous motif cut still closer to the quick by drawing an even more explicit link between the airliners used to attack the WTC and the bombers to be used to revenge the act.

This cybercartoon, showing an aerial shot of military planes releasing hundreds of bombs, is captioned "United and American Airlines Announce New, Non-Stop Service to Afghanastan" (*sic*), and when one looks closely at the image, we see that the logos of United and American Airlines have been superimposed on their tails. Literally, this cartoon implies that passenger aircraft might be redesigned to deliver bombs. But it also acknowledges the key insight that made the terrorist attacks

email: October 2

possible: that passenger aircraft might themselves become instruments of warfare.

A series of semi-animated cybercartoons entitled "Boeing Invitation" built on this idea. Attached to an email message as a PowerPoint file, when opened, one of these reads:

> To: Mr. Osama Bin Ladin (And Friends)
> We at Boeing have noted your recent interest in some of our products…
>
> [small images of Boeing 757 and 767 commercial aircraft pop up]
>
> We now feel compelled to introduce you to the rest of the line…

A second page now loads in which similar images of missiles and bombers appear, not all at once as in the previous cybercartoon but individually, eerily "flying in" to the viewer's screen. When the screen is full of threatening aircraft, a closing caption appears:

> Don't wait for an appointment:
> we'll just drop in.

The same idea was further developed in other variations.

Lists of Osama jokes had a long, if moderate, period of peak popularity, beginning about a week after their emergence and extending from October 11 to October 20,[23] although such lists continued to be posted on message boards at the rate of about once every three days through the end of the year. The popularity of cybercartoons is harder to gauge due to the difficulty of dating their circulation, but both Joseph Goodwin and I received the bulk of our examples during the period between October 9 and October 24, suggesting that these forms of humor also peaked at this time. Thus this cycle, unlike the earlier disaster-focused one, did meet with some success, circulating by e-mail and being posted on websites as well. This is a predictable result, since as we have seen, the cyclical dissemination of jokes is modeled on the prevailing economic and political order (Dorst 1990). Since the jokes are founded on politically dominant images of the military as all-powerful and the Other as primitive, dirty, and ignorant, we could expect such joke cycles to appear and mark a resurgent confidence in the dominant structures of this country.

Yet even though jokes in such a vein elicited laughter during this period, they did not appeal to all audiences and in fact made some witnesses profoundly uncomfortable, not because they were seen as inappropriate, but because their implicit political message was not accepted by all.

Of the "new" one-liner jokes, the cleverest and most successful was this one: "You know what Osama Bin Laden is going to be for Halloween? . . . A DEAD GUY!!!!" This joke circulated orally as early as the first week of October, attributed to television humorist Jay Leno (Hider 2001: October 3, 2001 10:51 PM). It gained even more popularity when it was told by the pro-military Republican Senator John McCain on the nationally broadcast *Letterman Show* on the evening of October 18. It plays on the traditional use of Halloween to impersonate common fears, and a common costume would be that of a corpse. The joke combines the ominous nature of this festival of death with the key idea of the earlier joke, "What's the difference between Osama and Christmas," in addition playing cleverly on the double meaning of "going to be." Thus the threat of the terrorist leader appearing (like Poe's masquer of the Red Death) in the guise of what everyone fears most is immediately defused with the secondary meaning: "by Halloween, Osama will be dead."

Female audiences were particularly uncomfortable with these kinds of jokes, as illustrated by one thoughtful reaction to this joke documented in a Canadian woman's online journal:

> I guess maybe I do know why the Letterman show bothered me. A comic depiction of an unfamiliar culture (Afghanis as camel-loving madmen) is just another way of objectifying them. And objectifying them muddies the definition of them as human beings—granted, human beings capable of terrible

things. Yet once they're seen as less than human, it's easier to visit atrocities on them under the justification of "revenge." Which, if you've been paying attention, is exactly what the terrorists did to our society on September 11th. . . . I hope, oh, I hope, we don't sink to that level. We have to be better than the terrorists, and treat them better than we expect in return, or what's it all for? How can we say we're better?

(Farries: October 19, 2001 3:33 PM)

Thus it is revealing that, as popular as the "Osama Jokes" were, they were not as popular as the Second Wave jokes that implied quite a different reaction to the 9/11 tragedy. An early example of such a joke originated in a political cartoon by John Deering of the [Little Rock] *Arkansas Democrat Gazette*—"Ultimatum to the Taliban."[24] The cartoon, which showed a group of bearded and turbaned men in a cave expressing horror over a note that says, "Give us Osama Bin Laden or we'll send your women to college," originally appeared September 20, but as with many items it began circulating actively a week later in a wide range of settings: photocopy and electronic form, as well as paraphrased oral form. Message boards record the widening use of this cartoon during the start of the Second Wave. At Lincoln Center in New York City, another observer saw two items posted on a bulletin board near the principal artists' dressing room. One was an inspirational quote by the late conductor Leonard Bernstein, but the other was Deering's cartoon (Schubin 2001: September 29). And on the same day the *Washington Post* reprinted this piece, possibly in response to its growing popularity in Internet conduits. One observer called it "a truly lovely editorial cartoon. . . . Oddly enough, this may be the truest thing I've seen in print in weeks" (*alt.gothic*: September 29, 2001 08:43:46 PST). More interestingly, on September 27, a participant in *alt.support.stop-smoking* observed a home-made sign posted on an office door:

TO THE TALIBAN—
HAND OVER BIN LADEN,
OR WE'LL SEND YOUR WOMEN TO COLLEGE!

(September 27, 2001 09:44:09 PST)

The sign paraphrases Deering's original caption rather than quoting it, indicating that the joke had already passed into oral circulation. In oral form, the punch line took a variety of forms: Simon Bronner, for instance, collected it as, "To the Taliban from the American people: / Give us Bin

Laden, or we will take all of your women and send them to college" (e-mail, September 30, 2001).

While not strictly traditional in origin, the emergence of "Ultimatum to the Taliban" at the end of September and the beginning of October, clearly marks the beginning of a more general Second Wave of American humor that did not build on the militaristic, revenge-oriented humor of the first wave. The target and strategy of its humor contrasts sharply with the abortive "gross" cycle and with hyperpatriotic items like "George W. Bush's Speech" and "Osama at Halloween." Most notably, it does not promise a firestorm to equal the Trade Center's demise, but instead shifts the focus to the Afghani government's policy of depriving women civil rights. The joke could be taken two ways. One could see, ironically, a visit by a group of college-educated women as a social threat comparable to that of a nuclear attack.[25] But the messages commenting on this cartoon clearly show a more humane interpretation: that the freedom of women in this country represents a strength comparable to traditional male-focused military weaponry.

Certainly this move away from a militaristic atmosphere affected the progress of the joke that was perhaps the most widely circulated during this second wave, which I will call "Osama's Sex Change." The core idea emerged, like "Ultimatum to the Taliban," during the First American Wave and likewise did not become popular until some weeks later. In fact, the first form appeared in a hyperpatriotic atmosphere similar to "George W. Bush's Speech," as part of a lengthy, politically incorrect message cross-posted on *alt.politics.nationalism.white*, and *alt.niggers*. It began:

> Once Osama bin Laden has been captured and tried, some judge or jury will eventually have to decide on an appropriate form of punishment for the cowardly supercrimes which he has committed. It should be obvious that all existing forms of capital punishment are far too lame and humane to ever possibly fit the crime. . . . Here are a few appropriate methods of slow punishment which I have thought of that might be more appropriate than modern day methods of execution. See how many more you can add to this list.

Some of the suggestions involved literal forms of torture, such as "Feed[ing] his body slowly into a jet engine[26] . . . or a wood chipper," while others, like "Paint[ing] him white and put[ting] him in a cage full of niggers" patently appealed to the racist sentiments of this narrow conduit. Demonizing bin Laden, from this point of view, was no less wrong than demonizing Others in this country, as the Canadian online journal quoted earlier suggests. However, it was the following suggestion that seems to have entered a shadowy oral/virtual tradition to emerge later:

> Give him a sex change operation (without anesthesia) then put his body on public display in the streets of Kabul . . . it is said that over there, women have no status at all and that the Taliban has been rounding up all the widows and dumping them alive into mass graves. Perhaps the Taliban would oblige everyone and do the same to Osama bin Laden turned into a female.
>
> (September 17, 2001 21:21:07 PST)

This suggestion thus combined the two elements seen in visual humor of this First Wave: pedicating bin Laden (and so effeminizing him) and seeing him dead. Alan Dundes, commenting on rituals in which the loser in a feud is emasculated, then killed, comments, "it is evidently not enough, symbolically speaking, merely to kill an enemy . . . [and] the defeated individual is not *just* emasculated he is specifically *feminized*" (1997, 35). Thus this suggestion fits into a broad range of masculine aggressive behavior documented by Dundes, in which the ultimate revenge involves (literally or symbolically), castrating one's enemy, turning him into a woman, and then killing him/her.

Gestated further in private conduits, "Osama's Sex Change" emerged again at the beginning of October, now in a new context that presents it as the "perfect" revenge:

> I have pondered long, over just what would be the best "Ultimate Revenge," . . . the most perfect punishment for Osama Bin Laden, once he has been found and captured alive? Should we kill him??? Nay, for then he merely becomes a martyr and a hero to the extremists. What we should do is to capture him alive, and then folks, after he has been convicted of all of his crimes, he should be sentence [*sic*] to this most perfect punishment. And what punishment is that, you ask? Why give that 'expletive deleted' a full blown sex change of course! Then send him back to Afghanistan, and force him to live out the rest of his sorry-aced [*sic*] life as a woman under the Taliban government, . . . Whadda-y'all think about my idea, huh???
>
> (*miami.general:* October 01, 2001 14:16:06 PST)

This version of the "sex change" idea for the first time argues that the hypermilitary response is self-defeating, since it simply answers one act of cruelty with another and invites yet another terrorist attack in a widening circle of violence. The appeal of this suggestion is that it turns bin Laden's own anti-democratic sentiments against him, both effeminizing him and making him live under the rules that Islamic extremists have themselves formulated. This form of the joke was further streamlined and emerged the following day in an explosively popular ecotype that began by challenging even more explicitly the militarism of existing "Osama jokes":

> A creative solution. And it's peaceful!
>
> Re: Osama. Killing him will only create a martyr. Holding him prisoner will inspire his comrades to take hostages to demand his release. Offering a huge reward for his capture will only encourage him to give himself up so his cohorts can get the money.

And this version streamlines the suggestion, making the text more suitable for quick reading and forwarding in e-mail form:

> The solution?
>
> Let the SAS, Seals or whatever covertly capture him, fly him to an undisclosed hospital and have surgeons quickly perform a complete sex change operation. Then we return 'her' to Afghanistan to live as a woman under the Taliban.
>
> (*rec.crafts.metalworking:* October 03, 2001 12:46:27 PST)

Significantly, this version, even though it circulated on a male-dominated message board, included a link to www.rawa.org, the website of the Revolutionary Association of the Women of Afghanistan, an activist organization advocating the return of gender equity in that country. In an editorial titled, "We're All Afghans Now," Dr. Susan Block appealed to American leaders and the general public to support the goals of RAWA in negotiating a final government to replace the Taliban. However, even she found room to comment on this joke, which she called "a marvelous idea":

> It's a joke, of course, but it rings with a delicious sense of sexual justice. Plus, it helps heal that awful castrated feeling so many of us Americans have felt since our biggest phallic buildings were so painfully cut down. In that sense, it's a sort of sick but somewhat therapeutic anti-terror vengeance fantasy. (Block 2001)

Dr. Block's comments show how "Osama's Sex Change" more than any other joke managed to elicit a genuinely national response to the threat posed by the terrorist attacks. It acknowledges the way in which the strike was seen, symbolically, as a thrust against the nation's masculinity and concedes that the proper response is to do the same to the nation's assailants. At the same time, it holds out the possibility that a limited revenge on Osama could avoid the consequences of the firestorm promised in much of the other WTC humor. Thus the solution is both "creative," and a fresh way of achieving the desired revenge, and "peaceful," in sparing lives on both sides. It fulfills masculine fantasies, but also speaks to feminine outrage at the sexual repression that the Taliban represents. While earlier versions spoke to the political concerns specific to their message boards, the streamlined ecotype could be seen as humorous by a wide range of conduits and so spread rapidly, peaking in popularity only two days after this version first appeared and remaining popular from October 4 to October 10 but continuing to show up regularly through December. Indeed, this joke proceeded to become the single most popular WTC verbal humor item on the message boards surveyed, eventually showing up on 629 sites, over five times as many appearances as the "Osama Joke Lists."

The last really popular WTC joke in the Second Wave, "Alligators in the Potty," appeared just as the popularity of "Osama jokes" was beginning to wane. It took its origins from an contemporary legend, dubbed "Mall-o-ween" by the virtual observer Barbara Mikkelson,[27] which emerged explosively on the Internet on October 9-10. This legend warned that Afghani terrorists had planned two strikes, one targeting airplanes on September 11, the other striking at shopping malls on Halloween. For folklorists, the most interesting part was the contextual envelope in which the legend was enclosed, which was a virtual catalogue of "contemporary legend" markers:

> I think you all know that I don't send out hoaxes and don't do the reactionary thing and send out anything that crosses my path. This one, however, is a friend of a friend and I've given it enough credibility in my mind that I'm writing it up and sending it out to all of you. My friend's friend was dating a guy from Afghanistan . . . [*text of legend follows*]
>
> (*alt.folklore.urban:* October 09, 2001 21:23:18 PST)

Like "Mall-o-ween," "Alligators in the Potty" predicts a terrorist attack on a fast-approaching date. Indeed, it opens with added urgency, since the earlier legend, emerging on October 10, gave its audience a full three weeks to decide if the warning was credible. The new parody legend, emerging October 16, gave its readers less than two weeks to decide if the CIA was correct in saying that alligators would rise out of toilet bowls on October 28 and bite unsuspecting Americans on the ass. Again, however, the verbal text gave far more space to the contextual envelope of the warning, clearly carrying the "friend-of-a-friend" envelope of "Mall-o-ween" into the realm of burlesque:

> I usually don't send emails like this, but I got this information from a reliable source. It came from a friend of a friend whose cousin is dating this girl whose brother knows this guy whose wife knows this lady whose husband buys hotdogs from this guy who knows a shoeshine guy who shines the shoes of a mailroom worker who has a friend who's drug dealer sells drugs to another mailroom worker who works in the CIA building. He apparently overheard two guys talking in the bathroom about alligators and came to the conclusion that we are going to be attacked. So it must be true.

A further satirical twist appears in some early texts, which add a tag clearly cut-and-pasted from an authentic governmental or corporate transmission:

> This message (including any attachments) contains confidential information intended for a specific individual and purpose, and is protected by law. If you are not the intended recipient, you should delete this message. Any disclosure, copying, or distribution of this message, or the taking of any action based on it, is strictly prohibited.
>
> (*alt.wisdom* October 16, 2001 16:54:21 PST)

Needless to say, the parody envelope and the authentic warning *not* to distribute the warning combined to make this joke one of the most popular WTC items during the latter part of the month, peaking in popularity only two days after its first appearance and remaining popular for a week. Interestingly, as "Alligators in the Potty" premiered on message boards, responses showed that it appealed strongly to female readers. On *alt.wisdom*, one of the first boards on which it appeared, Cher, the woman who contributed it, was showered with a series of virtual praise from other women for finding and sharing the item. The joke minimizes the importance of rumors about terrorist attacks, and so by extension the danger of further terrorist attacks themselves. A reader on another message board commented sardonically that this warning "Seems to be as reliable as a lot of the other 'facts' reported in 'mainstream' media in the past month" (*alabama.sports.alabama*: October 16, 2001 18:00:31 PST).

In a month when state and national officials had repeatedly announced the need to guard against an imminent repeat of the 9/11 strike, such comments indicate that many Americans found the need for continued vigilance counterproductive. Ironically, during the same period the American government moved in a directly opposite path, beginning air bombardment on October 7 and ground fighting on October 19. In addition, the sharp peak of this item's popularity at the precise moment when the allied attack shifted to ground action also suggests an implicit resistance to military solutions. This joke and others in the Second American Wave document the increasing rate at which Americans shifted away from militarism as their primary response to the terrorist attacks. This is not to say that the "Osama jokes" ceased to circulate: indeed, they still exert their influence from a multitude of well visited websites. But as October wore on, the Second Wave suggested that the primary problem was not Osama bin Laden but the protracted war of jitters that the government's policies was doing little to calm. Thus the jokes moved away from celebrating military might, combined with male-specific obscenity and ethnic slurring and toward a recognition that there were other important problems in society besides the threat of renewed terrorism. The primary creative impetus of American folk humor was channeled into jokes that implied that warfare abroad and constant alertness at home were increasingly irrelevant. The path humor took suggests an increasing split between official policy and Americans' sentiments, even as public polls continued to suggest near unanimous approval of war policies.

5. THE MOVE TO CLOSURE (OCTOBER 10-30, 2001)

One prediction I had made was that joking would be especially popular early in October (a prediction that we have seen fulfilled) and that it would disappear by the end of the month. Interestingly, the last half of this prediction proved wrong: in fact joking continued throughout the month and to some extent into November, though with less of the emergent flare of some of the jokes surveyed. It remains to look at two examples of these late-appearing jokes. The first, which I'll title "Bin Workin," was the single piece of humor that represented an international response to the WTC attacks. Growing out of an ethnic quip that circulated in Australia as early as October 6, the joke proved extraordinarily successful. An ecotype appearing on October 7 reached virtually all English-speaking countries within the week following.

In origin it grew out of a tradition of anti-ethnic humor, in this case directed at Australian Aboriginals, in much the same way as the British

Wave used details from the American terrorist strike to perpetuate colonial stereotypes of the Irish. Unlike jokes such as "Killing the Afghans" and "Hijacking the Blimp," however, this joke proved flexible enough to adapt to ethnic Outsiders in many English-speaking countries. Thus on some level it was not about the World Trade Center tragedy at all, but rather about a multitude of local conflicts that involve power struggles with Others. In essence, it argued that the known Outsider (whose identity shifted as the joke was relocalized) was a more immediate threat than the unknown Islamic terrorist. More interestingly, the joke tended to lose its anti-ethnic edge as it spread, with the role of the potential (if incompetent) terrorist shifting from ethnic Other to members of the group among whom the joke was distributed. Like the Second American Wave, the joke's popularity implied an attitude that minimized the danger of terrorists and suggested that we should stop focusing on the aftermath of the WTC tragedy and return to work on less dramatic but more important problems in our home communities.

Forms of this joke first appeared on Australian-based message boards debating local politics. The immediate context was a dispute over the current government's policy of providing welfare and public support to Aboriginals, whose traditional lifestyle is under pressure from modernizing influences. While the official governmental policy is to assist Aboriginal colonies, a growing number of white nationalists have attacked such efforts in much the same terms as conservatives have assailed welfare policies for ethnic minorities in the United States. Smoking and drinking are commonly mentioned together as besetting sins of Aboriginals (see Fettell and Pfeiffer 2002), and the improbability of finding them working, or earning a living, is a commonplace among Australian white nationalist propaganda. In addition, the "bin" + verb or noun is a commonly reported feature of Aboriginal dialect.[28] The joke, therefore, played on the similarity between the "bin" (= Arabic "son of") and the common substitution of "bin" for "have/has been" in Aboriginal dialect:

> Police have since released the names of two of the terrorists – bin Smokin and bin Drinkin. An accomplice, bin Workin, could not be found.
>
> (October 06, 2001 16:45:16 PST)

> They're here, all right.
> bin Laden's cousins have infiltrated aboriginal communities.

ASI [29] operatives, on the lookout for these 'cousins', have been putting these questions
anyone here bin Drinkin
anyone here bin Stealin
anyone here bin Jailed
whole communities have stepped forward.

(*aus.politics:* October 12, 2001 02:57:07 PST)

What became the most frequently forwarded ecotype of this joke first appeared on October 7 in a thread titled "Terrorists" posted on an Australia and New Zealand forum of the *Travel & Immigration Discussion & Answers* message board sponsored by BritishExpats.com:

TERRORISTS FOUND ON PALM ISLAND

Latest news reports advise that a cell of 4 terrorists has been operating on Palm Island in North Queensland.

Police advised earlier today that 3 of the 4 have been detained.

The Northern Regional Police Commissioner stated that the terrorists Bin Sleepin, Bin Drinkin and Bin Fightin have been arrested on immigration issues.

The Police advise further that they can find no one fitting the description of the fourth cell member, Bin Workin, on the island.

Police are confident that anyone who looks like Workin will be very easy to spot in the community.[30]

(October 07, 2001 19:13)

Two elements—the desire to turn back to "business as usual" and the joke's applicability to other populations of ethnic Outsiders—made the joke funny in an international sense. Thus the joke could be easily adapted to a new situation and rerouted through many conduits, which explains the explosive speed with which the joke spread to other parts of the British empire and hence to North America. By October 9, the joke had circulated in both New Zealand and in the United Kingdom, where "Nowhere Man" posted to *rec.music.beatles* a version localized in Liverpool but virtually identical to the Australian text.

The presence of independent Aussie versions, and the apparent absence of recomposed versions from other countries, shows that the joke initially circulated in oral context, like the items in the British Wave that appeared in many textually variant forms. By contrast, all the "Bin Workin" variants localized outside of Australia contain language found in the October 7 "Palm Island" text. This makes it almost certain that this Aussie version of the joke was the model for all the subsequently circulated international versions.[31]

Within the next day, versions were posted adapting the Australian text to settings in Glasgow and in Newfoundland, Canada, and on October 11 the first United States version appeared. The joke proved easy to adapt to American situations, simply replacing the image of the ignorant Aussie aborigine with an equally stereotypical Black image:

> *This was just on CNN NEWS at 2:11PM:* Latest news reports advise that a cell of *five* terrorists has been operating *in the Harlem area.* Police advised earlier today that four of the five have *already* been detained.
>
> The [...] Regional Police Commissioner stated that the terrorists: Bin Sleepin, Bin Drinkin, Bin Fightin and *Bin Pimpin* have *already* been arrested on immigration issues. The police advise further [*etc.*]
>
> (*e-mail,* October 24, 2001 but dated "10/17/01" in the header)

While such versions are localized in non-Australian settings, it is significant that such phrases as "Regional Police Commissioner" and "immigration issues" are retained, even though no such position exists in American police forces and "immigration" refers to quite a different issue and ethnic conflict in this country. However, the notion that Others have "bin" doing improper things allowed those who passed it on to connect it with a large variety of local conflicts. Thus one recomposition of it by a British humorist targeted "our office" as the place where "bin Sleepin" and his associates are at large:

> From Safety Council.
>
> We've been notified by Building Security that there have been 4 suspected terrorists working at our office. Three of the four have been apprehended. Bin Sleepin, Bin Loafin, and Bin Drinkin have been taken into custody. Security advised us that they could find no one fitting the description of the fourth cell member, Bin Workin, in the office. Police are confident that anyone who looks like he's Bin Workin will be very easy to spot.
>
> (*alt.support.depression.manic:* October 20, 2001 00:58:36 PST)

Within days this form became the dominant ecotype, replacing the "Palm Island" version. It too was easily adapted to local office concerns, and produced a roar of virtual laughter.

This development paralleled, and in part reinforced, other items in the Second American Wave of jokes, which marked most Americans' willingness to reach closure and return to "business as usual." None did so more clearly than the item I'll label "Knitting an Afghan." Like other WTC jokes, it seems to have circulated quietly as a quasi-improvised quip several weeks before it circulated widely. On the very active American message board *alt.current-events.wtc- explosion*, for instance, one participant complained about the way in which airport security officials were scrupulously frisking passengers, looking for anything that could be construed as a weapon. "I talked to my mother today who has a friend going overseas," he continued, "who is trying to find knitting needles to use on the plane that won't be considered a weapon. What a strange thing for an old lady to have to worry about!" (September 27, 2001 21:22:39 PST) . "They are probably afraid she will knit an Afghan," a respondent commented, provoking a series of appreciative and supportive remarks (September 28, 2001 09:20:06 PST).

This pun, like the one in "Killing the Afghans," implicitly defines the response to terrorism as more of a problem than the risk of hijacking itself. And like other jokes it came up periodically in virtual conversations complaining about airlines security measures. It did not take long before people began creating their own reasons for introducing the pun into conversations, thus turning this conversational quip into a self-contained joke. The first context in which I saw this happen was, appropriately enough, the list *rec.crafts.textiles.needlework*:

> A friend mentioned to me today that she'd heard from someone who'd had her knitting needles confiscated before boarding an airplane. Apparently officials were afraid she'd knit an Afghan. :))
>
> (October 11, 2001 10:46:34 PST)

"Knitting the Afghan" circulated modestly on private e-mail, but the most successful ecotype of this joke appeared a few days later in the form of an alleged news release:

> This just in (from my sister-in-law):
>
> CHICAGO - The war on terrorism took a strange and sad turn Friday as airline officials at O'Hare International Airport refused to let a 73 year old grandmother board her plane as she had in her possesion two, six inch knitting needles. Apparently authorities were worried that she may knit an Afghan.
>
> (*alt.shoe.lesbians.moderated*: October 14, 2001 18:33:22 PST)

From this point on, the joke in this form appeared regularly on message boards, and like "Bin Workin" it displayed not so much a brief, cycle-like popularity but a slow, steady spread. By the end of the month, "Knitting an Afghan" was continuing to spread and find acceptance, and in fact during the next month it appeared on an additional forty-two message boards. This "slow and steady" joke circulation was somewhat unexpected, given the way in which previous disaster humor had emerged, spread quickly, then disappeared from the scene. Perhaps this persistence of the risible moment indicates how deeply the event affected people, particularly Americans. More specifically, it signaled a growing dissatisfaction with official definitions of the crisis, particularly impatience with the extended security alerts and the way in which they targeted ordinary citizens as no better than associates of bin Laden. Increasingly, the popularity of such humor suggests, Americans wanted to return to a state of being where traveling grandmothers and lazy office workers could be seen as ordinary people, not as potential terrorists.

CONCLUSION

This essay has been largely descriptive in focus and methodology, but these were shaped by my theory of joking and predictions ("Model"). Thus it is now possible to sum up this survey in terms of how the data has confirmed or problematized these theoretical predictions.

A latent period did exist, during which joking was strongly and angrily expressed. A risible moment, however, emerged around September 17-18 in both the United Staes and Great Britain. Even so, most jokes circulated quietly up until October 1, after which they increasingly spread outside their original conduits and were more frequently picked up by professional media.

The jokes emerged in waves, including distinct American and British waves of humor. The multi-wave phenomenon was most clear in the development of American humor, where a hyperpatriotic cycle was followed and surpassed by one expressing doubts about the military response and longing for return to normalcy, rather than the expected focus on "gross" elements referencing violent death.

While the most popular jokes peaked during the first and second weeks of October, "Alligators in the Potty" and "Bin Workin" both displayed considerable popularly during the third week. Thus, once the risible moment had been created, new jokes spread rapidly through exisiting conduits. Unexpectedly, a number of third wave jokes, including "Knitting an Afghan," remained in circulation, though at a less active pace, through the end of the year. The continued movement of

WTC jokes suggests that American military action complicated and delayed the process of reaching closure.

My prediction that WTC jokes would focus on the media-broadcast images of explosions and the collapse of the towers proved partially true, though in way I did not anticipate. Jokes of the first American wave focused on the use of passenger airplanes as weapons of war, using fantasy revenge to visit the dominant images of the attacks on Osama bin Laden and other ethnic Outsiders. Since no dominate media image depicted the other attacks, few jokes emerged for either the Pentagon or Flight 94 crashes. Hence, the emic term for anti-terrorist humor, "WTC jokes."

WTC jokes recycled plays on words and ethnic stereotypes from previous joke cycles. Much of this came from cycle jokes that emerged during Desert Storm. While elements of previous disaster joke cycles did surface, it was not to the extent anticipated. The motion toward military actions in response to the terrorist strikes may have led Americans to see the events less as a disaster and more as acts of war; hence the appropriate models for joking were found in military rather than disaster joke cycles. Unsurprisingly, anti-Arab stereotypes underlie many of the jokes, while the British Wave drew on traditional numbskull humor directed against the Irish. In addition, "Bin Workin," the most widely distributed joke of the Second Wave, was popular precisely because it could be adapted to a wide variety of ethnic humor stereotypes, and eventually developed into a broader form not dependent on ethnic slurs.

References in both American Waves to existing Internet materials such as "America, the Good Neighbour" and "Mall-o-Ween" appear to reflect the increasing dominance of the Internet, at least in the United States, in spreading rumors and information about disasters. In addition, complex electronic texts proved the most successful items, but only after they had evolved into a frequently-forwardable ecotype. By contrast, in both Great Britain and Australia, oral communication appeared to be the dominant means of generating and circulating jokes, with most of the jokes being recorded rather than spread by the Internet.

It is remarkable that both American Waves and the British Wave remained essentially distinct. In part, this may be due to the fact that much of the humor relied on knowledge of language and historical events less familiar to residents of the other nation. Perhaps the anti-militarism of the British Wave was both offensive to those participating in the First American Wave and incomprehensible to those sharing jokes in the

Second American Wave. In any case, while the Internet clearly influenced the folk process of disaster-based joking, it did not, in this instance, produce a great deal of humor reflecting a "community of the world."

The Internet arguably made the development and spread of jokes more efficient and more dynamic. Particularly the unexpected proliferation of computer-generated cybercartoons was a phenomenon that will need much closer study in the future. The increasing use of Internet-specific acronyms and graphic devices to signal approval or disapproval of jokes creates a performance context analogous to that familiar to traditional fieldworkers documenting joke sessions with audio- or videotape.

Virtual communication is indeed a vehicle for making and maintaining cultural connections, in addition to oral, print, and broadcast media. In general, such a conclusion should not be surprising: Bronner (2002) reports several studies that found that use of e-mail and similar computer-mediated forms of communication in fact stimulated social bonding and allowed participants to maintain more relationships. Thus the suspicion of the Internet as isolating and destructive of "authentic" traditions seems just one more in a long list of nativistic stereotypes that have deterred the discipline from studying the phenomena that is actually most alive and most central to constructing a response to cultural stresses like the Trade Center attacks. Folklorists will hereafter need to take this important dimension of acculturation into consideration when examining future events in which traditional culture plays a major role. We also need to develop and refine methodology best tuned to do this. Further substantial discussion of such traditions, based on "virtual ethnography," is not only warranted but central to the progress of folkloristics.

Above all, the sheer omnipresence of relevant material, recorded in the heat of the moment but retrievable in calm reflection, creates an unparalleled opportunity for the computer-ready folklorist. This study, lengthy as it is, gives only the surface layer of this material and does not deal with the many other traditional responses to the September 11 tragedy. In particular, it deals only with English-language humor, although it is clear that similar joking must have existed in other important languages including Arabic. Much more needs to be written about folk responses to this national disaster, and about the ways in which both the raw, obscene burlesques and the more reflexive humor that followed interacted to help all the world's citizens adjust to a new landscape, revealed in the space opened up when we saw part of the Big Apple crumble.

PART TWO

Rites of Passage

3

CREATING SITUATIONS

Practical Jokes and the Revival of the Dead in Irish Tradition

ILANA HARLOW

The playing of practical jokes[1] involving the animation of corpses at wakes seems, at first encounter, to be a singularly bizarre practice, incongruous with its social context. Such amusements, however, were congruent with the behavioral norms of wakes as they were held in Ireland through the first half of the twentieth century. Furthermore, these *seeming revivals* of the dead quite possibly were part of a tradition of parodying "the revival of the *seemingly* dead" and "resurrection"—familiar themes in Irish folklore and popular culture. This essay documents that tradition through a presentation of narratives and dramas in which people who appear to be dead are ultimately revealed to be alive. The practical jokes under consideration should not be perceived as peculiar, for they exemplify aspects of Irish humor and an Irish proclivity towards provocative ludic behavior, introduced below by Brian Foley as the tendency to "create a situation."

"There was all sorts of different wakes," Brian Foley recalled as we sat in the home of his father-in-law Michael Walsh in Kilmacthomas (Kilmac), County Waterford one afternoon in 1992. (See "Notes" for transcription symbols.)

Brian: I can remember actually going to a wake here in the village—not here in the village but a mile or two out. And an old lady had died. And she suffered from, oh God, I'm not sure if it's rickets.

But her legs were spread very wide when she was alive. And as she walked she swung her two legs—she walked like that [Brian demonstrates a bowlegged walk with his pointer and middle finger]. Like John Wayne in a Western film. ◆

And . . . she died and rigor mortis had set in. And the body was discovered two days later. So they had to tie the legs before they put her in the bed for the wake. And they tied the legs together with binder twine down at the ankles.

And some clever fellow came into the wake and he was kneeling at the bottom of the bed and he slipped a penknife in under the clothes and he cut the twine ◆◆ and the two legs shot out and ◆ everybody scattered out and they said the woman wasn't dead. ◆◆ And the priest was called and all.

And ye know that sort of thing went on at the Irish wakes all the time.[2]

Another one was they tied a bit of binder twine around the neck, and the corpse was lying back with the hands up here [on its chest] and the twine was running down the length of the body out to the end of the bed. [-] the local character came in at an appointed time and he gave a tug and—the head went up. And everybody scattered and ran out. ◆◆

And ◆ then the body was left relaxed and everybody came in and said, "God, nothin' happened."

And while they were still looking, the body suddenly lifted again. [-]

At all wakes that sort of thing went on.

Ilana: Were you there when that happened?

Brian: No, no, I was never there. No.

Ilana: The legs one?

Brian: Yeah the legs one, yeah, yeah that one was in—she was a woman used to cure warts by puttin' snails on them.

Michael: Oh yeah.

Brian: Neil, Kate Neil ◆◆ up there in—I don't know what the name of the place is.

Ilana: Was that considered disrespectful or okay?

Brian: No I think the Irish didn't worry too much about the word 'respectful' or 'disrespectful.' They just did whatever would create a situation.

Ilana: Create a situation? ◆ To put it mildly.

Brian: Yeah, exactly. Yeah. That sort of thing went on all the time. ◆◆

Indeed, this was neither the first nor the last time I heard of such activities. Although I was surprised by the frequency with which they were reported to me, the reports of their enactment at wakes were less of a surprise. Séan Ó Súilleabháin's *Irish Wake Amusements* (1967b) had introduced me to various ludic activities that took place at these farewell parties. Throughout much of Europe, since medieval times and possibly earlier, feasting and drinking, dancing, singing and music, storytelling, riddling, and games were normal features of wakes.[3] The design of the Irish wake has been explained by reference to a pre-Christian Celtic fear that the dead might return to avenge insults suffered during their lifetimes or to harass those who had inherited their property (Christiansen 1946, 27; Ó Súilleabháin 1967b, 168–172). According to this theory, wakes were intended to appease the dead, "to show goodwill towards them, to sympathise with them in their decease" (Ó Súilleabháin 1967b, 171), and thus to ensure good relations between the living and the dead.

At the most basic level, the purpose of a wake is to watch the body during the period of time between death and burial. Since wakes lasted all night long, people attending them engaged in various activities simply to pass the time; and since Irish wakes are social events, some activities, such as playing games and drinking, were of the sort common to other social events. A number of activities managed to integrate the corpse, it being the guest of honor, into the social scene. This latter aspect of wake amusements will be elaborated upon below. Traditional wakes survived a slew of condemnations from the Church, including several bishops' synodal decrees that disapproved of the drinking, singing, and dancing which took place.[4] Eventually, however, wakes did become less boisterous when they started to be held outside the home—first in churches and then in funeral parlors. Still, wakes remain social affairs at which stories are told about the departed and drink is taken to toast their memory. Although wakes were occasions for merrymaking (Ó Súilleabháin 1967b, 159–160), it should be noted that amusements were restricted to the wakes of old people who had died of natural causes; the wakes of young people and of people who had died "bad deaths" were more somber and subdued.

THE REVIVAL OF THE SEEMINGLY DEAD

Practical jokes involving the seeming revival of the dead can be placed into a broader Irish context through juxtaposition with the widespread narrative theme of "the revival of the seemingly dead" which the jokes seem to parody. The violation of expectations which occurs when a pronouncement of death is found to be erroneous can inspire varied reactions of relief, horror, and humor. Various genres that deal with "the revival of the seemingly dead" and "resurrection from the dead" express different attitudes towards these themes. In myths, resurrection is usually attributed to a miracle, and thus is inspirational to the faithful. In the world of Märchen, where the boundaries between life and death, this world and the other, the ordinary and the supernatural, are easily crossed, resurrection is far from miraculous. Indeed, the resurrection of innocent victims is to be expected—it is accomplished by the actions of another character in the tale, is often related to disenchantment, and leads to joyful reunions.[5] In legends, the revival of the seemingly dead (more common than the miracle of resurrection found occasionally in religious legends) is usually a terrifying experience for those who encounter the revived. Their fear often has its source in the belief that the person has not simply revived from a deathlike state, but has actually returned from the dead; as illustrated in many ghost stories, when the dead return in spirit form, it is sometimes in order to exact vengeance.[6]

If ghosts are startling, the revival of the dead, or of the seemingly dead, is shocking. Ghosts and other revenants are culturally recognized categories of being. People who encounter such entities can name what they are experiencing. Reports of resurrection are much rarer. In some cultures there is no name for such beings.[7] They are either categorized under the general heading of "miracle,"[8] or are falsely assumed to be ghosts. Ghosts—those returned from the dead in spirit form—are not considered below.[9] Still, they are important to bear in mind, since jokes and comic dramas that deal with "resurrection" or with "the revival of the seemingly dead" seem to mock belief in ghosts as well as belief in the possibility of resurrection.

The Horror and Humor of Revival

A presentation of Irish narratives and dramas in which people who appear to be dead are ultimately revealed to be alive will demonstrate the prevalence of this theme. A likely initial response to the violation of expectations caused by an encounter with a person presumed dead is portrayed in Kevin Campbell's narrative below about the man who died twice. Would-be grave robbers are themselves victimized by the shock of seeing the corpse they uncover sit up in its grave. Even in a macabre legend such as this, the potential for a slightly humorous effect exists in the terror experienced by the villainous grave robbers. Their fear is unfounded, since they have witnessed not a return from the dead but merely a regaining of consciousness; thus for some people they are implicitly made out to be fools. Their shock is paralleled ironically and tragically when the prematurely buried man's mourning wife dies from the shock of seeing her revived husband. The husband subsequently dies of grief over the wife's death.

This narrative (AT 990; K426) is widespread in Ireland. I first heard it in 1992 from Kevin Campbell, originally of Lurgan, County Armagh, in

Northern Ireland, as we sat late at night in the common room of a youth hostel in Tralee, County Kerry, and he told story after story:

> But there are so many—I don't know how classic these things are as well, how typical. There's another one [-]—this particular one happened in my own town as well. This guy who . . . died twice you know.
>
> What happened was—it's kind of cruel in nature as well [Kevin chuckles]—this guy died and—he's put in a coffin—all the rest. And he's buried.
>
> Anyway, these guys come in afterwards—knew he was pretty well-to-do, so he would have been buried with rings and things like that on his person. And they dug up the coffin and they tried to get the ring off his finger and they couldn't. [-] They took his arm and they put it up on kind of a plank of wood and they had a big shovel and they just [Kevin slices the air with a downward motion of his hand] right down on his finger where the ring was. [-]
>
> The guy woke up immediately . . . he woke up and he rose up more or less out of the coffin and the guys nearly shit themselves-like, really. He jumps up out of the grave anyway and they run away.
>
> And anyway that guy got up himself—got up out of the grave. And he walked back. And he was wearing kind of a white kind of a cloth. They used to wear a kind of a white cloth—the same as now I suppose, a white kind of a thing—garment—after you die. . . . And he went back and he rapped on the door where he was living and his wife saw him and she dropped dead.
>
> She actually dropped dead. And it sounds bad-like but she died-like, you know? She died of shock when she saw him. [-]
>
> He was alive and he died shortly afterwards because of the fact that he blamed himself for that. And he was buried again.
>
> *Another Irish hosteller:* That's an old one. What it is, is they used to bury people who were in comas. They weren't dead yet and just the shock of having the finger chopped off used to wake them up, you know?
>
> *Kevin:* There's so many where he appears back again and the wife drops dead. That's particularly sad.
>
> And you're not even sure if that's particularly true-like. An awful lot of these are hearsays and some of them are true, some of them are a bit true, some of them are totally untrue. But they're great stories.

Two years later I was meeting in a pub with Martin Kiley, a former gravedigger who lives in Kill, County Waterford, and I mentioned this story to him. He responded by telling a similar story—one which does not focus as much on the shock of witnessing the revival of the seemingly dead as much as it affirms that such revivals *did* in fact occur:

> Well that was a true story. That happened here in Ireland. Ye know.
>
> That time they used to go into a trance, the people. They were only in a coma. They'd go into a coma and they'd have to cut their finger to wake 'em up. They found that cure for 'em.
>
> A girl died and she had a lovely ring on her finger and this fellow wanted the ring.
>
> And when they put her into the coffin he saw the ring and so he said, "I'll dig up that grave some night," he said, "and I'll get that ring."
>
> So he did. He went off to the graveyard where she was buried and he opened the grave and he opened the coffin and he took out her hand. And he couldn't get off the ring so he bit it off. And her finger started bleeding and she sat up in the coffin.
>
> And she served in a public house after. That really happened.

Kevin calls his tale and related narratives "great stories." What makes the revival of the seemingly dead a great story? And why does it have such comic potential? Wylie Sypher has actually proffered that resurrection belongs in the comic domain (Sypher 1956, 220). In *The Irish Comic Tradition,* Vivian Mercier writes that in order to appreciate parody, "It is necessary to recognize what is being parodied and to see the tendency to absurdity in the original which made the parody feasible" (1962,2). It seems no wonder, then, that there is such a great tradition of parodying the return from the dead—resurrection is a phenomenon which seems desirable yet absurdly impossible. In the selection of traditional and popular texts below that deal with "resurrection" and with "the revival of the seemingly dead," the motifs' potentials for comic effect are evident.

The miracle of resurrection is a familiar motif in Irish folklore. It was enacted, for example, in the December folk drama of the mummers' play, in which one character was stabbed and a mummer playing the part of a doctor brought him back to life. The resurrection was enthusiastically celebrated by the other mummers and by the audience, even though it was not a surprising twist of plot. Audience members were familiar with the annually performed play and knew that the fallen character would be revived. Its continued performance demonstrates the popularity of the theme. Revival of the dead and of the seemingly dead is a process that many people enjoy enacting and witnessing. Similarly, people enjoy listening repeatedly to traditional tales of the revival of the seemingly dead. The theme remains popular even when the plot is no longer surprising.

Some scholars have theorized that ritual plays like mumming, performed in the dead of winter, were at their inception a form of sympathetic magic enacted to ensure the renewal of the seasons. Other scholars support metaphorical rather than causal associations between the revival of the dead in the play and the renewal of spring at winter's end (Glassie 1983, 103, 180–81). It is also conceivable that the revival of the dead in the mummers' play recalls the paradigm of resurrection in Western culture—Jesus' miraculous rising from the dead. These ritual and religious associations tie mumming into serious realms of the cosmos; yet mumming was also a comic, ludic genre that included a clown or a fool as a standard member of the cast. In fact, the fool character used to be central in the life-cycle drama but, as time passed, became peripheral in mumming (Gailey 1969, 100).

The integration of religion and play in a single form might seem unusual, but it is actually quite typical, and supports insights into Irish humor made by Mercier that "comic literature in Gaelic shows the ambivalence towards myth and magic or sometimes towards Christian rites" (1962, 9).

This ambivalence was quite evident in a folk drama featuring a resurrection called "The Building of the Fort," which used to be performed at wakes. As reported by W.G. Wood-Martin in his *Traces of the Elder Faiths in Ireland,* the play, which "was filled with sarcasms on various Christian rites and customs," culminated in a battle between the leaders of each of the two groups of enemy soldiers portrayed in the play:

> After a well-sustained fight one combatant fell, as if mortally wounded, and was immediately surrounded by women in cloaks, with hoods drawn over their heads, who keened over the fallen warrior, whilst a bard recited his exploits, and pipers played martial music. It was then suggested that the prostrate man was not dead, and an herb doctor . . . was led in, and went through sundry strange incantations. The fallen man then came to life, and was carried off by his comrades with shouts of triumph (Wood-Martin 1902, 1, 314 ff.)

It seems particularly potent for a play featuring the resurrection of a dead body to be performed at a wake with an actual dead body in the room. Still, the play was a farce, a comedy. The resurrection was only one of many sarcastic references to Christian rites. Mercier writes, "the marvelous is but one stage in the development of many an Irish tale. In a later version the same story may appear as a parody" (1962, 12). Although parodies can develop only after the original has been established, they do not always replace the original. Tales that promote resurrection as sacred coexist with tales that mock it as absurd. Differential belief exists in society, and even individuals waver back and forth in their beliefs. As Leszek Kolakowski has written, in every era the adversarial yet complementary characters of "priest" and "jester" exist; the former is the guardian of absolutes, while the latter questions what appears to be self-evident (1962, 323).

A well-known tale involving "the revival of the seemingly dead" tells of a stranger who comes to a house in which a dead man is laid out. The man's wife asks the stranger to sit with the body while she goes to tell the neighbors of his death. When she leaves, the "dead man" sits up and tells the stranger he is only feigning death in order to catch his wife in her affair with another man (H466). Shortly after the wife's return, her lover comes to visit and the "dead man" beats the adulterous couple. This traditional story (closely related to AT1350), in which the husband plays a vicious prank on his unfaithful wife, was told as a personal narrative by Aran islander Pat Dirane to J.M. Synge, who used it as the basis of his play "The Shadow of the Glen" (Synge 1935, 57–60). Synge also plays with the idea of resurrection in his comic drama "Playboy of the Western World," in which the protagonist, Christy Mahon, seemingly kills his father twice, and twice the father rises from "the dead." Synge's dialogue, informed by his ethnography, illustrates the phenomenon noted earlier, that upon seeing someone presumed dead, it is more common to assume that the person is a ghost than to accept that he has revived. When Christy first sees his father after the supposed slaying, he fears him as "the walking spirit of my murdered da" and looks for a place to hide from that "ghost of hell" (Synge 1935, 47).

The theme of resurrection is probably most widely known from the comic recitation and song "Finnegan's Wake," which tells of tippler Tim Finnegan who falls off a ladder when drunk, breaking his skull. A fight breaks out at his wake, and amidst the brawl some whiskey spills on Tim and revives him (see Appendix). "Finnegan's Wake" has inspired related songs and performances. Michael Walsh of Kilmac sang me a song composed by a local postman who is now dead and gone. The song, whose chorus begins "Then Pat Malone forgot that he was dead . . . ," tells the story of a married couple who couldn't make ends meet. The husband pretended he was dead so the wife could collect his life insurance. But he forgot that he was dead when he smelled the whiskey at his wake (see Appendix.).

In Downpatrick, County Down, I met Bobby Hanvey, a photographer and member of a group that occasionally puts on a fundraising event called "Tim Finnegan's Wake." Bobby himself conceived of the idea. At these four-hour affairs, held at hotel pubs, Bobby, dressed in a shroud, lies motionless for most of the evening playing the part of the corpse. Those who attend are the mourners. The ambiance of an old-time wake is recreated. The pub is lit by candlelight; drink, clay pipes, and snuff are passed around, music is played, and songs are sung. If it is a Catholic crowd, someone dresses up as a priest; if it is a Protestant crowd, someone dresses up as a minister. The mourners wash the corpse. Prayers are said. "And people come up and after they get enough drink in them and they see me laying still they imagine I *am* dead," says Bobby. "A lot of them come up and touch you, you see, through the night, to see if you're dead." Towards the end of the evening Bobby, as Tim Finnegan, comes to life.

"Finnegan's Wake" and related texts play both with the notion of resurrection and with the notion that the whiskey (which is denounced by the church, and which can make its imbibers dead drunk), is also the holy water of life.

I heard another parody of resurrection through anointment in a joke about a hare and a priest. Fourteen-year-old Yvonne of County Armagh told the joke, and it was commented on by her friends Tracy and Laura.

Yvonne: There was this man, right? and he was driving along you know, goin' to chapel.

Rmmmmmmmm.

[Tracy tempers Yvonne's tendency to get carried away with dramatization with an "Okay, Yvonne."]

Yvonne: Okay. Slams on the brakes. [Yvonne makes a screeching sound]. He slams on the brakes. Oh no! He hit the hare—you know, a rabbit thing. Okay, he hit the hare ◆◆, the poor rabbit is dead.

And he goes, "Hail Mary, Hail Mary" and all that there. You see. And he didn't know what had happened. He was sittin, there cryin', and a priest came past. Okay.

Laura: Cryin' over a rabbit?

Tracy: Aww.

Yvonne: The priest goes, "Oh, what have you done?"

And he said, "I've run over a hare, what am I gonna do?"

And [the priest] tells him, "Hold on a wee minute and I'll put stuff on it you know, that could help it."

But anyway [-]—he put the stuff on the hare—and the hare got up and the hare ran on down the field and kept lookin back and wavin'. Ran on down the field, run back and wavin'.

And the man goes, "What did you put in that, anyway?"

"Permanent hare wave." ◆◆

Some of the texts above play with the belief in the miracle of resurrection, others with the belief in the return from the dead. Some parodic forms mock the revival of the dead by setting up situations in which the dead are not actually dead at all, but only *seemingly* so. The practical jokes under consideration are the *reverse* of such parodies; jokers take an actual corpse and only *seem* to revive it. Most parodic forms claim that resurrection or revival is absurd by showing that it never really occurs, but only *seems* to when those who were never really dead are somehow revived. The practical jokes show the absurdity of the idea of revival by making a corpse move involuntarily, thus demonstrating how very dead the person is and how impossible it would be for the corpse to actually revive and move on its own.

The Humor of Corpses

It should be noted that even when a corpse's movement is not the result of a practical joke, it could be considered amusing. Ned Flynn illustrated this to me as we sat with friends and family in his sister Mary's kitchen in Faha, County Waterford:

> My mother used to tell the yarn about this poor person died. An old person. And I think they were dead a long time. They were dead for quite a while and they were found.
>
> So the legs were stiff—they couldn't straighten them.
>
> So they had to lay him in the coffin anyway.
>
> And this fellow says, "I'll straighten them," he says. And he went out and he got a big stone, a big heavy rock of a stone and lifted it up onto his legs.
>
> And as he did, he [the corpse] sat up. ◆◆ Inside in the coffin.

Perhaps corpses, rigor mortis, and the image of a corpse suddenly springing up, like a jack-in-the-box upon being released from its binding, or like a see-saw when a weight is placed on its legs, is funny because of the mechanical quality of the motion. As Henri Bergson proposes in his essay on laughter and the comic effect, it is funny to us when a person acts involuntarily, without autonomy, like a machine.[10] He also suggests that "appearance seeking to triumph over reality" is comic (1956, 96). When corpses move, there is motion without life; the appearance of life triumphs over the reality of death.

THE SEEMING REVIVAL OF THE DEAD

The above illustrations of various horrific and humorous developments of the theme of the seemingly "undead" dead, widespread in Irish narrative, enable greater understanding of the fabrication of the "undead" dead through animation of a corpse, for they demonstrate that such practical jokes are thematically connected to other expressive forms of Irish culture. It is evident from the conversations surrounding the next account that the practical jokes fit into the spirit of old-time Irish wakes.

"What do you think makes a good story?" I asked the company assembled one night at the Flynns' of Faha, County Waterford. Ned Flynn, a brother from nearby Dungarvan, and the Flynns' friend Davey Whelan from County Tipperary responded to my query:

Ned: To hold people. To be able to hold people in suspense . . . until the end, ye know? [-]

Davey: Ye want a crowd in the house and you want someone dead-like in there.

Ilana: You'd wanna have someone *dead*?

Davey: You would.

Ilana: Why?

Ned: The *wakes*. He's talkin' about the wakes. In the wakes longgo—when a person died, they had what ye call a wake—in the house. Funeral parlors now take them [corpses] away. But at the wake they have drink—beer, and they have chalk pipes. [-]. They're made of chalk ye know, white chalk. And they were given out to the people that came to the wake to pay their respects to the corpse. And they had chalk pipes for the men and they had snuff—the old women used snuff—and they'd give snuff to the women. But the women used to smoke the chalk pipe too, didn't they Davey?

Davey: Oh yeah.

Ned: They were known as a *dúidín* [doodeen] and they usually—they've got a long stem on them, but there's no point in having a long stem, because it broke off. They usually broke half the stem. Ye'd have a little pipe and about that much of a stem on it. That was known as a *dúidín*. And that word was used in song as well: "his *dúidín* in his gob". His 'gob' is his mouth. [-]

Ilana: [-] And where do the stories come into it? What kinds of stories would people tell at wakes?

Ned: They'd tell stories about a wake—about this fellow died.

It happened in Dungarvan.

This happened actually.

He was a character. They were characters. A character now is a fellow up for devilment ye'd say—fooling and blaggarding [blackguarding], ye know—*innocent* fun now. There wouldn't be anything in it.

He stole in. He got in some time of the day and he put a bit of cord around the corpse's neck. And he brought it down the clothes to the [-] foot of the bed.

The room was full, anyway, late in the night when he came back in again. And he knelt down at the foot of the bed—at the end of the bed, to say his prayers. And when he were nearly finished, he cut the twine and he pulled it and the body sat up in the bed. ◆◆ And they all ran out.

Ilana: Oh God. Were you there?

Ned: I wasn't. No. ◆◆ My mother used to tell that story. ◆

I told Packie Manus Byrne[11] of Ardara, County Donegal, an account of a practical joke and asked him if he had heard of such things. I was not recording him at the time so what follows is my summary of the response he gave me—an account which his eyes told me was being playfully embellished:

> A man died sitting on the ground leaning against a wall with his knees pulled up to his chest. Of course, once rigor mortis set in they couldn't fit him in a coffin, so they built a coffin in which he could be placed sitting up—a coffin that was higher than usual, more of a cube shape than a rectangle. Someone managed to rig up a string to him and at the wake, when one of the women was saying the Rosary, he pulled it and that made the corpse turn over and face the woman. Everyone was upset, especially the woman. The blaggard was beaten up when they found him out.

Other types of pranks at wakes also caused observers to momentarily think the corpse had come back to life. Andy McGuire of Glencolmcille (Glen), County Donegal, and I were sitting by the hearth in his house above the village as he told me an old story about Paddy the Tay (Paddy the Tea), who had called in to say a prayer at the house of a man who had recently died. The wake was held in Teelin, just down the road from Glen.

The dead man once had gotten a fishhook caught in his finger, and as a result his finger was crooked. Paddy the Tay came to the wake wearing a swallowtail coat. Paddy was on his way out of the room that the corpse was in, to get a cup of tea; when Paddy's back was turned, some jokers or blaggards took the corpse's bent finger and stuck it through the button hole at the back of Paddy's coat, and the hand of the dead man "pulled" Paddy back into the room. This recalls a prank reported by Ó Súilleabháin which involved sewing a man's coattails to the corpse's shroud (Ó Súilleabháin 1967b, 67). Andy's account came as one among many remembrances of people who are no longer living:

> God bless him. Oh they're all dead and gone.
>
> There was another man lived out here in Teelin. I remember him.
>
> He was called Paddy the Tay.
>
> Paddy the Tay.
>
> There's a disease called diabetes. [He would] go into the house [they'd] always give him a cup of tea.
>
> He was a Teelin man.
>
> So this night in question there was a wake in a house in Teelin, you know there was a man dead in the house, so Paddy thought he would call in to say a prayer in the house.
>
> And ye know he had one of these swallowtail type coats on him that time, ye know, that they used to wear.
>
> And a man was dead in the house. On the bed. And he [the dead man] got a hook into his finger one time. They were fishing cod. And the finger bent over like this, do ye see? [Andy motions a crooked index finger.]
>
> And some of the blaggards out in Teelin—Paddy [went into the] other room for a cup o' tea and while he was out, a couple of them took the man's hand and put it into the button hole like this, do ye see? [-]
>
> Hand of the man in the bed pulled Paddy back. It's true.
>
> "Were you there?" I ask.
>
> No. I heard it, I heard it.

I heard another account from Eugene Gillan, originally of County Sligo, in Kinsale, County Cork. And when I mentioned such practical jokes to Kevin Campbell, who is at least a generation younger than the men who had told me about them, he said that he had heard of such pranks. He did not know what to make of them, however—whether they had actually happened or were just told as jokes. In New York, an Irish-American woman I met related it as something she had heard of as happening in Ireland, and an elderly Irishman in New York recollected seeing such a prank as a young boy in County Sligo. I had read accounts of such practical jokes in both Ó Súilleabháin's *Irish Wake Amusements* (1967b) and in Eric Cross's *Tailor and Ansty* (1964).

In his description of pranks played at wakes, Ó Súilleabháin writes:

> Even the corpse occasionally became involved through these pranks. One of the commonest stories in this regard tells how the limbs of an old person who had died were so bent through rheumatism or arthritis that they had to

> be tied down with ropes to straighten them for the period of the wake. In the dusk-like atmosphere of the wake house some trickster would secretly cut the ropes, causing the corpse, as it were, to sit up, terrifying those around. (1967b, 67)

A similar situation is recounted by the Tailor, the great character who, along with his wife Ansty, inspired the book by Cross:

> There was something like that happened in another wake years ago. They were waking a man who was found dead, sitting in a chair, and he had got stiff and his body was bent as he was sitting. He looked queer on the table with his knees sticking up. But if you pressed his knees down the rest of his body came up from the table.
>
> Well, the divil a bit, but someone devised a plan for settling the business and to keep him straight. They tied a rope around his knees and under the table, and another round his chest, and he looked as decent a corpse as ever lay on a table then.
>
> The wake went on, and a piece of the night was spent, and people were getting lively, when some boy cut the rope round the corpse's chest and he popped up off the table as though he had been shot. The company thought that he had come to life again and there was the devils' own hullabulo. (Cross 1964, 91)

Corpses have been made to move as though alive in other areas of the world, too. Petr Bogatyrev describes games in sub-Carpathian Russia in which the cadaver is made to participate, and includes a girl's account of a prank:

> They attach a string to the hand of the corpse and, while the psalter is being read, the boys pull the string and see! the corpse moves its hand. And they are frightened. (Bogatyrev 1977, 42)

Practical jokes were also played with corpses at wakes in the eastern Canadian province of Newfoundland and Labrador, much of which was settled by the Irish. Peter Narváez, who has compiled a catalogue of social interaction at Newfoundland wakes (1994, 268–271), has discussed the social functions of practical jokes along with other "tricks and fun" enjoyed at wakes in Newfoundland (1994, 263–93) [reprinted in this volume]. Monica Morrison writes that pranks played at Newfoundland wakes serve an anti-ritual function of relieving the solemnity of the event (1974, 288). There is a good deal of literature supporting the view that jokes are subversive of dominant structure and denigrate dominant values; jokes have even been described as *anti*-rites (Douglas 1991, 102).[12] Subversion alone, however, cannot adequately account for such jokes. As illustrated by the narratives and beliefs concerning the revival of the dead presented earlier, the jokes are thematically connected to other traditional forms in Ireland, and thus tie into a broader Irish cultural context.

THE WAKE

When a person dies a natural death, it does not prompt the violation of cognitive expectations that is experienced when a young person dies. It is part of the natural order of things for elderly people to die. The death of an intimate associate, however, does violate social expectations. Social relationships must be mutually enacted if they are to continue. When one member of a relationship dies, the survivor is left with the problem of how to maintain the relationship. Wakes are creative responses to the violation of social expectations that results when death spirits away a member of society. Wake activities, including practical jokes involving the animation of the corpse, were ways of integrating the corpse into the social scene while simultaneously ushering the dead person out of it. Such activities thus demonstrated, as parts of the rite of passage, that the dead person had acquired a new social status. The practical jokes under consideration focus attention on responses to both temporary and permanent disruptions of social relations; the former result from the playing of the practical joke itself and the latter are a consequence of death.

Practical jokes fit into the structure of oldtime Irish wakes. Wakes are recognized as forums for public grieving and as formalized means of showing respect towards the deceased and their families. Davey Whelan's remark above, that having "someone dead in the house" inspires good storytelling, indicates the Irish wake's status as a social function as well. It was a communal gathering that gave rise to traditional social activities such as storytelling, riddling, dancing, singing, and drama. Ó Súilleabháin enumerates the types of ludic behavior that occurred at Irish wakes: taunting and mocking; booby traps, mischief making, horseplay, rough games, and fights (1967b). A game in which mock priests performed marriage ceremonies was also played.[13] Even this *general* description of wake activities makes it apparent that playing practical jokes at wakes is not as improper as it might seem to those unfamiliar with the format of oldtime Irish wakes. This does not mean that pranksters, when found out, were never banished from a given wake or that they were never berated, for sometimes they were (as indicated in Packie Byrne's account above). It *does* mean, however, that joking was not considered completely inappropriate behavior. Practical jokes entailing the seeming revival of the dead actually complement "The Building of the Fort" mentioned above—the somewhat spoofing play sometimes performed at wakes, in which characters acted out a death, a wake, and a revival.

The corpse was often animated, or at least treated as though it were alive, in other wake activities, too. If a game of cards were played at the wake, for example, the dead was sometimes dealt a hand; if people were smoking, a pipe was put into the corpse's mouth; sometimes, the corpse was taken onto the floor to join in the dance (Ó Súilleabháin 1967b, 31–32, 172).

The wake marks a liminal moment in the social life of an individual. In the period between death and burial, a person being waked is physically still part of the community, is present at the social gathering, yet is unable to participate. (This, interestingly, is the reverse of the situation presented in supernatural legends that involve revenants. The dead in such legends are already buried, their bodies no longer in view. And in the absence of the body, the spirit or ghost of the person attests that the dead are part of society and can be active in social life). The wake must deal with the question of how to relate to a person in a liminal state of being, and how to integrate such a being into the social scene.[14]

Wake activities are a creative response to death and its disruption of social life. They enable friends to interact with the departed in such a way as to lessen the severance of mutually enacted social relations that occurs with death. Ó Súilleabháin writes that behavior at the wake showed that the deceased was still one of the company (1967b, 171–172). He posits that wake activities were an effort to show that "Death was but a trivial occurrence, which could be alleviated by the features of the wake" (1967b, 172). He theorizes that wake activities initially were inspired by a fear of the dead and of ghosts. The wake gave the deceased a good send off; this was necessary, since some people worried that the dead who were not waked or buried honorably would return for vengeance.[15] Such beliefs do not prevail currently, but the notion remains that the wake is one last opportunity to have a good time with the deceased. Ó Súilleabháin comments that the wake was the last occasion on which the dead and the living could share each other's company, and thus was an "attempt to do final justice to the deceased while he was still physically present" (1967b, 172). This sentiment is supported nicely by a comment Kevin Campbell made to me about these high-spirited affairs:

> And there's a lot of drinking going on even, and people laughin' and there's loads of emotion. But the next day it's dead, dead atmosphere, it's—as soon as the lid goes on the coffin it changes totally.
>
> You'll never see that person again. Not only that—there's a big difference between seeing somebody dead and not seeing [him] ever again . . . in any context.

Practical jokes played with corpses do not necessarily honor the dead, but they certainly are a way of interacting with them and actively integrating them into wake activities. Building on Ó Súilleabháin's notion that pranks actively involved the corpse in the wake (Ó Súilleabháin 1967b, 67), Narváez has made the intriguing suggestion that animating a corpse, far from victimizing or disrespecting the dead, actually enabled the deceased to take part in the fun as an "active participant in an alliance with the prankster" (1994, 272 and this volume 121).

Aside from the need to maintain a relationship with the departed, practical jokes were also inspired by, and contributed to, the merry-making going on at the wakes. Social gatherings that honor a deceased community member are often a mix of joy and sadness. Wood-Martin reported that at Irish wakes,

> Tragedy and comedy, all that is stern and all that is humorous in Irish character, are displayed in unfettered freedom. Transition from deepest sorrow to mirth occurs with the greatest rapidity, so that there is melancholy in their mirth, and mirth in their melancholy.(1902, 1:314)

DIFFERENTIAL BELIEF

The origin of wake activities, as theorized by Ó Súilleabháin, and legends dealing with the revival of the seemingly dead, convey belief in the return from the dead. Practical jokes involving animated corpses played on the fear some people had that the dead could come back and do harm to the living. Thus, the effectiveness of the practical jokes was enhanced by the existence of differential belief; the perpetrators of the practical jokes who apparently were *unafraid* of the dead took advantage of the fact that some of their neighbors *were* afraid. They exploited the existence of differential belief.

A good deal of folklore consists of collective representations belonging equally to many members of a given community; but as Richard Bauman has pointed out, it is also possible for difference of identity to be at the base of a folklore performance (1972, 38). Folklore may be differentially distributed, differentially perceived, and differentially understood; it can even be an instrument of conflict and aggression.[16] The success of practical jokes depends not only on the joker and victim having different information states[17] (Bauman 1988, 37, 40), but also on the fact that differential belief exists within a single society.[18] One person's belief is another person's silly superstition or *piseog*. The resource of differential belief is mined by practical jokers in Ireland, who play on others' *piseogs*. I was introduced to this form of entertainment before I even got to Ireland when the Irishman sitting next to me on the flight over told me accounts of such activity.

The potential for using differential belief as a resource in provocative play can be seen at a basic level in the following exchange between two children that I heard in Glencolmcille, County Donegal. Maria, age nine, reports a belief. Patrick, age seven and three quarters, blatantly defies and discounts it:

Maria: If a girl spits, blood comes out of Mary's mouth.
Ilana: And if a boy?
Maria: Blood comes out of God's mouth. And [-] if a boy and a girl whistles, Mary and God starts to cry.
Patrick: *I'm* whistlin'. [He whistles.]
Maria: See. They're cryin' now. God and Mary is up in heaven cryin' now cause you're whistlin'.
Patrick: Sure but we *have* to whistle.
Maria: Ye *don't* have to.
Patrick: If someone's far away—can't hear someone else—they whistle.
Ilana: So why do you think it's wrong to whistle? Do you know?
Maria: It says in the Bible and our teacher told us.

Patrick's dismissal of Maria's belief, his implicit categorization of it as a *piseog*, enables him to make a valid point about the practical necessity of whistling to get someone's attention, while he simultaneously gets a rise out of Maria. Mockery of belief seems to be at the base of many pranks. Michael Walsh of Kilmac recalled to me a practical joke that involved tying a thin length of twine to the door knockers of two houses across the street from each other. When the people in one house opened their door (note that the doors open inwards), the tension on the twine would cause a knock on the door across the way. The residents in that house would come to the door to find no one there. In a community where some members believe that ghosts exist, or that unexplainable knocks on the door could be an omen of death,[19] this sort of prank is more than an annoyance. Thus, it brings with it the added pleasure of playing on others' *piseogs.*

Similarly, when people believe that someone can return from the dead to do harm to the living, the animation of a corpse in their presence is not only an unexpected shock, it is also frightening. Practical jokes entailing the seeming revival of the dead (along with comic songs, narratives, and dramas that deal with the revival of the seemingly dead) seem to mock belief in ghosts as well as belief in the possibility of resurrection.

LEGENDS AND PRACTICAL JOKES

The contrast of sacred and ludic, actual and parodic, horrific and comedic expressions of the same themes of resurrection and revival, highlights relations between the genres of legend and joke. As mentioned above, practical jokes consisting of animating a corpse seem to play on the belief held by some people in Ireland that the dead can return to do harm, and on the resulting fear of the dead. In both legends and in accounts of practical jokes, people's initial reaction when they see their loved ones revive is not one of joy; instead they are frightened and run away.

Features of supernatural legends such as ghosts—the undead dead—confound and thus highlight the permeability of cognitive and cosmological categories. The practical joker who animates a corpse fabricates a being that confounds categories, and in doing so the joker seems to mock such legends. The legends suggest the possibility of the undead dead. The practical joker takes advantage of the belief in this possibility. The practical joke appears to actualize the possibility of the undead dead, but ultimately reveals itself as simulation. The potentially numinous is presented as humorous.

The comparison of legends and practical jokes, particularly in regard to the social contexts in which they are enacted, is illuminated by David Krause's comment that "the tragic figure must come to terms with the distressed world and affirm sacred values; the comic figure must escape from the oppressive world and mock sacred values" (1982, 30). Supernatural legends are in the realm of the sacred. Practical jokes, of course, are ludic. Johan Huizinga has delineated the relationship between play and the sacred, beginning with a view of archaic ritual as sacred play (1950, 19–20). The realms of the sacred and the ludic are not mutually exclusive; furthermore, they actually involve kindred processes. Both 'religion' and 'play' negotiate boundaries between categories, and help mortals transcend the limitation of situations in which they find themselves.

PRACTICAL JOKES

Practical Jokes as Theater and as Play

Although practical jokes are occasionally malicious, they basically are regarded as a humorous form, even by the victims, when they consider their own duping in retrospect. A practical joke is a little piece of theater performed in front of an unwitting audience. Its essence is subjunctive. Richard Schechner, influenced by Victor Turner, describes the subjunctive character, the "as if" quality, of the theater. The quality is integral to its nature, yet in a good, successful performance, "the 'as if' has sunk out of sight and all the audience sees is the 'is' of the show" (Schechner 1981, 36). Like the theater, the practical joke is a temporary construction, a bounded strip of experience in the key of make-believe.[20]

The violations of expectations resulting from the practical joke are temporary. The practical joke as a unit of behavior includes the eventual revelation to the victims that the experience was indeed part of a joke. Although it might affect ongoing social relations if the victims fail ever to see the humor in it, the practical joke generally does not have any effects "in the real world". This comic violation of expectations is self-contained. There is relief and humor in this, especially when contrasted with the actual and long-term violations of expectations described in supernatural and tragic legends.

In most social contexts deception is considered immoral and unethical, but when the deception is defined even retrospectively as "play," it is often considered a pleasurable and even admirable activity. The practical joke is considered "play," which, by its very nature, often entails semblance and deception (Huizinga 1950, 35). "Play" is linked conceptually and etymologically to "appearances." As Wendy O'Flaherty points out, "illusion" is an English derivative of *ludo,* the Latin word for "play." And the English word "play" also has associations with illusion—a "play" is a makebelieve drama, the "play of light" causes mirages, and "wordplay" often creates double images (O'Flaherty 1984, 119).

Narrative Response to Practical Jokes

Narrative responses to practical jokes—accounts of the practical jokes often told by people who were not themselves victims—define them as play; they thus suggest that social relations should not suffer because of them. Practical jokes, and people's endorsement of them as "innocent fun," are temporary abandonments of ideals of trust and community. Accounts of practical jokes praise those who violate the values; they are affectionately dubbed "the local character," a "clever fellow," a "blaggard," a "fellow up for devilment." Perhaps in part this is to emphasize that such pranks are recognized forms of diversion which should not have permanent disruptive effects on community life. The narratives encourage people to overlook feelings of victimization and to focus instead on the creative aspect of the prank and the characters who carried it out.[21] When victims narrate their own duping as an amusing event, they publicly show an appreciation of the humor in the prank. Thus the telling of such narratives is linked to the restoration of social relations temporarily disrupted by the victimization and potential alienation which accompanies pranks. While the narrated event can be divisive, the narrative event can be unifying.[22]

Richard Tallman suggests that practical jokes and the stories that recount them are two parts of the same expressive tradition (1974, 35, 249). The entertainment value of the practical joke clearly does go beyond the actual event itself, through its duplication in narrative form (Morrison 1974, 293). It seems that pranks are often funnier in the retelling than in the enactment. When I asked narrators if they had been present at the enactment of the practical joke they were recounting, most replied that they had not. The fact that they told me about practical jokes, even when they had not participated in or witnessed the particular practical joke recounted, supports the claim that telling about a practical joke is an extension of the tradition of its enactment. Their knowledge of the practical joke indicates that at some point people who were there at the wakes told the story to people who were not present. The situation was reportable, tellable. The accounts made their way into oral circulation; community members who did not witness the events found them worthy of recounting. The narrative accounts of such events also reinforce the notion among community members that such practical jokes *are* indeed enacted and that they are intended as diversion—that the appropriate response to such things is laughter. Part of the comic effect certainly lies in the pranksters' and listeners' delight in the reaction of the unsuspecting victims.

The antics of practical jokers differ from the deceptive activities of tricksters. Tricksters often engage in their deceptive activities for purposes of personal gain, and are usually just as happy if their victims never find out what has transpired (Tallman 1974, 270). Practical jokers, however, revel in the revelation to the victims that they have been duped; part of the structure of the practical joke as a genre is for the victims to experience the violation of expectations. Richard Bauman has noted this as well, and refers to this part of the practical joke as the "discrediting of the fabrication" (1988, 45, 48).

IRISH HUMOR

The comic effect also derives from paradox and illusion. As Bauman has noted, practical jokes depend for their effect on things appearing to be something other than what they actually are. David Krause points to paradox as a source of laughter in *The Profane Book of Irish Comedy* (1982). An animated corpse creates the illusionary paradox of the undead dead. Paradox, something that appears to be what it is not, leads us to perceive contradiction (Napier 1986, 1). As Mary Douglas has suggested, humor is often based on contradicting or challenging dominant cognitive or social structures, or on the juxtaposition of the seemingly incongruous or disparate (Douglas 1991, 95–96).

Krause characterizes Irish comedy as a rebellious, liberating, anarchic, impulsive, creative behavior or life force, which functions against a cruel and oppressive reality. In a section entitled "The comical denial of expectations," he writes:

> Irish comedy is based on what might be called an oxymoronic view of life: losers can be winners, vices can be virtues, folly can be wisdom. This paradoxical approach to dramatic laughter thrives on contradictions and exaggerations that allow the comic characters to insulate themselves from the inevitable villainies of the world as well as from their own palpable frailties. (1982, 255–256)

The character of the humor that Krause observes does not apply to Irish comedy alone, but to the humor of many cultures. Also, it is too much of a generalization to ascribe all the humor of a culture to a reaction against oppressive conditions. It is, however, descriptive of much Irish humor. Although Krause is referring to underdogs' use of deception and subterfuge as a survival tactic against political oppressors, it seems that his notion suitably describes the practical joke under consideration. Playing with death, making light of it, is a form of subversion. Though the entertainment value of the practical joke—its ability to create a situation—is probably its key function, the contradiction inherent in the seemingly undead dead and the temporary defeat of the inevitable—our mortal frailty—cannot be ignored.

CREATING SITUATIONS

When I asked Brian Foley whether the animation of a corpse would be considered disrespectful, he replied that the Irish "just did whatever [-] would create a situation." This understated description of home-made entertainment intrigued me. I pursued the idea with Brian, who responded, "I don't know what it is. I suppose boredom has a lot to do with it. People that didn't have lot to *do*—just *did* something, to *create* a situation."

He proceeded to tell me about another practical joke, played one calm night on three policemen who were "smoking their pipes and they were fly-fishing. Very relaxed gentlemen . . . And he [the joker] decided . . . the situation—the whole thing was too peaceful. He had to do something to upset it, get a little bit of excitement." The joker caused a big splash in the water by throwing a greyhound into the river from a bridge above. "The lads were fishing and one of them thought they had a salmon caught. And they were all pulling in their reels. ◆ And they saw a greyhound coming in. They didn't know where the greyhound came out of ye know? ◆ But everybody made their own fun I suppose."

Michael Walsh of Kilmac echoed Brian's sentiments in a discussion we had two years later about practical jokes played with corpses. He said that although "you wouldn't be welcome" to do that sort of thing today, back then "it would only be done for a laugh. . . . They made their own enjoyment" in the days before television or radio. This attitude was also conveyed to me by a Dubliner who had spent some time in jail, and described to me a practical joke played by prisoners on fellow inmates as "great crack"—good fun: "And it *is*, you know-like. It breaks up the monotony. It's entertainment you know. When you can't get a filim [film] like—make a fool out of somebody. ◆"

As communities gathered to honor one of their dead, amidst an environment of generous reciprocity in which guests paid respects and offered prayers, and hosts offered food, drink and tobacco, and stories were told, and cards were played, some guests chose to have some fun by introducing a disruptive element—the undead dead who would frighten the other guests. The framing of such behavior within a socially integrative custom is reminiscent to me of the ambiance which develops in many pubs. The reciprocity involved in patrons buying each other rounds is mixed with playfully abusive verbal dueling—known as slagging and blaggarding.[23] Behavior that brings people closer together, which reaffirms social relationships through mutual generosity, is mixed with the temporary abandonment of cohesive social values.

The provocative ludic impulse in Ireland is manifested in practical jokes, in "winding people up," in "codding" them, and in verbal dueling, among other expressive forms. When you wind people up you "get them going," you tell them something false or provocative to "get a rise out of them." When you "cod" someone, you try to make him or her believe what is not true. It can be thought of as a verbal practical joke.[24]

For instance, when I first met Davey Whelan in a County Tipperary pub, acquaintances of his asked, "How's the wife?" as they walked passed us. "She's contrary today. Don't go near her," he replied. He told me his wife was bedridden and that she was quite disagreeable; I commiserated with him. One day I visited with Davey in his home for several hours, and thought it odd that he did not go in to see his wife at all, for even a crotchety woman needs to eat. I asked after her health, and he told me she was contrary. When I got back to the Flynns, my hosts, I asked them about Davey and his wife. It was revealed to me that Davey had no wife at all, and certainly not an invalid one. "He codded you rightly," they laughed. On subsequent days I noticed that people often greeted Davey by asking, "How's the wife?" It was a running joke regarding his bachelorhood. Since I did not know this, I presented Davey with an opportunity to have some fun with me. The Flynns' amused response, "He codded you rightly," told me I shouldn't hold it against Davey, that it should not affect our relationship negatively, that his actions could be defined as a culturally recognized behavior called "codding," and that he had done a particularly good job of codding me.

Many Irishmen I encountered told me or demonstrated to me that they take great pleasure in verbal repartee. The Irish word '*craic,*' which is used in English as well (crack) to designate "fun," literally means "chat." Publican Gerry McCarthy told me he likes the spontaneity of *craic*, the "quick mindedness of people to come back with an answer":

> It's very hard to describe what it really is. It's just, I suppose it's people's imagination at work. [-]. It's generally saying something that immediately gets a response in another. [-] It's a certain animation. Somebody says something, somebody comes back with something else.

A quick example of this can be seen in the following joke I heard when I asked for lies in a pub in Kilmac.

> Did you hear that one? Did you hear that one about the world's greatest liar? He said, "I swam across Niagara Falls."
>
> "I know," said your man. "I seen ye."

The situation created by the enactment of folklore is often playfully agonistic. In some storytelling contexts, listeners respond by telling a story that they think outdoes the first story in its effect—in bizarreness, scariness, or humor. In discussing the verbal dueling known as "flyting," W. H. Auden noted a poetic aesthetic when he remarked that "the comic effect arises" from the fact that "the protagonists are not thinking about each other but about language and their pleasure in employing it inventively" (Krause 1982, 268). This is in keeping with Gerry McCarthy's statement that "You may often have talk of no consequence really, but just—fun." It seems not surprising that a form of verbal dueling, called "barging," did occur at wakes. Eugene Gillan, currently of Kinsale, County Cork, thinks that the form of insult or verbal harassment called "slagging," which sometimes develops into a verbal duel called a "slagging match," happens all over the world, but is more prevalent in Ireland. He attributes this to the ability he thinks the Irish have "to sense people within a few seconds of meeting them," the ability to determine "whether they're good humor or bad humor [-] They would sense that a person is a kind of a braggart and try to bring him down to earth."

In discussing the amusing pastime of "winding someone up," Eugene noted that some people "are easy got at." If a person is very serious, "you can tell them a story and get them going. You know what I mean like? You'd say 'such a fellow is a great judge of the weather' in front of someone who was actually a better judge."

It seems to me that there is something very "Irish" about wanting to provoke a response in others, to "create a situation" as Brian Foley put it.[25] This is quite evident when considering the practical jokes that are at the core of this essay. I was intrigued by my discovery that narratives of a corpse sitting up when a strap holding it down is broken are widespread in the American South. It is quite revealing to compare Irish and American versions, since in America the strap always breaks *by accident,* while in Ireland the strap is almost always broken *intentionally.*[26] *Hoosier Folk Legends,* edited by Ronald Baker, includes two Southern accounts (his numbers 20 and 21) summarized below.

Corpse Sits Up at Wake

A hunchback who has died will not lie flat in his casket so he is strapped down. A cat running around the room jumps onto the corpse. A friend of the deceased attempts to hit the cat with the broom. The blow of the broom breaks the strap and the corpse sits up.

Corpse Sits Up During Funeral Service

A hunchback who has died will not lie flat in his casket so he is strapped down. During the funeral service, just as the priest says, 'This body will rise again,' the strap suddenly breaks loose and the body shoots up in the casket. All the people flee from the church. (1982, 50)

Ghosts along the Cumberland, edited by Lynwood Montell, includes two related stories.[27] In #463 in his book, the contraction of a corpse's muscles makes it sit up, and in #466 (which is similar to Baker #20), a cat who jumps on the hunchbacked corpse causes the strap to break and the corpse sits up (1975, 202–204).

American Negro Folktales, edited by Richard Dorson (1967), includes one account, his #197C:

On the Cooling Board

A hunchback who has died won't lie flat on the cooling board so he is tied down. The string around his neck breaks and he sits up. (330)

Both American and Irish versions relate a situation which plays with appearance and reality. In both a dead person appears to be alive, but the Irish *create* this illusion; they encourage the schism, and emphasize the disjuncture, of appearance and reality.

It is noteworthy that in the Irish accounts (and in Bogatyrev's sub-Carpathian account), the cord is usually cut while someone is praying for the dead. This has at least two practical reasons behind it: during those moments of prayer the attention of all present would be focused on the corpse, and the act of prayer affords the prankster a valid reason to be near the corpse. Still, on those occasions when the prankster seems engaged in the act of praying even as the string is being cut or pulled, the idea of perpetrating the joke precisely at the moment when those present assume he has the most pious of intentions certainly seems to intensify the sport of it all. This practical joke mocks the sacred, and also temporarily mocks the oppression of death.

Brian Foley's characterization of the practical joke as being done to "create a situation" recalls the situational focus of Erving Goffman's sociological inquiries (1986). Goffman begins with the premise that when individuals attend to any current situation and try to make sense of it, they face the question "What is it that's going on here?" They must "frame" the situation, define it, before they can react to it appropriately. Goffman, inspired by William James, is concerned with what individuals "think is real," and with the ways that their subjective framing of situations is vulnerable. Goffman studied "fabrication"—"the intentional effort . . . to manage activity so that . . . others will be induced to have a false belief about what it is that is going on," leading to— "a falsification of some part of the world" (Goffman 1986, 83). His investigation shows that fabrications, to greater and lesser degrees, are a standard feature of everyday life.[28] Fabrication, the intentional falsification of reality, is also a standard feature in various folkloric texts. Goffman's work can elucidate both traditional forms of fabrication and instances of fabrication in traditional narrative. In Bauman's writings on the practical joke, which were influenced by Goffman's work, he notes that the practical joker "intentionally manipulates features of a situation" (1988, 36); this could also be thought of as the creation of a situation. For as Bauman notes, "'Fabrications', the creation of appearances, are designed to elicit reactions" (1988, 39).

Brian Foley's notion of "creating situations" struck me as particularly resonant. It is an apt description of the way in which folkloric texts are used to create, perpetuate, transform, or transcend situational contexts[29] and ongoing social, cultural, and historical contexts.[30] Brian's comments on his community's use of folklore suggest that the act of "creating situations," the intervention in the flow of experience, is a local aesthetic and perhaps even an ethic.[31]

Appendix to Chapter Three

FINNEGAN'S WAKE

Tim Finnegan lived in Walkin Street
A gentleman Irish mighty odd.
He had a tongue both rich and sweet
To rise in the world he carried a hod.
Now Tim had a sort of a tippling way
With a love of the liquor he was born.
And to help him on his way each day
He'd a drop of the crature every morn.

Chorus: Whack fol de da now dance to your partner,
'Round the floor yer trotters shake.
Wasn't it the truth I told you?
Lots of fun at Finnegan's wake

One morning Tim was rather full
His head felt heavy which made him shake.
He fell from the ladder and broke his skull
So they carried him home, his corpse to wake.
They wrapped him up in a nice clean sheet
And laid him out upon the bed
With a gallon of whiskey at his feet
And a barrel of porter at his head.

Chorus

His friends assembled at the wake
And Mrs. Finnegan called for lunch
First they brought in tay and cakes
Then pipes, tobacco and whiskey punch.
Mrs. Biddy O'Brien began to cry
'Such a neat clean corpse did you ever see
Yerrah, Tim, avourneen, why did you die?'
'Ah hold your tongue,' says Paddy Magee.

Chorus

Then Biddy O'Connor took up the moan
'Biddy' says she 'you're wrong I'm sure.'
But Biddy gave her a belt in the gob
And left her sprawling on the floor.
Oh then a mighty war did rage
'Twas woman to woman and man to man.
Shillelagh law did all engage
And a row and ruction soon began.

Chorus

Then Mick Maloney ducked his head
When a noggin of whiskey flew at him.
It missed him, falling on the bed
The liquor splattered over Tim.
Bedad, he revives and see how he rises
And Timothy rising from the bed
Says "Fling your whiskey round like blazes
Thunderin Jaysus, do you think I'm dead?"

PAT MALONE FORGOT THAT HE WAS DEAD

Michael Walsh of Kilmac sang me a song composed by a local postman who is now dead. They used to hold concerts in the halls, and the postman sang it several times on stage. Michael introduces it:

> This is a song, 'tis—it's a kind—I'll tell you now what 'tis about.
>
> It's a story about a man and woman living together. And things went very bad with them. They couldn't make ends meet. And the man was insured for a hell of a lot of money. And the woman—they had a chat one night and the man said to the wife, "You know," he said, "I wonder," he said, "if I pretended I was dead," he said, "you know?" he said, "Put me up in the bed," he said, "and tell your man that the man's dead." And it goes like this:
>
> Times are hard in an Irish town
> Everything was goin' down
> When Pat Malone was short for any cash.
> He finally his life insurance spent
> All his money to the cent
> And all of his business gone to smash.
>
> Then the wife spoke up and said
> "Now dear Pat if you were dead
> Tis a hundred thousand smackers I should take."
> So Pat got up and tried
> To make out that he had died
> Until he smelled the whiskey at the wake.
>
> Then Pat Malone forgot that he was dead
> He sat up in the wake room and he said,
> "If the wake goes on a minute
> The corpse he must be in it
> You've got to make me drunk to keep me dead."

So they gave the corpse a sup
Until they filled him up
Placed him back again upon the bed.
And before the morn was grey
Everybody seemed so gay
Sure they didn't really think that he was dead.

So they took him from his bunk
Still alive but awful drunk
And placed him in the coffin with a prayer.
And the driver of the cart
Said "He'll be dead before I start
I want to see that someone pays the fare."

Then Pat Malone forgot that he was dead.
He sat up in the coffin and he said,
"If you dare to doubt me credit
You'll be sorry that you said it
Drive on me boy or the corpse'll break your head."

So then they started out
On the cemetery route
All the neighbors tried the widow to console.
And when they reached the base
Of Malone's last resting place
And then they lowered poor Patsy down the hole.

Then Pat began to see
Just as plain as ABC
He had no time to reckon on the end.
As the sods began to drop
He broke off the coffin top
And quickly through the earth he did ascend.

Then Pat Malone forgot that he was dead
He quickly from the cemetery fled.
Twas a lucky thing be thunder
He was nearly going under
And Pat Malone forgot that he was dead.

Wasn't that a nice one?

4

TRICKS AND FUN
Subversive Pleasures at Newfoundland Wakes

PETER NARVÁEZ

Death used to be an integral part of life that united home and community, but today we deny it. Dying persons are routinely sequestered from the living in specialized hospital wards. Professionally trained morticians prepare cadavers to be "lifelike" for public display in funeral homes. Domestic funerary customs and rituals, community mechanisms of consolation and collective support for the bereaving, no longer appear to be with us. In Newfoundland, however, this loss is relatively new. Through the first half of this century, and on rare occasions even into recent decades (Buckley and Cartwright 1983), the traditional house wake in Newfoundland has been an important social context for the enactment of forms of mediation and magical agency, a liminal cultural scene in which various rites of passage for deceased persons have taken place. In a significant study of the traditional Newfoundland house wake, Gary R. Butler has shown how "a structured deployment of interior spaces" has assisted in resolving the sacred-profane tensions inherent in the deads' movement from worldly to otherworldly status (Butler 1982, 31). His analysis details the material and social transformation of the "front room" or "parlour" from a formal house space usually reserved for strangers to the exclusion of community members, to a sacred wake room "opened to the community and wakers to the exclusion of strangers" (Butler 1982, 29). A temporary sacred space in which a series of rites of separation were enacted, the wake room housed the deceased for three days and two nights, the funeral taking place on the third day. Although Butler notes slight differences between Protestant and Catholic modes of decorating the wake room and their explanations of customary practices, he stresses their similarity, maintaining that the wakes of both religious persuasions performed the identical social function of fulfilling the needs of community members to "pay their last respects" (1982, 31).

But to read Butler's account and other accounts such as those by James C. Faris, Melvin M. Firestone, and Anne-Kay Buckley and Christine

Cartwright, one might suppose that in paying their last respects to community elders, participants at Newfoundland wakes have conducted themselves with the greatest decorum (Faris 1972, 154–5; Firestone 1967, 78–9). Buckley and Cartwright acknowledge that during the late night vigil of a wake, youthful participants "enjoyed the unusual opportunities and freedoms available in the special context," and engaged in "pranks, drinking, and courtship . . . within the general range of acceptability shared by the community." They do not provide descriptions of these activities, however, apparently believing them to be peripheral to "serious" wake behaviors. Similarly, a more recent treatment of wakes in the community of Calvert by Gerald L. Pocius admits that men provided alcoholic beverages, "humorous anecdotes" were told, and participants experienced "enjoyment," but in the main his description accents death as a somber community occasion (Pocius 1991, 180–3). Undoubtedly, many Newfoundland wakes *have been* solemn events, particularly those held for the "untimely" deaths of infants, children, and young adults (see Ó Crualaoich 1990, 148–49). In contrast to such portrayals, however, many testimonies, particularly those from Roman Catholic communities, indicate that historically and within living memory, Newfoundland wakes have often been characterized by disorder, ridicule, and laughter. Van Gennep has noted that in fulfilling the contradictory social needs of keeping the dead alive and removing the dead, mortuary rites often involve the imbrication of mourning and license (1960, 148). In clear opposition to the hegemony of official religion, the dead have been kept alive at Newfoundland wakes through smoking, drinking alcoholic beverages, eating, talking, storytelling, singing, dancing, fighting, pranking ("tricks"), and playing games, activities that have merged sacred spaces with profane collective pleasures into festive, carnivalesque states that resemble Octavio Paz's description of the Mexican fiesta:

> . . . the fiesta is not only an excess . . . it is also a revolt, a sudden immersion in the formless, in pure being. By means of the fiesta society frees itself from the norms it has established. It ridicules its gods, its principles, and its laws: it denies its own self. The fiesta is a revolution in the most literal sense of the word. In the confusion that it generates, society is dissolved, is drowned . . . in its own original chaos or liberty. Everything is united: good and evil, day and night, the sacred and the profane. Everything merges, loses shape and individuality and returns to the primordial mass. (1961, 51)

Thus, Lambert de Boileu described the boisterousness and seeming impropriety of a wake in a "small harbour" in Newfoundland during the 1850s:

> I selected a companion, and away we went to the scene. Some few neighbours were invited, and kept up the wake until the rum and brandy were exhausted. Although Jem [a friend of the deceased] was only a few hours in advance, the spirits had commenced their baneful influence. . . . Poor Paddy [the dead man] was often appealed to, to say if any of the party had wronged him, and what for. Sometimes the corpse would be taken up, and, in drunken madness, embraced by one of his friends; then another would come up and dispute the right; then a scuffle would ensue, and the dead body would be thrust first in this corner, and then in that, but oftener would be laid flat in the middle of the floor. A little of this wake went a long way, and I speedily left the party, and walked home in the moonlight. (Bredin 1969, 85)

This once customary Newfoundland scene is a New World variant of the "merry" wake attended by Seán Ó Súilleabháin in County Mayo, Ireland in 1921, where "horse-play became the order of the night" (Ó Súilleabháin 1967b, 9–11, 67). Superficially, such behaviors not only appear profane, but aggressively blasphemous as well.

PLACATING THE DEAD

Two major interpretations of these activities, both resting on the premise of the continuity of pre-Christian Celtic religious tradition, have been advanced by Irish scholars: placation of the dead and counter-hegemony. Firstly, drawing from the research of Reidar Th. Christiansen (Christiansen 1946, 27; see Freud 1950, 51–63), Ó Súilleabháin advanced the theory that Irish merry wakes endured because of a continuing acceptance of a pre-Christian Celtic belief in the need to placate the dead. According to this view, fear of the dead is a central motive in the wake complex. It has shaped what today might be called a multiform folk idea or *traditum* (Butler 1990, 5) that made traditional wake amusements a cultural imperative, namely, that *it is necessary to normalize relations with the dead before interment in order to prevent the dead from harassing the living in the future.* As Ó Súilleabháin maintains, during wakes

> pity was mixed with a still stronger feeling of fear that the dead person might return to take revenge on those who had succeeded to his property. Thus the

> survivors did everything in their power to placate the dead. This could best be done while the dead body was still with them. Hence the wake. It was originally intended to give the living a chance of showing goodwill towards the dead and of sympathising with him in his decease. (Ó Súilleabháin 1967b, 171)

Tenacious pre-Christian practices that syncretized and admissibly co-existed with officially acceptable religious customs at Newfoundland wakes have been cited by Butler: an open window in the wake room "to permit the deceased's soul free egress from the house," and the removal of the deceased "foot foremost and only through the door" (Christiansen 1946, 17). But the European-Newfoundland custom that dovetails with Ó Súilleabháin's placation interpretation of wake behavior is the "tradition that those who come to view the corpse touch or kiss the body. This is said to be performed so that the living will never again see the deceased or be haunted by dreams about him" (Butler 1982, 31; see Gordon 1984, 24; 71–115 [19–20]).[1]

While perhaps not motivated by one aspect of the tradition reported by Ó Súilleabháin, that the dead were envious of those who succeeded to their property, Ó Súilleabháin's placation-of-the-dead explanation certainly applies to other social interactions with the dead at Newfoundland wakes. One wake participant explicitly confessed his fear of engaging in the common practice of inserting a pipe in the mouth of a deceased person because "you'd think that fellow would come back after [a] man be putting pipes in his mouth and he dead" (66–25 [C326]). Relatedly, a senior who was concerned with the potential of shenanigans at her own wake attempted to restrain some youths from future frolicking by threatening them with her return from the grave to "torment them" (67–22 [87]). Direct petitions to the deceased to ease relations, as in Lambert de Boileu's account ("Poor Paddy was often appealed to, to say if any of the party had wronged him, and what for"), certainly may have been prompted by mourners' fears of the dead and the need to settle outstanding accounts, whatever those accounts might have consisted of.

To clarify the full dimensions of the placation-of-the-dead argument in the Newfoundland context, however, it should be explained that those in attendance at a wake might have placated the dead not so much through behaviors in "honor" of the dead (Ó Súilleabháin 1967a, 52) as by simply behaving in an ordinary manner, as though the deceased was alive and a member of "the crowd" participating at a party, better known in Newfoundland as a "time" (Schwartz 1974; Wareham 1982). In this way, mourners could exhibit, in Ó Súilleabháin's words, "that the dead person was still one of themselves" (1967b, 171). The overall strategy in developing and maintaining this impression was to engage in participatory activities that either directly or indirectly animated the inanimate corpse. In understanding the apparent disorderly, rowdy, participatory component of many of these activities, one should recognize the social significance of humorous attacks in the contexts of Newfoundland friendship; passivity in the face of humorous attacks and teasing has traditionally conferred respect and therefore has elevated one's status within a friendship circle (see Firestone 1967, 113–14). The dead actively participated in a wide variety of friendship behaviors at Newfoundland wakes. They were aggressors, passive participants, and dupes, but whatever their role, most often the social events that the dead engaged in were characterized by the humorous attacks of friendship, attacks which fostered group solidarity and consequently placated the dead.

As amusing events and practical jokes, many of these activities have generated personal experience narratives (see Tallman 1974, 260–1), community and regional legends, and recollections of extraordinary occurrences. The following taxonomy of activities in which members of a group socially interact with a corpse during a wake represents a sampling of narratives and informational accounts compiled from archival and historical documents and a variety of contemporary oral sources.[2] Many of these activities qualify as "play" in Roger Caillois's sense, that is, a voluntary activity that exhibits a degree of uncertainty and results in amusement; it is economically unproductive, conducted according to rules or imagination, and bounded by time and space (Caillois 1961, 9–10). A variety of Newfoundland informants from predominantly Catholic communities are represented, and the activities they refer to are linked to the remembered past but are generally not associated with contemporary life. The taxonomic categories describe the *apparent* actions of mourner, corpse, and prankster protagonists from the viewpoint of a neutral participant. This approach attempts to compensate for the *post factum* knowledge of prankster activities revealed in the source accounts.

Social Interactions at Newfoundland Wakes

Mourner Protagonists

Mourners eat with and in honor of the deceased: 64-13 (C45); 70-11 (49) (midnight feed, beef and cabbage); 71-22 (21) ("a wake was a big scoff"); 71-42

(34); 71-44 (9) ("scoff which usually took over an hour"); 72-177 (5) (scoff); 74-74 (19) (Ó Súilleabháin 1967b, 16–18; also see Gordon 1984, 25).

Mourners drink alcoholic beverages with and in honor of the deceased, and make toasts to the deceased: 64-7 (C14, C21); 66-25 (C326); 71-42 (34); 72-177 (5); 73-101 (6); 71-23 (3-4); 73-64 (7); Bredin 1969, 85 (Ó Súilleabháin 1967b, 16–18).

Mourners use tobacco or tobacco substitute (tobacco or moss in "TD" clay pipes, cigarettes, snuff) with and in honor of the deceased: 63-2 (C2); 64-12 (C42); 64-14 (C98); 66-25 (C326); 71-42 (34); 72-177 (4); 73-13 (10); 74-74 (19); 74-74 (19); Pocius 1991, 181–82 (Ó Súilleabháin1967b, 14–5 ; also see Gordon 1984, 24).

Mourners exhibit physical affection toward deceased:

Mourners kiss or touch corpse on forehead: 71-115 (19-20) (see Butler 1982, 31 and Gordon 1984, 24).

Mourner picks up and embraces corpse: Bredin 1969, 85.

Mourners fight, corpse involved: Bredin 1969, 85 (Ó Súilleabháin 1967b, 71–2).

Mourners dance: 64-7 (C14, C21); 71-23 (3-4); 71-42 (36); 72-130 (8) (Ó Súilleabháin 1967b, 29–31, 67).

Mourners sing secular songs: 71-42 (36); 71-23 (3-4) (Ó Súilleabháin 1967b, 26–7).

Mourners tell riddles: 71-42 (36); 73-64 (7) (Ó Súilleabháin 1967b, 32).

Mourners tell stories: 63-2 (C10); 64-10 (C33); 64-13 (C45); 71-42 (36); 71-44 (9); 74-74 (19); Pocius 1991, 181 (Ó Súilleabháin 1967b, 26–7; also see Ó Crualaoich 1990, 156).

Mourners converse with corpse: Bredin 1969, 85.

Mourner reads mock will: 71-42 (33).

Mourners play games:

Mourners play card games: 71-42 (36); 71-44 (10) (Ó Súilleabháin 1967b, 31–2, 67).

Mourners play game with penalty of kissing corpse: 71-44 (10); 73-175 (24-5).

Mourners play game with penalty of biting the corpse's toes: 73-175 (24-5).

Mourners play game with penalty of staying alone with corpse in the wake-room: 73-175 (24-5) (Ó Súilleabháin 1967b, 67).

Mourners play "Share the Goat": 64-12 (C42) (Ó Súilleabháin 1967b, 58 ["Dividing the Goat"]).

Mourners play "Forfeits" ("Parson," "Parson's Sheep"): 64-13 (C45); 73-175 (24-5) (Ó Súilleabháin 1967b, 121–22).

Mourners play kissing game "something like Forfeits": 71-44 (10) (Ó Súilleabháin 1967b, 94–95 ["Frumso Framso"]).

Mourners play "Hide the Button": 64-13 (C49) (Ó Súilleabháin 1967b, 116–7).

Mourners play "Sheep": 71-44 (10) (Ó Súilleabháin 1967b, 69 [variant of "Clean Sheep, Dirty Sheep"]).

Corpse Protagonists

Corpse makes noises or speaks:

Corpse makes noises: 71-129 (22-3).

Corpse says, "Get me my pipe and tobacco": 71-22 (20).

Corpse asks for a cup of tea: 73-95 (11).

Corpse smokes pipe or cigarette: 64-7 (C14, C21); 66-25 (C326); 70-27 (1); 71-23 (3-4); 71-44 (13); 72-177 (5); 73-175 (24-5); McKenna 1990; Pollard 1986; Jordan 1985 (Ó Súilleabháin 1967b, 67).

Corpse drinks alcoholic beverages: 71-129 (22-3); 71-23 (3-4); 73-175 (25-6); Bredin 1969, 85.

Corpse plays musical instrument: McKenna 1990 (accordion).

Corpse greets mourner by waving hand/arm: 71-129 (22-3); 71-22 (4); 71-42 (37); McCarthy 3 September 1991.

Corpse sees through open eye(s): 71-44 (13); 73-64 (7); Pollard 1986.

Corpse shakes: 71-42 (37); 72-130 (8).

Corpse stands: 64-7 (C21); Matthews 1990.

Corpse sits:

Corpse sits on bed or in coffin: 71-44 (13); 72-130 (8); 73-175 (24-5); 73-187 (12); Pollard 1986).

Corpse suddenly sits up (see Christiansen 1946, 32):

It is later revealed that a prankster pulled up corpse with horse's collar, ropes, string, or fishing line: 64-14 (C98); 67-22 (87); 71-22 (4); 71-22 (20); 71-44 (14); 72-177 (5); 73-101 (6); 73-101 (7); 73-64 (7); 73-95 (11); Pollard 1986; Jordan 1985.

It is later revealed that the securing mechanism (rope, strap, flagstone) for flattening hunch-backed corpse was sabotaged by prankster or accidentally failed: 71-13 (45); 73-13 (14-5) (Ó Súilleabháin 1967b, 67; also see Baker 1982, 20–21; Ballard 1992; Stevens 1976, 31).

Corpse appears alive in her/his own clothing: 64-7 (C21); 71-42 (33); 71-42 (37).

Corpse leaves: 71-22 (21); 73-187 (12).

Corpse leaves wakehouse and frightens someone in act of retribution: 73-13 (9).

Corpse strikes mourner: 71-22 (21).

Corpse humorously dressed:

Corpse wears ridiculous hat: Walsh 1984.

Corpse wears multiple shirts: 67-22 (87); 71-129 (22-3).

Prankster Protagonists

Prankster moves deceased to wakeroom by rolling corpse downstairs: 67-22 (87); 71-129 (22-3); Oldford 1990.

Prankster gets into bed with corpse: 67-22 (87).

Prankster(s) steal(s) the two coppers (pennies) from corpse's eyes in order to amass one dollar for the purchase of a bottle of "moonshine": 73-101 (7); 73-187 (12).

Prankster physically molests (head, eyes, whiskers, feet) corpse: 64-12 (C42); 71-42 (33); 73-13 (16); 73-64 (7).

Prankster blackens faces:

Of sleeping mourner: 63-2 (C10); 64-7 (C21); 64-12 (C42); 64-13 (C45); 70-11 (49); 71-42 (33); 71-44 (11); 71-44 (9); 72-130 (8); 73-13 (9); 74-74 (19) (Ó Súilleabháin 1967b, 67).

Of corpse: 79-129 (22-3).

Prankster places candle in hand of sleeping mourner: 73-64 (7).

Prankster puts pepper in pipe of sleeping mourner: 70-11 (49) (Ó Súilleabháin 1967b, 66).

Prankster puts pepper in mourner's tea: 74-77 (23) (Ó Súilleabháin 1967b, 66).

Prankster burns pepper on stove to make everyone sneeze: 71-42 (38); 73-64 (7).

Prankster burns snuff on stove to make everyone sneeze: 73-64 (7).

Prankster put gunpowder in cigarette of mourner: 74-77 (23).

Prankster ties sleeping mourner's legs together: 71-42 (33) (Ó Súilleabháin 1967b, 67).

Pranksters play practical jokes using water:

Throwing cups of water: 71-44 (9).

Sitting mourner down in pan of water: 71-44 (9-10).

Prankster awakens mourner by holding liniment under nose: 64-7 (C21).

Prankster awakens mourner by pouring molasses over mourner's head: 64-7 (C21).

Prankster puts molasses on soles of mourner's shoes: 64-7 (C21).

Prankster puts thumbtacks inside mourner's shoes: 64-7 (C21).

Prankster spits tobacco juice into mourner's rubber boots: 71-42 (33).

Several of these categories refer to serious socializing activities, while others, emicly known as "mischief," "jokes," or most often as "playing tricks," exhibit the qualities of practical jokes, a folklore genre defined by Richard S. Tallman as "a competitive play activity in which only one of the two opposing sides is consciously aware of the fact that a state of play exists"; the knowing side's object of play is to cause the unknowing side "some physical and/or mental discomfort," especially, I would add, the extreme self-conscious discomfort of embarrassment (Tallman 1974, 260). Two analysts have judged the corpse as the victim of practical jokes at Newfoundland wakes (see Morrison 1974, 288), but the sampling for the above taxonomy indicates that the deceased were usually not victimized. Exceptions are categories of "corpse physically molested," "corpse humorously dressed," "prankster steals the two coppers from corpse's eyes," and "prankster blackens face of corpse." The participatory interpretation argued earlier (behaving in an ordinary manner, as though the deceased was alive and still one of "the crowd" participating at a "time") counters the notion that practical jokes entailing touching or manipulating a corpse necessarily victimize it. Clearly, from the standpoint of conventional religious ideology, the sacrosanct physical person of the dead is inviolable, and any contact with the dead except for the most serious reasons is "disgraceful" conduct. The force of this norm makes it appear as though corpses touched for ludic purposes are victimized, but this is an ethnocentric impression. What occurred in the majority of practical jokes cited is that *the corpse was an active participant in an alliance with prankster-protagonists,* usually men, who perpetrated jokes against an unknowing side. The victims, often women and seniors, were those who were surprised or shocked by the rising corpse, the corpse's greeting, the corpse's voice. Even in the games cited, the corpse willingly allowed his toes to be bitten by the "*victim*" of "forfeits." And in his actions and passivity, the corpse's status was elevated. Given the additional vantage of a new ontological state, the corpse became the supreme prankster who only needed a little help from his friends.

Thus, a need to placate the dead has undoubtedly played a role in liminal wake behavior that has mediated binary oppositions of life and death, tears and laughter, private space and public space, work and play, body and soul, sacred and profane.

COUNTER-HEGEMONY: POPULAR RELIGION VS. OFFICIAL RELIGION

"Shenanigans" and "mischiefs" in Ireland have also been interpreted in hegemonic terms, a theoretical frame suggested by Antonio Gramsci (see Byrne 1982; Gramsci 1990; Narváez 1992), as part of a continuing cultural antipathy between dominated, subordinated peoples adhering to sacred practices "derived from a cosmology and a metaphysics whose origins lay in Celtic religion" (Ó Crualaoich 1990, 145) versus representatives of the hegemony of official religion. Gearóid Ó Crualaoich, a major advocate of this position, has maintained that games played at Irish merry wakes, traditionally organized by a jesterlike "borekeen" (*cleasaí*), were a "manifestation of the tension or struggle between clerical authority and an ancestral value system in Irish traditional culture" (1990, 155). In discussing fairy beliefs, a related cultural component of Irish popular religion, Diarmuid Ó Giolláin has extended the conflict argument, contending that the traditional antipathy between Irish religion and official religion was "part of a struggle between the subordinated cultures of local communities and the hegemonic culture of the state" (Ó Giolláin 1991, 199). The historical, clerical judgments of the Irish Catholic clergy clearly support this thesis. Ó Súilleabháin has provided abundant documentation demonstrating that ideological signifiers such as "abuse," " insult . . . to God," "odious, pernicious and detestable practices," and "disgrace" were routinely used by church officials as weapons of condemnation in campaigns against Irish wake amusements (Ó Súilleabháin 1967b, 19–21; also see Christiansen 1946, 31; Gordon 1984, 25–8; Stevens 1976, 32).

Counter-Hegemonic Pleasures

By themselves, however, placation of the dead and the counter-hegemony of Celtic religious practices against official religion do not adequately explain wake amusements in Newfoundland. In particular, these explanations have not sufficiently taken into account manifest social functions and *intentionality,* that is, the conscious purposes for engaging in particular activities that informants have articulated. In fairness to Ó Súilleabháin, it is important to note that he did ask "several people who took part in various wake amusements in former times why they did so" (1967b, 166). He elicited four reasons: there was "no harm" in carrying on a traditional custom; people did not wish to behave differently "from the general pattern"; amusements "pass[ed] away the long night"; and amusements kept people awake (167). For Ó Súilleabháin, however, these reasons did not solve "the problem of the gaiety and entertainment at oldtime wakes" (1967b, 167). Beyond a consideration of the reasons he elicited, which he considered "sensible and hard to object to," it is understandable why Ó Súilleabháin tended to neglect the synchronic dimension. As a survivalist, he was primarily interested in contemporary data only to the extent that it provided information for reconstructing the past. Deriving its theory from social Darwinism, one of the foremost aims of survivalist folklore analysis has been to reconstruct past stages of western culture by inference through deciphering the original meanings of contemporary folklore "survivals." These cultural traits have been defined by Edward Tylor as seemingly "meaningless customs" that "had a practical or at least a ceremonial intention when and where they first arose, but are now fallen into absurdity from having been carried on into a new state in society where the original sense has been discarded" (1958, 94). In his analysis of Irish wake amusements, Ó Súilleabháin similarly observed that living examples of traditional customs and belief deserved study for "they were items in the traditional code of behavior of our ancestors. . . . Now outmoded, their main value is to give us an insight into the mind and ways of thinking of our forefathers in times gone by" (1967b, 169). Thus Ó Súilleabháin's study provides the stimulating hypothesis that the collective placation of the dead was a primary, original purpose of wake amusements.

Such an analytical, latent social function, however, offers no adequate rationale for why such practices were sustained over long periods of time. The set of activities designated as "wake amusements" are too complex to be simply regarded as "mindless," thoughtless, tradition-directed behaviors. Indeed, aside from the magico-religious custom of touching the dead to alleviate the possibility of dreaming about the deceased, the vast majority of informants' testimonies reveal that placating the dead has *not* been a predominant manifest function of social interactions at Newfoundland wakes. In keeping with the findings of Ó Súilleabháin, some Newfoundland participants emphasize the practicality of some gregarious wake behavior. They maintain, for instance, that interactions involving smoking were practiced not only for social reasons, but for the practical purposes of alleviating the odor of death and preventing one from contracting a dead person's disease (70-27 [1]). In these instances, placation was not operative. As in Ó Súilleabháin's sample, several Newfoundland informants claim that wake amusements primarily "passed the time," enabling one to fulfill the rule of staying awake and providing company for the deceased (see Ó Súilleabháin 1967b, 167). Besides being practiced for perceived reasons of formal religious injunction, such deferential acts of companionship or attendance may be construed as symbolic forms of affection, friendship, and love; they need not be viewed as placation.

The argument that wake amusements represent counter-hegemony in sustaining Celtic religious practices suffers from a similar analytical deficiency. There are no manifest indications from Newfoundland informants that participation in wake amusements has been part of a struggle to maintain ancient popular religious practices in face of the hegemony of official religion. Ó Crualaoich's interpretation of counter-hegemonic Irish merry wakes is less a general cultural theory than a well-constructed, interpretive, historical account of the origins of a form of cultural conflict in Ireland. For Newfoundland it is important, but of limited use in providing contemporary evaluations.

What specifically, then, maintained the traditional house wake in Newfoundland with such vitality? It will be advanced here that its popularity was significantly sustained by *pleasure.* Most often, the stated social purposes and consequences of late night wake activities in Newfoundland have been expressed in terms of pleasure. Typical comments include: "great fun to a wake boy" (63-2 [C10]); "there was a crowd at the wake and they were having a great time" (71-13 [45]); "people came from all around to have a good time, even strangers" (71-22 [21]); "tricks and fun . . . at wakes" (71-42 [33]) The intentional collective pleasures of many traditional Newfoundland wakes may be interpreted as exhibiting features which were at once *evasive,* i.e., pleasures in which the sociocultural is sidestepped in favor of sensory-biological indulgence, and *subversive,* i.e., antagonistic pleasures that display the social consciousness of a subordinated group engaged in rebellious acts against dominance and dominators. Evasive pleasures recall Roland Barthes's use of the French idiom *jouissance*—ineffable, context-specific experiences of physical pleasure perhaps best described as "thrilling" and "orgasmic" (Barthes 1975; see Heath 1977, 9). While such pleasures might not be considered "productive" in terms of actually altering social relations, they are vitalizing and often provide at least a temporary sense of empowerment.

Given certain social contexts, the consumption of alcoholic beverages promotes *jouissance.* John Szwed has noted the importance of drinking alcohol to communication in a Newfoundland community, because it has functioned as a "leveling, specifying, focusing activity" (Szwed 1966, 438). In terms of developing differential identity through evasive pleasure, a small group focus is intensified by drinking because, as Erving Goffman has noted, it is an "engaging activity" which "acts as boundary around the participants" (Goffman 1961, 25). The following humorous family legend concerning a wake in Jigging Cove conveys the significance of alcohol at Newfoundland wakes.

> Well you see there's another chap lives over there, over there about a mile across the harbour in Jigging Cove. They had a family [of] about five or six and the old man there, their father, was probably sixty or seventy years old and he died. And they came over, to report his death of course, and there was my father and a few of the boys over here . . . they made a coffin for him and took it over and put him in the coffin. And the house they used to live in there was no room to put the coffin, only right along by the stove, one of these old Waterloo stoves . . . and the head of the coffin was right close by the stove. And so there was quite a lot of this black gin for sale we used to bring from [the French island of] St. Pierre. Now the black gin would be in black bottles . . . but the gin would be white just the same you see. . . . Now the black gin would be twenty-five [cents a bottle] and, of course, that's what the people would go for. So they all gets a few bottles of gin and they goes over and starts with the wake, and they puts an old clay pipe in his [the dead person's] mouth. Now then, we're going to have a dance and there's no one to play for them but he [the deceased] had a son, I imagine twenty years old, and he had to play [the fiddle]. If he didn't play they were going to kill him and that was all there was to that. So the young fellow started to play and they started to dance and they danced and danced and their gin was gone and there was so much fire and heat [from] this old stove that the man, the dead person, there was a crust on him and he was starting to turn bright red. . . . They got two fellows gone over to the harbor again for to get more gin for to keep their supply good but they was late in arriving [returning]. And they goes out by the door to sing out for them [the wake attendants], and they sings out and everytime they sing out, of course, (now we right down under a big hill) and somebody would answer them. Finally they sang out and they blared out and the other fellow would answer them and the louder they'd sing out, well the louder the other fellow would make fun of them, which was their own echo under the hill and they got frightened to death and thought 'twas ghosts and they came on home and left the boy [son] there by himself. [64-7 (C14)]

An additional element to this narrative has been provided to me by the collector, John D.A. Widdowson: apart from the tape-recorded interview, he was informed that during this wake potatoes were thrown at the corpse (see Ó Súilleabháin 1967b, 10). This account portrays various forms of *jouissance* (drinking, dancing), and the transgression of the official religious taboo prohibiting the desecration of the dead does not result in actual negative sanctions. Initially, placation does not appear to be at work because, as with so many Newfoundland wakes, the "mourner" protagonists at the wake have not known the deceased very well, and they have attended primarily for pleasure. While these wake attendants are ultimately "frightened to death," because of their fear of the dead (ghosts), there is no implication that their previous maltreatment of the deceased and his son might be linked to their excessive anxiety. According to the unsympathetic sophisticated narrator, who finds their plight humorous, the real fear of the protagonists results in foolish reactions to a phenomenon (echo) that has a naturalistic explanation. While the storyteller might be advocating greater decorum at wakes, he is also simply ridiculing the absurd actions and judgments of inebriates.

At least three jocular ballads sung in Newfoundland, two European-derived and one native, also depict the evasive bodily pleasures of *jouissance* at wakes. The most famous, "Finnigan's Wake," a broadside import (Laws Q17; 67-24 [C373]; 70-8 [C780]) obtains much of its humor from the contrast of hegemonic piety and counter-hegemonic *jouissance* at a merry wake. That is, reverential, conventional religious practices (setting candles, tears, a mournful outburst) are set off against the popular, traditionally disparaged physical pleasures of drinking, smoking, and dancing, and the shenanigans of drunken revelry, fighting, and throwing things. In addition, the climactic punch line of the jocular ballad ("Do ye think I'm dead?") prompts laughter because we are doubly surprised. First, we laugh because of the collision of two incompatible planes of thought: our shared expectations that the living are animated and speak, and that the dead are inanimate and mute; i.e., we don't expect the dead to rise and to speak as if alive. Second, and compounding this collision, we hardly anticipate the "dead" to verbally mock the living for having made an obvious mistake about corporeal status!

As presented on a field recording by MacEdward Leach, "Finnigan's Wake II"—a song also known in Newfoundland as "Finnigan's Wake," but in Irish songsters usually called "Molly McGlocklin"—is the narration of a young widower who tells of the circumstances of his marriage to Molly McGlocklin and how he eventually fought his wife's lover, one Barney McFinnigan, to the death (Leach 1966, 8). The latter had to resurrect himself from the dead at his own wake to defend Molly from her pugnacious husband. At one point during the melee the husband-narrator is killed ("How long I was dead I don't know"). He too came back to life, defeated "Finnigan," and within six months murdered Molly and at the gravesite "slapped her" dead body on the bones of "Finnigan." This morbid morality tale of a "decent, laboring youth" who is now "single again," spending his time "rakin and batterin," is probably more revealing of traditional gender roles than anything else, but it again documents a wake as a central cultural scene of pandemonium and violent *jouissance*.

Newfoundland's best known balladeer, Johnny Burke (1851–1930), "Bard of Prescott Street," often recollected actual events in his songs, peppering his compositions with local references and dialect (Mercer 1974; Kirwin 1977; Taft 1990). In some of his best known humorous songs, such as "The Kelligrew's Soiree" and "The Teapots at the Fire," he enjoyed presenting the slapstick, free-for-all antics of particular social gatherings. Like these ballads, Burke's realistic portrayal of a local wake, "The Night Pat Murphy Died," furnishes yet another cultural scene where *jouissance* predominates.

THE NIGHT PAT MURPHY DIED

(Air: Paddle Your Own Canoe)

The night that Paddy Murphy died,
  I never will forget,
The whole gang they got loaded drunk
  And some ain't sober yet.
And while the bottle was passed around,
  Sure everyone would stay,
And Murphy came down with the pipes,
  To open up the play.

Chorus:
That's how they showed respects to
  Paddy Murphy,
How they showed their honor and
  their pride,
And then they looked at Pat and all
  the others
And everything at the wake was fun
  The night that Murphy died.

'Bout two o'clock in the morning,
  some dirty sneakin' tramp
Rose up the lid of the ice box
  To see poor Paddy's lamp.
They stopped the clock so Mrs. Murphy
  Couldn't tell the time.

And at a quarter after two,
They argued her it was nine.

Oh the day of Paddy's funeral,
It was a wonderful sight,
And the people all looked lovely,
And the pallbearers dressed in white.
They brought him to the graveyard
And laid him in the clay,
And they said good-bye to Paddy,
And they all walked away.

(Burke 1960, 55; Kirwin 1982, 119]

Ritualized *jouissance,* where "everything" at Paddy Murphy's wake was "fun," collective drinking ("the bottle was passed around") and inebriation ("some ain't sober yet") was the order of the day. A member of the Murphy family provided clay pipes "to open up the play," and it appears that much of the play centered on practical jokes; two are cited. One is the stopping of the clock to extend the period of merriment and to befuddle the widow. Another prank is perpetrated by a "dirty sneakin' tramp" who raises the ice box lid "to see poor Paddy's lamp," a possible allusion to the exposure of the corpse's penis, a shocking "trick" that has reportedly been practiced in Ireland (Millman 1977, 190).

The Counter-Hegemonic Pleasures of Courtship

Evasive and subversive pleasures are often inextricable. Certain rebellious pleasures that display a social consciousness of subordinance may be overtly expressed through verbal forms such as jokes and wisecracks. Like evasive pleasures, however, subversive understandings are not exclusively communicated through verbal codes. Physical presentational codes (e.g., odor, tactility) might outweigh verbal ones, especially when groups engage in prohibited behavior with the full knowledge and cooperation of a community, as has been the case with the physicality of merry wakes. Because laughter is one of the most obvious nonverbal demonstrations of collective, physical pleasure, Mikhail Bakhtin's sense of the "carnivalesque" is germane here, for it unites *jouissance* and subversive pleasure. According to Bakhtin, the carnivalesque possesses a "material bodily principle" in opposition "to severance from the material and bodily roots of the world" (1984, 9). Like medieval carnivalesque forms of ritual spectacle, Newfoundland wakes reflected a materialistic, collective "all-people's character" that resisted spiritual authority through comic expressive forms. In turn, these carnivalesque pleasures at Newfoundland wakes have often been intertwined with courtship and sexual relations.

Most pranksters in Newfoundland have been young men trying to impress young women by making them laugh and/or by frightening them. Through such courtship customs at house wakes, Newfoundland youth have rebuffed the moral sway of official religion, as well as resisted the moral monitoring of older members of family and community. Certain kinds of house wakes offered a traditional sanctioned context for courtship. Thus, if there was "an old person who had his years spent, you were more likely to look ahead to his dying for some fun" (74-77 [23]). The death of a younger person was considered tragic, but the timely failing of a senior brought on the hopeful expectations of youth that a wake was in the offing (see Ó Crualaoich 1990, 148–9): "that was wonderful to hear tell of somebody dead" (64-10 [C33]); "you'd be waiting for them to die, to stay up the night for a bit of fun" (64-13 [C45]); "when you'd hear tell of an old man or an old woman sick in the wintertime, every time you meet somebody, 'did you hear tell of how Skipper so-and-so or Mrs. so-and-so is? Are they dead yet?' You'd be waiting for them to die. Because that meant a couple of good nights" (Keating 1992).

Some of the pleasurable activities anticipated at wakes involved foodways. One informant equated wakes with eating a "scoff" (see Kirwin 1982, 438–9), that is, a "feast": "a wake was a big scoff" (71-22 [21]). Typically, a scoff in honor of the deceased was eaten at midnight ("You'd go into wake, and however many was in that house twelve o'clock that night they all had something to eat" [Keating 1992]). Often lasting over an hour (71-44 [9]), this meal altered the mood of the mourners. It is appropriate that eating preceded a night of pleasure for, as Mikhail Bakhtin has perceived, special food events exhibit transformational potency:

> In the act of eating . . . the confines between the body and the world are overstepped by the body; it triumphs over the world, over its enemy, celebrates its victory, grows at the world's expense. This element of victory and triumph is inherent in all banquet images. No meal can be sad. Sadness and food are incompatible (while death and food are perfectly compatible). The banquet always celebrates a victory and this is part of its very nature. . . . It is the triumph of life over death. In this respect it is equivalent to conception and birth. (Bakhtin 1984, 282–3)

After the scoff, elder mourners and the immediate family retired, knowingly leaving youthful participants to "sit up" or "wake the corpse." It was then that "the fun began" (71-44 [9]). After the scoff "the older people went home and the people belonging to the house were tired, so they went to bed, went to sleep, and the crowd took over; they had a ball from then to daylight while old skipper so-and-so was in there, cold as ice" (Keating 1992). Buckley and Cartwright have reported that "often one of the more easygoing adults [participated] in the vigil to make sure things didn't go too far' (1983, 11). As the following narratives reveal, however, such invigilators were not always appreciated, and they could become the victims of pranks. An unanticipated twist occurs in the second narrative; the believing dupe is more provoked by the prank than frightened.

> During one evening of a wake at her distant relative's house [over forty years ago], [Eileen] along with a few of her friends entered the house and into the room where the body was. Also present in the room was an elderly gentleman sitting in a rocking chair, who, every few minutes, would fall asleep or "nod off." [Eileen] quietly slipped a piece of string around the corpse's finger and secured it tightly. Then they would wait until the old man opened his eyes and they would pull on the string thus raising and lowering the arm of the dead body. This act eventually caused the old man to leave and go upstairs to bed. [Eileen] told me that the man never did tell anyone of the events he experienced that night probably in the fear that they would think he was crazy. (Milley 1991)

> Now once a service was done about 1865 to an old fellow Mickey——— who lived in a small town in Newfoundland. Now Mickey was a bit odd or so they used to say. Grandfather always called Mickey "a cute fool." He was always ailing with one thing or another and the neighbours always helped him out, yet, Mickey managed to live until he was well up in his eighties, and one night died in his sleep. Well, anyway, Mickey as the saying goes was "cocked, leathered, and shaved." His ailing was over and he was lying peaceful in a brand new habit. Well, at that time the neighbours would go to visit the family in mourning and stay for the night. Sometimes the younger ones would stay until twelve and after that the older folks would come and stay until morning. Well, at Mickey's wake two fine lads in their twenties were staying until twelve and after that my grandfather would take the midnight watch. So the two lads, knowing that my grandfather was coming alone for the rest of the night, decided to play a prank on him. When they knew my grandfather was on his way, they decided to liven Mickey up. By sticking his old pipe in his mouth, tying a very thin but strong cord around Mickey and attaching it to outside the window sill. Well,

> after the lads had met my grandfather at the door, they wished him a "good night" and they were on their way. Grandfather stood outside the cabin to light up his pipe. There was no one else around and he knew Mickey was not going anywhere. Well, he turned to enter the cabin when he saw Mick with [his] pipe in his jaws slowly rising up from the coffin. Well, grandfather made one jump straight for Mick, grabbed the pipe from his mouth and pushed him down, [saying] "damn you Mick, you couldn't go nowhere when you were alive and you're not going anywhere now!" (Jordan 1985)

Distanced from the usual moral restraints imposed by the nightly supervision of elders, youth laughed, joked, played, teased, and courted in the context of the corpse until dawn. The pleasures of courtship were often at the heart of these activities: "the nights were long, the family was in bed, so I guess everything was done; there was tricks and riddles and . . . there was even some loving done" (73-64 [7]). Courtship is highlighted in the following narrative concerning a prank during an Anglican wake in the community of Shearstown during the 1930s. It is particularly revealing with regard to attitudes toward the deceased individual as well as to the dead in general. In addition, and as de Certeau has observed about narratives concerning games, it should be kept in mind that the oral circulation of such stories furthered specific antics of the merry wake by providing "schemas of action," teaching "the tactics possible within a given (social) system" (De Certeau 1984, 23).

> Believe it or not at the wakes years ago the young people would come. Not so much the old people, the young people, especially if they were in love. [laughs] I'm laughing because this one night was out of this world. . . . This old man, he was a real old, they'd call them in them days "cusses" when they were real real snotty you know, right bawling at everybody. . . . He never had a kind word for anybody! [laughs] Anyway he died you know. [laughs] I'm sorry but it's funny even now! So he died you know. Everyone was glad! [laughs] No one was sad. [laughs] . . . And they were all sitting, now the couples was together you know. . . . And the way they had the casket put, it was this way. [motions, laughs] They done it for fun I think. Afterwards they said a couple of the men done it for fun. [laughs] And no one noticed a thing you know. . . . The couples you know, they was so happy and kissing and hugging, just sweet lovely innocent love you know. All of a sudden, this thing [casket] started moving down off the three chairs. They had him on chairs and he moved down about [motions], the end of the casket hit the floor and [he] stood up straight! [laughs] Oh my goodness gracious! . . . Well the sweethearts was no longer sweethearts! They beat it for one small door! Everybody beat it for that one

> small door. Well I tell you there was some bruises everyone trying to get though the door! . . . He could've stepped right out of the casket but he didn't, he just fell forward! . . . Well they laughed, they laughed! (Ameen, 14 November 1992)

One erotic Newfoundland ballad centers on courtship behavior at wakes. Entitled "Shoot the Cat," the song offers insights into wakes as possible scenes of scandal.

> Nellie was the prettiest girl that ever you did see,
> Oft times she asked to a dance or a spree,
> And she was asked a question and the answer for to make,
> And she kindly asked her Mrs. could she go to the wake.
> Yay, yay, fell the dee, don't you know what I mean?
>
> Yes, you may go but be civil and beware,
> For Johnny is going and you know he will be there.
> He will kiss you and he'll court you, and he'll keep your belly warm,
> And perhaps you will be sorry coming home in the morn.
> Yay, yay, fell the dee, don't you know what I mean?
>
> Oh the dance being over and all cleared away,
> Johnny took his Nellie onto some bed of hay,
> And said Johnny unto Nellie let me lie you on your back
> And I'll show you the game what they call "shoot the cat."
> Yay, yay, fell the dee, don't you know what I mean?
>
> Oh six months being over and seven on the rail,
> Nellie's rosy cheeks they began to look pale,
> Her apron strings they wouldn't tie, and her stays they wouldn't lap,
> And they put it to the game what they call "shoot the cat."
> Yay, yay, fell the dee, don't you know what I mean?
>
> Oh eight months being over and nine coming on,
> Nellie was the mother of a bouncing young son,
> And said Mrs. unto Nellie let me name it for sake,
> And we'll call it "Shoot the cat coming home from the wake."
> Yay, yay, fell the dee, don't you know what I mean?
>
> This young bugger he grew up to be a man,
> And coming round the corner with his rooster in his hand,
> And every girl he'd meet he would give to him a shake,
> Saying, "Daddy shoot the cat coming home from the wake."
> Yay, yay, fell the dee, don't you know what I mean?

(69-34 [C554], collected by Jesse Fudge from Robert Childs, Ramea, December 22, 1977; hear a variant, 82-186 [C5846], collected by Peter Narváez from Dorman Ralph [originally from White Bay], St. John's, July 23, 1982; for a commercially released variant hear "Daddy Shot the Cat" on O'Brien and Power 1990)

A nonsense syllable refrain with a teasing query ("Yay, yay, fell the dee, don't you know what I mean?") accents the taboo subject of the song and the pleasures involved in decoding its connotative meanings. While in British usage "shoot the cat" has meant "to vomit," a similar phrase that may be relevant to this song is "whip the cat," an expression referring to engaging in a practical joke (Partridge 1972, 157). Given the more obvious sexual meanings of "cat" which, like "pussy," has long signified female genitalia, and "cock" (Dorman Ralph variant), the sexual significations of which had banished its usage in the speech of polite society by the late eighteenth century (Rawson 1989, 73, 85-90), this ballad's title and plot further support the association of Newfoundland wakes with the pleasures of courtship games, dancing, sexuality, and pranks. Beyond the implicit admonition to obey parents and the warning to beware of men, the lyrics of "Shoot the Cat" explicitly liken wakes to dances or "sprees," and acknowledge the potential sexual dangers that wakes present as late night cultural scenes in which youth have free reign until the morning.

It is important to stress, however, that despite the potential for the scandalous kind of behavior represented by "Shoot the Cat," traditionally it has been parents, having experienced the good times themselves, who have tacitly sanctioned "tricks and fun" ("the family was sometimes aware of what was happening but basically it seems that they did not mind" [73-64:7]; also see Ó Súilleabháin 1967b, 11). In sanctioning such courtship behaviors, adults have accepted the more overtly subversive counter-hegemonic elements of these festivities. Many of these subversive pleasures have been expressed through antithetical humor against official authority. As Bakhtin has perceived, "precisely because of its unofficial existence, [folk humor has been] marked by exceptional radicalism, freedom and ruthlessness" (1984, 71). One traditional technique of folk laughter has involved creations "parallel to the official forms" (1984, 74), and this is evident in the following account of "Forfeits," a game that parodies the relations of a clergyman (parson) and his flock.

> One of the favorite games played at wakes on St. Brendan's was called "Forfeits." For this game one man was appointed leader and called "the Parson" and another was appointed his helper and called "the Parson's Sheep." All the other people in the room would be given a strange name—probably made up by "the Parson" or taken from the Bible. The game went something like this: the Parson would say: "Parson lost his boots and spurs. Some says ——— has it." Here the Parson would say one of the names he had given someone in the room. "Some says———'s got it." The person the Parson had just named would have to give a name [one of the fictive names the Parson had given out earlier] here of someone in the room . . . within five seconds or he would be penalized. The penalty would be the forfeiting of something belonging to you like your ring, watch, shoe, etc. In order to get your belongings back you would have to do a "forfeit." This was a dare of some sort. Usual "forfeits" were: kissing the corpse, biting the corpse's toes, staying in the room alone with the corpse, etc. (73-175 [24-5]; see Ó Súilleabháin 1967b, 121–122)

If pleasure, rather than placation of the dead, was the primary social function here, then "tricks and fun" at Newfoundland wakes may be regarded as part of a traditional struggle between those adhering to traditional customs of pleasure versus the hegemony of official religion, for an oppositional spirit framed the pleasurable qualities of these practices. A struggle of signification over these activities (i.e., were they "fun" or a "disgrace"?), and the active intellectual consent of the subordinate that would eventually contribute to the demise of wake amusements, is implicit in the apologetic explanations evident in several accounts ("tricks weren't meant to be offensive," "nothing disrespectful"). Participants might well have been persuaded, therefore, that even if tricks were fun, they were on the edge of disgrace. Official religion's position was in keeping with Christianity's long tradition of condemning laughter within its ideological spheres (Bakhtin 1984, 73; Camporesi 1989, 42). In such conflicts, hegemonic religion in its biopolitical attempts to supervise and regulate the mechanics of life and death, or to exert what Michel Foucault has called "bio-power" (Foucault 1986), has made the physical body the site for the negotiation of power relations, and this has necessitated social contracts at local levels. Hence in Ireland, Ó Súilleabháin has argued that "above all, the influence of the Church" spelled the demise of "the lively, merry, boisterous wakes of former years" (Ó Súilleabháin 1967b, 164). Rather than advancing the cosmological unity of life and death through the immortality of the soul and its traverse from one world to another as official religion did, merry wakes dramatized the contradictions of life and death through the physical interactions of the living with the dead. These displays also affirmed, however, that death is an inescapable part of life. Thus one informant, maintaining the healing powers of such procedures, observed that wakes "were sad for some and a party for others"; "having a gay old time" was "the way we helped out" (Keating 1992).

THE CORPSE AS HUMOROUS PROP

Having a "gay old time" was heightened by the emotional intensity of physical interactions with the dead at wakes. Even narratives concerning pre-wake preparations of the dead emphasize the idea of the corpse as prop. One technique of dealing with heavy bodies on narrow stairs was to provide cushioning for the cadaver and let its own weight and gravity do the rest. As the last of the following statements indicates, sometimes rolling a corpse down a stairway was not intentional.

> I can remember a man from my father's generation telling me how they dressed up Old Man ——— in seven or eight shirts after they washed him and when they were bringing him to the wake room they threw him downstairs. (71-129 [22-3])

> Will———, aged 55, rolled a heavy corpse downstairs and put seven shirts on it, pinning them at the neck and pushing the pin through the neck of the dead man himself, saying it would keep the shirts secure. (67-22 [87])

> An older woman who lived next door to my mother on the island of Foote's Cove, "Aunt ———," as everyone called her, was a very tall, heavily built woman, who was also partially blind. Anyway, Aunt——— died in her sleep one night and early the next morning my mother's father and a friend of his, Joe Foote, were called upon to bring the body downstairs so that it could be prepared for the wake. Because the steps in the house were very narrow and steep the two men reasoned that the only way to move Aunt——— was to lower her down on her feather mattress. When they had lowered her part ways down the incident must have struck them funny for they began to laugh and Joe said, "Lester boy, I can't hold her! Get out of the way!" Aunt——— ended up at the foot of the stairs in a heap covered by her feather mattress with her sister-in-law saying, "Oh poor Aunt———! What have you done with her?" (Oldford 1990)

Humorous accounts of post-wake activities also reflect the slapstick prop imagery of cadavers hurling through space. The following variant of a well-known Newfoundland legend describes an incident that I have also heard attached to François and Bay de Verde.

> This person died. This was in the wintertime. And the only bit of ground that they had around there was on a hill some place or other where the graveyard was situated. So they had to wake the fellow you see before the burial. They had to have a wake and everybody got plastered out of their skull. So finally after a time they decided that finally they'd put him in the ground. So they started up the hill; they had the fellow on the sleigh. They got about halfway up and whoever was pulling the thing along, I guess the line broke. Something like that happened and he [the corpse] started down the hill and one fellow hollered, "Stop him! Stop him! For God's sakes he'll be killed!" (Budgell, 8 July 1991)

THE DEMISE OF THE MERRY WAKE TRADITION

Ó Súilleabháin contends that the advent of one-night wakes in Ireland, brought about "when people conformed" to the bishops' advice that the corpse should be brought to the local church "the evening before the interment," spelled the demise of the merry wake because fewer could attend. As he explains, "the games and other festivities ceased, as they demanded that the corpse be present; now it was in the local church awaiting burial next day" (Ó Súilleabháin 1967b, 164–5). A parallel development occurred in Newfoundland, but as the following three testimonies reveal, there was local counter-hegemonic resistance to clerical injunctions. Some wake participants actively attempted to maintain two night wakes in their homes.

> At the wake—only one night—there was plenty of rum and food. They sang and told stories, both men and women. They had "such a great time at the wake" they decided to keep Aunt Joanie for another night, instead of bringing her out to the church the following morning. The daughter was staying with friends so they all went to work and left the corpse in the house. The angry congregation and priest waiting in the church sent someone else in for the corpse and Aunt Joanie was buried when they got back home in the evening from work. (71-42 [43])

> It occurred about 60 years ago when the man was just a young man. He said that at a particular wake they had such a time they wanted it to go on for another night. On the day of the burial they went to see the man "Billy" who was supposed to drive the horse and carriage to church. They threatened the

> man not to show up—and the man didn't. The people were even in church waiting. My lady informant told me, "I knew what had happened—I knew there wouldn't be any funeral." The priest, however, grew impatient and told a man to go look for Billy. They didn't find him, but they quickly organized a new procession and the ceremony went on with some delay. Most people suspected what had happened but my informant remarked, "Old Billy didn't tell; I guess he knew better, the poor old bugger." (73-64 [7])

> . . . these practices were frowned upon by some people, and they tried to prevent these things from happening by having wakes in the church but this never caught on and wakes are still held in the homes at St. Brendan's. (73-175 [26–7])

Even after hegemonic religion's victory in incarcerating the body within church walls, however, some of the old tricks continued to be played:

> A few years ago in Gander Bay, a body was laid out in the church. Some people broke into the church, took the body out of the coffin and propped him up in the coffin for all to see. (Norris, 7 November 1991)

> These people dared one another to go into church after midnight where there was a woman laid out for funeral services the next day. Loretta's great uncle Martin took up the challenge and proceeded to enter the church. He eventually went into the church and emerged a few minutes later and after he returned outside Martin and his buddies went home. Anyway, the next day word had gotten around that somebody had turned Aunt [Margaret] over in her coffin last night. When Martin heard about this, his face lit up with a smile. (Fewer, 11 November 1991)

THE MERRY WAKE IN CONTEMPORARY NEWFOUNDLAND POPULAR CULTURE

Although today many of the customs of pleasure which used to be practiced at good wakes in Newfoundland have been relegated to memory, entertaining interpretations of those occasions live on in the popular culture of Newfoundland and Canada through the humor of a Newfoundland dramatic group known as CODCO. Founded in 1972 (Peters 1990), CODCO's second production, *Sickness, Death and Beyond the Grave* (1974) featured two scenes involving a wake and corpse humor (Peters 1992, 127–34). But CODCO's most direct references to "tricks and fun" have been on "Wake of the Week," one of their miniserials featured on their television series "CODCO," occasionally running on the

Canadian Broadcasting Corporation's (CBC) national television network since 1988. The miniserial was hosted by two fictional Newfoundland seniors, Cass and Betty Furlong, played by Cathy Jones and Mary Walsh, who attended wakes as their principal diversion. As an example of CODCO's use of tradition, one of their routines involved a wake wherein the Furlongs convinced one of their living male relatives to play a corpse so that they could host a house wake. Enacting the most spectacular and most widespread wake prank in Newfoundland, the corpse suddenly sat up in his coffin; one of the mourners immediately became hysterical with fright.

Mourner: He sat up! He sat up!

Cass: Of course he sat up! It's a wake! It happens all the time!

Betty: It's a joke, a bit of a wake joke. [laughs]

Mourner: No! No strings, no tricks, no . . .

Betty: You're living in the past my darling, with the ropes, the tricks, and everything. They do it all now with laser beams!

Cass: It's an Irish wake now complete with holograms!

(CODCO, 18 November 1989)

Like so many elements of some of CODCO's finest creations, this scene derived directly from Newfoundland experience.

CONCLUSION

Clearly, ethnocentricity biases thinking with regard to such an emotionally charged subject as death, and many contemporary reactions to the materials of this paper often evidence a nervous discomfort that could be attributed simply to the culturally unusual. However, it is ideology, a process that transforms power relations into that which is "normal" and "common sense," that triggers such ethnocentric reactions. Educational institutions conservatively maintain such power relations by cultivating *plaisir* or contemplative pleasure, rather than the physical enjoyments of *jouissance*. As opposed to the abstract nature of *plaisir*, John Fiske has noted that "popular pleasures are often much more located in the body . . . in the physicality . . . of me, right here, now" (Galbo 1990/91). This distinction between individual contemplative enjoyment and collective, participatory physical pleasure is also influenced by the grammars of technological and sensory media. As Marshall McLuhan wrote about the practical joke: "To literary people, the practical joke with its total physical involvement is as distasteful as the pun that derails us from the smooth and uniform progress that is the typographic order" (McLuhan 1964, 44).

Using the same metaphor, rational critiques of culture are often derailed by the false neutrality of the "respect other cultures" posture. The significance of this portrayal of Newfoundland wake amusements and their capitulation to the hegemonic forces of official religion is that death in Newfoundland, which used to be an integral part of life, is much less so today (see Peere 1992). The bureaucratization, specialization, and compartmentalization of modern death have largely removed death from community contexts and, as has been noted by other analysts of analogous developments elsewhere, *this causes social problems.* What Robert Blauner has written in regard to funerals is also true for traditional wakes: "in modern societies, the bereaved person suffers from a paucity of ritualistic conventions in the mourning period. He experiences grief less frequently, but more intensely, since his emotional involvements are not diffused over an entire community, but are usually concentrated on one or a few people" (1977; see Ariès 1974; Kiliánová 1992).

The paradoxical social needs of vitalizing the dead and disposing of them have been accomplished in Newfoundland through multifaceted rites of passage. For an extensive period, and in face of official religion's attempts to regulate the physical and social body, the Newfoundland wake kept the dead alive through merging sacred space and profane collective pleasures, pleasures that appear to many youthful Newfoundlanders today to be little more than another bizarre aspect of a strange past.[3]

5

PARDON ME FOR NOT STANDING

Modern American Graveyard Humor

Richard E. Meyer

My first impulse was to entitle this essay "Dead People Can Be Really Funny Sometimes." After my friends suggested counseling, I abandoned the original plan in favor of the present title—though not without some regret, because there really was an important point buried within this seemingly insensitive frivolity. Death may not be funny, but people often are, and it is in the human response to this rite of passage—sometimes collectively, but most often individually—that we find the basis for much of what we would call death-based humor. And nowhere, I would contend, is this phenomenon more visible than in the graveyard.

We begin, then, with a paradox. Graveyards, after all, are places of dread and loathing, or so we have been conditioned to believe. A great deal of our traditional folklore supports this reaction. Throughout much of the twentieth century, older superstitious dread, combined with contemporary death denial, affected behavior to the point where graveyards (now known as "cemeteries" or, most recently, "memorial parks") became the most conspicuously avoided elements of the modern constructed landscape. Surely, this would seem the most unlikely of environments to spawn idiosyncratic and sometimes quite aggressive (i.e., "in your face") expressions of humor. Yet humor is definitely there, its presence becoming increasingly evident in recent times. Modern graveyard humor's manifestations are principally verbal, supplemented in some instances by visual elements. Its focal point is in large part the individual gravemarker, with a range of expression that covers the full spectrum from subtle wit to blatant tastelessness. The vast majority of instances are the result of deliberate decision making, either on the part of the commemorated individuals or others close to them. Yet there are occasional examples of clearly unintentional humor, or of humorous responses stemming from changing cultural perspectives. Finally, there is the matter of the graveyard as staging point for humorous expression by others. Put another way, you don't have to be dead to be funny!

VERBAL HUMOR

For a gravemarker, whose primary purpose is to serve as a posthumous material surrogate for the person departed, to have any efficacy, it must provide at least the most basic and minimal inscribed data—a personal identifier and, perhaps, a date. Indeed, a number of the earliest markers found in North America consist of no more than a set of initials and a death date crudely cut into a piece of roughly hewn fieldstone. As gravestones started to become more elaborate—as early as the 1670s—specialized carvers, a number of them trained in England and other European countries, graced their handiwork with increasingly more detailed visual decorations, accompanied by a proportionate degree of length and complexity in verbal inscriptions. Over the next 250 years, the verbal inscriptions, which were largely rhyming epitaphs ranging from simple couplets to many lines, and the visual decorations found upon the same stones evolved in lockstep. Harsh reminders of mortality and a stern insistence upon rigorous piety gave way to softer, and often romanticized, expressions of sentimentality and a confident belief in the attainability of paradise. If you sense, given the thrust of the present essay, that something is missing from this pattern, you are entirely correct. Until the last several decades of the twentieth century, death, at least if judged by the material testimony of the graveyard, was an eminently serious business. Humor in any form, whether blatant or in more subtle guises such as whimsy or even delicately playful wit, is simply not a significantly identifiable element in American (or European, for that matter) gravestone inscriptions throughout the greater part of their history.

Which brings about the need for an important digression at this point. How can the confident declaration that concludes the preceding paragraph possibly be correct? Have we not, many of us at least, actually *seen* examples of such older graveyard humor, epitaphs whose wit and pungency cannot fail to make us chuckle and bring a smile to our faces? Indeed we have, and the sad fact is that we have been duped, for they are in almost all instances entirely spurious. Let us take but two examples: "I Told You I Was Sick," and "Here Lies [supply any name], Wife of [———], Who on [supply any date] Began to Hold Her Tongue." Though the first of these has actually begun to appear on recently placed markers (life, after all, does imitate art more frequently than we might care to admit), the long history of these two gravestone utterances, and countless others of their ilk, is due to their having been repeatedly quoted but never properly documented.

The chief culprits in this are a number of small and cheaply printed booklets—sometimes in the shape of gravestones—with grotesque titles such as *The Itty-Bitty Bathroom Book of Bodacious Tombstone Epitaphs* (okay, that's a bit of an exaggeration, but close enough to make the point). They are not particularly difficult to find. Look in the card section of lower-echelon gift stores, or in the glide path to supermarket checkout stands, wedged in somewhere between the junk food and copies of the *National Enquirer.* Seldom providing any documentation for their humorous "epitaphs" (at most a town or city name, and sometimes a year), they quickly go in and out of print, cannibalizing each other even as they provide a sort of dubious immortality to this corpus of ephemeral graveyard humor. Oddly enough, there are occasional real epitaphs indiscriminately intermixed with the phony ones. This becomes doubly frustrating since, as colonial American gravestone expert James Slater has recently pointed out, the ability to "ferret out actual epitaphs from fake ones cannot be assured from these little books" (2001, 9). As if things were not bad enough already, in the past decade a great many of the spurious epitaphs from the "Itty-Bitty" books have migrated to a number of decidedly non-scholarly Internet web sites, where they enjoy a parallel cyberspace existence, reaching ever-widening audiences of gullible believers and compounding the problem of authenticity beyond hope of remedy. The irony in all of this is the fact that—as we shall shortly see—it is entirely unnecessary, for there is plenty of material in American graveyards which is every bit as funny, and a lot more real, than these largely fabricated examples.

Several years ago, while strolling through a cemetery in Albany, Oregon, my eye was caught by a contemporary flat marker for an individual named Henry J. "Pappy" Padrta, who had died in 1986 (figure 1). The sandblasted image of a man panning for gold first attracted my attention, as I was quite preoccupied with visual indicators of occupational and recreational pursuits on gravemarkers at the time. But it was the short inscription at the bottom of the stone that caused me to burst out laughing: "Pardon Me For Not Standing." Yes, the figure in the image *is* kneeling, but it was immediately obvious that the accompanying statement had a somewhat different reference. Clearly a sense of humor—and the ability to deal with the emotionally complex issue of death in a manner quite outside the norms of conventional expression—lay behind this arresting contemporary epitaph. The idea wasn't totally original: around the middle of the twentieth century a number of popular American magazines engaged in the practice of asking celebrities to compose their own

Figure 1. Gravemarker of Henry J. "Pappy" Padrta, Waverly Memorial Cemetery, Albany, Oregon.

epitaphs (Klisiewicz 2001, 26), and variants of this particular epitaph are attributed to a number of figures, including writer Ernest Hemingway and silent film star Clive Brook (Self-Composed Epitaphs 1984, 5). Additionally, a number of the "Itty-Bitty" books throughout the years have featured this oh-too-cutesy epitaph supposedly found on a stone in Ruidoso, New Mexico (no cemetery named):

Here Lies
Johnny Yeast
Pardon Me
For Not Rising

I would have liked to learn the circumstances behind the choosing of this particular epitaph on the Padrta stone, but, unlike a number of the instances to be discussed shortly, my efforts some fifteen years later to reconstruct the story of this 1986 marker proved fruitless.[1] Gravestones, like crimes, become increasingly difficult to investigate as time elapses and the trail becomes "cold".[2] Still, my encounter with this small contemporary marker had the effect of alerting me to the presence of real and consciously created humor in the graveyard; my senses were sharpened in anticipation of more.

I was not disappointed. Soon, as I began to focus my attention more closely upon verbal inscriptions (prior to this time my eyes, particularly in more recent burial areas, were programmed to focus on visual motifs to the virtual exclusion of most other detail[3]), it became apparent that "Pappy" Padrta's interjection of humor into his final material testament was no fluke. Rather, it was part of a growing trend in modern American graveyard commemoration. The majority of such humorous inscriptions are relatively short and unrhymed (thus, in a technical sense, not true "epitaphs"), and they cover the entire spectrum from cleverly witty to blatantly crude, e.g.:

The Difficult He Did Right Away;
The Impossible Took A Little Longer
(1994, John Mitchell, Forest Home Cemetery, Forest Park, Illinois)

. . . .

I Said I'd Live To Be 100. What Happened?
(1992, Hardy Martens—aged 76—Dallas Cemetery, Dallas, Oregon)

. . . .

This Wasn't In My Schedule Book
(1995, Helen Louise Jones, Lone Fir Cemetery, Portland, Oregon)

. . . .

Loved Everyone /
Loved His Friends and Hated His Enemies
(1974, Sadie Raye and Carl E. Lynn, Eureka Cemetery, Newport, Oregon)[4]

. . . .

This Is Indeed A True Bummer
(1977, William Scott "Hooter" Gibson, Fernwood Cemetery, Lansdowne, Pennsylvania)

. . . .

Don't Get Caught With Your Pants Down
(1990, Willard W. Ricketts, Clagett Cemetery, Keizer, Oregon)

. . . .

Put Your Ass On Some Class
(1988, E. Kalani Padaken, Valley Isle Memorial Park, Paia, Maui, Hawaii / in conjunction with incised Harley-Davidson motorcycle logo)

Figure 2. Gravemarker of Ed McKinley, Hilltop Cemetery, Independence, Oregon.

. . . .

Born A Fighter—Died A Fighter
—Now I Am Really Pissed—
(1985, Jacob B. Fisher, Woodlawn Cemetery,
Las Vegas, Nevada)

Slightly up the ladder of complexity from these utterances is the rhyming couplet found beneath the image of a bucking bronco on the 1981 stone for former rodeo cowboy Ed McKinley in Hilltop Cemetery, Independence, Oregon (figure 2):

Ain't No Horse Can't Be Rode
Ain't No Man Can't Be Throwed

McKinley's epitaph is actually a fairly well-established proverbial couplet in American cowboy and rodeo lore (Cunningham 1996), turning up in everything from cowboy poetry to practical advice columns (Underwood 1999, 32).[5] Paired with the visual image, it evokes a sense of the self-deprecating humor found in any number of western texts pairing horses and riders (one thinks immediately of songs such as Curley Fletcher's "The Strawberry Roan"), a quality strongly present in the personality of McKinley himself, who chose the design and inscription for his marker while still alive as a wry commentary upon the ups and downs of his sporadic career as a rodeo performer (McKinley 1988).

Another, even more complex instance of self-composed and preordered comic gravestone verse is found upon the marker for Paul Lennis Swank (1906–1984), a member of an occupational folk group with a tradition of esoteric lore every bit as rich as that of cowboys (Meyer 1989b,76–77). The town cemetery of Canyonville, Oregon, where Swank's marker is found, is filled with material testimony to this community's traditional ties to Oregon's logging industry. There are markers fashioned of log segments or of crosscut sections suspended by chains from pipe frames, parts of logging equipment transformed into folk markers, as well as commercial markers incised with images from logging life. Verbal references are also abundant, and sometimes quite ingenious in their application of occupational imagery, as on the 1986 stone for Virgil R. "Mutt" Campion:

No More Logs Do I Pull
No More Whistles Do I Hear
With My Savior Now I Rest
A Yarder Engineer

But the epitaph on Paul Swank's gravemarker carries this process to a whole new level:

Here Under The Dung Of Cows And Sheep
Lies An Old Highclimber Fast Asleep.
His Trees All Topped And His Lines All Hung,
They Say The Old Rascal Died
Full Of Rum.

When I first encountered this stone some years ago in the course of research for an article on logger gravemarkers in the Pacific Northwest, I was struck by the fact that a death date was not present, indicating the possibility that the person celebrated upon it was still alive. This indeed turned out to be the case, and in subsequent interviews Mr. Swank outlined to me the process by which he came to create his own gravestone (Swank 1983). The epitaph was, he claimed, self-composed, although he admitted freely to the influence of the often quite humorous logger poetry he had enjoyed listening to throughout his adult life. He chose these lines because they represented, as he put it, "me," but felt it necessary to have the stone made and placed upon his plot while still living because he feared that otherwise his wishes would either not be carried out or might be somehow watered down. There already had been enough watering down, he said: when he submitted his original order to the monument dealer, the operative word in the next-to-last line of the epitaph was "bastard," but, the carver being unwilling to use this language on a gravestone, he was forced to compromise on "rascal." This may have indeed been the case, but I have always suspected that, like some of Richard Dorson's informants in the Upper Peninsula of Michigan (Dorson 1952), this old timer was having a good time putting on the "perfesser" fellow who had come down from the ivory tower to do a little fieldwork in the real world. Regardless, the paired elements of occupational pride and good-natured humor present on Paul Swank's gravemarker (his death date was added in 1984) are more than sufficient to bring a smile to those who come upon it.

Perhaps the most interesting modern effort in this vein is the 1983 marker found in Logan, Utah's City Cemetery for Russell J. Larsen. The front side of this small upright stone is unremarkable, consisting of Mr. Larsen's name, his dates, and a brief record of his naval service during World War II. Oftentimes, cemetery visitors—even experienced ones—fail to take the time to examine the reverse side of upright gravemarkers, in which case they would unfortunately miss the inscription (figure 3) which makes this marker anything but ordinary:

> Two Things I Love Most,
> Good Horses And Beautiful
> Women, And When I Die I Hope
> They Tan This Old Hide Of Mine
> And Make It Into A Ladies Riding
> Saddle, So I Can Rest In Peace
> Between The Two Things I Love
> Most.

Again we have an example of a humorous epitaph based upon older elements of oral tradition. Folklorist Barre Toelken (1995, 37–38) has pointed out the use of remarkably similar lines in a poem entitled "The Two Things in Life that I Really Love" by contemporary cowboy poet Gary McMahan, and is convinced that, in both instances, ". . . the poem comes out of cowboy tradition" (2000). The connection, especially in cowboy verse, between women and horses is well established and continues to find currency, as in the opening lines of this recent cowboy poem by Fred Engel entitled "Remember the Cow":

> A Friend Of Mine Once Offered A Toast,
> To The Two Things In Life That He Loved Most,
> "Women And Horses," He Blurted Out. . . . (Engel 1997)

Figure 3. Gravemarker (reverse side) of Russell J. Larsen, Logan City Cemetery, Logan, Utah.

Larsen's use of this linkage, however, definitely takes it to a wholly different level. His decision to have the verse—with its clever use of a blatantly erotic image—inscribed upon his tombstone says much to his sense of humor and his desire to leave a lasting material testament to an important element of his worldview. There is definitely more here one would like to know, but again the trail has become cold. Since I first encountered this stone in 1992, I have tried in vain to learn more about Larsen and his intriguing monument, but the closest I have come is a brief conversation I had with a groundskeeper (who did not wish to be identified) in the Logan City Cemetery: "Yes, I knew him," he said. "He was a real character. It was his liver that got him."

VISUAL HUMOR

The impact of a gravestone's statement is often most powerfully achieved through a mutually reinforcing pairing of verbal inscription and visual image. This is a principle the Puritans understood well, their elaborately carved gravestones often incorporating such symbiotic combinations as a skull and crossbones perched above the injunction *Memento Mori* ("Remember Death"), or a spent hourglass with the statement "My Glass Is Run." The Victorians practiced similar pairing, and frequently accompanied the image of a rosebud broken at the stem with the words "Budded On Earth To Bloom In Heaven" upon children's gravemarkers. In our own time, one is more likely to find markers which employ this pairing technique to emphasize the importance of recreational or

Figure 4. Gravemarker of Neil E. Edwards, Mt. Pleasant Cemetery, Seattle, Washington.

occupational pursuits—the image, say, of a person bowling with the legend "Scoring In Heaven," or of a 18-wheeler semi-truck with the phrase "Last Load Delivered."

Humor—most often of the whimsical variety—may also be readily achieved on contemporary gravemarkers through use of this principle of paired elements. An excellent example is the 1986 upright marker found in Seattle, Washington's Mt. Pleasant Cemetery for Neil E. Edwards (figure 4). Depicted upon the face of the polished black granite surface is the meticulously detailed image of a 1957 Studebaker, with clearly visible letters and numerals on its license plate, and the words "I've Had A Great Ride" beneath. The monument was executed by Quiring Monuments of Seattle, a firm known throughout the industry for its leadership and creativity in the modern trend towards highly personalized gravemarkers, but the design concept itself was the result of a careful collaboration between Quiring Monuments and Mr. Edwards's family. David Quiring, owner and president of the firm (and a third generation memorialist), recalls:

> Neil Edwards was the owner of Mt. Pleasant Cemetery and he and my father and our families were close friends for many years. Consequently he was quite familiar with death and dying and in his case he had time to contemplate his own demise. In his final months he told everyone who lamented with him "Don't worry about me; I've had a great ride." He came from humble beginnings and was proud of his successes. His family thought that this quote aptly summed his philosophy and was a positive thought to leave on the memorial. (2001)

As regards the image of the automobile etched upon the monument, Mr. Quiring, noting with fondness that "Neil was quite a character," continues:

> He was always avid about cars. I remember when Chrysler promoted the hemihead engine (one of the most powerful of the early 60s and now one of the rarest and most valued engines among collectors), Neil's son (my age) bought a racing Plymouth with that engine. Neil had to get the Chrysler luxury edition with the same engine (extremely rare car now). He loved to squeal around the cemetery in that car. He sold a grave plot to a widow whose husband had owned the 1957 Studebaker Golden Hawk and was able to buy it before she put it on the market. It had one of the first superchargers available and was blisteringly fast for 1957. He loved that car! In fact, his son still has it. (2001)

The juxtaposition of image and epitaph in this instance, though the elements arguably stem from two separate sets of circumstances, results nonetheless in a coherent and metaphorically powerful statement that, in its whimsical assessment of a life well-lived, clearly captures the spirit of this remarkable self-made individual.

Another example of visual/verbal juxtaposition for whimsical effect may be seen on the double-sided husband and wife marker for Dan and Vera Short in Rochester, Washington's Grand Mound Cemetery. When Dan died in 1984, Vera Short commissioned the stone and had it placed in the cemetery. On his side she had etched an image of a welding truck (her husband's business), but she also created a most interesting montage on her side of the marker. Above an extraordinarily well-detailed depiction of a VISA card are the words "Charge It!," and below, "Send The Bill To Heaven." "He always joked, 'No wonder I'm just a poor welder with Vera and her VISA," she remembers. "When we went to pick up his ashes, the man said, 'Do you want to pay cash or charge it?' I paid cash. Dan might have gotten mad if I charged that!" (1996).

The 1981 gravestone for L.D. "Mac" McCoy (figure 5) found in Coos Bay, Oregon's Sunset Memorial Park represents a very clever and carefully calculated visual/verbal construction. Beneath an open, spread five-card poker hand are inscribed the words "I'd Rather Be In Reno." In concept, the epitaph is certainly not original: older variants have been attributed to, amongst others, W. C. Fields ("On The Whole, I'd Rather Be In Philadelphia"), though it is not found upon his gravestone (Koykka 1986, 137–138), and I have seen contextually appropriate applications on any number of contemporary markers ("I'd Rather Be Flying"—images of

Figure 5. Gravemarker of L.D. "Mac" McCoy, Sunset Memorial Park, Coos Bay, Oregon.

Boeing 737 and small private plane, 1986, John Ray Utterstrom, Sunset Hills Memorial Park, Bellevue, Washington; "I Would Rather Be Hunting"—image of hunting bow and arrows, 1983, Keith W. Barker, Price City Cemetery, Price, Utah). The reference to Reno (Nevada), however, is even more than usually personal. According to his eldest daughter, Mac McCoy dearly loved to play poker: "Every Friday or Saturday he used to play poker with his friends," she recalls, "and he went to the casinos in Reno often" (Carlin 2001). It was so much a part of what made him a special individual that, prior to his funeral, she put a deck of cards in his suit jacket pocket to be buried with him. The love of the game would, of course, also explain the visual image on Mr. McCoy's stone. But look more closely: the hand depicted appears to be a royal flush (the highest hand in poker), until you see to the final card, which would be the ten of hearts to complete the flush. Instead, it is the two of spades. "He died, so I guess you could say he drew a losing hand, that's one way you could put it," his daughter said. We both agreed, however, that the irony of coming so close to a royal flush and then totally bombing out with the deuce of a different suit would certainly have appealed to her father's highly developed sense of humor. The marker, she says, was designed by the family (she credits her brother with being the primary creative force in the process) as a fitting memorial to a man who enjoyed his time on earth and held a very special role in their own lives.

One of the most striking examples of visual humor in the modern American graveyard involves juxtaposition of a somewhat different sort (figure 6). In rural Scipio Cemetery, on Route 37 in Allen County, Indiana, near the Ohio border, stands a small, nondescript 1982 upright granite marker for Archie A. Arnold. What makes this grave site

Figure 6. Gravemarker, with flanking "expired" parking meters, of Archie A. Arnold, Scipio Cemetery, Allen County, Indiana.

remarkable, to say the least, are the two old style parking meters, each frozen with their red "expired" flags showing, embedded in the concrete base to either side of the marker. Obviously, this assemblage required some serious planning! My Indiana informant, who wishes to remain anonymous, says she has it on good authority from her great aunt, a local resident, that Mr. Arnold was a well-known Allen County character with "a quirky sense of humor." He apparently secretly designed his own mortuary complex and made all appropriate arrangements prior to his death, specifying in his will that his creation was not under any circumstances to be tampered with. His outraged and mortified relatives, so the story goes, tried to fight this provision in his will , but a judge ruled that there was no legal basis for violating Mr. Arnold's stated desire. That, coupled with the fact that the cemetery—unlike many—apparently has no regulations which might allow for removal of this highly unorthodox grave decoration, has insured that it remains undisturbed to this date. Precisely where and how Mr. Arnold obtained the necessary hardware to complete his final statement remains a mystery.

INTENT AND PURPOSE

In view of the examples discussed to this point, as well as numerous others which might be cited, it should be evident that expressions of humor are an identifiably present element in the contemporary

American graveyard. What, then, are we to make of this phenomenon? What do these artifacts tell us of the persons who created them and, on a broader level, of the shifting parameters of American cultural attitudes towards death and commemoration? Gravemarkers, throughout the larger part of their existence, have served to reinforce the cultural attitudes dominant at the time of their creation. Thus, despite being material surrogates for departed individuals, their texts have, in the vast majority of instances, reflected communal rather than personal perspectives and values. This is why, for instance, variants of the old Puritan epitaph

> Hearken Stranger, As You Pass By,
> As You Are Now So Once Was I,
> As I Am Now So You Must Be,
> Thus Think On Death And Follow Me

may be found on literally thousands of colonial New England gravestones, while a limited number of visual symbols—clasped hands, heaven-pointing fingers, weeping willows, and heavenly gates ajar, principally—dominate the iconography of American Victorian markers in all regions of the country. Until the last four decades of the twentieth century, gravemarkers, with only minor deviations, were predictably conservative and conventional. Beginning in the early 1960s, however, and growing at an exponential rate ever since, there has been a movement in American material commemoration away from collectively conventional expression towards its individual, personalized opposite. Folklorist Carol Edison, noting that "The need to stand apart and be recognized as an individual, not a number in a computer, is a common complaint for twentieth-century man," was one of the first to offer a scholarly analysis of this phenomenon (1985, 186), and I have also addressed the issue (1984a, 1984b, 1989a, 1989b, 1990, 1991a, 1991b, 1993). Indeed, as any fieldworker who has spent a significant amount of time in the contemporary sections of American cemeteries can confirm, there has been a virtual explosion in recent decades of such personalized expression. We now see sandblasted or laser-etched visual images depicting every sort of recreational and occupational activity imaginable: verbal inscriptions running the gamut from snatches of popular song lyrics to long (and sometimes incredibly bad) self-composed poems; and grave goods of the sort once only encountered at the burial sites of Roma and other folk groups with highly esoteric funerary practices.

Not everyone is pleased with this trend. It has, in fact, engendered a long-standing debate within the professional structure of the monument and cemetery trades. Some see it as tasteless and undignified, yet another appalling indicator of the alarmingly materialistic and "now-centered" preoccupations of today's society, while others embrace the opportunity to apply their creative energies in new directions, at the same time satisfying the needs of a new generation of patrons (Hanks 1987; Kimball 1997). Regardless of one's position on this issue, the trend is clear and not likely to diminish at any time in the foreseeable future. As one contemporary monument dealer recently noted, "Seventy-five percent of my work today involves some sort of personalization, and forty percent is definitely custom," whereas, when her father ran the business a generation earlier, "it was all standard—right out of the book" (Buckley 1996:1A).

The new symbolism of gravemarkers, then, is highly personal and idiosyncratic, and, in most instances, concrete rather than abstract. It is a conceptual framework widely favored by a whole new generation of monument patrons, and in this sense, at least, shares with earlier eras the adoption of an accepted vocabulary of memorialization that reflects and supports a collective worldview. The essential difference is that, for the first time in the history of American funerary commemoration, the focus of that vocabulary has become dominantly retrospective rather than prospective. Modern gravemarkers, in ever greater numbers, are a celebration of life, not death, the hereafter, or abstract metaphysical principles. Highly particularized football helmets and oil rigs are today's equivalent of winged death's heads or weeping willows, while "The Wind Beneath My Wings" has replaced *Memento Mori* on the gravestone inscription top ten hit list.

Humor has its part in all of this, though it does up the stakes just a bit, for the risks of misunderstanding or censure are potentially greater. Persons who select markers of the type discussed in this essay, whether these individuals be the deceased themselves or others who act on their behalf, are certainly endowed with a more-than-common sense of humor. But this quality is often matched with an equally entrenched streak of independence, and perhaps a bit of courage as well. It all comes down, in the end, to individual personality, a point which folklorist J. Joseph Edgette made clear a number of years ago in his analysis of epitaphs, such as the one chosen by retired West Virginia coal miner Julian C. Skaggs ("I Made An Ash Of Myself") to mark the site of his cremated remains (1989, 90–91). Edgette's findings, I submit, have been validated over and over again by the markers and individuals we have been examining here. Modern American graveyard humor, while clearly embraced by the contemporary trend towards personalization of all sorts in monument design, is almost always directly linked to personalities whose strength is such that they can find a laugh even in death.

UNINTENTIONAL HUMOR

There is, of course, another type of humor found in the graveyard, one not stemming from a conscious and deliberate attempt to create such an effect. This unintentional humor can take many forms, and may be the result of any number of initiating factors. In earlier eras, for example, stonecarvers, working character by character with mallet and chisel, quite frequently made mistakes which were the equivalent of modern-day typos without the luxury of backspace keys or typeover features. These generally resulted in misspelled names or incorrect dates. Occasionally, however, a moment of absentminded chiseling might produce a more humorous effect, as on the 1781 marker for James Erwin in East Derry, New Hampshire's Forest Hill Cemetery. What appears at a glance to be one more instance of the ubiquitous utterance "My Glass Is Run" turns out, upon closer examination, to be the far more interesting "My Glass Is Rum"!

Changes in language over time can produce a similarly unintentional humorous effect. Visitors to seventeenth and eighteenth century cemeteries, for instance, are often vastly amused by markers noting that the deceased was "Casually Shot" or "Casually Fell Down A Well," not realizing that the term "casual" was an archaic synonym for "accidental." Old—fashioned familial terms ("consort" = "wife"; "relict" = "widow"; etc.) or given names (Experience, Submit, Exercise, etc.) will frequently produce the same results (one wonders what these inhabitants of colonial America would make of "significant other" or "Heather").

By far the largest number of instances of this type of graveyard humor result from unintentional double meanings buried within otherwise well-meaning inscriptions. A somewhat celebrated occasion of such language is found upon the 1866 marker for Edward Oakes in West Cemetery, Middlebury, Vermont:

Faithful Husband Thou Art
At Rest Untill We Meet Again (Wallis 1954, 169)

More recent instances might include the 1984 flat stone for Peter Kindante in Portland, Oregon's River View Cemetery ("You Can't Keep A Good Man Down"), or the 1989 upright marker for Troy David Gray, aged 18, in Crown Hill Cemetery, Salem, Indiana ("I'm Outta Here").[6] Nor is the possibility for this type of unintentionally humorous interpretation limited to the gravemarkers themselves. Regulatory signs posted within cemeteries, for instance, are sometimes not as carefully thought out as they might be:

NOTICE
All Grave Markers Will Be Installed
Flush With The Ground & Grass Over
The Grave. Anyone Violating These
Rules Will Be Subject To Removal
(St. Wencelaus Cemetery,
Scappoose, Oregon)

. . . .

PLEASE TAKE TRASH WITH YOU
This Is A Cooperative
Graveyard And All Must
Share To Keep It Clean
(Yankton Cemetery,
Yankton, Oregon)

Inappropriate and/or incongruous language may inspire a humorous reaction from the viewer, an example in point being the inscription on the 1934 marker in Crown Hill Memorial Park, Dallas, Texas, for notorious gun moll Bonnie Parker (of Bonnie and Clyde fame):

As The Flowers Are All Made Sweeter
By The Sunshine And The Dew,
So This Old World Is Made Brighter
By The Lives Of Folks Like You

Incongruity also sometimes becomes evident in the unfortunate visual juxtaposition of landscape elements (e.g., figure 7). Ask any cemetery fieldworker who has been at it for a while, and they will generally admit to having at least one photo in their collection of a yellow "Dead End" or "No Exit" road sign standing alongside a cemetery setting.

Finally, we must consider the fact that sentiments once expressed in all seriousness may seem funny to others, perhaps wholly or in part for

Figure 7. Unfortunate juxtaposition of city street sign and mortuary landscape, Cohasset Central Cemetery, Cohasset, Massachusetts.

that very seriousness itself. This is evident in a number of epitaphs (sometimes very elaborate ones) on the monuments of professed atheists or others who, for lack of a better term, we might call "God Haters." Consider, for example, the rather idiosyncratic 1872 East Thompson, Connecticut, inscription for Jonathan Richardson:

> Who Never Sacrificed His Reason
> At The Altar Of Superstition's God,
> Who Never Believed That Jonah
> Swallowed The Whale (Klisiewicz 2001, 25; Wallis 1954, 102)

In a somewhat similar vein, the badly weathered 1913 granite marker for confirmed bachelor William Hartley depicts a man in Victorian formal attire, standing atop a rock and facing (across a chasm) a woman with outstretched arms. The inscription beneath reads:

To An Independent Good
Looking Old Batchelor
Who In His Younger Days
Preferred Living A
Single Life Rather
Than Get Married And
Have A Petticoat Boss
Ruling Over Him The
Rest Of His Life And
Perhaps Through An
Endless Eternity

(Myrtle Point Cemetery,
Myrtle Point, Oregon)

A celebrated final example is the 1873 gravestone of Joseph Palmer (figure 8), located in Evergreen Cemetery, Leominster, Massachusetts. Palmer, a well-known local eccentric and reportedly a very difficult person to deal with (Malloy 2001), apparently delighted in flaunting current standards of fashion and decorum by cultivating a full beard as a younger man (Edgette 1989, 90). His defiance reached a head in 1830, when he was attacked by four locals who attempted to shave off his beard. He successfully defended himself with a knife, was arrested, and spent more than a year in the Worcester County jail for refusing, as a matter of principle, to pay a fine stemming from the incident (Malloy 2001). Upon his death, Palmer managed to achieve the last word on the matter by causing to be erected above his grave a white marble monument that features a bust portrait of himself in full hirsute splendor, accompanied by the words

Persecuted for
Wearing the beard

OTHER HUMOROUS USES OF THE GRAVEYARD

By way of a brief postscript to this essay's central arguments, it might be noted that the dead are not the only ones who have found the graveyard a fertile ground for humor. Editorial cartoonists have, since the 1870s, consistently employed images of gravestones and cemeteries as metaphorical vehicles for their often sardonically tinged brand of humorous commentary, and nonpolitical cartoon and comic strip artists have not been far behind. Of the latter, perhaps the most active of all in

Figure 8. Gravemarker of Joseph Palmer, Evergreen Cemetery, Leominster, Massachusetts.

using this device is Wiley Miller, creator of *Non Sequitur*, a cartoon and comic strip series syndicated by the *Washington Post* Writers Group. My personal Wiley favorite among the dozens I have chuckled over—and one I might have missed entirely had it not been for the diligent clipping efforts of my late mother-in-law—is a four-part strip entitled "A Modern Life Lesson. . . ." In the first two frames, a briefcase-toting business executive hurrying through the cemetery pauses to contemplate the inscription "Stop And Smell The Roses," carved in oversized letters upon a very large, upright, tablet-style gravestone. The third frame shows him doing just that, bending with a peaceful, almost beatific, expression upon his face to inhale the fragrance of a beautiful red rose planted immediately in front of the marker. In the fourth and final frame we see only the man's feet, hands, and briefcase protruding from the flattened tombstone, which has toppled forward and squashed both him and the rose. This sort of black humor may not be to everyone's taste, but in my view it beats "I Told You I Was Sick" any day.

Upon occasion, the graveyard wanderer stumbles upon the curious handiwork of certain individuals whose clandestine creations, shrouded in anonymity, straddle the dubious boundary between vandalism and art. Some of these performances are visual, but the preferred medium is verse. A few examples will have to suffice. Some years ago, in the old pioneer cemetery located on the campus of the University of Oregon in Eugene, I noticed an early twentieth century marker that featured a variant of the old Puritan epitaph mentioned earlier in this discussion:

Remember, Friends, As You Pass By,
As You Are Now So Once Was I,
As I Am Now, You Soon Shall Be,
Prepare For Death And Follow Me.

Ho hum—But wait! Beneath, hastily scrawled with felt-tip pen, perhaps the work of an aspiring creative writing major, was a postscript Cotton Mather would definitely not have approved of:

To Follow You I'm Not Content
Until I Know Which Way You Went!

In a similar vein, the mid-1980s saw a rash of such bardic and largely ephemeral (the felttip pen again being the instrument of choice) additions to conventional Victorian epitaphs on tombstones throughout southwestern Oregon pioneer graveyards. Presumably the work of one individual (the styles share a certain, shall we say, distinctiveness), they were all outrageously bad—and thereby good—to the point where it is difficult to choose a representative example. However, in the interest of brevity, consider the following old/new collaborative effort found in the Jacksonville Cemetery:

Weep Not For Her Who Dieth,
For She Sleeps And Is At Rest;
The Couch Whereon She Lieth,
Is The Green Earth's Quiet Breast.

. . . .

And Now Away She Flieth
Into The Wild Wild West
While We Survivors Sigheth
At The Coroner's Inquest.

Finally, one group which has a proclivity for generating esoteric humor within the graveyard setting is composed of those very individuals who are at one and the same time intensely occupied with the serious study of cemeteries and gravemarkers as highly relevant features of American culture. Cemetery scholars and fieldworkers have a dark and irreverent side! They delight in such activities as photographing each other in absurd, unflattering (and sometimes compromising), graveyard-specific postures, and they can tell you with uncanny accuracy exactly how many fieldworkers can be crammed into a certain large chair-shaped monument in a New Hampshire cemetery which shall remain unnamed. Nor is such behavior the sole province of one discipline: cultural geographers, linguists, and sociologists are every bit as bad as folklorists, and I have even known an art historian or two to occasionally descend to such levels of depravity. Recently, one wag within the Cemeteries and Gravemarkers section of the American Culture Association—a large and multi-disciplinary assemblage of scholars who regularly present upwards of thirty separate conference papers at their annual meetings—has begun to poke fun at the group's very *raison d'être,* issuing first a bogus set of conference paper abstracts (see Appendix), several of which constitute elaborately esoteric in-jokes, and then an outrageous parody of the section's annual "Call for Papers" format (figure 9). I could say more, but I really must stop now: after all, I must work with these people!

CONCLUSION

In this essay I have tried to make the point that real humor does exist in the contemporary American graveyard, that a great deal of it is the result of conscious and deliberate decisions on the part of persons wishing to make a final and lasting statement which is consistent with their living personalities, and that the whole fits within the larger framework of an ever-growing emphasis upon individuality and personalization in monument style. Whatever form this humor may take, it is for all of us—whether those who cause it to be or those who delight in its various manifestations—a most happy and welcome phenomenon, for it is but one

CALL FOR PAPISTS

The Pius XII Caucus of the Cemeteries and Gravemarkers Permanent Section of the American Culture Association is seeking proposals for its special paper sessions at the ACA's 2002 Annual Meeting, to be held March 13-16 in Toronto, Canada. Topics are solicited from any disciplinary perspective except for Protestants, Nostradamists, and other religiously subversive sects, whose adherents need not apply. Especially encouraged are papers on the following topics: The clash between sacred and secular elements on contemporary Italian-American gravestones; Why Catholic cemeteries are not as dull as they seem; The recount of contested gravestones in Chicago's Catholic cemeteries following the 1960 presidential election. Send proposals to:

The Chair
The University
The Department
The Address
The Phone Number
The Fax Number
The E-Mail Address

Figure 9. Parody of Annual "Call for Papers," Cemeteries and Gravemarkers section, American Culture Association.

of the many indicators of this age's growing rejection of the death-denial behavior which characterized so much of twentieth century American society's attempts to deal with the great mystery of death and dying. Past ages had their own solutions and means of coping with this profound experience: if a sense of humor and a belief that life is not invalidated by death is ours, then I, for one, am all for it.

Virtually every time a reporter interviews me on the topic of gravestones, they ask me what epitaph I have chosen for myself. After first reminding them that these stones do indeed "speak" to the living (see Meyer 1989b; 1991b), I like to tease them with deliciously Puritan-sounding quotations from Shakespeare, Richard II's "Let's talk of graves, of worms and epitaphs." Or, even better, his "I wasted time, and now doth time waste me" (to be accompanied, of course, by a suitably disquieting visual image of Father Time with his scythe, or at the very least a spent hourglass). Of late, I tend to favor Mercutio's final pun from *Romeo and Juliet*: "Ask for me tomorrow and you shall find me a grave man." Any of these might also have sufficed as a clever way to bring this discussion to an end. But a far better—and shorter—example springs to mind. The gravemarker for Mel Blanc (figure 10), a man who brought us decades of laughter, shall have the final word here. Listen, and just perhaps, in its finest Porky Pig voice, you will hear it say

"That's All Folks!"

Figure 10. Gravemarker of Mel Blanc, Hollywood Memorial Park, Hollywood, California.

Appendix to Chapter Five

COVER LETTER

Dear members of the Necropoli and Sepulchral Monuments Section, American (Counter)Culture Association (ACA):

Because he suspects that a horrendous and most unfortunate mixup between the computerized mailing lists of two important academic organizations to which he simultaneously belongs (and chairs sections within) may have resulted in your recently having erroneously received the abstracts of papers to be presented in the Teeth and Jaws Section of the upcoming annual meeting of the American Crocodile Association (ACA), THE CHAIR has asked that I send you the enclosed abstracts for *our* paper sessions, along with his most obsequious apologies and abject grovelings for any confusion(s)—past, present, or future—caused by this unspeakable lapse.

Most humbly and sincerely,

THE CHAIR's footstool

ABSTRACTS

AMERICAN (COUNTER)CULTURE ASSOCIATION
Necropoli and Sepulchral Monuments Section

THE CHAIR
The University
The Department
The Address
The Telephone Number
The Fax Number

ABSTRACTIONS OF PAPERS/PRESENTATIONS
2000 MILLENIAL MEETING
[Not!] April 1, 2000
The Big Easy

AHI, T. Una: Center for North/South Studies
University of Hawaii at Mauna Loa
Pele, HI 96240

"On the Cutting Edge of Gravestone Carving Technology: The Macadamia Method"

Once falsely touted as a powerful aphrodisiac, the juice extracted from Hawaii's native macadamia nuts is being put to a radically new use in the Hawaiian gravestone carving industry. When forced at extremely high pressure through a special nozzle, the juice triggers a complex chemical action upon the surface of the stone, resulting in the conception of incised images so dramatically realistic that passerbys in local cemeteries often mistake them for the real thing. Though "macadamia etching" has so far proven successful only when applied to Hawaii's native lava rock, it is anticipated that similar techniques using extracts from walnuts, pecans, and peanuts may be adapted for use on traditional mainland stones.

BROWN, Bud: Department of Physical Education
Mideastern Ohio State Technical and Vocational College
Wintergreen, OH 43801

"The Final Score: Graves of Famous Football Players"

Just like in life, the graves of famous football players sometimes feature their famous football feats. I'll show you a few examples, like the one for Douglas "Wrong Way" Corrigan (or was he that flyer guy, hell I can never keep 'em straight!), who once scored a touchdown (well, a safety, actually) against his own team by running the length of the football field the wrong way (his tombstone faces a different direction from everyone else in the graveyard, I think maybe that's symbolic or something), and then also there's the presidential seal on the pre-need tombstone of Gerald Ford which substitutes the University of Michigan Wolverine for the American Eagle. I've got others too.

DORQUE, Jerry W.: Tru-Valu Software, Inc.
9908 Flakely Ave. N
Seattle, WA 98008

"Research in Progress"

If I register and show up for the conference, my paper will deal with my current research. I'm not going to say what that research concerns because feedback from the last conference where I didn't show up indicates certain people were unreasonably upset they didn't get to hear my previously announced paper, and I don't want anyone to worry their little heads about whether it's going to happen again or not. So, if I'm there you'll get to hear about it. And if not, hey, that's just tough!

FUBBENHEIMER, Gretchen N.: School of Cognitive Learning Experiences and Gender Studies
Desdemona College
Othello, MO 65001

"Gravestones as Symbols of Sexual Oppression in the Poetry of a Neglected Victorian Writer"

Unbeknownst to her family and friends, (Mrs.) Sarah N. Goatlips, prominent Philadelphia socialite and widow of Victorian financier Horace T. Goatlips, composed scores of poems which were discovered after her death lining the litterboxes of her seventeen cats. Though virtually ignored by chauvinistic male editors of poetry anthologies and literature textbooks, these verses are remarkable for their use of gravestone imagery (obelisks, table stones, gates ajar, etc.) as powerful and disturbing symbols for male oppression and (unconscious) female submission.

FURD, Ellsworth J.: Department of Geography and Tourism
Yukiuk Community College
Arctic Station, AK 99601

"The Emperor Crab Cemetery: Breaking New Ground in Ecotourism"

During the catastrophic "Good Friday" earthquake of 1964, the tiny fishing hamlet of Emperor Crab, Alaska sank 276 feet and disappeared beneath the waters of Katchemtrap Bay, leaving only the town cemetery miraculously perched atop a vertical shaft of basalt rising from the ocean floor. "Winch-Downs" to the site from hovering flightseeing helicopters are increasingly popular amongst tourists seeking exotic travel options.

LaDONNA, DONNA: RR #3
Wheatley, KS 66241

"My Slides"

Hi! These are some of the slides I took in a couple of cemeteries last year on my summer vacation. I think they're really neat! Some are a little dark, but I think the battery may have been running a little low in my camera, I don't know. There are several lambs, some trees which I think may be petrified or something, and something really unique—a stone with a color photograph on it!

La GRENOUILLE, Gaston: Académie des arts agricole et militaire
St. Cyr plus petit
FRANCE

"'Mort pour le Nid': The French Carrier Pigeon Cemetery at Oiseau sur Oeuf"

Perhaps the most curious of the many World War I cemeteries dotting the landscape of northern France is the *Nécropole Nationale des pigeon voyageur militaire,* wherein rest the heroic remains of some 476 carrier pigeons who gave their lives in the service of La France during The Great War. Amongst the precisely aligned rows of nest-shaped gravemarkers may be found the final resting place of Hércule, ace of aces, who flew more than 63 successful missions before being shot out of the sky by the infamous Baron Manfred von Richthofen (may his boche name life in infamy forever!), as well as the massive granite egg representing "le tombeau de pigeon inconnu."

LAMSON, Joseph, XVIII: 1658 Tucker's Ford Rd,
Malden, MA 01010

"Hezekiah Effingdon: The Master Turkey Carver of Bildad, Massachusetts"

In addition to the usual assortment of winged skulls, hourglasses, coffins, and (in his later, degenerate period) willow and urn designs, the work of Hezekiah Effingdon (1698/9–1768) is remarkable for the exquisite representations of wild turkeys he carved in the tympanums of some 60% of the slate gravemarkers found in the area immediately surrounding Bildad, Massachusetts. While debate rages as to the symbolic meaning of these arcane motifs, there can be little doubt that Hezekiah's turkeys are far superior in design, execution, and taste to the rats carved by his Bildad rival, Jehosaphat Hopkins (1704–1759).

MOONEY, Joe Bob: Cell Block C
Chumagee County Correctional Institution
Chumagee, OK 73803

"'No Stone Unturned': A Revisionist Look at Cemetery Vandalism"

Virtually all studies of cemetery vandalism conducted to date are flawed by the erroneous assumption that such acts are essentially antisocial in nature and possess no redeeming qualities whatsoever. In this paper, which is based upon research conducted with colleagues at the last three institutions with which I have been associated, I shall argue that a number of highly desirable results, including powerful male bonding, release of potentially dangerous testosteronal pressure, and enhanced economic opportunities for liquor stores and cemetery restorationists, are in fact the inevitable byproducts of these misunderstood community relations activities.

PUTZ, Jasper N.: Center for the Study of Arcane New Englandia
113 Lanterne Street
Boston, MA 02119

"'By Their Droppings Ye Shall Know Them': A New Look at Slater's 'Guano Thesis'"

In the mid-1980s, researcher James A. Slater energized the worlds of gravestone and ornithological studies when, in a paper presented to a special joint meeting of the Association for Gravestone Studies and the Audubon Society, he advanced the notion that seemingly random specimens of bird droppings found on old gravestones actually represented complex, sentient patterns of symbolic communication. This paper challenges certain fundamental tenets of the Slater thesis, arguing—among other things—that a significant number of these motif clusters were actually the result of squirrels.

PUTZ, Jasper N., Jr.: Department of Anthropology, Sociology, Folklore, and Speech Communication
North Dakota State College of Education
Ubetcha, ND 58199

"A Sociological Analysis of Automobile Graveyards"

Analysis of samples from 206 automobile graveyards in Oklahoma, Puerto Rico, and The Yukon demonstrates patterns of natality, mortality, and banality bearing significant statistical compatibility (when utilizing the ??? test of reliability) with those found in human graveyards in the same locales. Further, seasonal patterns of planting, harvest, conception, and drunk and disorderly arrests seem linked to these identical patterns, though sometimes in reverse order. Charts, graphs, and slides of chicken entrails will be used to illustrate and validate these findings.

REYEM, E. Drahcir: Department of Leisure Studies
Polk University
Monmouth, OR 97361

"Total Saturation Fatalities as Recorded on Early Oregon Gravemarkers"

Along with disease, accidental and deliberate shooting, and the more traditional forms of drowning (e.g., in a river, lake, hotel bath, etc.), total saturation—a medical condition wherein the body absorbs an excess of concentrated moisture and explodes, often causing death—ranks as one of the most frequently occurring types of fatality recorded on early Oregon gravemarkers. Analysis of death dates on the stones reveals that more than 80% of such fatalities took place in the months of December through March, Oregon's notorious rainy season. Sophisticated water repellants have virtually eliminated this affliction amongst modern residents of the Beaver State.

WEST, Rex D.: Department of Texan Studies
Bluebonnet State University
Longhorn, TX 78464

"You Can't Judge a Symbol by its Shape (Usually)"

Visitors to Mt. Holymaple Cemetery in Dunder, Illinois are frequently amazed by the 27 ft. high solid granite Texas-shaped gravemarker for Leonard Fudde, mistakenly assuming it to be one last sign of allegiance by a wandering son of the Lone Star State unfortunate enough to be buried on foreign soil. Actually, it may be classified as an occupational symbol. Mr. Fudde, a noted contortionist who billed himself "The Human Pretzel," was best known for his famous stunt wherein he contorted himself into the shape of Texas with his left eyeball precisely denoting the location of the state capitol, Austin.

WIGGINS, Astral: 16 Crystal Canyon Rd.
Sedona, AZ 86077

"Spirit Rubbings: A Breakthrough in Thanatological Research?"

By utilizing and readapting the basic time-tested techniques of gravestone rubbing, a growing number of thanatological researchers are embracing the principle of spirit rubbing as an effective alternative in instances where spirit photography might yield faint and/or insubstantial results. This paper discusses the basic materials, methods, and controlled substances essential to mastering this revolutionary technique.

ZORCH, Uzitzizus: Department of Ethnolinguistic Theory
The University of Chicago at Milwaukee
Milwaukee, WI 53520

"'I Spit Upon Your Shoes!': Ritual Insulting on Uzitzistani Gravestones"

In the tiny former Soviet bloc country of Uzitzistan, ritual insulting is a customary form of greeting and linguistic "icebreaking" at gatherings such as effigy burnings, committee meetings, and family reunions. It is an especially important element in courtship rituals. Given this emphasis in life, one is not surprised to find splendid examples of such insults frequently used as epitaphs upon Uzitzistani gravemarkers. In many instances, these represent personal favorites of the deceased, and a number of them are either direct or debased quotations from famous works of Uzitzistani poetry.

PART THREE

Festivals

6

WISHES COME TRUE
Designing the Greenwich Village Halloween Parade

JACK KUGELMASS

The "striking florescence of celebration" in the modern world (Manning 1983, 4) is rapidly transforming both the physical topography of America and the annual holiday cycle of its citizens. Throughout the Midwest, for example, local communities seem almost frenetic in their creation of ethnic theme parks and "historic" pageants and, where appropriate, their rebuilding of habitations and public buildings with Swiss, German, Norwegian, and a variety of other ethnic motifs. Larger cities throughout the country have created "festival" markets and historic districts, while "artists'" neighborhoods have become the hallmark of a thriving city. Chicago, Milwaukee, and Minneapolis all have their "SoHos." And, like the East Coast metropolis that dominates the economic as well as the cultural life of America, cities everywhere now foster a host of public events to celebrate the cultural diversity of their populations.

This preoccupation with celebrations was already noticeable toward the latter part of the nineteenth century—evidence of the impact of immigrant festive culture on America (Conzen 1989, 73). Its adaptation by Americans of all persuasions is in part a reflection of the search for novelty and experience—hallmarks of consumer capitalism (Manning 1983, 5)—and in part a representation of the modern notion that authenticity must be found in some other time and place (MacCannell 1976, 3). Little wonder then that the rhetorical modality of these events is so strongly traditionalistic, or that the "rediscovery" of the city among the new commercial class has created a virtual simulacrum of a nineteenth century urban gentry.

The very "florescence of celebration" would suggest the existence of some variation of morphology, and it might be useful at this point to outline even a preliminary system, which I will develop further toward the end of the essay, for categorizing public events. Among the principal types of public events are:

1. Civic celebrations, undoubtedly the most common of public events. These are officially sanctioned, and have increasingly become "a distinctive genre of mass communication" that help engender a "we-feeling" among the many and disparate segments of the nation state (Chaney 1983, 120–121). They are correctly considered rituals of unification, glossing over divisive issues and presenting participants and viewers with legible collective symbols (Lawrence 1982, 163). Much like royal pageants and military parades, such celebrations are used by elites to underline the ideal social order of a given community (Cannadine 1983; Da Matta 1984, 219; Warner 1959).
2. "Ethnic" festivals, including social groups based on religion, class, and gender whose participants wish to claim a place for themselves within the American social and cultural pantheon (Wiggins 1982). These events, although semiofficial, may contain elements that do not lend themselves to incorporation into American civil religion (i.e., they may become overly rambunctious or overtly political, such as the Irish Republican Army's participation in New York City's St. Patrick's Day parade).
3. "Carnivalesque" festivals that shun or are shunned by the official pantheon. Such festivals, which may represent groups that at other times seek to legitimize themselves within the social and cultural hierarchy, deny the legitimacy of that hierarchy. In her studies of the artists' and counterculture's spoof of Pasadena, California's annual Rose Bowl parade—the Doo Dah festival—Denise Lawrence argues that "alternative parades" like this one have become increasingly common since the mid-1970s (1982, 173; 1987, 133). There is, however, considerable evidence that such events were quite common in the past (Bakhtin 1984; N. Davis 1975; Ladurie 1979), and that they typically occur alongside mainstream events (S. Davis 1986), particularly among socially marginalized groups (Lipsitz 1990). Given their parodic nature and their relative openness, costumers' iconography is less legible (or at least more narrowly targeted) than civic or even ethnic celebrations (Lawrence 1982, 166).

This essay is an ethnography of a "carnivalesque" event, the Village Halloween parade in New York City. In analyzing the parade's evolution and changing structure, I am attempting to explain what the event "has to say," or, in Mary Douglas's words, how it "bring[s] out of all the possible might-have-beens a firm social reality" (1982, 36). I conclude by suggesting a connection between the emergence of new expressive forms of, and recent transformations in, the cultural construction of selfhood.

Parades are not easy to document, particularly night parades that attract hundreds of thousands of people, such as the Village Halloween parade in which most participants wear costumes having only a thin connection, if that, to the spirits and monsters we normally associate with Halloween. Also, there are those intangibles that are so much a part of this parade: the almost continuous blaring music of marching mariachi, reggae, and even klezmer bands interspersed among the other elements of the parade; noise, particularly the cheers from the audience for outstanding costumes and, more typically, catcalls for outlandish transvestites; color-vivid reds, golds, purples, and others intended by their creators to dazzle against the black backdrop of night; and the audience, many of whom are themselves dressed in Halloween costumes and masks. Indeed, squad cars from the local police precinct are sometimes driven by police wearing vampire fangs. The city itself becomes part of the celebration, as here and there people display pumpkins and other holiday decorations from their terraces. In Greenwich Village, the home of the parade, whole streets have balconies with puppets of political leaders saluting the crowds below, while a huge spider climbs the tower of the public library eerily lit by orange spotlights. What pervades the event is not so much the world upside down (Kunzle 1978) as the world upside down and right side up suddenly juxtaposed. The result is a powerful sense of irony and humor through a collective recognition of the rather easy transposition of order and chaos, when, like in a dream, familiar things can sometimes seem entirely unfamiliar. Halloween is New York's answer to Mardi Gras. Like its New Orleans counterpart, the celebration "is a way of dreaming with others, publicly and responsively" (Kinser 1990, xv).

To provide the reader with as full an account as I have of the event, to create, so to speak, a text out of which much of the discussion will proceed, let me share the notes I took during the 1987 parade, when I tried to record every costumed participant I saw. An hour or two before the parade begins, the marchers gradually fall into formation along West Street just north of West Houston Street. I decided to use the opportunity to record as much as I could while the event was "stationary." Since people arrive at their assigned locations somewhat randomly, my notes are not an accurate description of the order of the parade. However, because I intend to analyze the parade in terms of its content rather than its form, this does not constitute an impediment to my analysis.

The parade begins with its current organizer, Jeanne Fleming, in costume, followed by Ken Allen, a leading member of the parade's board, dressed as a Mexican god. Nearby are transvestites with huge protruding fake breasts, gaudy skirts and hats, and huge cigarette holders. I try to interview them unsuccessfully. (Most participants are "in character," and the parade is not the time to get a "backstage" view.) I begin to follow "The Fashion Police," dressed in white cloaks and white firemen's helmets, who are ticketing people for wearing unstylish clothes. I receive a ticket for my buckskin jacket, which the "police" attribute to participation in Woodstock and denigrate as "sixties retro." I walk along West Street and see a group of mixed gender middle-aged teachers from New Jersey assembling their costumes. They introduce themselves as Gladys Night and the Pits (each member of the group is dressed as a different celebrity pit dog, including Pit Vicious, Dolly Pitton, Daddy Warpits, Rock Pitson, Scarpit O'Hare, Pitter Pan, etc.). Others include: a couple dressed in flight helmets, goggles, and bomber jackets with a large-scale silver styrofoam airplane protruding from their front and rear; "Vera Carp," a shy transvestite; a man in a white radioactive uniform; "Tortilla Flats," a red open truck with a devil growling and a skeleton dancing to the music coming from a trailing mariachi band; the Chrysler Building with jumping stockbrokers (1987 was the year of the stock market crash); a character from "Gilligan's Island"; a monk calling himself the "Late Father Barnaby"; United Farm Workers with a huge skeleton holding a sign that reads "I ate grapes"; and "New Wave Primitives" in a car covered in burlap, tinsel twigs, and a Balinese mask. Inside the car, characters have painted faces and are wearing bone earrings and chain necklaces. One group of transvestites, accompanied by a man dressed in a long brown costume with toilet paper dangling from it, explains: "We're out with our date. He's dressed as a turd because everyone knows that all men are shits."

I see more costumes, including: "Jesus for Everybody," a group distributing Jesus brochures; a Chinese dragon; a junior high school percussion band; a man wearing a shower curtain and a bathrobe; a woman calling herself "Post Industrial Fortune Teller" holding a tray with a lit candle, a jar, and a straw basket containing Chinese fortune cookies; "Lady Death"; "Hershey Bar"; a one-man walking Korean salad bar made from painted foam; "Pink Pig Floyd"; clowns; Indians; a man with a tall green head, which he explains is a migraine headache; a mariachi band singing "La Bamba"; a skull holding a placard that reads, "More Nukes"; a giant tube of "Crest Tooth Paste"; Renaissance costumes; Sun Ra from Sweet Basil (one of a handful of advertisements in the parade); a ghoul cocktail party; characters from the "Wizard of Oz"; the "Condom Fairy" distributing free balloon condoms; "The Village Light Opera Group"; a transvestite nun; "Death" as Chicago's future; a man eating a baby and a woman with a sign that reads "eat me"; a pizza with its baker and a family of eaters; a Peruvian band; a graffitied wall with a half-torn poster advertising Visa; an African band; monsters holding human heads; a group dressed as individual cards from a deck that shuffles itself by running to change places; a Caribbean steel band; "Sky Tracker"; "Ghost Busters"; "Death"; a transvestite mermaid; a cowboy transvestite; a family of monsters; a family of clowns; assorted monsters; a Chinese dragon; a transvestite trick-or-treating; a group of men dressed as huge lipstick cases; a "Free Tibet" group; an air bubble with a captive couple; white African dancers; African stilt dancers; "The Big Apple Corp Gay and Lesbian Marching Band"; a fairy godmother; Campbell's Soup; a headless man in a trench coat carrying his head in his hands; male ballet dancers with women's names; a giant can of Raid; a strutting male peacock; cardboard penguins; a steel band with Ronald Reagan as the drummer; vampire women; ghouls; Ronald Reagan holding a gun and a Bible; a silver-and-gold brocaded man; "Hot 103 FM" (an advertisement for a local radio station); a recycling group; two queens and a bishop; Scottish bagpipes; the "Loisida Band" (the name refers to the Puerto Rican community's colloquial name for their Lower East Side neighborhood); transvestite "Wizard of Oz" characters; a group of "Trojaneze" lubricated condoms; a man raising money to fight AIDS; "Caliente Cab Co." (an advertisement for a Mexican restaurant); Queen Kong.

In previous years the parade culminated at Washington Square Park with music and various performances, such as the appearance and descent of a spectacular devil on the Washington Square arch. Now, due to changes in the route, the parade stops at Union Square, where musical bands entertain spectators. For many, the Halloween spectacle continues elsewhere, at numerous private parties in homes throughout the city; the more daring head to Christopher Street in the heart of Greenwich Village. The Christopher Street promenade is an annual event that parallels the parade, and there are more than a few people—both spectators and performers—who attend this while avoiding the parade altogether. Although the promenade probably preceded the parade, its growth each year demonstrates a certain linkage between the two events. (Greenwich Village has a long, albeit erratic, history of impromptu Halloween celebrations, and there is undoubtedly a link between the recent emergence of such carnivalesque celebrations and the increasingly public nature of gay culture.[1] The parade, as I shall indicate below, straddles the line between civic festival and carnival; the promenade makes no claim to respectability. On the contrary, it celebrates the irreverent and the lascivious. As New York's gay Mecca and the site of numerous gay-oriented bars and shops, Christopher Street is like an inner sanctum. On Halloween night, the sanctum transforms itself into a public stage, and the city, if not the world, is its audience. Here are my notes:

1. Spectators lining Sixth Avenue awaiting the parade.

2. These costumes are modeled on Brazilian Carnival costumes, demonstrating the wide range of influences on the current parade.

3. The police love the Halloween parade and consider it one of the safest public events held each year.

4. Some costumers improvise poses, performing for sections of spectators as they march up Sixth Avenue.

5. Costumed man on Christopher Street after the parade.

6. After the parade, celebrity ghoul, Greenwich Village.

8. On October thirty-first, ghouls are everywhere in Greenwich Village, since many residents scurry about to private costume parties.

7. Phalluses and vaginas are ubiquitous; mere exposure and, of course, size, contribute to a sense of the ridiculous and evoke tremendous laughter from spectators.

From Seventh Avenue all the way west to the river, Christopher Street is closed to traffic. The throngs of spectators, which number in the tens of thousands, make entire blocks almost impossible to traverse. There is a physical contact here that is partly ecological—a narrow street and a huge throng—and partly ideological—bodies, which seem more public than private, to be gazed at, even touched. The event is referred to as "the promenade" because it features transvestites who strut along the street, often in pairs, either acting nonchalant or actively seeking the attention and applause of spectators.

At the corner of Christopher Street and Seventh Avenue there is a man dressed as Tammy Bakker, with gobs of makeup and huge eyelashes, holding a Bible, the pages of which are from Gay American History. Nearby is "Jessica Hahn Dog" posing for Playdog. Further along I see a man dressed as a giant tube of KY jelly. In the crowd, I spot characters from the "Wizard of Oz" and a "nun" standing on a balcony sprinkling holy water onto the crowd below. Next to her a man with a huge phallus who is dressed in a bathrobe is sodomizing a transvestite. When he stops, "she" climbs the fire escape begging for more. He goes into his apartment, reemerges masturbating, and then throws the liquid contents of a cup onto the crowd to simulate ejaculation. He then hangs from the fire escape, squats, and simulates defecation. Another man pretends to masturbate with an electrically lit phallus. A transvestite, dressed like a French courtier, performs fellatio on him. On the opposite side of the street, two bare-chested young men wearing tight blue jeans are exhibiting their lean, muscular bodies by scaling, monkeylike, the fire escape outside their third-floor apartment. The crowd below shouts its approval. When one of the climbers faces the street, people begin to chant, "Show your dick!" One of the men begins to unzip and zip, sadistically teasing the onlookers, transfixed by the promise of a live peep show. Elsewhere, a young man pulls his pants down and sticks his buttocks out the second-story window. The crowd, delighted, demands a repeat performance.

Many who are present at the promenade appear to be passing tourists, often the scattered remnants of the parade seeking a little more time in the spotlight. An "Arab" walks by with a rug protruding from his middle as if he were riding a magic carpet. A group of transvestites is dressed as Girl Scouts. Two Kabuki actors, wearing bright silk gowns with their hair tied in knots, pose as a group of Japanese tourists takes their photograph. One man is dressed as a Hasid. I also see: a plain white costume with the words "generic costume"; two transvestites dressed as middle-aged dowdy ladies; a transvestite nun with metallic hair and a mustache, wearing the Hebrew letter "khay" (a common American Jewish symbol). Toward the westernmost part of the street I spot two young men dressed as grotesque space aliens with flashing red eyes, silver boots, sequined hats, black zippered coats, and long rubber fingers. When I ask them where they are from, they explain with Hispanic accents, "We're not from here. We're from outer space." For the next few minutes we engage in a perfectly absurd discussion about the difficulty of finding parking for space ships in Manhattan, the relative age of space aliens, the time it takes to get from one universe to another, and the best place to eat blood in Manhattan.

From my descriptions, we can see that there are some very clear distinctions between the parade and the promenade. Partly because it is framed in space and time and partly because it does have a degree of organization (in theory participants register before the event; in practice many just show up unannounced), the parade is a complex mixture of iconography—some parodic and/or metaphorical join otherwise unrelated domains of experience; others are more directly representational or metonymical and use one element to stand for something larger. Sometimes metaphor and metonym blend ambiguously. The presence of a huge tube of Crest toothpaste, for example, is as much a celebration of the aesthetics of everyday life as a satire on it. As Da Matta argues, following from Turner, abstractions and dislocations "bring on a consciousness of all the reifications of the social world" (1984, 214). Completely unstructured and very chaotic, the promenade is purely metaphorical and ludic. Its iconography is entirely of a world upside down. Although I will have much more to say about the two events later, let me conclude for the moment with the rather curious observation that neither has a particularly close connection to Halloween.

Although Halloween has long been a much-cherished holiday for children in this country, its origins are tied to the British Isles, and, in particular, to Ireland, where the holiday developed as a blend of native and Catholic beliefs. For the Druids, 31 October marked the end of the year, a time when herdsmen had to find shelter for their livestock for the winter. It also marked a symbolic death, a time when the world of the living and the spirit world were less divided, and the living, therefore, felt compelled to propitiate the dead by offering them food, hence the origin of trick-or-treating (Santino 1983) and the iconography of death that pervades the holiday and its Celtic precursor, Samhain. Particularly noteworthy about *Samhain* is its position between the equinox and solstice. Marking the boundary between winter and summer, Samhain represents a moment of transition charged with a peculiar kind of energy (Rogers 2002, 21). That very energy undoubtedly contributed to the attachment to it of key liturgical moments in the Christian calendar connected to the commemoration of saints and the recent dead. At the same time, its place in the seasonal calendar made it an appropriate point for the slaughter of animals in preparation for the winter, the gathering of crops, and the rethatching of cottages (Rogers 2002, 47)—elements, along with others such as masquerade and courtship, that intertwine notions of death, rebirth and celebration. Nineteenth century Irish immigrants brought Halloween to America, and with it came an associated tradition of disguise, pranks, a sense of the supernatural, and games and rituals that had more to do with the fortunes of love than death (Rogers 2002, 48).

Halloween's relegation to the domain of children may reflect a general disenchantment with the world of spirits within American culture, much the way fairytales are treated. Perhaps it reflects Richard Dorson's thesis[2] that Old World demons have proven to be extremely reluctant to cross the ocean (Dorson 1983), or, if they did make the journey, as did Norwegian trolls in Wisconsin, their relegation to the netherworld of lawn furnishings may have made the trip seem hardly worthwhile. Its recent revival as an American festival speaks less to the possibility of religious enchantment than it does to the license the event provides, a type of behavior that became quite familiar in the 1970s, when the Village Halloween parade emerged. Moreover, the license is as much a chance to misbehave as it is a chance to display oneself or one's vision of the world, to occupy public attention, which is, as John MacAloon suggests, the most precious of human goods (1982, 262). Through the use of masks, Halloween allows people to transform themselves, to assume personae, to enter a fantasy world with enthusiasm. It offers a time out of time "when we can enter into our experience for its own sake, not for what it produces" (Abrahams 1982a, 163). According to Babcock, this fantasy world "does more than simply mock our desire to live according to our usual orders and norms; it reinvests life with a vigor and a *Spielraum* attainable (it would seem) in no other way" (1978, 32).

For most people, even the relatively innocuous masking for a costume party is a venture well beyond the world of the familiar. For many of its participants, the time out of time of the Village Halloween parade provides a public spectacle through which culture takes on a semblance of wholeness, and public rituals, either largely scoffed at, as in the case of ethnic parades, or ignored, as in the case of state rites, seem once again meaningful.[3] Moreover, the profusion of individual identities in postmodern culture, the fragmentation of families through divorce, migration, and single gender couples, as well as the dislocation of communities through gentrification—a process particularly evident in Greenwich Village throughout the 1970s—has created a need for such productions, for invented traditions that legitimize new social and class formations and give collective expression to the physical spaces they occupy (Hobsbawm and Ranger 1983). Community events satisfy the "need to feel part of something" (Bonnemaison 1990, 32). It is precisely the need for new traditions, which became increasingly acute as the economic, social, and cultural landscape of New York City was transformed during the late 1970s and 1980s by a booming Wall Street and its ancillary industries, that has enabled one man's idea to have such dramatic impact on the life of a great metropolis.

In 1973, Ralph Lee, a puppeteer and theater director, rounded up 150 friends and acquaintances and convinced them to march through the streets of Greenwich Village on Halloween night carrying or wearing some of the giant puppets he had designed for his plays. In doing so, Lee began a tradition that was gradually to assume a life of its own, to grow beyond a scale anyone had thought possible. Lee responded by designing ever-more-spectacular puppets, including a forty-foot articulating snake capable of reaching down and kissing young children in the crowd, a giant Irish sea god riding in a chariot, and a twenty-foot three-masted ship complete with rats scurrying to abandon it. To help create the proper backdrop, Lee also designed the giant spider, which each year sat atop the Jefferson Market Library, and other creatures that emerged from buildings or otherwise made an appearance during the night's activities. In the early years, the parade lasted no more than an hour. People generally learned about it by word of mouth, or as they happened upon these Halloween revelers on the way home from work. Within a few years, the once-intimate parade took nearly five hours to traverse the same route. The length of time was due only in part to the increased number of marchers; it had much more to do with the number of spectators.

To cope with the logistics of large crowds, changes were made, albeit reluctantly: barricades were introduced to separate spectators from participants; a police permit was acquired; and notices were posted by the traffic department banning cars from parking along the parade's route. Eventually the route itself was changed to allow more room for spectators. By 1986, the parade was considered too large an event to hold in the heart of old Greenwich Village. Originally the parade began at

Westbeth, the subsidized artist cooperative apartments near the Hudson River, wound its way along the narrow streets, and ended up in Washington Square Park. For security reasons, the route was switched, so the parade would begin on Sixth Avenue, a bland modern boulevard that could better accommodate the half-million spectators who were coming from all over the metropolitan area to view the parade. It then detoured up Tenth Street—a token reminder of its former route of narrow twisting streets of old brownstones—turned up La Guardia Place, and ended at Union Square. In 1987, after considerable pressure from property owners in the Tenth Street block association, the Tenth Street route was dropped and the parade was completely restricted to broad boulevards—West Houston, Sixth Avenue, and Fourteenth Street. Although the new route is better suited to a parade of this scale, some who recall the early years continually lament the changes. For them, the new route symbolizes the end of a once-intimate and extraordinary ensemble of puppet performances.

With increased size and visibility, the parade now has to undergo a review by Community Board Two, the local Greenwich Village planning board. In February 1987, I attended the first community board meeting at which the parade's organizers were invited to discuss their plans for the fall. The meeting was used by a handful of opponents to voice discontent about the event's size and its potential impact on a historic district. Despite the testimony from members of the police department, who openly attributed the low crime rate in Greenwich Village on Halloween to the parade, the parade's opponents assumed that the event was a powder keg waiting to explode. They complained, too, about the evolution of the parade, arguing that "it had become political," and that they would "prefer a real Halloween parade, something for children." In order to consider the issues more carefully and to solicit other opinions, the board decided to hold a special open meeting in April, at which the parade would be the only issue on the agenda.

When the community board met again, both opponents and supporters of the parade came with reinforcements. For the most part, the parade's opponents were Greenwich Village property owners; the supporters were tenants. As at the February meeting, opponents complained about the changes in the parade, the fact that it had grown too large, and that it had become too political and bawdy. Some suggested turning the parade into something else, either a local event or a children's parade. What lay behind much of the opposition, indeed what was a recurrent theme in the complaints, were two seemingly contradictory issues: the nature of the parade's politics, that is, its seriousness, and the parade's playfulness, particularly its licentiousness. "We do not want this parade," exclaimed one block association leader. "It's lost its meaning. It's a Mardi Gras. And Halloween is for children. It's not a Mardi Gras!" The notion of a Halloween parade for children in part reflects the earlier dominating presence of giant articulating puppets that delighted young and old. It also suggests that despite its creator's disavowal of officialdom and city sponsorship, the parade has at its core a coherent vision of civic order. The promenade is very much the converse. Indeed, the very combination of alternative vision and lack of structure makes such an event potentially explosive (Handelman 1990, 55).[4]

Despite their threats, the parade's opponents failed to stop the event. Indeed, one board member, who was himself opposed to the parade, admitted at a public meeting that an informal poll he had conducted showed neighborhood residents to be overwhelmingly in favor of the parade. The only persistent complaint he recorded was displeasure over changes in the parade's route: local residents liked the old route of winding streets, and they generally liked to view the parade from the comfort of their apartment windows.

If opposition within the community board proved ineffectual, a much more serious threat was posed by the increasing alienation of the parade's founder from his creation. When I met Ralph Lee in the summer of 1986, he had just resigned as head of the organizing committee, and was uncertain whether there would be another Halloween parade. What became clear during the interview was that he had begun to consider the parade a monster of his own creation. It had gotten too big, too much out of his control. Lee had meant the parade to be a ritual-like collective enactment of primitive myth. The giant puppets he saw as part of a pantheistic belief system centered around nature and incorporating ideas and images from primitive religions. Marching through the streets carrying the spirit-puppets offered the Greenwich Village community a chance to cleanse itself (the parade was led each year by hags on stilts sweeping the streets with brooms made of twigs).

Lee was particularly bothered by the increased size of the parade. In 1973, audience and participants were one. Recently, the parade had become overwhelmed by spectators. The parade had turned from ritual to theater and, in that sense, it no longer served the purpose he had envisioned for it. Not only were the crowds passive spectators, but they had even become somewhat ominous. The 1982 parade's stage manager recalls what it was like to lead the event and confront masses of people at one major intersection.

> The truck came to a halt. I said, 'Please move out of the way.' And as the truck inched forward there was a chant that was started in the crowd yelling, 'Stop the truck!' I realized that 10,000 people were yelling at me. They wanted to hurt me because I was on top of this truck.

Despite prior concern over the possible impact of Lee's resignation, the event continues to grow. The smooth transition has much to do with the organizing skills of Jeanne Fleming, the parade's current director, who describes herself as a "celebration artist" and "orchestrator of events." Fleming, who has a master's degree in medieval studies, sees a direct connection between medieval carnival celebrations and the Halloween parade. She became involved in the parade as a participant, and began organizing the event after she met Lee in 1982 and he indicated his desire to let go of it. As Fleming recalls:

> And I said, 'You can't let that parade die!' So I said, 'Maybe I could help with it.' And then I realized I was saying maybe. And I just said, 'No, I'll be there. On September 1st in New York and I'll help you do it.' So I did.

By the time Lee resigned, Fleming had already been doing most of the administrative work for the parade for several years, such as generating grants, securing official permits, finding sponsors, and contracting artists and musicians to design and participate in floats. Lee, meanwhile, focused all his efforts on making puppets. Fleming was very much inspired by Lee's work and, at least initially, did not resent Lee's abandoning the administrative work to her. The two shared certain ideas, including a sense of the significance of the parade for participants. According to Fleming:

> Parades let people see themselves as a performance rather than as machines. It lets them see the imaginative side of themselves. You can go to a disco and dance and be feeling like you're creating something of yourself out there, but it costs you a fortune to get in, and there are social constraints. On the night of Halloween there are no social constraints. People can be as weird, as sweet, as mean, or whatever. They can look into their craziest mind, their deepest desire and realize what that is.

According to Lee:

> The parade charges people up. It warms their insides; energies are allowed to flow between people. The masks in that situation give people permission to play with each other and assume roles that allow them to give vent to things that they might be holding back. The obvious example is the gay people. For them to be able to be out there in the street doing their dream person is pretty fantastic. And not just them, but if somebody wants to be Ronald Reagan to the nth degree, he can do it; he can act that out, or be Nixon, or be some witch or guru, or whatever you want to be. I don't think people are aware of what they are doing a lot of the time or what they are revealing about themselves. The choices they make as to what their disguises are going to be are heavy-duty choices. For example, a costume years ago—I might have only seen a photograph of it—it was covered with patches of different kinds of fur and sewed on to it was this kind of vegetation. I'm not sure what he was, but it was something from inside himself that was allowed to surface.

Despite this shared sense of the value of the parade for individual self-expression, Lee and Fleming had very different notions about the significance of the parade for the larger community and the city. For Lee, the parade was closely tied to his interest in spirits, primitive ritual, and nature. From that standpoint, the "Old World" charm of Greenwich Village provided an extraordinary setting—a stage upon which to perform.

> There are trees on the streets in the Village. Halloween has a lot to do with nature and the changes of the season, and the fact that there are all those bare branches at that point is a great backdrop for Halloween. You see a figure against those branches, you can imagine yourself in the countryside.

Although Fleming argues that the Halloween parade has special importance because it is "the last event before people shut themselves up in apartments for winter, and that by releasing energy it prevents evil by acting as a safety valve for restless energy," she believes the parade has less to do with reacquainting city people with the power of nature than it does with acquainting them with the very place they inhabit.

> Parades let people reclaim urban spaces not just as a place of work but to renew their relationship with the environment. By animating all senses, parades change people's relation to the city, letting them look at the city in a new way. Parades allow all different groups of people to get together in public in an important way, crossing all political, economic, religious, ethnic barriers. There are very few events in the city that do that.

The differences in Lee's and Fleming's respective points of view are critical for understanding the radically different perspective each had on the parade's evolution. For Fleming, the growth of the parade into a huge spectacle is a sign of its success. For Lee, that growth is a sign of failure, because the parade has moved increasingly away from the intimate ritual he devised. By 1987, he simply wanted nothing more to do with the event. According to Fleming:

> When Ralph decided to drop out of the parade I begged him to save the giant sweepers. And he wouldn't do it. I promised him I'd hire professionals to wear them, they'd be paid, and I'd have a stage manager, you know, every assurance he could have had about the costumes. And I said, "You know Ralph, to do that, you're like cursing the parade because I believe in the power of these things." And he said, "I know that it might be happening, that that's a problem but I won't do it." And that was another real break for me with him. It was a real break of faith with what celebrations are about. With what this parade is about. It was a real spiritual, philosophical break that happened between us.

The "spiritual, philosophical break" was by no means one-sided. Lee was more than just tired of the work involved in organizing the parade and the annual transformation of his Westbeth loft into a factory for erecting his giant floats. The fact is that the parade had long since made a "spiritual, philosophical break" with its creator.

In conducting my interviews with people who have designed some of the more impressive costumes and floats in recent parades, I found it striking how little they knew of Ralph Lee or his work. Indeed, sometimes they began participating without ever having seen the parade before. Ross Berman, a fashion stylist, describes missing the parade altogether in his first attempt to see it because he was too busy doing the makeup for his Connie Francis drag routine. Another one of his friends dressed as Veronica Lake, and a female friend came as Marilyn Monroe. Although once in costume there was plenty to do in the Village even without the parade, he found his first venture into the world of Halloween celebrants disappointing.

> We hadn't yet gotten to our conceptual Halloween. It was fun, but I felt there was something missing. It wasn't clicking. There were a hundred other people dressed exactly the same way, doing exactly the same thing, and we felt we weren't reaching a degree of design that we could in creating something for Halloween. So next year we decided we could do something conceptual, and there'd be four of us. And we went through everything in the world and we

> decided on '60s stewardesses. And then we came up with the idea of TWAT, which stood for "Transvestites Will Attempt Travel." And we decided to design the costumes in a very '60s sort of way, but sort of update them. I was the funniest, so I was Connie, and we all had names: it was Connie, Barbie, Luvie, and Tippie. And I was Connie, formerly of Lingus Airlines. So that's where that went. And we started planning it in August, and a friend of mine made the patterns for the costumes for us and basically did the sewing.

The costumes were bright yellow, with each member wearing either red, purple, blue, or green stockings, scarf, and gloves. "Tasteful" earrings were acquired from wholesalers.

> We wanted to be "conceptual," but not be Lana Turner, Marilyn Monroe, or Jane Mansfield. We wanted to do something that would sort of be camp and sort of fun and sort of more accessible to people, because we felt that it would be a very accessible thing to be flight attendants, where they have not met Marilyn Monroe or Joan Crawford. And as it turned out we were very well received. It was beyond our wildest dreams that people would applaud us as we walked through this parade and screamed for us. And people recognized us out of costume afterward that we had never met before but could come up to us and say, "You were the TWATs. You were wonderful!" It was incredible.

For Ross Berman, the parade is closer to theater than ritual. The costumes should "make a statement and be conceptual." The statement is spoof, and lacks a conscious political intent. "It just so happened last year when we did the TWAT thing that was when TWA was on strike. So everyone was saying, 'Oh, how political of you.' But we were . . . like it just happened this way."

Robert Tabor is another young designer whose costumes for large groups—pink flamingos, goldfish, and slices of pizza—have won a good deal of public recognition. Although he suggests that there are some commercial benefits to winning prizes at places like the Palladium (a local dance and concert hall that gives out awards for the best Halloween costumes)—"It's great exposure. People come up to you and take your name down"—he sees the parade more as

> a chance to develop any character, wish, whim that may be inside you. The chance to bring it out, express it, and in a sense masquerade your true self as people know you. And it's a chance to really be totally creative, no boundaries whatsoever and just try to in a sense fool, fool the people that know you.

The presence of such costumes and performances has promoted the evolution of the parade from ritual to theater, and finally to something akin to a theatrical review or cabaret with the framework of limited time and set space. What we see, of course, is a "folklorization" of an event through communal re-creation (Wilson 1979, 456). Indeed, the parade has come to assume some of the chaotic, ludic quality that characterizes the annual Christopher Street promenade of transvestites on Halloween night, and, to an increasing degree, one blends into the other. Indeed, many head to the promenade as soon as the parade is finished. At the moment, the principal difference between the two events has to do with the degree of the carnivalesque. The parade is structured linearly in space and framed by time. It ends when the last marchers reach Union Square. Despite attempts to continue the event with musical performances at Union Square, the crowds tend to disperse quickly; they have come to see a parade, whereas those who choose to party have numerous private options and have little need for it. In contrast, the promenade bursts forth from Christopher Street onto neighboring streets and avenues, and has no set beginning or end. There are no walls separating spectators and performers, consequently the sense of structurelessness and communitas is much stronger at the promenade than at the parade. The Halloween celebration is a good example of what MacAloon (1984) refers to as ramified performative type: the parade is spectacle; the promenade is carnival. There are other performative genres at work here, too.

Although these Halloween festivities may be looked upon as attempts to reestablish "old beliefs" and rites, something that has a certain appeal within postmodern culture generally, the fact is that the entire event—which includes private parties, the parade, and the promenade—in its current form is now a grand urban spectacle, and much closer to festival than ritual. As Roger Abrahams notes, "The primary vocabulary of ritual underscores such motives as continuity and confirmation; the transformations put into practice are responsible for maintaining the flow of life. Festivals on the other hand, commonly operate in a way antagonistic to customary ritual confirmation" (1987, 177). Rituals heal rifts in the social fabric; festivals may open wounds, at least for the moment, and often at the more stable moments in the group's life (188). Indeed, were the holiday to occur in the heat of the summer, a traditional time of friction in the city, the explosion some residents fear might very well take place.[5]

Despite the festival quality, there remains a certain ritual component, almost an archaeology of its founding intent. Indeed, Lee's legacy is the continuing benign nature of this event. It is possible, therefore, to divide the costumes into two major categories: those which mythologize and therefore speak to the ritual element of the parade, and those which parody or satirize and reveal the festival element of the parade. I would argue that the two elements are competing, or at the least contradictory, rhetorics that suggest two radically different points of view on the part of participants and ultimately of viewers. The fact that they occur together underscores the power of the event: festival without ritual is hardly worth the effort. Indeed, it is precisely the resulting ambiguity that gives the event its power.[6] At the same time, each element has its own mode of symbolization. Ritual requires metonymic representation, a part standing for the whole, which lends itself to ready meaning; festival calls for metaphor, a realignment of preexisting categories (see Manning 1983, 26). Mythology is represented metonymically, parody metaphorically. These tropes are keys for understanding the political semiotics of public events; the use of one more than another will push the event in a particular political direction. Civic ceremonies, for example, rest heavily on the use of metonym; they are fundamentally conservative, and derive their authority from common wisdom. Public events that use a good deal of metaphor are those that push against the tenets of conventional understanding.

The Halloween parade suggests the complexity of a semiotic system. For example, the mythologizing component is evident in Ralph Lee's puppets as well as in the costumes of most of the other participants, including the nonbenign spirits and monsters that appear in the parade. Ralph Little, a Trinidadian artist, in 1986 created a giant demon representing the vices of contemporary culture, particularly drugs. One might call costumes like these "statements" rather than "questions," or "indications" rather than "subjunctions," altering slightly the wording of Victor Turner's evocative formulation (1982, 82). Since their relationship to official culture is by no means univocal, it might be best to see the issue of indication versus subjunction as a continuum, rather than as an absolute division. The same is not the case for those costumes that celebrate contemporary mythology, particularly the heroes of film, comic books, and television. Of these, "Star Wars" and other sci-fi costumes were the most common in 1987. Some of the more unusual costumes included a group of people wearing white, blood-splattered shirts and black pants, screaming and holding pigeons; they were acting out a scene from Alfred Hitchcock's film, *The Birds.* Aside from the last-named group, these costumes of popular mythology have a closer fit with the world as known. They postulate nothing new, and so the issue of statement versus question becomes one more of division than of continuum.

The satiric and parodic is the component of the parade that is more meditative on, and generally more critical of, contemporary culture and values than are the mythological components. Whereas the mythologizing element of the parade props up icons or invents new ones, the parodic is iconoclastic and political. The parodic, for example, was represented in 1987 by the United Farm Workers float led by a huge skeleton with signs suggesting that grapes are sprayed with chemicals that cause cancer among farm workers. More typically, critical floats use the rhetoric of satire: giant human roach motels, for example, were a commentary on the pest of urban life, and the three-dimensional mockup of Greenwich Village with giant skyscrapers looming ominously over it was created by a political lobby called "Save the Village."

The specific politics of the parade are conditioned partly by the general politics of popular culture, which, as John Fiske argues, work "on the micropolitical level, not the macro level, and . . . [are] progressive, not radical" (1989, 56). The parade is also conditioned by the political economy of the design community, whose members contribute considerably to the overall quality of the spectacle. Although I do not have precise figures here, it is clear from even a random sampling of outstanding costumes that many of their creators are professionals rather than one-time amateurs. Designers are often independent contractors rather than workers, and their dreams are readily slanted toward the possibility of ownership of the means of production; they are less alienated, therefore, from the labor process. Also, their relationship to work is more complex than other occupations, so that work and leisure are not entirely in opposition to one another.[7] Since they see themselves as artists or craftspeople, they are likely to use fulfillment or creativity as major factors in choosing a job. Moreover, self-expression is a high priority for these designers, and if there is an overall characteristic to their politics, or indeed, to their sense of self, it stems from a perception of the world radically divided between those who work to create and those who labor. In the words of Robert Tabor, "The parade brings out creativity. It promotes unleashed creativity for everyone, even if there is no creativity at their jobs. . . . It opens up a part of the self for people." Tabor's statement suggests Herbert Marcuse's belief that "art is committed to an emancipation of sensibility, imagination and reasoning . . ." (as quoted in Limón 1983, 38). It also suggests the tenacity of craft and its peculiar consciousness, both as a form of resistance, despite the bureaucratization of work, and as a political agenda, determined to impact itself upon the consciousness of others.

Although there is a tendency for anthropological literature to see this type of festival as total inversion of the everyday (Babcock 1978), or, in a Marcusean sense, as a "vehicle for recognition and indictment" (Limón 1983, 31), it makes more sense to place it in the context of Abrahams and Bauman's analysis of festival behavior on St. Vincent and La Havre Islands (1978:195). They argue that the disorder and license of the parade is not the antithesis of the order that is supposed to characterize the rest of the year, "and that many of the people who engage in license during the festival are the community agents of disorder during the remainder of the year." Indeed, Halloween provides a nexus for the urban community, when the forces of order—in this case the commercial and business classes who inhabit the more desirable parts of the city—and disorder—artists and gays—come together, revealing how closely intertwined, as Raymond Williams suggests, hegemonic and oppositional elements are within culture (Limón 1983, 44).

The design community's participation in the parade has increased the quality and self-expressiveness of costumes. It has also amplified the parodic and, in particular, the campiness of costumes, many of which juxtapose the least-likely combinations: blending of genders, as in tranvestitism; and blending of once discrete physical domains, as in human cocktails, human salad bars, human slices of pizza, giant walking phalluses and condoms, gumball machines, fashion police, human poodles. "Camp," Susan Sontag writes, is essentially "love of the unnatural, of artifice and exaggeration" (1982, 105). "The whole point of Camp," she argues, "is to dethrone the serious" (116). Camp blends domains that are hegemonically relegated to discrete and mutually exclusive categories, particularly in regard to gender, and it is in regard to gender that the Greenwich Village Halloween Parade dons its most satirical and, in a sense, political costume.

It should be noted, however, that the political issues raised by designers, particularly gay designers, are presented in a masked way—appropriately so, given the fact that this is Halloween, and perhaps, too, because the Gay Day parade in early summer has become a more appropriate setting for overt political statements, including the public demonstration of gay or lesbian affection, bonding, and sexuality.[8] So camp/parodic in the Halloween event is integrated with the mythological, and the rhetoric of the parade remains ambiguous.

Earlier I suggested a tripartite typology of public events—civic, ethnic, and carnivalesque festivals. Civic and carnivalesque events are similar to Handelman's (1990) typology of presentational and representational events: the former constituting an idealized model of social reality, the latter playing with and distorting reality. My middle category, "ethnic festivals," mediates between the other two categories, and contains elements of both. Handelman's typology includes a third category, but not a middle one. Instead, he posits a category of events that model—worlds unto themselves that may be used to bring about transformations in the real world. Although extremely evocative, there is something awkward about this typology: presentations and representations constitute opposite ends of a continuum; model suggests a separate axis that bifurcates both presentations and representations. It seems to me that presentations that model are typical of revolutionary regimes committed to creating a "new man." Presentations that do not model, for example, the Macy's Thanksgiving Day parade, are those committed to a preexisting vision of social reality. A similar dichotomy could be made for representational events. The material in this article suggests that Lee had constructed a parade that blended the transformational thrust of a model with an event that fits the ethnic festival category of my earlier typology. His discomfort with the parade's evolution hinged on its having moved increasingly toward the carnivalesque side of the spectrum, whereas the model had become overwhelmed by the sheer size of the spectacle. Lee is not the only one for whom the transformational thrust of the model has significance. Indeed, those at the margins of the social and cultural system are particularly concerned with what Jameson refers to as "authentic cultural productions" (1979, 140)—another term, I would think, for model. Given that they are marginalized groups, the models they produce are likely to contain a good deal of oppositional material. They are carnivalesque and they fall, therefore, easily on the side of representation on the representation-presentation continuum. Given the above typology, one might well expect a rather complex agenda on the part of some people at the Halloween celebration. Let me return to my field notes to illustrate this point:

An hour or so after the parade has ended, I am standing on Christopher and Bleecker Streets together with thousands of other people. In the middle of the intersection I notice a man dressed in a white ballerina costume looking suspiciously like a fairy godmother dispensing wishes with a magic wand. He doesn't pay much attention to me, I suppose, because I'm busy with a notepad rather than a camera; I cannot exchange stardom for a spell. "Do I get a wish?" I ask. "Yes. Anything your heart desires." "I want your phone number." "My phone number?" "Yes. I'm an anthropologist and I'm doing some research on the Halloween parade. I'd like to talk to you."

Two weeks later I call Fred to confirm our appointment, and we agree to meet for brunch at a local bagel shop. Just as I am about to hang up, Fred tells me to look for someone with brown curly hair wearing red glasses. Of course, I still have a mental image of someone in a white gown with a magic wand.

At the restaurant, Fred spots me first. Out of costume he looks magically transformed: a tall, slender, good-looking man about 40. We exchange greetings, order food at the counter, and head to a table. I learn that the fairy godmother is a playwright who lives in a still-not- gentrified block in "Alphabetland" (between Avenues B and C). He has been involved in the parade either as spectator or participant for the past ten years. Fred's description of how his costume came together this year reveals the essential self-parody of his humor.

> The costume was designed by someone who's done a lot of work for dance companies. It's sort of a takeoff of a ballet dress from the 18th century. It was beautiful. Sort of a white satin with glitter and silver sequins. I wore a blond wig with glitter and a wonderful crown—like a headdress, which actually was from the Snow Queen. I made the wings myself from foam that had been used as packing for a stereo. I used wire and glitter. When I glued the glitter I smiled because I thought, "Yes, there's something so fanciful and frivolous about glitter that it's like the antithesis of being down-to-earth." They looked kind of frumpy and weren't straight. It looked kind of like I had done a lot of flying around. I liked the bedraggled aspect. I wanted to be slightly frumpy, as if I had gone through the mill a bit myself and had still come to the fact that goodness is the bottom line. And I wore white tennis sneakers sort of like yuppie women who go to the office in sneakers. I thought, "Well, the good fairy has got to save her feet, too." I made the wand from a wood dowel and an aluminum tinfoil Christmas tree ornament at the end. My friend Norman has all these costumes in his apartment because he ran a children's theater. It's sad to see all those costumes and realize that it's really the people that make the costumes come alive and not the other way around. Some of the jewels were falling off the crown. They looked sad in the apartment. But once I got it on and I got out there it came alive. I realized it is the spirit of the performer.

Fred talked to me about the loss of two close friends who died of AIDS, and how his participation in the promenade was a way for him to emerge from mourning by helping others.

This year there seemed to be a lot more observers than participants. But even so, I must say I was touched by the crowd. I was going up to people with all their facades and defenses, and 98 percent of the people just melted. There were three Black kids, very, very angry teenagers. I went up to them and with my wand I went bonk, bonk, bonk, and they melted. One guy came as a ghoul. I bonked him on the head and nothing happened. I did it again, and he just stood there. He wouldn't give me an inch. He was just stubbornly staring me down. So I said, "Oh, come on." And I bonked him. And he melted. A Korean woman came up to me and said, "What does it mean when you bonk them on the head?" I said, "It means you get your wish darling!" "Oh," she said, "do me, do me." Then another woman dressed as a frog hurled herself at my feet and she said, "Make me into a prince!" I kept going like this [Fred motions with his outstretched arm as if he were waving a wand], but it didn't work so I figured I would try it again. I thought, "Maybe if she wanted to be a princess it might have worked. It's too complicated, I can't deal with it. It's two wishes." I could do it. But I thought she needed to live with it a little longer.

Also, I thought it was touching. There would be a group of friends and they would say, "Oh, get him. He really needs it." I could tell that this person was really hurting. Whether it was for personal breakup or heartbreak or some physical situation. And they came up to me with such earnestness. Like you know, "Make this better!" And it was a very rewarding thing to hit them with the wand. It seemed to cheer them up anyway.

Fred talked about Halloween, his belief in astrology, and the Christian idea of death and renewal with All Saints Day following Halloween. His comments revealed the degree to which for him, and for designers and artists, and particularly for gay people, the Halloween parade offers a moment for creation, a collective dreamtime. During Halloween, the skills of labor otherwise used to fashion consumable commodities are suddenly transformed and harnessed through leisure for self, and for collective self-expression. For gay people, Halloween is a moment of utopian wishfulness, a time when their vision of the world has the possibility of moving from periphery to center and capturing, even if only for a few short hours, the hearts of an entire city. As Fred describes his experience:

Maybe that's mixing up a lot of symbols, but it seems like out of negativity is a lot of potential for good. And I just felt like my costume was a lot more successful than the people who were trying to be scary. I felt like there was a magnetism and a magic coming from me. And it was a very rewarding thing

> to hit them with this wand. It seemed to cheer them up anyway. People have this innate reverence for the power of this mythological figure. And I guess that was what I was thinking of. It was really the power of goodness, was really what captivated me about it and also instructed me. I had no idea that I would get such a response going out as some embodiment of merry and goodness. It was really very gratifying. A friend of mine who was with me and is very spiritual, kept saying, "Fred, you're really healing people." And I felt it, too. I wish in this world instead of that being a momentary thing, it could be a way of living for people. I even had a fantasy of going to midtown dressed as the good fairy. I may even do it. I think there's a magic in Halloween that allows people to suspend things and allows certain fantasies and let their own wishes come true.

CONCLUSIONS

Unlike most parades, the Village Halloween parade makes no claim to respectability. Rather than challenge the city by occupying elite turf and marching up Fifth Avenue—the typical route of ethnic events—the Halloween parade consecrates its own terrain. Unlike other parades, this dramatization of boundaries, in its origins, defined not an ethnic group but a way of life, particularly a Bohemian, artistic, and, frequently, gay way of life. One can only surmise that it is not accidental that the stimulus to create this annual celebration of Greenwich Village culture is a recent phenomenon: one hardly needs to dramatize the obvious. Whereas the gay relationship to Greenwich Village is not in dispute, except, that is, through the AIDS epidemic, Greenwich Village as a bohemian artist colony is a thing of the past. In recent years, New York neighborhoods have undergone transformations that are leaving whole sections of the city unrecognizable to their longtime residents; neighborhoods, such as Greenwich Village, long known for their bohemian or ethnic character, are no exceptions (Zukin 1982). Despite the high cost of housing in the city in general and in Greenwich Village in particular, this charming neighborhood of nineteenth century row houses has managed to maintain its link to the artists and writers' colony that once formed the nucleus of its identity only through Westbeth, a subsidized loft building for full-time artists. The fact that the parade originated there and fanned outward through the neighborhood suggests the contentious aspect of the parade: its attempt to incorporate and consecrate space that in real life is no longer its own. Outside the narrow spatial and temporal boundaries of this parade, Greenwich Village has become part of the ordinary work-a-day world, and not the artists' world of "work as play." Ironically, this is precisely why the parade grew so quickly, why it found such a ready niche within the expressive life of a great metropolis, and why it so readily gave voice to hegemonic as well as oppositional culture. Although intended as a celebration of the spirit of a unique community, in effect, the parade has become much more than that. It has simultaneously become a celebration of an emergent mainstream, of the new social classes that have substantially transformed the city and, in doing so, have destroyed, in effect, the social basis of the city as a locus for an artists' community.[9]

Finally, let me add something of a purely speculative kind. The general rise in popularity of Halloween throughout the United States suggests a transformation in American culture in the individual sense of self. If the 1950s celebrated the nuclear family as the hedge against world apocalypse,[10] and the 1960s gave rise to oppositionality through a collective youth culture, the 1970s saw the emergence of the New Right and a crass individualism in which the self became increasingly severed from collective obligations. This privatization has taken an interesting twist in regard to popular culture, and particularly in regard to gender. With the demise of a procreative imperative, sexuality becomes a matter of choice and lifestyle (Harris 1982). At the same time, the emergence of transnational cultures is contributing to a "world marked by borrowing and lending across porous national and cultural boundaries" (Rosaldo 1989, 217). The optional is increasingly part of the modern experience. Indeed, the expansion of the threshold of the sexual self is intricately connected to expansion of the self in other domains as well, and this manifests itself in all kinds of expressive culture, including religious beliefs and practices. Perhaps, then, the popularity of Halloween can be seen as an implicit rejection of a collective self prescribed within the Judeo-Christian tradition. Neopaganism offers, if not a world without limits, a self without social encumbrances, then at least a cultural border zone in constant motion (Rosaldo 1989). To understand the roots of that self, clearly one ought to look at the underlying structure of late capitalism. To see its continual manifestations, one must also examine "New Age" religion. Ultimately, it is within the framework of neopagan culture—and certainly as a manifestation of an emerging post-Christian culture—that we will need to place Halloween to fully understand the position it is assuming within the pantheon of American holidays.

7

MAKING MERRY WITH DEATH
Iconic Humor in Mexico's Day of the Dead

Kristin Congdon

Children eat sugar skulls with their names printed on the candied foreheads, public figures endure attacks with predictions of their impending demise, and papier-mâché skeletons appear, inviting the dead to live amongst us. These *calaveras* (literally "skulls," but also used in reference to whole skeletons) walk the dog, play musical instruments, and perform other day-to-day activities. Mexico's Day of the Dead festival, also celebrated in many parts of the United States (Beardsley 1987, 64), is a time to honor death while mocking it with great abandon.

It would be difficult to point to another culture that celebrates with so much amusement and gaiety what many other people feel is the most difficult rite of passage. In Mexico, the more hilarious the confrontation of the dead with the living, perhaps the greater the pleasure and engagement with the celebration. Death is unavoidable, and the response of many Mexicans and Mexican-Americans is to accept it as a permanent companion. This relationship is friendly, comical, ironic, and full of mockery. Octavio Paz described it this way:

> To the inhabitant of New York, Paris, or London death is a word that is never used because it burns the lips. The Mexican, on the other hand, frequents it, mocks it, caresses it, sleeps with it, entertains it; it is one of his favourite playthings and his most enduring love.[1] (1961,10)

This essay will explore how humor is used in Day of the Dead rituals with special attention to the function of the iconic *calavera* or skeleton (see the article by Stanley Brandes in this volume for the literary *calavera*). I will analyze how humor is an inseparable part of the aesthetic process of the Day of the Dead celebration, allowing for a breakdown of opposing forces, opposites that are somehow overcome and conquered in the popular Mexican and Mexican-American worldview. The two pairs of opposing forces, which I will analyze, are life and death and the upper and lower economic classes. In Day of the Dead rituals, the boundaries between these entities, typically seen by most Europeans as opposites, are broken down through the aesthetic process of reversal. In a reversal, something that is thought to be ugly becomes pleasurable, or even beautiful. If the aesthetic is not inverted or reversed, it is at least blurred (Lippard 1990, 200–201). As this aesthetic reversal takes place in ritual space, the boundary between the artist and the participant is also deconstructed during the fiesta experience. Humor is the catalyst for this aesthetic process. Were it not for the success of the humor, the reversal would perhaps not be accepted, and the power of the ideas about death would be diminished. These ideas will first be explored and then further grounded in the widely celebrated *calavera* prints of José Guadalupe Posada and the Linares family's papier-mâché *calaveras.*

IDEAS ABOUT DEATH

There are wide differences between the way Europeans and Mexicans approach death (Brandes 1998a, 364; Garciagodoy 1998a, 192–193). For Europeans, death is an omen that has nothing to do with social issues, but can have a symbolic sense to it, or a moral teaching. In contrast, according to Héctor Grimrac, Mexicans view death as a "splitting of the personality" (Garciagodoy 1998:192). Whatever they cannot do themselves in regard to their social situation, they can impute that limit to death. It is death, represented in the skeleton, which, with the use of humor, can make the daring kind of social statements with which it would be too risky and certainly improper for the living to involve themselves (Garciagodoy 1998, 192–193).

This explanation, though, makes a complex topic seem too simplistic. Mexico's indigenous people had strong ideas about death in pre-Hispanic times that involved a melding of life and death. These ideas have changed over time, as they have incorporated practices and ideology of Spanish origin. For example, Spain also has a tradition of using humor with an anthropomorphized character, Death, which exposes social wrongs on an allegorical level (Garciagodoy 1998, 192). However, the Aztecs held the strong belief of life coming from death—and therefore the view that life and death are co-dependent. In fact, in this way of thinking, death feeds life. It was this belief that allowed for the sacrificial spilling of blood, and the offering of beating hearts to the gods. These ritualistic acts ensured ritual participants that the world would continue to exist as it should. The sun would shine in the sky, and the maize would grow tall to feed the people (Scalora 1997, 65).

For Mexicans, then, death is simply a part of life. It is not separate from life, as an entity from somewhere else, a force that somehow comes to you at a certain time. Rather, it constantly lives within you, in the form of a skeleton, a *calavera*. María Antonieta Sánchez de Escamilla, from Puebla City, teaches her nursery school children not to fear death. She tells them that "our loved ones never really die while we remember them." When her children feel uncomfortable about death, she tells them to touch themselves, and explain why they are afraid when each of them "owns a skull and a skeleton." She further says that "We all carry death within us," and when they [the children] understand that we are all made of bones, death makes more sense (Carmichael and Sayer 1991, 119).[2]

At a young age, children are taught to respect the dead and that if they do not do so, it could result in severe danger (Scalora 1997, 76). Having an understanding that the dead do not go away forever, that they can return to visit, and that death can be welcoming, permits both children and adults to have a feeling of security. It makes that which might be foreboding and terrifying more welcome in everyday life. In a country where health care and sanitary conditions are poor, death and dying are all too prevalent. The fact that death returns in a humorous manner makes it easier to approach. The living are able to take part in the joke.

The connection between life and death is explained and heightened in several ways. Many believe that the dead remember the living in the same manner that the living remember the dead (Carmichael and Sayer 1991, 105). The living make *ofrendas* (literally "offerings," but also altar-like constructions for the dead, usually placed on a tabletop), and it is believed that the dead respond by leaving signs of their presence for the living (see figure 1). It could be the unexplained snuffing of a candle, a strange shadow, a tipping over of a glass, a soft whisper, or the sensation that you have been touched by a presence you cannot see (Scalora 1997, 79). Before the dead reach their final destination, they visit places important to them when they were alive. They may be able to make these visits in various forms, perhaps as a hummingbird or a cloud. It is believed that the Toltecs handed down these ideas to the Aztecs and that, in some manner, the idea of the dead surrounding us in various forms exists today (Carmichael and Sayer 1991, 55).

Ancient beliefs of the Totonac, who today reside in the state of Veracruz, maintained that living relatives were expected to help the dead in their journey on to the next life, at *Kalinin*, the world of the dead. It

Figure 1. *Ofrenda* by Catalina Delgado Trunk, set up at the Florida Folk Festival in White Springs in 1996. Photo by Kristin G. Congdon.

was believed that the immortal part of the being is what travels—the spirit-soul or that which is the seed of life. When it gets to its destiny, it is guided by the gods (Carmichael and Sayer 1991, 62). Both the living and the gods, therefore, assist the dead on their journey in the afterlife.

Death is embraced by the Mexicans for other reasons besides having the responsibility to assist relatives on their journey to a better place. Life is often seen to be so difficult that, relatively speaking, death may not be so bad. Suffering, therefore, is a part of life, and death releases you from the pain. In support of this idea is a common Mexican proverb that asks, "Why should I fear death when life has cured me of frights?" (Garciagodoy 1998, 175). Another formulaic expression with similar sentiment reflects the view of a bereaving mother: "I loved the little angel; but I am glad that he is happy, without having to experience the bitterness of life" (Carmichael and Sayer 1991, 54).

Partly because Mexicans understand that death is imminent, they embrace it in a manner unlike Europeans and Anglos. Instead of expressing angst about death, as Camus did,[3] Mexicans face it with humor (Garciagodoy 1998, 186). And it is with this sense of humor that the living welcome the dead into their homes during the Day of the Dead. This is a time for reunion, connections, celebration, and constructing meaning in one's life. Humor is used to find a comfort zone in which to express a respect for death, by making it a part of living. Humor is also used to mock death, as it mocks the living, especially those from the upper economic classes who, like everyone else, cannot escape it.

Mexicans on the lower economic rungs of life understand that the plans they make and the dreams they have are only possible if they have life to see them through. Unlike the upper economic classes of people, they do not have access to the kinds of lifestyles and medical facilities that, to some degree, might ensure a healthier life. Nonetheless, they also know that a stable economic life will not necessarily grant anyone a long and healthy life. In this regard, the rich and poor are the same; they both face death. Neither group has control over it, a fact which can be empowering to people who struggle every day to have their basic needs met. Death is an equalizer. Consequently, all the pomp and circumstance, the fancy clothes, and the daily activities of the rich become somehow trivialized, even ludicrous. These are key lessons presented by the ever-smiling *calaveras* (Garciagodoy 1998, 186).

There is another reason why the *calaveras* are so merry. They are festive because they are the dead welcoming the living when they die. As Arsacio Benegas Arroyo explained, "When I die I want there to be music, I want people to dance, to get drunk and to feel no sadness" (qtd. in Carmichael and Sayer 1991, 130). It only makes sense, then, that Mexicans would embrace the *calaveras* who are involved in these merrymaking activities.

Day of the Dead

The Day (or Days) of the Dead is one of the most significant yearly celebrations for Mexicans. It is not necessarily a celebration unique to Mexico, but "it is now and has long been a symbol of Mexico" (Brandes 1998a, 362). While Day of the Dead celebrations clearly make connections to the Catholic Church, the Day of the Dead has aspects of ritual which go beyond church doctrine. Although the Catholic Church does not embrace all aspects of the fiesta, Day of the Dead celebrations are generally tolerated.

Ofrendas

During Day of the Dead celebrations, graves are decorated and family vigils occur, special foods are made, a form of ritualized begging or solicitation occur, and *ofrendas* are created, usually in a spiritual site within the home of the deceased relative (Brandes 1998a, 363). *Ofrendas* differ from place to place. In Veracruz, for example, sugar cane, banana leaves, palm leaves, and coconuts are often used to make an arch around the altar space. In Puebla, *papel picado* (cut paper) is placed around the altar.[4]

Usually, an *ofrenda* is placed on a table that serves not only as an altar, but also as a place for food to be served, specially baked for the deceased. Also arranged as part of the *ofrenda* are rosaries, pictures of saints, *milagros* (charms), and statuettes. Bright and colorful flower arrangements combine *cempitsuchil* (marigolds), *terciopelo* (cockscomb), gladiolas, and *nube* (a gypsophilia-type flower). These flowers are placed around the altar, along with items that the deceased person would enjoy; often these relate to his or her life's work or hobbies. The scent from the flowers, mixed with *copal* (incense), is unmistakable, and said to entice spirits into the house. Sometimes, in order to make the invitation even more clearly marked, the flowers are extended from the doorway of the home to the street (Congdon, Delgado-Trunk, and López 1999, 313-314).

According to Chicana artist Amalia Mesa-Bains, there is symbolic significance in the way an *ofrenda* is constructed. The canopy or arch may be expressive of celestial imagery, and the repeated use of aged surfaces is reflective of time and erosion. She notes the continuous placement of memorial objects on the *ofrenda* as important in that they focus the work on the deceased. Mesa-Bains also observes the formalist aesthetic dimensions of *ofrendas,* in that there is often a striking balance between scale and volume and a serialization of objects placed in a pleasing formal arrangement (1997, 126). Catalina Delgado-Trunk makes several *ofrendas* for Day of the Dead celebrations every year. Often they are placed in public spaces for the purposes of educating the community (see figures 2–6.).

In some respects, *ofrendas*, like other Mexican home altars, can be read as if they were family albums complete with deities and "an iconic portrait of negotiations between family members and the divine in which requests and promises are traded" (Beezley 1997, 100–101). This is a site where the secular and the sacred worlds come together. All kinds of relationships

Figure 2. Day of the Dead *ofrenda* by Catalina Delgado-Trunk, 1996. This *ofrenda* was installed in Orlando, Florida's City Hall in an effort to educate the public about the Day of the Dead. Photo by Kristin G. Congdon.

Figure 3. Detail of figure 2.

Figure 4. Detail of figure 2.

Figure 5. Detail of figure 2.

Figure 6. Detail of figure 2.

are negotiated in this altarspace (Beezley 1997, 93). As it is made, the creator is mindful that the purpose of every object placed on the *ofrenda* is meant to entice the absent spirit(s) to visit (Gutiérrez 1997, 46).

It is traditional for people to purchase new objects for the Day of the Dead celebration, such as new cooking dishes, jugs, kitchen utensils, small and big cups, and incense burners. Creative crafts are also purchased, such as candlesticks, trees of life, candied skulls, and *calaveras* (Pomar 1987, 24). New toys are purchased for both living and deceased children to play with (Pomar 1987, 28). Although it is often not economically feasible, even the clothes people wear are supposed to be new (Carmichael and Sayer 1991, 18). The demand for new purchases creates a vibrant marketplace where the activity of making and selling goods is heightened. The marked increase in activity, in both public and private spaces, marks these special celebratory days in a way that cannot be ignored (Garciagodoy 1998, 202).

All-night vigils of praying and feasting take place in cemeteries across Mexico. Flowers are placed on the graves along with other decorations such as crosses. Graves are swept and headstones repaired. Tomás Ybarra-Frausto reports that often, along with drinking coffee or stronger libations, groups will tell stories about the living and dead. Often strange happenings will be reported, including tales of the *levantada del muerto* (folktales of the dead sitting up in the coffin at the wake).[5] There is always talk about the afterlife (1991a, 24).

During the festival, Fredy Méndez from the State of Veracruz said, "we all treat all living beings with kindness. This includes dogs, cats, even flies or mosquitos" (qtd. in Carmichael and Sayer 1991, 80). He further explained that if people are not pleasant to each other, the dead know it, and will become unhappy, perhaps even sick (Carmichael and Sayer 1991, 80). This belief enhances the sense of connectedness that is pervasive in Day of the Dead celebrations. The dead and the living are intertwined to such a degree that what the living do directly affects the dead. A decreasing number of people set their dinner tables with place settings for the dead, but it does still happen. Some of the deceased's favorite possessions are placed on the chairs (Carmichael and Sayer 1991, 21).

In Mixquic, four people carry a coffin with a cardboard skeleton in it. They mourn the dead by pretending to cry, but they do so in such a way that it is humorous and people laugh (Carmichael and Sayer 1991, 140). Happiness and pleasure are mixed with mourning and sadness. They become hard to distinguish, just as it becomes more difficult to clearly define the difference between the living and the dead, for on these days, the dead are thought to intermingle with the living. They come to joke, celebrate, and feast with family and friends. These activities bring great comfort to the living. And as the festivities take place, everyone is reminded of the democratic spirit of death. No one is immune to it, regardless of economic privilege. Elena Poniatowska explained it this way: "We are here only on loan, only passing through. The earth tries to catch us, that's why we shouldn't hold on so hard to life. Dying is good, but it is a matter of luck" (1991, 56).

Skeleton as Aesthetic Reversal

Death's presence is visualized in many areas by the skull and skeleton, or *calavera,* which dates back to pre-Columbian times. Mexicans dance with skeletons, children eat sugar skulls with their names printed on the foreheads, and the famous painter Frida Kahlo painted herself sleeping under a papier-mâché skeleton which rested on the canopy over her bed (Congdon, Delgado-Trunk, and López 1999, 315).

The practice of eating sugar skulls with one's name on it may be interpreted in several ways. It may be a reminder that death resides inside every person, and that the skull (read as death) is part of us. Garciagodoy suggests one possibility of meaning associated with eating the skulls, as she reflects on the practice as cannibalistic:

> The eater wants magically to appropriate characteristics of the morsel as when an Aztec runner ate a bit of the calf muscle of a sacrificed warrior who was a good runner. During Days of the Dead, by consuming a sweet skull the eater is inoculated against fear of death because she or he has taken in the peace of death or the dead. Another desire can be to dominate or destroy what is eaten, in which case the ingestion leaves the eater alone in the field. If one consumes a skull, one pronounces one's immortality. (1997, 138)

The eating of sugar skulls may also be likened to eating the sweet Day of the Dead bread, sometimes made in the shape of bones. While it gives the consumer pleasure to eat the tasty bread or sugar skull, there is clearly more to it than pure taste enjoyment. Garciagodoy points out that philosophers since Aristotle and psychologists since Freud have noted the seriousness of both play and humor (1998, 137). These activities, playful and lively as they are, carry more meaning than satisfying a sweet tooth or hunger.

Another way of looking at the act of eating skulls and death bread is to liken it to the Holy Feast. In this sense, to eat is a powerful act and a powerful verb. It has to do with consuming, assimilating, and becoming God (or as in the Catholic faith, to become nearer to God as in receiving grace). As God saved the world, he fed a people who were in their agony (Garciagoday 1998, 137). This interpretation is one that demonstrates that God cares about all His people, especially those who have little in this life. To "take him in," therefore, is to be redeemed. To eat of the dead, then, is seen as an empowering act. It is to risk, to believe, and to live again in the next life with those who have died before. To have this knowledge is to be able to rise above life's difficult circumstances. It is better than being rich and privileged in this life, because life is so short. To eat of the dead, knowing this, is certainly cause for celebration, a kind of reversal where the poor and disenfranchised become equal to the ruling class—on a level beyond the one experienced in this life.

Just as the bread signifies life in death, so too does the presence of the skeleton. If one dances with the skeleton, makes it and eats of it in this life, the continuity of life after one dies is ensured. There is humor in the celebration and the accompanying equalizing knowledge, which is continuously represented by the lipless grin of the *calavera.* The smirk is a sign of "resistance to the usual order of things" (Garciagodoy 1998, 204).

During the Day of the Dead, instead of the living looking after themselves, they take care of the dead, making sure they are fed, honored, and remembered. But in doing this, the living are also cared for in a way that goes beyond day-to-day mundane concerns. The humble classes have not only gained the power to live forever, but they have spoken, in a bold and visible, but humorous way, to the ruling class. Garciagodoy suggests that if the *calaveras* spoke in words to the dominant culture, they would mock the upper classes by saying:

> You think us quaint? You think us colorful? You think us chronologically anterior and therefore inferior to you? Here is what our stereotypes look like, what they feel like, and they are as dead as the reductionist minds from which they originally came. And as alive. Here they are, stripped down to the bones, having come back to haunt you and bite you back. (1998, 201)

These are skeletons that do not sit still in their coffins. They do not decay. They take up the activities of the living and denounce the power of politics, science, position in society, and any kind of logic the upper classes take as truth. They turn the world upside down, and they laugh out loud while doing so. The dead are not placed on the fringes, the outskirts of town. They are not forgotten, and they are not out of sight. They have managed to tip the world to its side, making that which is often seen as marginal—the dead and the underprivileged—the focus of attention (Garciagodoy 1998, 198).

Images like the *calavera* in Day of the Dead celebrations have the power to tease certain emotional responses from us, such as desire, faith, laughter, hatred, and empathy. These emotions commingle with other firmly established cultural ideas, and they produce meaning (Doss 1999, 29). For Mexicans, the meaning, in large part, comes from being on the lower rung of the economic ladder and being able to transcend it. It is this recognition, deeply imbedded in their sense of identity, that helps to define the aesthetic attraction.

In Chicano culture[6] this aesthetic, associated with an economic and political positioning, takes the form of what is called *rasquachismo.* Recognizing that the codes set by the established community to keep up appropriate appearances can never be met, *rasquachismo* acts to shatter the attitude. If you live in an environment that is always on the verge of coming apart, things must be held together with whatever can be found or tapped into, both physically and emotionally. If the job is tenuous, the car is old and rusted, and the toilet is always breaking, a sense of humor is needed for survival. *Movida* is the word used to represent a coping strategy; it is to buy time, to make options, and to find a way to keep a hopeful outlook. Resilience comes from resourcefulness. As Tomás Ybarra-Frausto explains, this process of making use of available resources that results in *rasquachismo* "engenders hybridization, juxtaposition, and integration" (1991b, 156). It results in an aesthetic that flies in the face of the dominant culture. It is the ability to re-invent in an irreverent kind of way, placing unlikely objects and ideas together. It is a kind of survival, both physical and emotional. Ybarra-Frausto further observes:

> To be *rasquache* is to posit a bawdy, spunky consciousness, to seem to subvert and turn ruling paradigms upside down. It is a witty, irreverent, and impertinent posture that records and moves outside established boundaries. . . . *Rasquachismo* is a sensibility that is not elevated and serious, but playful and elemental. It finds delight and refinement in what many consider banal and projects an alternative aesthetic—a sort of good taste of bad taste. It is witty and ironic, but not mean-spirited (there is sincerity in its artifice). (1991b, 155)

In this tradition, the lower economic class transforms things that are considered to be garbage by the cultural elite. Automobile tires become plant containers and old coffee tins become flowerpots (Ybarra-Frausto 1991b, 157). For Texas Mexicans, this act of recycling is an artistic practice that not only connects makers with their homeland, but also demonstrates their differences with the dominant Anglo culture (Turner 1996, 62). Like the aesthetic of *rasquachismo*, the appeal of the low-rider tradition can also be said to be a reversal. Unlike a luxury car, valued by a wealthy jet set, the low-rider is "low and slow" (Sandoval and Polk 2000, 12).[7]

The same aesthetic sensibility and worldview described as *rasquachismo* is seen in the Mexican *calavera* and Day of the Dead celebrations. That which might been seen as bad taste is somehow played with and reversed into good taste.[8] While in some company it might be rude or inappropriate to flaunt or laugh at death, or to conspire with the dead, an aesthetic reversal, especially in a ritual space,[9] can make the unacceptable acceptable. Additionally, those who might be set aside or forgotten, like the dead, are remade, enjoyed, and visible.

Calaveras are created for reversal; they offer the realization that it is absurd to perceive things as opposites, like life and death (Garciagodoy 1998, 199). *Calaveras* represent the dead in living form. Opposites collapse. The construction of opposites or dualisms is a way of seeing the world that has been constructed by Europeans. To see opposites, we must view things from the outside. In this manner, the viewer, as subject, sees the world as object. This approach further divides the body and the mind, and the conscious from the unconscious (Turner 1982, 100), but the *calavera* mocks that way of seeing and thinking, and reconstructs the world as a continuum. Dualisms (life/death, the haves/the have-nots) disappear, and a more connected, integrated world takes its place.

The same reversal takes place in art. For example, the classical body of the privileged elite is typically fleshed, even in the rare occasions when artists represent the figure in death. The figures are often posed at rest, or enjoying their leisure, whereas the *calavera* is skeletal, active and working, unless it is a member of the upper class who is, nonetheless, still de-fleshed. Seeing the humorous depictions of all *calaveras* in bare-bone form trivializes what they do, whether they engage in work or play (Garciagodoy 1998, 203). The mockery and inversion of the reversal deconstructs the rules of the upper classes as it equalizes relationships. For the underdogs, there is clearly great pleasure in this process.

To an outsider, the Day of the Dead might seem crass, ugly, disrespectful, and perhaps even nonsensical. But to understand the way the ritual functions is to understand how the reversal works in the aesthetic worldview of the participants. Garciagodoy explains:

> The grotesque is transgressive in and of itself, uniting life and death, displaying the nonbeautiful, nonclassical, unglamorous practices of the subordinated in, no less, the form of nonbeautiful, nonclassical, unglamorous, living skeletons. In addition, making death the center of attention turns the usual order of things upside down and inside out, for the privileged classes prefer to pretend that death is too far in the future to be relevant, feeling protected by their wealth, their access to medical resources, and their generally low-risk lifestyles. (1998, 203)

The aesthetic, then, is based on social defiance and humor. It is glitzy, unsubtle, and raucous fun.

The idea of a "quality" art experience is mocked, as it is recognized to be class-bound. Lippard suggests that the word "quality" is used simply to describe what the ruling class values, as they lay claim to the aesthetic turf in the structured world they have created. However, she further notes, what constitutes "quality" substantially differs among classes, cultures, and even genders (1995, 301).[10] For those who embrace the Day of the Dead celebrations, quality means dramatically changing the rules. It means embracing many artistic characteristics that define the identity of the everyday lives of the lower classes, including welcoming the dead.

The fact that Day of the Dead activities are performed in sacred time allows for the coming together of the living and the dead. As a Yaquis Indian commented, "There are certain days when the wall between worlds becomes so porous that the living and the dead can pass through without being subject to the laws of space or time" (qtd. in Garciagodoy 1998, 40). Just as in abstract form the living and dead become more indistinguishable, so too do the performers and the participants in Day of the Dead celebrations. Everyone shares equally in the ritual group's belief systems and practices. Any customary isolation is removed and camaraderie is reinforced (Turner 1982, 112).

Many Mexican and Mexican-American artists, rooting their work in Day of the Dead and other Mexican rituals, have successfully utilized the aesthetic of reversal. Their work embodies the humor and mocking necessary to promote the Day of the Dead *calaveras*' message about death. José Guadalupe Posada, for example, made prints of *calaveras* that are widely recognized today, and the Linares family continues to make papier-mâché *calaveras* that are appreciated throughout the world. Understanding the artistic process and the life history of these artists is useful in further assessing how humor is used to reverse ruling class belief structures, while making peace with the inevitability of death.

JOSÉ GUADALUPE POSADA

Generations of printmakers have been inspired by the Mexican artist José Guadalupe Posada. An extremely prolific artist, he created about 15,000 prints in thirty years (Traba 1994, 15). Born in 1852, Posada lived through and illustrated two violent revolutions. He died (1913) before the end of the second revolution, the mass uprising of 1910–1921 (Brenner 1967, 185).[11] Posada came into the world at a time when the inventive tradition of satirical newspapers was well underway in Mexico. *El Calavera,* founded in 1847, used the skeleton in modern dress as a symbol of the moral, critical voice of the newspaper. Visual content was stressed, yet artists preferred to remain anonymous; the editors and news writers were continuously being arrested for their revolutionary words, and the disrespect they repeatedly showed to the ruling class and the clergy. They made fun of physical defects and private foibles, and satirized those they believed to be engaged in wrongdoing. Names of newspapers changed, and editors, like the artists before them, attempted anonymity in order to remain safe from reprisals.

In 1871 Posada worked as head lithographer for a weekly periodical called *El Jicote* in Aguascalientes, the town where he was born. It folded after eleven issues, and Posada moved, with his employer, to León, where a new press was started. His early work shows his familiarity with earlier caricaturists from Mexico City (Ades 1989, 111–113).

By the early 1890s the number of cheaply illustrated papers increased dramatically, with Posada greatly associated with their popularity (Ades 1989, 114). His work was aimed at various kinds of popular culture forms such as songbooks, children's stories, and parlor games, including playing cards (Carmichael and Sayer 1991, 11, 126).

Posada's images were varied. Most of his work in Mexico City was done for publisher Antonio Vanegas Arroyo, who requested broadsides of sensational news items such as a mining disaster, a collision of a tram and a hearse, and a woman who gave birth to three babies and four iguanas. He created images of Robin Hood-style bandits, and terrifying deaths by firing squads that were repeatedly used by Vanegas Arroyo, with new names of new victims. Broadsides of *calaveras* would be used in various publications and later sold on street corners (Ades 1989, 117).

Don Blas, a middle son of Antonio Vanegas Arroyo, described Posada when he knew him as a likable man, bald with a fringe of white hair, and diligent with his work.

> He was very industrious. He began to work at eight o'clock in the morning and worked until seven at night. My father would enter the shop (we set up a shop for him after he had worked a while with us) with whatever he wanted to print, and say, 'Señor Posada, let's illustrate this', and Posada would read it and while he was reading would pick up his pen and say, 'What do you think about this little paragraph', and he would dip his pen into the special ink he used and then give the plate an acid bath and it was finished. He got three pesos a day whatever he did, and in that time it was a lot because whoever had as much as seventy-five pesos a month was at least a general. Posada was very good-humored and peace loving. He hated quarrels, and treated everyone well. He was no snob. (Qtd. in Brenner 1967, 188–9)

Posada scanned the workings of society in much the same manner that he visually probed skeletal features. Often what he saw was corruption, pain, poverty, and disaster, which he exposed with wit, irony, insight, and courage. Just as the bones of humans provided the structure and framework for their existence, the skeletal figures of the ruling class composed the structure of society, with all its flaws and misgivings. What Posada saw was so damaging, and so cruel, that, reflecting on the traditions of his people, and utilizing the popular culture of his day, he ingeniously mocked it with lipless creatures from the dead.

Posada's interpretation of events greatly pleased the revolutionary public. The rulers were often depicted as puppets; Posada made them bow and smile, appear all too plump, or somehow foolish looking. The revolutionary figures, however, along with the working class, were depicted as heroes, in somber grandeur. Brenner noted how he used this twisting of viewpoint, complete with humor, to help along revolutionary activities:

> By implication not evident in the text he was illustrating; by interpretation grown of conviction; because of his shafted laughter; because of enormous pity and tranquil clairvoyance, Posada is the prophet of the sudden shift in the national scene that comes with the revolution. There is a different reliance on miracles. Hope walks out of its mystic garments and girdles itself with bullets. (1967, 193–4)

With the use of the laughing, mocking skeleton, he made political statements that spoke clearly to the public. He commented on the abrupt transition of power to a new president, and he did a series of *calavera* images that directly related to the Revolution. Another series depicted the human cost of the civil war. In dialogue with photographs of the Revolution, he replaced the fleshy soldier, boy recruit, and firing squad with skeletal figures (Ades 1989, 122). In *Metamorphosis of Madero,* he showed the division between the classes—the poor in wide-brimmed hats and the rich in distinguished top hats (Ades 1987, 123). The Mexican muralists picked up on his class distinctions and his biting political criticism, and continued, to some degree, in the tradition he had made so popular.

Posada's images of the *calaveras* inspired many Latin artists who came after him. For example, Diego Rivera's mural *Dream of a Sunday Afternoon in Alameda Park* depicts Posada's famous skeleton *La Catrina,* the upper-class woman *calavera,* in a wide-brimmed hat, beside him as a child. Many artists continue to use Posada's images, especially *La Catrina,* in their *ofrendas* (See figure 7). José Clemente Orozco claimed that Posada was like the greatest artists in that he understood the "admirable lesson of simplicity, humbleness, balance, and dignity" (Poniatowska 1991, 57, 62).

Like the muralists, Posada drew on traditions that came before him. The Aztecs had carved partially skeletal figures in earthenware and stone (Garciagodoy 1998, 101), and skeleton figures were prevalent in eighteenth-century funerary catalogues. Before that, they were traditionally used in medieval art. Skeletons had been animated as if they were living long before Posada made it so popular in Mexico (Carmichael and Sayer 1991, 58). But Posada seemed to have the gift to take the skeletal sweets that were prevalent in his youth and build on their characteristics and purpose. His genius was that he was able to make the *calavera* work so effectively as a statement of his people and his time (Garciagodoy 1998, 101–102). Creating scenes from traditional ballads, revolutionary statements, and popular songs, he communicated to everyday people. His *calavera* Day of the Dead riddles, though, gave him his universal standing. One such popular riddle explains the Mexican's approach to death:

This brilliant general
Won a thousand battles
The only one he lost
Was with death's rattle

Figure 7. *Ofrenda* for art teacher Jouita Idar by Catalina Delgado-Trunk, 1997. Note paper cut of *calavera* in the large hat, making reference to Posada's important work, *La Catrina*. Photo by Kristin G. Congdon.

Now you can't tell
Whether he's a genius or a nut
Today on a skull
His general's hat does sit
And despite his medals
He's changed quite a bit.
(Qtd. in Poniatowska 1991, 62)

While Posada is now internationally known, his beginnings were relatively humble. Born to nonliterate parents in central Mexico, even in his adolescence he performed professional work as an engraver and draftsman. Despite his artistic success, he died in poverty in 1913. His skeletal remains were tossed into a common grave with other penniless individuals (Garciagodoy 1998, 96–98). This ironic, yet perhaps fitting, "ending" to his life is somehow poetic. It seemed to be Posada's choice to remain relatively unknown during his lifetime, by doing work for the mass public rather than the elite few (Brenner 1967, 192).

Arroyo went on publishing Posada's works after his death, yet no one seemed interested in the identity of the artist. In the 1920s, muralist Jean Charot, who had recently come to Mexico from France, rediscovered him, as later did the famous painters Diego Rivera and Clemente Orozco. In 1943 there was an extensive exhibition of Posada's work at the Palacio de Bellas Artes in Mexcio City, and his fame grew from there (Carmichael and Sayer 1991, 126).

In a manner fitting Posada's legacy, the muralists who were inspired by him also sought to democratize art, by making their art public with the intent to speak to the masses, including those who were illiterate. While they drew inspiration from his political zeal, his use of the laughing *calavera*, and his devotion to Mexico's poor, some also worked to overturn the exclusive power of the galleries and museums that controlled "good art" and "good taste." Yet it is one family of artists, the Linares family, who have most clearly followed in the footsteps of José Guadalupe Posada.

THE LINARES FAMILY

Diego Rivera introduced the Linares family to Posada. When he was studying at the Academy of San Carlos in Mexico City, Rivera said he frequently visited Posada in his studio, which was close by the school. In the 1950s, Rivera commissioned the Linares, also of Mexico City, to make him a papier-mâché Judas,[12] and indirectly, during this transaction, he showed them Posada's art (Masuoka 1994, 86). This influence was to have a long-term effect on the artwork of the Linares family. Many of the figures they now make are three-dimensional interpretations of Posada's drawings (Carmichael and Sayer 1991, 127).

The Linares family has created papier-mâché objects for over a hundred years (Masuoka 1994, 121).[13] They are known as *cartoneros*, makers of *cartonería* objects, traditionally used as props during fiesta celebrations. Constructed from paper, cardboard, and papier-mâché, which is made of a wheat-flour paste and paper, they are formed and painted for specific celebrations.[14] A *cartonero's* work follows the fiesta calendar: Mardi Gras, Holy Week, Independence Day, Day of the Dead, and

Christmas. There are also fiestas for local saints which a *cartonero* works on all year long (Masuoka 1994, 1–2).

The most well-known member of the Linares family was Pedro Linares, who lived from 1906 to 1992. As a child he recalled surrounding clay pots with papier-mâché to make *piñatas*. His family made papier-mâché Judases for Easter celebrations (Masuoka 1994, 9). Pedro was seen as the head of the family business. Three sons, Enrique, Felipe, and Miguel, and three grandsons, Leonardo,[15] Ricardo, and David, are considered the key members of the artistic Linares family business. Don Pedro was the family's central figure until his death in 1992 (Masuoka 1994, 17–18). Women in the Linares family also work on the *cartonería*, but their domain is mostly the home, and the papier-mâché work they do is mostly routine work to help out with orders when the men need assistance (Masuoka 1994, 27–33).

Typically, Day of the Dead papier-mâché figures are *calaveras* and skulls, mimicking the sugar skulls with names on them (Pomar 1987, 41). While this celebration and the Linares objects most clearly focus on the dead, all the work of the Linares family is deeply rooted in traditional beliefs about death. Perhaps this is why they were so easily drawn to the work of Posada.[16] It makes sense that Posada's two-dimensional renderings would successfully translate into sculptural form, since they were inspired by Day of the Dead papier-mâché figures and candied skulls (Masuoka 1994, 90). There are many successful examples of Felipe Linares' interpretation of Posada's works, which he usually quite literally translated. Posada's *La Calavera Don Quijote*, for example, depicts a *calavera* in armor with lance in hand, riding a skeletal horse while skulls fly all about. Although Felipe Linares did not capture the fast movement of Posada's horse, he certainly captured the action of the skeletons flying about, grinning widely as they go. In *"Panteon" de Diablito Rojo*, Posada (and, in turn, Filipe Linares) depicted a devil with wings who throws the police into a burning pot. While the *calaveras* boil *en mass*, other mocking figures both look and flee.

Not only do members of the Linares family reproduce Posada's illustrations in papier-mâché form, but they also make many other *calaveras* engaged in familiar day-to-day activities. Just as Posada did before them, members of the Linares family satirize the flaws of Mexican society. In Day of the Dead celebrations, the Linares' *calaveras* represent living friends and political figures depicted as if they were dead. By creating key figures in Mexican politics, especially those who have violated the trust of the working class, a mythology is created and transmitted to the public. The choice of subjects they make demonstrates concern for their community, and represents their ability to participate in the political dialogue of their times.

The Linares family also depicts natural disasters that have occurred in Mexico City. Their *Earthquake Scene*, for example, represents varied perspectives on the 1986 catastrophe. Large-scale unfleshed skeletons are depicted as trapped under fallen bricks, while another figure attempts a rescue. A coffin is carried, medical staff look on, and soldiers attempt to prevent looting as a *calavera* walks off with a television. One woman carries water in a bucket due to the destroyed plumbing. All *calaveras* carry out their activities with wide grins and a full set of teeth.

Popular culture inspires all members of the Linares family. They create scenes for places like a local discotheque, where a jazz band leans out the windows of a Volkswagen bug while a couple dressed in 1940s clothing dances on a car's top. They watch Mexican films on the studio televisions as they work. The wall where Felipe Linares works is full of images that come from newspapers. There are photos of a mushroom cloud from an atomic bomb, tanks and WWII Japanese airplanes, boxing scenes, cartoon illustrations, and logos from canned foods. He even saves interesting small matchbook covers with different dinosaurs depicted on them (Masuoka 1994, 68–69, 103). The family is clearly engaged with the world around them, and they use their art to make a humorous statement about it. That statement is deeply rooted in politics, popular culture, folklore, and, more specifically, a traditional Mexican approach to death.

Susan Masuoka discussed death with Pedro Linares in 1989 when he was eighty years old. Masuoka was working on the book *En Calavera*, a catalog associated with an exhibition of the Linares' work at the University of California-Los Angeles Fowler Museum of Art. Pedro Linares asked when the exhibition was to take place. Masuoka replied that it was five years away. With surprise that it was planned so far in the future, Linares remarked that he might be dead by then. If he were dead, he questioned, would he still be invited? Masuoka replied that she would send him an invitation, dead or alive. He seemed pleased and replied, "If I am dead I'll go *en calavera*. . . . If I die before your opening, they'll make me [in the form of] a papier-mâché skeleton and send me to Los Angeles like that." Everyone chuckled. He continued, "Whether in life or *en calavera*, I'll be there, I promise you. The important thing, though, is that you really do invite me." Masuoka reports that by that time everyone who heard the conversation was having a hearty laugh (Masuoka 1994, viii).

CONCLUSION

Humor is central to many of our folk beliefs and the practice of everyday communication systems (DuPré 1998, 47). It allows us to approach topics that might otherwise be uncomfortable. Humor is also a great equalizer. Freud claimed that humor can both distort reality and transcend it (Kuhlman 1984, 3). The Mexican attitude toward death, represented in Day of the Dead celebrations, uses humor to challenge the perceived reality experienced on this earth by the poor, by accepting and recognizing death as an equalizing truth that no one escapes. Death is humorously invited into the home and community with *ofrendas*, *calaveras*, feasting, and ritual activities at the cemeteries. Without involving humor, death would not be so acceptable. And for the working-class people of Mexico, because death is so pervasive in their everyday lives, avoiding the oppression of expected death would be difficult.

Calaveras are central to making humor work in Day of the Dead ceremonies. Garciagodoy proposed that humorous *calaveras* mask not only the difficulty of facing death, but also subordination and marginalization. Equalizing the status of the oppressed and the oppressors, *calaveras* question stereotypes of the downtrodden while poking fun at the wealthy. Those of the so-called leisure class are told that they are not the only group entitled to have fun. In fact, some *calaveras* flaunt the idea that there is plenty of fun to be had by everyone (1998, 204). They even ask the wealthy to join them in their merriment. But in this invitation is the understanding that if members of the ruling class partake, they will be exposed to mocking *calaveras*. They make visible class hierarchy. It is clearly the poor who do dangerous work, who live in the worst building structures, most susceptible to earthquakes and other disasters. It is the poor who engage in repetitive, unpleasant kinds of work that are dismissed and devalued, and it is the poor who die more readily because of an inability to pay for quality medical attention.

The *calavera*, in a humorous way, gives the wealthy time to think about their role in this subordination. They may purchase the works of Posada, the Linares family, and many other traditional artists. They may admire their poetry and ballads, their music, and their sense of humor. But ultimately, in enjoying the expressions of their humble compatriots, they must also consider the messages and belief systems represented.

The term "art" used to mean "to join or fit together," and the word "culture" comes from growth and cultivation (Lippard 1984, 358). In industrialized societies, these terms are too often associated with the elite. But today, some theorists, such as Thomas McEvilley, affirm that art's primary social function is to "define the communal self, which includes redefining it when the community is changing" (1992, 57). Likewise, William Ferris claimed that "art can make a community more human by bringing groups together" (1980, 19).

While many artists still concentrate on the individual expression, many more, along with critics, museum curators, and theorists, are becoming interested in ways that art connects instead of divides. Susan Friedman referred to the spaces where difference can come together as "borders." She wrote, "our survival as a species depends on our ability to recognize the borders between difference as fertile spaces of desire and fluid states of syncretism, interaction, and mutual interchange" (1998, 66). Perhaps some of those spaces are the borders between life and death, and wealth and poverty. Perhaps the laughing *calavera* can entice us to come together to face ideas and issues that we might more habitually want to avoid. If it is time for a restructuring of our world priorities and our relationships to one another; if it is time to move with less effort into each other's worlds and belief systems; and if we are brave enough to risk it, perhaps the *calavera* might help us along with a toothy grin.

8

CALAVERAS
Literary Humor in Mexico's Day of the Dead

STANLEY BRANDES

Feliz Día de Muertos
(Happy Day of the Dead)
STOREFRONT SIGN, Cuernavaca, Morelos (Mexico)

HUMOR, AGGRESSION, AND MORTUARY RITUAL

In *The Act of Creation*, Arthur Koestler states that humor "must contain one ingredient whose presence is indispensable: an impulse, however faint, of aggression or apprehension" (1964, 52). This assertion, controversial in its time, provides a condensed reformulation of insights presented earlier by Freud (1973), Wolfenstein (1954), and other psychoanalytic thinkers. Subsequent analyses of humor (e.g., Dundes 1971; Legman 1968, 1975) have confirmed the veracity of Koestler's formulation. There can be no doubt that humor derives at least some of its impact from its aggressive character. Teasing, for example, provides an outlet for personal criticism. As a genre, teasing is a form of "permitted disrespect," an ingredient essential to what anthropologists and folklorists know as the joking relationship (Apte 1985, 29–66). Almost half a century ago, Radcliffe-Brown defined this relationship as "a relation between two persons in which one is by custom permitted, and in some instances required, to tease or make fun of the other, who in turn is required to take no offense" (1965, 90). Keith Basso (1979) has shown that the person who teases walks a delicate tightrope. To remain on good terms with the victim, the speaker must know well his or her target. This means assessing which personality traits are safe subjects for ridicule and which are not. It also means understanding the conditions and context under which ridicule can take place, without creating offense. Similarly, ethnic humor (e.g., Apte 1985, 108–148; Brandes 1980, 53–73, 1983), sexual humor (e.g., Fine 1976; Legman 1968, 1975), and political humor (e.g., Brandes 1977) all have prominent deprecatory themes. All types of jokes—that is, verbal narratives with a humorous punchline—invariably include aggressive content. They may be either self-effacing or, alternatively, function to comment negatively on some despised outside group. In either case, the narrator must select theme and audience carefully, in order for the joke to be perceived as humorous and listeners' feelings to remain unscathed.

Rituals, religious or secular, are among the most prominent occasions for the release of aggression through humor. The ritual itself provides a safe frame by dictating the specific form of humorous expression and occasions on which it can emerge. Aggressors and victims are stipulated in advance, so that everyone—actors and audience alike—knows more or less what will transpire and when. To be sure, effective humor always contains an element of surprise. Teasing or joke telling falls flat without it. Clown figures, among the most common bearers of humor in religious ritual, need to innovate and improvise in order to produce laughter (Bouissac 1976; Brandes 1979). Gestures, actions, and words are only funny if they are perceived to be spontaneous. And yet, in the context of ritual, spontaneity is always contained by predetermined rules as to form, content, and timing. These rules provide safe boundaries, which assure that aggressive sentiments will be contained and not seriously threaten the social and political order. Occasionally, however, as with Carnival (Ladurie 1979), the action breaks through invisible barriers and produces rebellion, or, at the very least, enhanced awareness of prevailing injustices (Davis 1975).

Mortuary rituals, on the face of it, would seem inappropriate occasions for the expression of humor. However, anthropologists and folklorists have long been aware of what we might call "counter-intuitive instances," in which jocular inversions are intrinsic to the proceedings. Jacobson-Widding reminds us, for example, that throughout sub-Saharan Africa a "funeral is a complete inversion of prescribed and normal social behavior. The hierarchical order, controlled behavior, and the prudish etiquette of normal social life are transformed at funerals into the chaos of people shouting, embracing one another, rolling on the ground, tearing their clothes off, performing ritual jokes, and excelling in obscenities" (Jacobson-Widding 1990, 63). In Madagascar, we are told, the "most striking aspect of Malagasy funerals is the bawdy and drunken revelry enjoined on the guests. Malagasy participants state that these lively events are necessary because the deceased is in transition. He or she is isolated and lonely and needs to be amused and entertained" (Metcalf and Huntington 1992, 112). Europe provides comparable examples. Quigley states that, in traditional Scandinavia, a wake "was often an opportunity for courtship. In medieval Europe, most notably Ireland, mourners engaged in drinking, smoking,[1] storytelling, song and dance, and mockery" (1996, 64). Through the middle of the twentieth century, in fact, Irish wakes were major occasions for jocularity and amusement (Ó Súilleabháin 1967b), including practical jokes involving the animation of corpses (Harlow 1997).

In Mexico, particularly rural Mexico, ritual humor is a well-known feature of annual celebrations involving the veneration of saints (e.g., Brandes 1998b, Bricker 1973). Much less has been written about humor in Mexican mortuary ritual, with the exception of one notable event: the Day of the Dead, celebrated on November 1–2 each year. The Day of the Dead really consists of two Days of the Dead: All Saints Day (November 1) and All Souls Day (November 2), both standard Roman Catholic feast days.[2] This occasion, which exists outside of the framework of religious orthodoxy, also forms part of the overall cycle of events. Throughout this season, especially during the final week of October and the first week of November, humor, in both literary and artistic forms, pervades daily life. *Calaveras* are the main idiom through which humor is communicated.

CALAVERAS

Calaveras, which literally means "skulls," is the term the Mexicans use to refer, first of all, to the famously whimsical craniums made of sugar, candy, and papier-mâché that are sold in markets and on street corners throughout this season. Artistic *calaveras* such as these are used to decorate home altars, family gravesites, and storefront windows. When made of sugar paste (*alfeñique*), chocolate, or amaranth seed dough (*tzoalli*), they are also eaten. *Calaveras* are often customized by being inscribed on the forehead with the name of a friend or relative. In this form *calaveras* are presented as gifts to the people whose names appear on the skull. (There is a famous photograph of artist Frida Kahlo, lying on her deathbed, staring at a *calavera* that bears her name.) It is hard to imagine a more graphic representation of combined humor and aggression than that embodied in this type of *calavera* (see Kristin Congdon on iconic *calaveras* in this volume).

Another form of *calavera,* less famous outside Mexico, is literary. It is, in essence, a humorous epitaph, dedicated to the "memory" of a living personage. The literary *calavera* is always written in rhymed verse and often organized into quatrains. Though *calaveras* nowadays are generally short—four to twelve lines at most—they can vary from simple couplets to epics stretching several pages in length. A good example of a two-liner comes from the Veracruz newspaper, *La Opinión.* On 3 November 1912, the editor published a *calavera* in honor of a long-forgotten political figure, Don Angel C. Colina: "*Dicen que se ha muerto entero/ Por defender a Madero*"—"They say that he died whole because he defended Madero."[3] The poet normally dedicates a *calavera* to a friend or a relative, whose name provides the title of the epitaph.

Although, as we shall see, *calaveras* are sometimes complimentary, they are usually bitingly satirical and mock the victim's weaknesses through humorous teasing. Friends and relatives occasionally present *calaveras* to one another during the Day of the Dead. However aggressive they might seem, short verses of this sort almost always operate to reinforce friendships and other social ties. They are joking relationships. By presenting a *calavera* to a friend or relative, the poet implies that there exists such a strong bond between the two that not even a mocking jab at the victim's weaknesses will threaten the relationship. In turn, by accepting the *calavera* with good humor, the victim states in essence that he or she feels so close to the poet that the bond can well withstand an innocent personal jab.

The principal form of *calavera* is the published *calavera,* which appears at the end of October and beginning of November in newspapers and periodicals throughout the nation. Ever since the late nineteenth and early twentieth centuries, enterprising writers and artists have taken the opportunity of the Day of the Dead to produce broadsides and small magazines exclusively devoted to the dissemination of these sometimes clever, sometimes corny epitaphs (Wollen 1989). The authors of *calaveras* are generally anonymous. Anonymity, which is surely an intentional editorial decision, enhances the impression that the authors of these mocking verses express generally held opinions. The verses come to be perceived as the voice of the people.

One recent innovation is *calavera* contests,[4] sponsored by newspapers throughout the Republic. Poems are solicited from readers and the winners are published under a byline. One winning contribution to the nationally distributed newspaper *Reforma* (1 November 2000:16) is a *calavera* dedicated "to *las calaveras.*" It gives an excellent overview of the nature and meaning of these whimsical epitaphs:

A LAS CALAVERAS	TO THE CALAVERAS
Noviembre siempre es el mes *ya conocido y notorio* *cuando se habla a la vez* *de calacas y el tenorio.*	November is always the month already known and notorious when skeletons and *el tenorio*[5] are spoken of simultaneously.
Pues son nuestras tradiciones *el escribir calaveras* *donde hay muertos de a montones* *mas nadie muere de veras.*	Well, it's our tradition to write *calaveras* in which there are mountains of dead people but no one really dies.
Rescatar nuestras costumbres *esto cumple esos fines* *hablar de cielo y de lumbres* *y déjense de "jalogüines."*	To rescue our customs that satisfies those goals to speak of heaven and fire and leave behind "Halloweens."[6]
Es broma, lector, lectora, *no hay agravios encubiertos* *y no le carguen los muertos* *a quien escribe ahora.*	It's a joke, readers, there are no hidden insults and let the deceased not denounce the present writer.
Si acaso en esta ocasión *con tus huesos aquí asomas* *has de disculpar las bromas:* *¡Calaveras, bromas son!*	For it's the case that on this occasion with your bones showing you have to forgive the jokes: Calaveras, they are jokes!

Maestra Hortensia Galindo Garrido, Colonia Lindavista (México, D.F.)

Calaveras directed at the reading public occasionally express praise and admiration. Consider, for example, the *calavera* dedicated to beloved writer, Elena Poniatowska (*El Metiche,* 1 November 1995):

La pelona aunque con reuma *para leer no se hace rosca* *nos dejó sin la ágil pluma* *de Elenita Poniatowska.*	The hairless one [i.e., Death], although with rheumatism is still able to read, [she] left us without the agile pen of Elenita Poniatowska.

Use of the diminutive "Elenita" is a sign of public affection and adds to the generally positive message of this *calavera.*

Historian Miguel León Portilla, widely acclaimed for his mastery of pre-Columbian life and thought, also receives praiseworthy treatment in the press (*Calaveras Encanijadas,* 1995:4):

El ínclito historiador	The illustrious historian
tras de ser galardonado	after receiving an award
en un foro del Estado	in a State forum
habló con mucho valor;	spoke with great worth;
a la medalla hizo honor	he did honor to the medal
como quedó allí patente	as was obvious there
y hasta el mismo Presidente	and even the very President [of the Republic]
la festejó su entereza.	celebrated his integrity.
Descansa en paz, de una pieza,	Rest in peace, people of valor,
muere la gente valiente.	Die whole.

Highly accomplished intellectuals and people in the arts, like Miguel León Portilla and Elena Poniatowska, are the kind of subjects most likely to receive favorable epitaphs. Occasionally people of lesser renown are also rewarded with affectionate *calaveras*. From Ciudad Juárez, bordering on the state of New Mexico, comes the following poem in honor of a local citizen (*El Mexicano*, Ciudad Juárez, Chihuahua, 2 November 1933):

PEDRO RODRÍGUEZ

Siempre vivió silencioso	Silently he always lived
y silencioso murió	and silently he died
este amigo generoso	this generous friend
que Pedrito se llamó.	called Pedrito.

As with the Elena Poniatowska's *calavera*, this one uses the diminutive form of the subject's name, indicating a kind of tender respect.

On the whole, however, *calaveras* are designed to ridicule well-known figures from the world of politics, sports, the arts, and other high-profile professions. Poets use mocking *calaveras* to draw attention to negative aspects of the victims' public record. In the case of political *calaveras* in particular, the verses are a form of what I have elsewhere called "peaceful protest" (Brandes 1977). They not only make fun of known foibles and weaknesses of their leaders, but also express cynicism about politics itself at both the local and national levels.

In this respect, political *calaveras* help to create a shared political community. *Calaveras* directed at elected officials in Oaxaca, in the south of Mexico, might well mean nothing to a Mexican from the state of Coahuila, located on the northern frontier. Some *calaveras* are aimed at truly local communities, such as members of particular professions in small towns and cities. These *calaveras* assume the character of in-group humor. Consider, for example, a *calavera* published in a local supplement of the national newspaper, *La Jornada*. The *calavera* bears the title, "The Photographer and the Skull":

EL FOTÍGRAFO Y LA CALACA

Estaba Enrique Agatón	Enrique Agatón was
frotando su camarita	stroking his camera
en eso que sale la bella genio	when the beautiful genius [i.e., Death] appears
y le hace una preguntita:	and asks him:
¿Qué quieres hacer tú	What do you want to do
con ese aparatito?	with that apparatus?
Quiero sacar lindas fotos	I want to take fine photographs
Y chance tu retratito.	and attempt your portrait.
Ese deseo te concederé	This wish I will grant you
espérate un ratito	wait a minute
Pero si no salen bien	But if they don't turn out well
me hago el muertito.	I'll fall dead.

This *calavera* concerns a photographer virtually unknown outside his hometown, Cuernavaca, capital of the small state of Morelos. Published in a newspaper supplement with restricted distribution (*La Jornada Morelos,* 5 November 2000), the *calavera* is obviously directed to the photographic community in Cuernavaca, where Enrique Agatón lives and works. By contrast, verses that mock the president of the Republic and the national political process are directed to Mexicans and followers of Mexican politics everywhere.

POLITICAL CALAVERAS, 2000

Election year 2000 provided particularly fertile ground for *calavera* poets, given that on 2 July of that year the PRI (Partido Revolucionario Institucional), which had ruled Mexico for 76 years, finally lost both presidential and congressional elections. The winners were members of rival right-leaning party PAN (Partido de Acción Nacional), headed by presidential candidate Vicente Fox Quesada. Among the immediate factors that finally caused the downfall of the PRI were recognition of corruption on the part of PRI leaders and officials, together with the self-imposed exile of former President Carlos Salinas de Gortari (1988–94); the lengthy imprisonment of Salinas' brother in Almoloya de Juárez, the country's most famous high-security prison; and almost daily revelations of illegal accumulations of wealth on the part of government authorities. During the Day of the Dead season 2000, anonymous poets and the reading public expressed anger and criticism at the PRI through the biting medium of *calaveras*. Almost every periodical published epitaphs to the PRI itself. A writer contributed the following *calavera* to the newspaper *Nacional* (2 November 2000):

PRI

El PRI estaba preparado,	The PRI was prepared,
se gastó un dineral.	It spent a fortune.
Sin embargo el dos de julio,	Nevertheless on the second of July
acudió su funeral.	It attended its funeral.
Su cadáver deshicieron,	They took apart its cadaver,
fue un desmembramiento "atrox".	It was an atrocious dismembering.
Y sus huesos se los dieron,	And they gave its bones,
A los amigos de Fox.	To the friends of Fox.
Dicen que murió de viejo,	They say it died of old age,
o que un cáncer lo mató.	Or that a cancer killed it.
O que por un mal reflejo,	Or that because of a bad reflex,
una bota lo aplastó.	A boot crushed it.

The word *atrox* in the second stanza derives from the word *atroz*, standard Spanish for "atrocious." *Atrox* is meant to rhyme with Fox, the name of the presidential winner which appears two lines below. This kind of poetic license appears frequently in *calaveras* and is part of what makes them funny.

There are elements of this *calavera* that speak to a knowing public alone. The reference to cancer in the last stanza harks to the popular belief that the PRI fell because it was rotten and eaten up from inside its ranks, just as cancer destroys its victim from within. The boot in the last line refers to the dress code maintained by Vicente Fox, the presidential winner from the opposing party. Fox comes from the ranching state of Guanajuato and never wears standard shoes, only cowboy boots.[7]

From the *Union de Morelos* (2 November 2000) came another epitaph for the PRI:

EL PRI	THE PRI
Ahora sí se murió,	Now, yes, it died,
Estiró toda la pata	It lay down flat [lit. 'extended its entire leg']
Dejole a los suyos	Leaving to its members
Puras dudas, nada mas.	Only debts, nothing more.

Era el gran partidazo *Pero el cambio no aguantó* *El merito dos de julio* *La parca se lo llevó.*	It was the great important party But it couldn't take change On the very second of July It was taken away by death.

Calaveras published in November 2000 commented on every sort of shortcoming manifested by the PRI and its leaders. In the preceding *calavera*, the party's rigidity and financial imprudence are main targets of criticism. Still other poems emphasize the intrigue and insider profiteering which were demonstrable practices of the PRI (*Milenio,* 1 November 2000).

En panteón semidesierto *un gran hoyo se ha cavado* *pa' que quepa junto al muerto* *tanto secreto del Estado.*	In a semi-deserted graveyard a large hole has been dug in order to fit next to the deceased so many state secrets.
Y la Muerte ya ha ordenado: *"Escarban más por aquí,* *hay que dejar reservado* *un huequito para el PRI."*	And Death has ordered: "Dig further over here, we have to reserve a little empty space for the PRI."

Calaveras, ever adapted to changing circumstances, often comment on the most current political news. In October 2000, the papers were filled with reports of a recorded conversation between Raúl Salinas, imprisoned elder brother of former President Carlos Salinas de Gortari (1988–94), and Raúl's wife, Adriana. Segments of the conversation (the veracity of which was later confirmed by scientific analysis) convey Raúl's open condemnation of his brother Carlos's conduct. The scandalous episode is inscribed in the following *calavera*:

RAÚL SALINAS

Según una información *fueron varias las catrinas* *que llevaron al panteón* *al mayor de los Salinas.* *Quedó en sepulcro enrejado* *sin abogado y sin lana,* *pero bien comunicado* *con el sepulcro de Adriana.*	According to some information there were several female dandies who carried the eldest Salinas [i.e., Raúl] to the graveyard. He remained behind bars in his tomb without lawyer or money but in good communication with Adriana's tomb.

According to now obsolete Mexican political tradition, the outgoing president would hand pick his successor, who automatically became the

PRI electoral candidate. The designated candidate was certain of winning. In the year 2000, however, President Ernesto Zedillo proved incapable of delivering the majority vote to the PRI candidate (the outcome was specifically perceived as the result of his ineffectiveness). For this, he came under bitter attack by members of his own party, who accused him of intentionally losing the election. *Calaveras* all over the country were quick to express this sentiment. Consider the following epitaph, published in the national daily, *Reforma* (1 November 2000):

AL PRESIDENTE ZEDILLO

A Zedillo llevaron a enterrar	They carried off Zedillo to be buried
a un camposanto lugar.	in holy ground.
Cansado de tanto luchar	Tired of so much struggling
dicen que se dejó ganar.	they say that he let himself stop winning.

In the view of some citizens, Zedillo was too good for the PRI. Presidential elections under his leadership were, in popular opinion, the most democratic that Mexico had experienced in three generations. Hence, the following concluding stanza from a lengthy *calavera* (*Reforma,* 1 November 2000):

AL PRESIDENTE ERNESTO ZEDILLO

Se llevó a Zedillo la calavera,	[Death] carried off the skeleton Zedillo,
se lo llevó muy lejos de aquí,	carried him far from here,
buena persona que era,	good person that he was,
ni parecía del PRI.	he didn't seem to belong to the PRI.

That which some citizens interpreted as goodness, however, others condemned as weakness and cowardliness. By Mexican standards, politicians who manifest these basically "feminine" characteristics deserve nothing but scorn and disdain. Another *calavera* (*México Hoy,* 2 November 2000) targets the outgoing president thus:

ERNESTO ZEDILLO

Entre brujas y vampirios	Among witches and vampires
demonios y mil horrores	Demons and a thousand horrors
la muerte arrastra unos huesos	Death drags some bones
entre cantos y vítores.	Among songs and cheers.
El pervertió su suerte	He perverted his luck
pues nunca quiso entender	well, he never wanted to understand
que el poder que había usurpado	that the power that he had usurped

lo era para ejercer.
Prefirió el poder castrante
del que no sabe qué hacer
incongruencias y temores
sin talento y sin saber.

was there to be used.
He preferred the castrated power
of one who doesn't know how to use it
incongruity and fears
without talent and know-how.

At the turn of the millennium, PRI leaders were for the most part hated for their corruption, hypocrisy, and authoritarianism. At the same time, many Mexicans are attracted to political strongmen for their leadership, decisiveness, and ability to wield power effectively. Politicians like Zedillo, who demonstrate an inability to exploit their power to full personal advantage, are pitied for their impotence. And the term impotence inscribes the meaning perfectly. By incorporating the phrase *poder castrante* (castrating power), the *calavera* emphasizes the association between political and sexual power. Mexican politicians enjoy no escape from criticism: either they are too weak to rule effectively or too authoritarian for the common good.

CALAVERAS AND THE POWER ELITE

Powerholders in general have always been free game for critics with literary flair around the time of the Day of the Dead. Consider the following *calavera* from the 1940s dedicated to the Tijuana police commander (*El Condor,* Tijuana, 1 November 1943):

COMANDANTE DE POLICIA

Este pobre "chaparrito"
y su corte celestial
en el infierno está frito
lo porque todo hizo mal.

This poor "shorty"
and his heavenly court
fry in hell
because of all they did wrong.

Persiguiendo a las mujeres
por orden de su patrón,
abusaba de su puesto
pa' tener un galardón

Pursuing women
by order of their boss,
he abused his office
to get a large reward.

Mas todo tiene su fin
y la parca lo cogió
en tan triste situación
que hoy exclama el pobrecito:
sácame de aquí, patrón.

But everything must end
and Death caught him
in such a sad situation
that today the poor guy exclaims:
get me out of here, boss.

Abuse of power—power over women, power to obtain wealth illegally—is among the most salient *calavera* themes.

This theme also emerges in critiques of the clergy. From *El Chivo* (2 November 1996), a Oaxaca periodical, comes the following humorous epitaph. Its victim is Archbishop Héctor González Martínez.

Dicen que este santo cura
en su vida fue capaz,
que dentro de su locura
con el diablo, hizo la pazà.

They say that this holy priest
while alive was capable,
given his craziness,
of making peace with the Devil.

Este vivió de limosna
que le dimos los humanos
por eso con mucha sorna
fue botana de gusanos.

He lived from the alms
that humans gave him,
for this reason with much scorn
became an appetizer for worms.

Luchó contra la maldad
ilustrísimo prelado
más nunca dió caridad
como lo hubo pregonado.

He fought against evil
this illustrious prelate
but never gave charity
as he advocated.

Así su ríspida lengua
quedó tieza, de una tira,
este no tuvo mengua
en predicar la mentira.

Thus his *ríspida* tongue
became rigid all at once,
this one never let up
preaching lies.

Bartolomé lo enterró
cuando adoraba el dinero,
boca abajo lo enterró
allá por el basurero.

Bartolomé buried him
when he idolized money,
he was buried face down
there by the garbage pit.

Así con toda la calma
a la eternidad fue en pos,
este que no tuvo alma
y ni fue al reino de Dios.

There with great calm
He went for eternity,
This one who had no soul
And didn't even go to the Kingdom of God.

It might seem paradoxical, even perverse, that a sacred occasion such as the Day of the Dead should give rise to anti-clerical sentiment. However, literary *calaveras*, such as the one reproduced above, constitute part of a Bakhtinian, carnavalesque anti-rite. They are just one of many manifestations of the profane which emerge as counterpoint to sacred actions and belief. The Day of the Dead awakens contradictory emotions and allows them to flourish simultaneously.

CALAVERAS AND COMMERCE

Clearly, too, the Day of the Dead, though fundamentally a religious occasion, has long been imbued with a commercial dimension. Literary *calaveras* derive from the mid- to late-nineteenth century, during which José Guadalupe Posada (1852–1913) "became the master of the *calavera*. Personalities and professions of the time were portrayed as skeletons and accompanied by humorous verses" (Sayer 1993, 26). Posada's *calaveras* were printed on broadsides and reproduced in the popular press. In fact, throughout the last half of the nineteenth century in Mexico, broadsides were known generically as *calaveras*. The first illustrated newspaper in Mexico was even called *El Calavera*. From the time of its founding in January 1847, until it was suppressed by the government thirty-one issues later, *El Calavera* specialized in satirizing political currents of the day, and particularly poking fun at the nation's leaders through drawings, verse, and essays (Childs and Altman 1982, 54).

A generation ago, Edward Tinker remarked that during the Day of the Dead,

> *calaveras* appear to add their sardonic flavor to the gaiety of the occasion. Printed on colored paper, adorned with the grisly insignia of death, they carry verses satirizing people in the public eye, speaking of them as though they were dead, and often ending with burlesque epitaphs. They are peddled on the streets and read in cafés with many a chuckle. The newspapers, too, take this opportunity to run caricatures and caustic verses in *calavera* vein, about politicians and government officials against whom they have some grudge. No one illustrated these better than Posada, for his grotesque improvisations, fertility of imagination, and the human quality he imparted to his grinning, dancing cadavers, made him the supreme master of this kind of work. Another talent he possessed was for depicting the life and types of his countrymen—a genius he used to arouse the public conscience to realization of the wrongs of the downtrodden. (1961, 25)

What commentators often overlook, or at least de-emphasize, is that *calaveras* were and still are profitable items. Whether as broadsides or as newspaper features, *calaveras* are a predictable feature of the Day of the Dead. The Mexican public demands and expects them at this time of year and are willing to spend money to read them.

Hard to determine though such matters may be, it is fair to say that Mexicans, now an overwhelmingly literate people, demonstrate at least as great a craving for literary, satiric verse as for visual representations.

Although literary and artistic *calaveras* often accompany one another, the visual caricatures popularly known as *calaveras* are usually small and insignificant on the page when compared with text.

This formatting represents a significant change over the course of a century. It is true that text and drawing sometimes occupied equal space on the broadside page in Posada's day. However, drawings most often overshadowed satirical verse, probably in response to market demand from a non-reading public. In published media, at least during the season of the Day of the Dead, the written word in the form of literary *calaveras* has replaced *calavera* drawings in prominence.

Literary and visual *calaveras* seem to occupy distinctive, if overlapping, niches as popular artistic genres. Childs and Altman (1982, 54) believe that literary *calaveras*, published mainly on broadsides, emerged in the mid-nineteenth century mainly in response to the freedom of the press that came with Mexico's independence from Spain in 1821. Technical advances in printing were also partly responsible for this development. Over the course of time, literary *calaveras*, which had been a year round phenomenon, became increasingly restricted to the Day of the Dead. Certainly throughout the mid- and late-twentieth century, the rhymed, satirical epitaphs known as *calaveras* flourished during late October and early November alone.

This is not the case with *calavera* caricatures. Mexico has been home to iconographic representations of skulls and skeletons since pre-Columbian times (Brandes 1998b; Carmichael and Sayer 1991; Westheim 1992). To this extent, José Guadalupe Posada's images drew on and flourished within a long artistic tradition. Posada's great innovation was to situate this art in the context of immediate historical circumstances. His arena was a young nation with an unstable, rapidly transmuting political framework. Posada's art became just one of numerous forms of popular resistance (Beezley, Martin, and French 1994) that have flourished throughout Mexican history. As William Beezley puts it, the rhymed, illustrated obituaries "offered the common people the opportunity, without fear of censure or reprisal, to express their dissatisfaction with political and social leaders and to define their grievances, real or imagined" (1997; 98).

To this extent, published *calaveras* are a social and political leveling device. Through ridicule and satire, they denigrate and chastise, thereby symbolically toppling powerholders from their self-constructed pedestals. Literary *calaveras* assert the very egalitarian principle that Mexicans attribute to death itself. From the press of Posada's printer,

Antonio Vanegas Arroyo, comes the following *calavera,* published in a pamphlet dated 1905. Because it is exceptionally long, only a fragment is reproduced here. There can be no better description of the common fate that awaits all humanity.

GRAN BAILE DE LAS *CALAVERAS*	GRAND DANCE OF THE SKULLS
Allí irán los abogados	There will go the lawyers
Con toda su vanidad;	With all their vanity;
Allí irá la Facultad	There will go the [university] Faculty
Y los Doctores borlados.	And the certified Doctors.
En revuelta confusión	In mixed-up confusion
Estarán las calaveras,	Will be the skulls,
Y las meras petateras	And even the straw mat makers
Disfrutarán la ocasión.	Will enjoy the occasion.
Será una gran igualdad	It will be a great equality
Que nivele grande y chico	That levels big and small
No habrá ni un pobre [ni] rico	There will be neither poor nor rich
En aquella sociedad.	In that society.
De este mundo en extensión	In this widening world
El oro a todos pervierte	Gold perverts everyone
Pero después de la muerte	But after death
No hay clases ni condición.	There are neither classes nor rank.

The same message comes across in a moving *calavera* published nearly a century later in *El Imparcial,* from Oaxaca (31 October 1996):

Toditos los que hoy están	All those who today are
en este apretado osario	in this crowded ossuary
ya vivieron su calvario;	already lived their calvary;
iguales ahora serán	will now be equal
el lego y el sacristán	the layman and the sacristan
el sardo y el comandante	the guardsman and the commander
el reportero y el director	the reporter and the director
todos en este instante	all at this moment
llegaron a su panteón	will arrive at the cemetery
con las patas por delante,	with their feet stretched out in front,
calaveras del montón.	piled-up skulls.
No importa que fuera ministro	It doesn't matter if he were minister
magistrado o presidente	judge or president
todos pelaron el diente	all smiled fawningly
y llegaron a lo mismo:	and arrived in the same place:
el que vivió con cinismo	he who lived with cynicism

o en una cueva de fieras,	or in a cave of wild beasts,
señoritas o rameras	young maids or whores
dieron el azotón	fell over dead
y ahora son calaveras,	and now they are skulls,
calaveras del montón.	piled-up skulls.

By advertising the personal weaknesses of the rich and powerful, printed *calaveras* symbolically situate these public figures on the level of the common man. Through poetry they bring about, in effect, the equality that death will seal once and for all.

Still, for the living, social inequality is hard to escape. True, printed *calaveras* for the most part emphasize the common condition in which all humanity finds itself. And yet, these mock epitaphs occasionally break out of this mold to point out ways in which the Day of the Dead provides the occasion for the display of wealth and prestige. The best example comes from *La Opinion* (4 November 1913), a Veracruz newspaper printed in the early years of the revolution (1910–20).

NO VOY	I AM NOT GOING
¿Ir al Cementerio? ¿a qué?	Go to the cemetery? For what?
necedad en mí sería	it would be foolishness for me
ir a ver tanta viuda	to go to see so many widows
enlutada y compungida,	in mourning and remorseful,
frente a otros tantos sepulcros	in front of so many other tombs
donde moran sus fosillos	where their little fossils rest
adornándolos con flores,	adorning them with flowers,
poniéndoles siemprevivas,	placing down *siemprevivas,*
moco de pavo, gardenias,	cockscomb, gardenias,
flor de muerto y margaritas	orchids and daisies
Compradas Dios sabe cómo	Purchased God-knows-how
y qué clase de pastilla,	and with what kind of money [*pastilla*],
para mirarla después,	[only] to look at them afterwards,
riéndose a toda mandíbula	laughing wide-mouthed
con quienes, de aquellos muertos,	together with those people, who are
son suplentes en caricias.	substitutes for the deceased in caresses.
¿Ir al cementerio? ¿a qué?	Go to the cemetery? For what?
¿a ver tanta hipocresía?	to see so much hypocrisy?
No soy afecto de observar	I am not fond of observing
ese llanto de mentira,	that false weeping,
no quiero ver el dolor	I don't want to see the pain
sin consuelo de la hija,	without the daughter's consolation,
que ante la tumba del padre	which before the father's tomb

manifiesta en este día,
para al poco rato verla,
por las calles y avenidas,
prostituyendo aquel nombre
que guarda esa tumba fría.
¿Ir al Cementerio? ¿a qué?
¿a ver ciertas damitas
luciendo vistosos trajes
cuando a ese lugar debían
asistir, si nó de luto,
porque no se vean bonitas,
al menos no haciendo alarde
de que los valen cerilla
el respeto a los difuntos
y el ídem a sus familias?
No, marchantes, no estoy loco,
si para desgracia mía
y desgracia de otros muchos
que vivimos en la invieta,
la ciudad es un panteón,
desde por las hortalizas
hasta cerca de Vergara,
en el que duermen sin vida
los timbres de muchos nombres
matados en estos días.

is manifested on this day,
only a little later to see her
on the streets and avenues,
prostituting that name which
watches over that cold tomb.
Go to the cemetery? For what?
to see certain ladies showing off
flashy suits
when in this place they should
attend, if not dressed in mourning
because they won't be seen as beautiful,
at least not showing off
that respect for the deceased and
their families is of little importance?
No, *marchantes,* I am not crazy,
if through my misfortune and the
misfortune of many others
we live in the *invieta,*
the city is a cemetery,
from the vegetable gardens
to near Vergara,
where the stamps [*timbres*] of many names
killed on these days sleep without life.

As portrayed in this *calavera,* the Day of the Dead takes place against a backdrop of revolutionary violence and killing. Under such circumstances, death takes on a special meaning, which makes humor and satire more difficult.

Nonetheless, the *calavera* is true to its genre in its display of irreverent sentiments. It provides a scathing critique of the kind of social pretense that is carried out under the guise of traditional religious observance. If most *calaveras* serve to level humanity, this one acts as a commentary on the *calavera* genre. It operates to demonstrate not only the sensitivity of *calaveras* to historical circumstances and to the mood of the times, but also to show that nothing—not even the *calavera* itself—is above judgment. The *calavera* is poetry as protest, made all the more effective by its jocular guise.

BROADSIDES AND NEWSPAPERS CITED

Calaveras Encanijadas (Mexico City)
El Chivo (Oaxaca)
El Condor (Tijuana, Baja California)
El Imparcial (Oaxaca)
La Jornada (Mexico City)
La Jornada Morelos (Cuernavaca)
El Metiche (Mexico City)
El Mexicano (Ciudad Juárez, Chihuahua)
Mexico Hoy
Milenio (Mexico City)
Nacional
La Opinión (Veracruz)
Reforma
Union de Morelos

9

EXIT LAUGHING
Death and Laughter in Los Angeles and Port-au-Prince

DONALD J. COSENTINO

For Rodney Flambert

I would like to achieve immortality by not dying.

WOODY ALLEN

Let this essay on death and laughter begin as a tale of two cities: Los Angeles, California, where I live a few blocks from Hollywood Boulevard; and Port-au-Prince, Haiti, where I conduct research on Vodou.[1] Though they exist at opposite ends of an economic spectrum, both these extreme cities sustain singular lifestyles, and singular preoccupations with postlife arrangements. I have been an eager participant-observer in both their life and death styles, and offer this essay as a *memento mori* to lessons they have taught me.

Los Angeles

In Los Angeles, death has been subject to a treatment whose first premise is disguise. Half of us get incinerated in front of no one, our ashes discretely scattered over redwoods or grey seas. The other half get pumped full of formaldehyde and boxed out on narrow pink bunting, ready, it seems, for a tanning salon. Thus transformed into "loved ones," we get planted in cemeteries, which more and more resemble theme malls or miniature golf courses.

Insofar as the gap between appearance and reality is the territory of laughter (*chez* Freud, et al.), these measures to deny death are inherently funny. Consider Walt Disney's cryogenically frozen corpse awaiting some elixir (from Tomorrow-Land?) which will kick-start his DNA. Or Marilyn Monroe, our sleeping beauty, shelved into her marble crypt all blotted over with lipstick traces from still adoring fans. Or, indeed, the fate of the L.A. hoi poloi immobilized in their last great traffic jam just off the Glendale Freeway at Forest Lawn. With its glades and fountains, poets corners and babyland, Forest Lawn is the Camelot of modern mortuary science, a Disneyland for the Dead unmarred by any reference to the sober state of its decomposing inhabitants.

Most Angelenos don't seem to get that joke, at least not the way foreign observers have. There was, for instance, English expatriate Jessica Mitford, who made a career out of documenting the demented practices of Forest Lawn (*inter alia*) in her classic *American Way of Death.*[2] It was Mitford who pointed out the remarkable parallels between mummification in Pharaonic Egypt and embalming in twentieth century America, and the unfortunate similarities between the skin of the embalmed and the texture of cottage cheese. It was her friend Evelyn Waugh, the brahmin of twentieth century satire, who forever memorialized Forest Lawn (thinly disguised as Whispering Glades), in his classic *The Loved One.*[3] Early on in that gruesome and hilarious novel, the hero Dennis Barlow composes an elegy for his suicided friend Francis Hinsley, who has been all tarted up for his leavetaking by mortician extraordinaire, Mr. Joyboy:

> They told me, Francis Hinsley, they told me you were hung
> With red protruding eye-balls and black protruding tongue
> I wept as I remembered how often you and I
> Had laughed about Los Angeles and now 'tis here you'll lie
> Here pickled in formaldehyde and painted like a whore,
> Shrimp pink incorruptible, not lost nor gone before. (1948, 85)

Barlow makes his living as mortuary assistant at the Happier Hunting Ground, a pet cemetery. From that position, he manages to seduce Joyboy's cosmetology assistant, Aimée Thanatogenos. Unable to choose between her mortician lovers, the distraught Thanatogenos injects herself with a fatal dose of formaldehyde. Barlow takes charge of their Loved One's incineration, making sure that the bereaved Joyboy receives an annual postcard from the Happier Hunting Ground: "Your little Aimée is wagging her tail in heaven tonight, thinking of you."

An even weirder sendup of L.A. death styles was concocted by Jeffrey Valance in *Blinky: The Friendly Hen,* his elegiac booklet dedicated "to the billions of hens sacrificed each year for our consumption." After finding a nice frozen hen (shades of cryogenics) at his neighborhood Ralphs supermarket, Valance drives to an L.A. pet cemetery where he orders a complete funeral service for his newly adopted dead pet. This includes a powder blue casket with pink satin lining, a pillow (where Blinky's head would have been placed if she had one), a lot, internment, flower vase, viewing room, and a grave marker which reads:

1976 – 1978
BLINKY
THE FRIENDLY HEN

Such sentimental leavetakings do not come cheap. While the frozen Blinky cost $2.17 at Ralphs, her funeral cost $227.40. But a compensatory miracle did follow: when Blinky started to thaw in her coffin, she had to be placed on a paper towel. Her perfect imprint thus remained on the bloody towel, forming what might be called the "Shroud of Blinky," which, like the Shroud of Turin, incorporated a scarcely visible negative image in sepia monochrome. Unfortunately, Valance does not tell us where this pious image might still be venerated, but a simulacrum of the hen's funeral was featured in the 2000 exhibition "Made in California" at the Los Angeles County Museum of Art.

Port-au-Prince

Port-au-Prince lacks the resources, if not the imagination, for any such Hollywood treatment of human or chicken remains. Embalming is largely unknown, and in all that infernal heat, funerals are usually pretty hurried affairs. Besides, who but Americans could afford such fabulous necropoli as Forest Lawn? Haitians still manage to maintain a pretty lively scene down at their city cemetery. Natty tombs echo to hymns, wails, and the percussive beat of improvised bands, as the dead are wedged into their pretty new homes. Above-ground sepulchres are jauntily painted or tiled and decorated with tin wreaths, many embossed with photos of those laid to rest. Compared to this garish display, death in L.A. is Dullsville. All show and no action. An endless Sunday in the suburbs. Angeleno dead have run out of options, while in Haiti, death has just opened up new opportunities.

In their sepulchres, the Haitian dead achieve levels of bourgeois comfort which eluded most of them while they were alive. Eternal rest, however, is illusory. Port-au-Prince has a desperate housing shortage for the dead as well as for the living. Constricted cemetery space and the pressing needs of new corpses mean that old bones are pushed to the rear of tombs and finally into a central ossuary where they mingle with bits and pieces of the other nameless dead. Emaciated beggars watch while robbers smash crypts searching for gold teeth or jewelry, and then shake out the coffin for a new paint job and a quick resale.

In Haiti, life and death are fleeting. When rioters smashed into the family tomb of François "Papa Doc" Duvalier after the 1986 revolt against the tyrant's son "Baby Doc," they found the tomb empty. The former dictator's body was gone. Few believed Papa Doc had simply turned to dust. Most supposed Baby Doc had spirited his father's remains off to France, along with most of the national treasury. After all, Duvalier dust would add quite a malevolent jolt to any *wanga* (Vodou charm devised to effect harmful magic) that Baby Doc might need or want during his exile. Others recalled that as pallbearers lifted the coffin to commit Papa's body to the family tomb during his 1971 funeral, a dust devil arose out of nowhere. Terrified mourners turned tail and scattered, certain that Duvalier's spirit had jumped out of the coffin and was making its way back to the National Palace.

The disappearance of the dictator's remains was not remarkable to Haitians. In Vodou belief, the transitory fate of the corpse mirrors that of its souls (each individual has three), which are constantly on the move. At death, the personal part of the soul is ushered out of the corpse and into its afterlife by an *oungan* (Vodou priest). After a forced retirement of a year and a day under the waters, the personal soul may be recalled by family members, and thereafter repose in a *govi* (earthen jar) kept on a Vodou altar. Through ritual ventriloquy, a muffled ancestral voice from the *govi* may continue to counsel family members, until it is reincarnated in another body and the cycle recommences.

Such spiritual recycling is dependent, however, on avoiding capture by a *malfacteur* (evil wizard), who may kidnap a soul in transit, transforming it or its abandoned human casing into a *zonbi* (zombie). *Zonbi* are most commonly understood to exist in the form of captured spirits (*zonbi astral*), and not as the walking, soulless corpses favored by romancier/auteurs such as George Romero (*The Night of the Living Dead*; *Dawn of the Dead*, et al.), although those kind of *zonbi* are also understood to exist, and are much pitied for their dreary fate.

Hollywood images now inform Haitian mythology, reviving vestigial Congo beliefs regarding the reanimated dead, the way that Mme. Blavatsky and her cohort of Theosophists revived waning devotion to the *devas* (Hindu deities) in nineteenth century India. I first visited Haiti in 1986, the year Wade Davis's bestseller docu-novel, *The Serpent and the Rainbow,* had stirred up renewed interest in the *zonbi* cult. Sensing a thrill-seeking tourist, a young Haitian tout approached me on the street and whispered, "Hey, *Blan* [Whitie], wanna see a *Zonbi*?" with the same leering intonations other touts in other places offer dirty postcards or the services of virgin sisters.

THE GEDES

So the cemetery is a spiritual transportation hub, where souls are constantly taking off, landing, or being hijacked. Directing all this traffic is the Bawon Samdi, the grimmest member of an aristocratic pantheon of Vodou *lwa* (spirits), which includes such cousins as: Agwe, Admiral of the divine navy; Ogou, Generalissimo of the spirit armies; and Mistress Ezili, most imperious of the celestial call girls. Bawon Samdi is himself Lord of Death and presides over all Haitian cemeteries, along with a whole clan of related spirits who together bear a startling collective resemblance to the Addams family of cartoon and TV fame. There is, for instance, Bawon La Croix, his imbecilic brother, who keeps the cemetery grounds; and Gran Brigitte, Samdi's ghoulish, red-eyed wife. Then there are the Gedes, whose antics transform the cemetery into Haiti's theatre of the absurd.[4]

Everyone agrees that the Gedes are a family, and related to the Bawon Samdi. After that, no one can swear to the precise nature of that relationship. Sociologist Michel Laguerre says that the Bawon and Gran Brigitte (formerly a ritual prostitute) are the parents of all the Gedes and, together with their children, have surveillance over all the dead (1980, 95). André Pierre, Vodou artist and priest, essentially agrees with this genealogy. Pointing to the cross in his own yard, he explained that Gede served as 'Executive Secretary' to the Bawon (in conversation, 1987). Melville Herskovits, father of African and Caribbean studies in America, described the Bawon as a sort of evil amanuensis of Gede, a ghoulish dwarf dragging chains, with whom deals can be struck for the death or zombification of one's enemies:

> The Baron kills, but it is Gede who must dig the grave. He must consent to the judgment of death, and he is just. Even if the Baron has marked a victim, Gede can refuse to concur. 'If you do not merit death, Gede will refuse it,' say the Haitians. (1937, 247–48)

One measure of their contested relationship is laughter. Bawon Samdi never laughs or shows compassion. He leaves that sort of behavior to the Gedes, who constantly override his otherwise inexorable timetables. Another measure of their relationship is clothing. The Bawon is always in black, looking like a mortician, a politician, or a thirty-second degree Mason (all of which in fact he is!). When the Gedes manifest themselves in groups (something the other *lwa* never do), they look like refugees from some far-out revival of Sgt. Pepper's Lonely Hearts Club Band:

> The dominant colors of their outrageous outfits are purple and black, and they have powdered faces. They wear top hats, bowler hats, airplane pilots' hats. They wear two or three hats at a time, and they often put on dark glasses with one lens missing. Around their necks hang pacifiers and baby rattles; in their hands they carry wooden phalluses. With a coffin hoisted on their shoulders, bands of Gede stage mock funeral processions through the heart of the city. Flocks of Gede, sometimes accompanied by musicians, accost innocent bystanders. Women are surrounded and not released until they have paid the toll—a kiss on the lips for every Gede. Awkward young boys are talked into spending five cents to have a look at the secret in the cigar box—a Barbie doll with real pubic hair. (Brown 1991, 362)

As is apparent from the Barbie bush and wooden phalluses, the Gedes are goofily erotic. They crack dirty jokes, dance the *banda* (a pelvic rock similar to the Brazilian *lambada*), and generally do all they can to shock prudes and mock romantics. As sacred children (note their pacifiers and rattles), the Gedes merge with the dead and the other *lwa* to form the holy trinity of Vodou: *Les Morts, Les Mysteres, et Les Marasa*: the Dead, the Lwa, and the Sacred Children. Finding life and sexual sport in death, the Gedes have come to personify the resilience of the Haitian people; their mocking response to the misery delivered by society, history, and Bawon Samdi.

Being clowns, the Gedes find their funniest shtick in death. In his great Vodou inspired novel, *Continental Drift,* Russell Banks perfectly captures their graveyard routines:

> [Gede] leans wickedly on the jambs of the gate before the abyss, smokes his cigar, peers through sunglasses and in his reedy, nasal voice says, *You,* and *Not You,* and *You,* and *Not You.* He waves and pokes and even shoves you through the gate and over the abyss with his thick, stiff hickory stick, and then holds back with his stick you who are to stay on this side, lifting your skirt above your hips, if you are a woman, smacking his lips voraciously and poking the men and boys on their crotches and butts, turning his back and flipping the tails of his long black coat in a shameless prance. With his motley, his costumes and

> beggar's bowl, he derides worldly ambition; with his complaints about the exorbitant costs of keeping up his dynaflow, he parodies materialism. He dresses women as men, men as women, and asserts the insipidity of biology's brief distinctions. (1985, 369–370)

How is it that Haitians imagine death in such active ways, while we Angelenos try to pretend it never happened? Answers might be found by visiting Port-au-Prince on All Saints and All Souls Days (November 1 and 2). These Catholic holy days are also public holidays and, along with Carnival, are an excuse for some of the greatest binges of the year. Both days belong to the Samdi family, and are thus celebrated (sometimes in conjunction with Halloween on October 31) as a kind of Three Ring Circus for the Dead.

The first ring is the cemetery. The second is the *ounfo* (Vodou temple), which reserves the entire month of November to celebrate the family of Gede spirits. The last ring is *urbi et orbi*: the city and the world—the bars and brothels decorated with crepe streamers and Bela Lugosi masks; the *Ti Palais* (Presidential Palace); the Vodou healing centers; those overcrowded leaky boats which may or may not make it to Miami; the vibrant, mean streets where it is not unusual to pass Gede's ambling "horses," as those whose bodies are "ridden" (possessed) by any *lwa* are called. Gede's horses are apparent from their pimp-roll shuffle, and telltale Ray-Bans. All these places are his realms, for at this unpromising moment in the awful history of Haiti, Gede emerges from the cemetery as the most revealing personification of the *pep ayisan* (Haitian people). As Francis Huxley wrote:

> No other lwa is so close to man as Gede, for no others are so knowing, so active, and so intimate. The other lwa all idealize some part of man's nature, and thus have to have a heaven to live in, but the Gedes have no heaven other than the body of man, whether in the grave or out of it. (1966, 220)

Or as Mama Lola, the celebrated Brooklyn *manbo* (priestess) has testified, "Some people got Ogou. Some got Papa Danbala . . . not everybody. But everybody got Gede. *Everybody*!" (Brown 1991, 376).

CEMETERY MAN

> *Marley was dead to begin with. There is no doubt whatever about that. Old Marley was dead as a door nail. This must be distinctly understood, or nothing wonderful can come of the story I am going to tell.*
>
> Charles Dickens, *A Christmas Carol*

Maya Deren, a surrealist filmmaker and modern dancer, came to Haiti in the late 1940s to study dance ethnology. She wound up staying for three years, became a Vodou initiate, and wrote *Divine Horsemen*, perhaps the most eloquent book on the religion ever published in English. What Dickens knew about Marley, Deren came to know about Gede. If He were not dead—indeed not Death itself—then nothing wonderful could come of her tale:

> Gede is the dark figure which attends the meeting of the quick and the dead. This is the lwa who, repository of all the knowledges of the dead, is wise beyond all the others. And if the souls of the dead enter the depths by the passage of which Gede is guardian, the lwa and the life forces emerge from that same depth by the same road. Hence he is Lord of Life as well as of Death. His dance is the dance of copulation; in the chamber dedicated to his worship, the sculptured phallus may lie side by side with the three grave-diggers' tools. He is the protector of children and the greatest of divine healers. He is the final appeal against death. He is the cosmic corpse which informs man of life. The cross is his symbol, for he is the axis both of the physical cycle of generation and the metaphysical cycle of resurrection. He is the beginning and the end. (1953, 37ff)

Deren's account of a deity who is manifest in the most disparate things—death, copulation, dance, and healing—is reaffirmed by any number of contemporary witnesses. Regarding his cemetery connections, Gladys Maitre, *manbo*, doyenne of a cabal of Vodou hierarchs in Port-au-Prince, and my generous patron, observed, "In the cemetery you will see the Gede all over, but they stay in the cross. That is their place. When you wear your cross it can protect you from other things, but not from Gede. When you wear your cross, you always have Gede" (in conversation, 1987). Gede's provenance, however, should cause no fear, for as André Pierre explained, "Gede is your own parent. Your very own family. He is the god of death because it is in the cemetery where you find your own parents asleep" (in conversation, 1987). Indeed, Gede has become the most beloved *lwa*. Note the affection for this wild and crazy death guy randomly quoted from Mama Lola:

> Papa Gede is a cemetery man. He live in the cemetery, but that not mean he's bad. Sometime he say a bad word, but . . . he love everybody. He love to help people. When people sick—all [kinda] sickness—that's his job to help. . . . He very good man. He love children a lot. He love woman a lot. He a very sexy man. (Brown 1991, 330)

What can Lola mean? How can death be sexy? To most of us, linking death with sex is macabre, even oxymoronic, though as Georges Bataille argues, it may also be the most erotic of all metaphors:

> Eroticism, unlike simple sexual activity, is a psychological quest independent of the natural goal: reproduction and the desire for children. From this elementary definition let us now return to the formula I proposed in the first place: eroticism is assenting to life even in death. Indeed, although erotic activity is in the first place an exuberance of life, the object of this psychological quest . . . is not alien to death. Herein lies a paradox, that without further ado I shall try to give some semblance of justification to my affirmation with the following two quotations:
>
> *"Secrecy is, alas, only too easy,"* remarks de Sade, *"and there is not a libertine some little way gone in vice, who does not know what a hold murder has on the senses."*
>
> And it was the same writer who made the following statement, which is even more remarkable:
>
> *"There is no better way to know death than to link it with some licentious image."* (1986, 1)

Perhaps it is the intuitive genius of Haitians to recognize the doubleness of death in the various members of the Samdi family, to see Bawon as death's finality, and Gede as its generative possibility? [5] Not for nothing do Francophones (including Haitians) call orgasm *le petit mort* (the little death). In such a dichotomy, Bawon manifests death's apparent discontinuity and Gede its profound continuity, within the enduring cycles of (re)generation. Bataille again explains: "Discontinuous beings that we are, death means continuity of being. Reproduction leads to the discontinuity of beings, but brings into play their continuity; that is to say, it is intimately linked with death" (1986, 13). In light of this argument we may better appreciate why the phallus rises next to the funeral spade on Gede altars, or why all those black goats are lying dead on the floor at the end of a Gede ceremony:

> The victim dies and the spectators share in what his death reveals. That is what religious historians call the element of sacredness. The sacredness is the revelation of continuity through the death of a discontinuous being to those who watch it as a solemn rite. (Bataille 1986, 22)

What do these solemnities of death and generation have to do with Gede's various public obscenities? How do we account for his behavior in Mama Lola's Brooklyn basement, so hilariously described by Brown?

> *Msye Gede, Ti Malis Kache Bo Lakwa, Papa'm Te Rekonet Mwen, Gwo Zozo* . . . "If people don't remember my name," Gede whined, "I'm not going to stay!" And with that, he grabbed his walking stick—the one carved to look like a huge erect penis—and headed for the door. "No, no, Papa Gede, stay!" Then she giggled and said in a rush of words: "I mean, Mister-Gede-Little-Mischief-Hidden-Near-the-Cross-My-Father-Acknowledged-Me-Big-Cock . . . stay!"
>
> Halfway out the door, Gede wheeled around and planted his walking stick firmly on the floor. Spreading his legs to make the other two points of the tripod, Gede began to roll his hips in the lascivious dance step Haitians call the *gouyad.* "Little hole, little hole, little hole," he sang, "Big hole, big hole, big hole." The men whistled and hooted, and the women smiled. Soon everyone was swept into the simple, energetic song. With the roomful of people singing full voice, Gede took three little wide-legged jumps forward until the wooden phallus protruded directly from his crotch, and the song jumped to a new level, with a faster beat: "Little hole, little hole, little hole...." Just as abruptly as he had started, Gede stopped singing. He marched back into the center of the group, snapping his cane smartly under his arm. Then he poked it mischievously at a woman and asked her to hold his *zozo.*" (1991, 258)

Bataille again offers a complex rationale for such naughtiness:

> Obscenity is our name for the uneasiness which upsets the physical state associated with self-possession, with the possession of a recognised and stable individuality. . . . Eroticism always entails a breaking down of established patterns, the patterns . . . of the regulated social order basic to our discontinuous mode of existence as defined and separate individuals. (1986, 17–18)

André Pierre's explanation is much simpler, and goes more directly to the relationship between sex and laughter: "Why not? [Gede] only does in public what we all do in private" (in conversation, Croix-des-Missions, July 1986). It is the disjunction between the poetry of romance and the physics of intercourse that Gede finds so funny:

> Life for Gede is not the exalted creation of primal ardor; it is a destiny—the inevitable and eternal erotic in men. He is the lord of that eroticism which, being inevitable, is therefore beyond good and evil and is beyond the elations and despairs of love. Of this he is neither proud nor ashamed; if anything, he is amused by the eternal persistence of the erotic and by man's eternally persistent pretense that it is something else. (Deren 1953, 103)

On a quite drunken All Souls Day some years ago, my old friend Rodney Flambert offered a yet more graphic example of Gede's sense of humor. He asked if I had any idea what it might be like to make love to a Gede? I answered with a curious "No." He laughed as he remembered that once, halfway through his conquest of a new lover, she became possessed by Gede. Soon her sighs of love turned to the familiar and, under the circumstances, terrifying nasal laughter of Gede. Loudly enjoying the familiar in-and-out motion, Gede urged her now reluctant lover on to more vigorous performance in the grossest imaginable language. Master and mistress had changed places and Gede was thoroughly amused.[6]

In the immortal lyric of Tina Turner, we might then ask of Gede's sexuality, "What's love got to do with it?" If Gladys Maitre is right, the answer is "Not very much at all":

> Gede dance isn't sexual. It's funny. A way to make you laugh. When Gede doesn't want to dance, he get mad. He stays like that, looking at you and smoking. The dance is just to make people laugh. Because he know they love him, just because he says all those bad things. To make them get excited. You can't have Gede go after love, what are you going to do with all this pepper? So, he has nothing to say of love. Because some Gede come with pepper in the *clarin* (raw rum); they wash their face, all their body, with *clarin*. What can you do? Wash your face with pepper? Only a Gede can do that! But he can leave you with the pepper. Some Gedes always leave their horses with the pepper. So, he has nothing to say of love. (In conversation, Port-au-Prince, November 1987)

So the beast with two backs only serves to make Gede laugh. As the curtain raiser on all hypocrisies, Gede disdains naivete, even among innocent children whom he especially loves and protects:[7]

> It is reported from the North of Haiti that children are thought to be incapable of sin before they have had their first sexual experience. Why then the crude and pathetic custom carried out on the bodies of children who have died sinless? The corpse of a girl is deflowered with a stick, while the dead boy's penis is stretched up to his waist and there firmly tied in place. The parents, who have made their children guilty by this summary mimicking of sexual experience, do so for the best of reasons: it stops children from becoming little *diabs* and *diablesses*, phantoms who are so avid for pleasure that they seduce the living and abandon them, after a night of lascivious illusion, to awaken sprawled among the white graves of a cemetery. (Huxley 1966, 102)

Huxley's apparent shock at Gede's attitude towards infantile sexuality is often shared by other visitors to Haiti, as noted in Deren's acerbic observation: "Gede's unfailing discernment of attitudes toward sexuality accounts, I believe, for the sexual emphasis which visitors have found in vodou, for nothing will more quickly provoke Gede's appearance and his defiant, overt obscenities than the presence of white visitors, particularly those of Puritan tradition."[8]

Cemetery = death + sex + regeneration: this is the equation for which Gede is the only correlate. As much as we might try to unpack its apparent contradictions, we cannot. The elements conjoin in a single "root metaphor," as Sandra Barnes defined that term in her discussion of the Yoruba (and Haitian) god, Ogun:

> A root metaphor names the things that are likened to one another. The name gives the root metaphor permanence and therefore it can do its job many times over. When a psychiatrist says his patient is suffering from an Oedipus complex he can name and summarize what otherwise might take pages to explain, and he can use the label repeatedly. By the same token, when Haitian devotees call a despotic leader Ogou Panama, after a real figure, they condense into one label a complex historical essay on the uses and abuses of power. . . . By naming the metaphor, Haitians were free to augment its content. (1997, 20)

In a similar fashion, the root metaphor *Gede* glosses all his contrarious qualities, which nonetheless get summarized in the word "*balanse*":

> André Pierre . . . once used the word "balanse" when describing the death of a mutual friend. At first what he said puzzled—even shocked—me, but later I realized that his use of the word was a key to its meaning within Vodou. "Death came to our friend's door," Pierre said, and then laughed, "*Gede te balanse kay-sa!* [Gede balanced that house!]" Death shook everything up. And from the clash and commotion more life emerged, much as Gede uses his cemetery persona to add extra titillation to his sexual one, and vice-versa. André Pierre was saying that death actually enlivened our friend's house. (Brown 1995, 223)

THE FIRST RING: PORT-AU-PRINCE CEMETERY

Now let's cut to the Port-au-Prince cemetery on All Saints Day 1987. By dawn throngs are already gathered at its various tombs and shrines. Bits of cassava bread bob in rum puddles left at the cemetery crossroads, offerings to Legba, divine switchboard operator, who must open the barriers between the visible and invisible worlds before Gede (or any other *lwa*) can take flesh in the human world. A mass of supplicants is praying at the ossuary, where discarded bones remind the living of all the lost and nameless lineages of Africa.

The largest crowd is gathered around a huge concrete cross erected for the Samdi family in this and every Haitian cemetery. One by one, weeping, sucking on sequined rum bottles, or lewdly thrusting their pelvises in open invitation to Gede, supplicants reach out to add another tiny candle to those already sputtering all over the cross. Black and yellow rivers of wax have given the cross a gooey sheen, like frosting on a birthday cake at a party that has gone on too long. Some of the dripping wax has mixed with rum spilled as a libation. For despite his antics, Gede has a reputation as a good listener, whose practical and compassionate advice is often sought.[9] Having thus paid their graveyard greetings, supplicants will stream out of the cemetery, which is only the hub from which Gede emanates to every corner of the city. Many are headed towards the Vodou temples where birthday parties are already underway for all the members of the Samdi family.

THE SECOND RING: GEDE IN THE *OUNFO*

When Gede manifests at an *ounfo*, there is no mistaking his presence. He dons a top hat or threadbare "smoking jacket," but his favorite fashion accessory is sunglasses because they look cool, of course, and in his own way, Gede is very chic. There are also other reasons. Shades may help him see when he moves from the gloom of the grave to the glare of the temple. Sometimes his shades have only one lens. Some say one lens helps him to see both above and below the ground. Others say the glasses have one lens because the penis has one eye, and so Gede is also called "dickhead." Still others say the Ray-Bans are a put-on of the TonTon Macoutes, Duvalier's hated private militia, who favored shades as an essential part of their gangsta wardrobes.[10] These contradictory explanations are probably all true.

Gede may also have cotton stuffed up his nose, or a strip of linen around his chin, for he is corpse as well as gravedigger. From time to time, he may emit a gasping death rattle, or speak in the insinuating nasal voice favored by tricksters throughout the Black Atlantic world. He stinks. As Gladys Maitre says, "Gede don't smell nice. He smell like dead meat." His language is foul. He is a notorious liar, extremely insulting, and like tricksters everywhere, a glutton. He stuffs food into his mouth with both hands, washing it all down with his favorite drink—*clairin* (crude rum) steeped in twenty-one of the hottest spices known.[11] When he cannot put any more food in his stomach, he puffs on cigarettes and cigars. He is also accused of being a vagabond, shameless, a thief—but for all this, everyone seems to love him. When he manifests, the temple *ounsis* (initiates) sing:

Call him brave-o—he's a bold fellow
His banana butt is bold
His bit of chicken is bold
His cup of *clairin* is bold
His sweet potato bit is bold
I call Brave-Gede:
Come and Save the Children! (Metraux 1972, 115)

When they sing for him he does the *banda*, a dance of the hips which closely mimes sexual intercouse, and he may sing for them in return:

My dick says to my cherie's clit
Come and get it, my dick is hard
I spend the whole week working:
Monday, Tuesday, Wednesday, Thursday, Friday.
On Saturday, I give you money to buy some food.
On Sunday, I must fuck you all day long.[12]

At the *ounfo*, the Gedes manifest themselves *en famille*. At one such ceremony held in 1987, I witnessed the Bawon Samdi, holding his phallic cane like a baton, leading a troupe of Gedes through a martial display of bumps and grinds. This *ounfo* had been a favorite of Baby Doc; the crowds of onlookers up in the caged balcony were roaring in derision at this parody of the military that had replaced him. A few weeks later the army and Macoutes aborted the scheduled national election by massacring scores of voters at polls set up not very far from this *ounfo*. Evidently Gede had forseen it all.

The most famously celebrated of Gede's intrusions in the nation's political life came during the administration of President Borno (1922–1930). At the end of a long day of Gede ceremonies, celebrants sing and dance out of the cemetery and temples into the streets of Port-au-Prince. One such group of "horses" possessed by Nimbo, suavest of the Gede brothers, swept through the gates of the National Palace in their tails and top hats, waving hankies and intimidating police and pedestrians. They were demanding money from the President, who like many middle-class Haitians, was reputed to serve the *lwa* secretly. Unable to bear their cavorting and taunts, the hiding President Borno gave in and sent out money. Nimbo's political victory is remembered in a favorite Vodou song:

Papa Gede is a *bel garçon*
Gede Nimbo is a handsome chap,
When he's dressed all in black,
He resembles a senator,
For he is going up to the palace . . . (Deren 1953, 106)

Borno's successors learned little from Gede's laughter. As the power of authority has grown more arbitrary, cruel, and coercive through the Duvalier years (1957–1986) and the nightmare military regimes which followed, Gede's popularity on the streets has only increased. As state authority has refined its mechanisms of oppression, so too has Gede sharpened his flip-off of established authority into elemental, and often hilarious, manifestations of the common contempt for brummagem civility. Since the police have become regular agents of social oppression, Gede's role has increasingly become associated with the antics of social rebellion: vagrancy, pilfering, lewd and lascivious behavior, public drunkeness, impersonating officers of the state and priests of official religions, practicing medicine without a license. . . . The list goes on, but the point is clear. The Gedes are bums, louts, even outlaws, and they are all the more popular for their bad manners.

Given the oppositional character the Gedes have come to play in Haitian life, we should not be surprised to learn that the other holiday devoted to their antics is Carnival, the feast of reversals, the time when the world is turned upside down. Nor should we be surprised that the one politician Gede has championed in the streets is Jean-Bertrand Aristide, the anti-candidate, who urged his hordes of hungry supporters to go up the hill to Petionville (Port-au-Prince's wealthy suburb) and help themselves to the larders of the MREs (Haiti's "Morally Repugnant Elites"). Politically, Gede and his son, Aristide, are both Jacobins, motivated and justified by Lenin's famous query, "What is the crime of robbing a bank, compared to that of owning one?"

THE THIRD RING: *URBI ET ORBI*

It was February 1991, and Port-au-Prince was in a mood to celebrate. Jean-Bertrand Aristide, Catholic priest and street fighter against Baby Doc's dictatorship (1971–1986) had just been elected President by a landslide in Haiti's first ever democratic election (December 1990). Cynics in the hilltop mansions attributed his startling victory to the "E.T. factor": black and bony with a droopy eye, "Titid" (as everyone calls him by the Kreyol diminutive) was so homely you just had to love him. Yet the streets were euphoric. All over town Carnival revelers were wearing *kok kalite* (red rooster) masks. The *kok* is a symbol of Titid's political party; all his political posters juxtaposed his face to that of the rooster. There were many flocks of rooster masks parading the streets of Port-au-Prince.

Like all great romances, this one had utterly heinous monsters to confront the hero. Roger Lafontant, one of the Duvalier old-timers called "dinosaurs," had rallied the Ton Ton Macoutes for a preemptive coup against Titid. Mme. Ertha Pascal-Trouillot, the acting president, went on radio with unseemly haste to announce her surrender to the dinosaurs. Titid went into hiding. The streets exploded. Furious mobs rooted out and sometimes murdered suspected coup supporters. Then, for once following the wishes of the people, the army arrested Lafontant. So on February 6, Titid's inauguration was celebrated in the pink-and-cream colored Cathedral whose clam-shaped towers are laughingly called the twin vaginas. The horrified elite looked on at the Te Deum Mass while ecstatic crowds pressed at the church doors and hung from the concrete limbs of the outdoor crucifix shouting "*Yo sezi; Yo sezi!*" ("They are shocked; They are shocked!").

Three days later Carnival began. Satin-clad harlequins whipped the ground. Mulatto beauty queens threw rose petals from their electrified floats. The *negs* (common folk) threaded about the floats, re-enacting scenes from the recent crises which had become the national soap opera. A loony-looking couple dressed in tattered tux and wedding gown stood under a satin umbrella. It was an ersatz Baby Doc and Michelle Bennett, his bourgeois wife, re-celebrating the disastrous marriage that helped bring down the dictatorship. Close by, a bald-headed Lafontant look-alike marched with a group of mock Macoutes in their red scarves and Ray-Bans, cradling cardboard uzis. Intermittently, amidst these diverse groups, Gede would pop up, his face all white except for the Ray-Bans. Mr. Bones in top hat and smoking jacket; the bogus pol bumping and grinding with all the other revellers celebrating the election of his child as President of Haiti.

Titid was of course the hero of the carnival. Bedraggled red roosters hung from the standards of many marching bands. Often the *kok* was held over the *pentard* (guinea fowl), national symbol of the 1791 revolution against France, which had been co-opted as the standard for the Duvalier regime. In the earthy idiom of Carnival song, Mme. Pascal-Trouillot, the last President, was mocked as "Mama Caca" (Mother Shit):

Ertha Pascal-Trouillot,
Mama Caca,
Look how you let the *pentard*,
Into the national roost.

On a wooden platform across from the Presidential Palace a signboard had been painted with all these same characters from the political circus. Lafontant was tied up nude to a pole. His *zozo* (penis) was also bound with cords. Trouillot, her *coco* (vagina) hugely magnified, was bent over and bare for the dive-bombing *kok kalite.* Carnival symbols are not subtle.

Counterposed to the mock politicians in the little street dramas were more familiar monsters. At first I thought I was watching play-Arabs dressed in sheets and pancaked white faces. A parody of the Gulf War being played on CNN? Then I saw the familiar black top hat tugging the rope that bound these hapless "Arabs": Bawon Samdi. Then I noticed the skeleton by his side carrying the coffin: Gede. It was *Le Troupe Zombie,* raucously mixing the ghouls of Haitian folklore with celluloid phantasms from Hollywood. Haitians are bemused by American fascination with zombies, who constitute only a small class of their mythological *bakas* (monsters). If Americans want to buy these beliefs, Haitians don't mind selling them. Herard Simon, a Vodou strongman instrumental in procuring the puffer fish "*zonbi* medicine," which Wade Davis made famous in his adventure-documentary, *The Serpent and the Rainbow,* laughed as he told me, "We sold [Wade] the plans for the B-25, but we kept the F1-11 secret."

Following *Le Troupe Zombie* came the Chaloskas, monsters with huge red lips and great buck teeth. They also wore eye masks, big hats, and Sgt. Pepper military regalia, and chased each other and the laughing crowds with waving sticks. I first saw the Chaloskas in Jonathan Demme's brilliant film, *Haiti Dreams of Democracy.* Demme caught them performing in the 1987 Jacmel Carnival. They were wearing the same mad military gear, said to be in imitation of a nineteenth-century general.[13] Yet the objects of their satire were clearly contemporary. Marching around in a half-assed goose step, the demented Chaloskas sang, "There are no Macoutes in this troupe." In the inverted logic of Carnival, their denial affirmed their identity.

The honcho Chaloska then pulled out a notebook and barked indictments to his peons, "You are accused of telling the truth . . ."

And they brayed back through their big buck teeth, "*Wawawawawawawa,*" like a stand of donkeys.

The general shouted, "You are accused of not kissing our ass."

And the peons responded, "*Wawawawawawawa.*"

I recognized the interrogation. Maya Deren describes the Bawon Samdi lining up his idiot Gede children and instructing them in human ways, "I love, you love, he loves—what does that make?" Like dutiful schoolboys the Gedes responded, "L'amoouuurrr." I, too, had seen the Gedes line up at Gesner's temple. Holding his phallic cane like a baton, the Bawon led a troupe of Gedes through a martial display, every few steps pausing to execute a bump and grind. The brass band hired for the ceremony was playing "Jingle Bells." The audience upstairs in the balcony kept the martial tempo by chanting, "*Zozo, Zozo, Zozo.*"

Zozo means cock, and it means fuck, and everyone—men and women, sweaty faced, laughing hard—was shouting it in Carnival. Just as every character, political, military or celestial, stripped of his pretenses is an avatar of Gede, so finally is every motive and every action reduceable to *zozo.* Not *l'amooooour,* or *la vie,* or even *l'honneur,* only *Zozo.* Gede may be foul-mouthed, but he is the sworn enemy of euphemism. He lives beyond all ruses. He is master of the two absolutes: fucking and dying. Group after group danced down the Rue Capois, singing the grossest of his anti-love songs:

When you see a smart ass chick,
Pick her up and throw her down,
Pull down her pants,
And give her *zozo* . . . .wowowo!

One could wonder that women as well as men were shouting the misogynist lyrics, but Gede rides women as well as men. Among the Fon of Dahomey, whose descendants brought Vodou to Haiti, it is young women who strap the dildos on in masquerade. *Zozo* means cock no doubt, but what else does it signify? Is the *zozo* a flip off of established order? Of *la misère*? The antidote of life in death? Since everything is reduceable to Gede, and Gede cannot lie, he makes it possible to laugh even at the most terrible things. With Gede everything enters Carnival, even AIDS (SIDA), the viral crossroads of both his domains. Thus the marchers in "Kontre SIDA" sang:

Oh Mama, lock up my dick,
So I won't fuck a trick,
If I fuck, I'll get AIDS
So go fuck your Mama's ass!

Troupe "Kontre SIDA" marked their lyrics with the *banda,* Gede's bump and grind. One young reveler waltzed around with a rubber dildo on his head. Another was waving a wooden *zozo* from a Gede shrine with a condom rolled over it. The temptation of course was to say, "Oh, this is Haiti," but it would be truer to say, "This is Carnival." Celebrated with as gross a humor as Rabelais' jokes about syphilis (the AIDS of the Renaissance) in *Gargantua,* this is the real festival of reversals, not the packaged goo from New Orleans. In this new age of pandemics and holy wars I was glad to be there, looking at the underside of things.

I watched the last hours of Mardi Gras on TV at the bar of the Olaffson, the absurdly turreted Charles Addamsish hotel made famous by Graham Greene in his novel *The Comedians.* I had been roughed up on the streets, had my pocket picked, had been shoved away from the balcony of the Holiday Inn, where the photojournalists and tourists were shooting film. So I went back to the Olaffson and watched the rest of the affair on the tube. It was nice: the froufrou of rum punches complementing the images on the screen. Bourgeois floats sailing by with their mulatto crews, oblivious to the black, saucy street ensembles swirling in and out about them. All those Kreyol *negs* moving to the same *zozo* songs I heard at a Gede ceremony just before the 1987 Massacre. Carnival and Vodou ceremony, both for Gede; even explicitly so. The TV screen panning the crowds in front of the Holiday Inn suddenly split, and the lead singer of *Boucan Guinée* appeared in the white face of Gede Nimbo, most dapper of Bawon's children. He sang what was the theme song of the 1991 Carnival, "*Pale . . . Pale* " ("You Talk and Talk"):

> You talk and talk and talk and talk;
> But when you finish talking,
> When you stop, I'm still here. And
> from the ground, I'll come out.
> And from the ground, I'll walk around . . . .

Boucan's image and the corpse of Gede merged with all the Carnival revelers on TV. Laughing, groping, pickpocketing, fighting, goosing, puking, guzzling, dancing, dying: Gede then and now and everywhere. In this poorest country in the New World, misery becomes a trope for three days. The dinosaurs and Macoutes, the *zonbi* and the Chaloskas are defanged by Gede and a chorus of the laughing people. Finally, at 5 A.M. on Ash Wednesday, the vanities of Carnival are thrown into a giant bonfire in front of City Hall. Ashes for Gede . . . to start again.[14]

GEDE BALLYHOO

Gede on television; how perfect. All the Samdi family is used to ballyhoo. There was Papa Doc's patronage of course, his embarrassing attempts to look, act, and intimidate just like the Bawon. Rachel Beauvoir-Dominique (1995, 411) describes a cabinet meeting where Papa Doc dumped three buckets of white powder over his head, and conducted the entire session as the solemn and poised Bawon Samdi, terrifying the ministers with his nasalized intonations. "It was the same Bawon who, as chief of Vodou death divinities, presides over the realm of death and transfiguration: he who is asked to 'take the brats who insult elders to the cemetery' and who also leads to the 'divine' knowledge of self: *konnen moun yo, konnen bondye* (know man, know god)."[15]

Long before Papa Doc's copycat outfits, foreign observers had written fevered accounts of the Gedes: Herskovits, Hurston, Courlander, Deren, Metraux, to mention only the serious scholars, had all been transfixed by the Gedes' contrarious behaviors. Novelists Thomas Sanchez (*Mile Zero*), Russell Banks (*Continental Drift*), and William Gibson (*Count Zero*) had likewise created Bawon Samdi protagonists to preside over fictive American apocalypses. Then Karen Brown concluded her celebratory meta-biography of *Mama Lola,* the Vodou priestess in Brooklyn, with an ultimate chapter devoted to Gede, as I had the ultimate chapter of *The Sacred Arts of Haitian Vodou.*

That was just the writers. How much more flattering to the Gede family was the ancient adolescent Mick Jagger leaping around the "Voodoo Lounge" video in the frayed tuxedo of the Bawon Samdi. Or Bobby Brown in Ray-Bans and top hat humping the floor, while the chorus chanted "Do it, do it, do it" on *Saturday Night Live.* Before Gede's TV debut, there was the Bawon riding Geoffrey Holder in *Live and Let Die.* Who can forget his white powdered face laughing at James Bond in the movie's last frames? Or the grotesque portrayal of the Baronesque chief of police in Wes Craven's new age zombie flick, *The Serpent and the Rainbow.* All these foreign scholars, writers, and artists are only picking up what every Vodouist knows: Gede has become at once the closest and most revealing personification of the *pep ayisan* at century's turning.

His ubiquity is mirrored in the staggering array of imagery Gede has appropriated. Most commonly he is saluted in the chromolithographs of Gabriel and Gerard, both handsome young saints in black clerical dress. Posed before skulls and lily sprays, they look pallid, even anemic.

Sucked of their blood by one of Anne Rice's 300-year-old Caribbean vampires? Virginal seminarians ravished by Lestat? These saints are Hollywood poster-boys for Death, victims of the lecherous Tom Cruise in *Interview with a Vampire.* Such stagey surrogates must flatter Gede, or make him roar with laughter. So, too, must the plastic bust of the Star Wars villain, Darth Vader, complete with red light bulb glowing under his lowered visor, which has been set up as his shrine by celebrated Port-au-Prince and Miami flag maker Clotaire Bazile. Across from Vader, on the door leading to a private room where Bazile keeps Gede's coffin, is a life-size painting of rap star M. C. Hammer, wearing sunglasses and a very righteous Nation of Islam hat: Hip-Hop Gede.

He's everywhere. As Karen Brown notes, "Gede, like a sponge, absorbs whatever is new on the social horizon. There is a Gede who is a dentist, and one who is an auto mechanic, and now there is even a Protestant missionary" (1991, 376). Of course he has acquired AIDS, the disease du jour. Recent Carnivals in Jacmel have paraded Papa Gede HIV in a wheelbarrow with an IV drip attached to his arm, on life support but no doubt looking to score with someone in the crowd. In some *ounfos* December 25 is now celebrated as the Bawon's birthday, the cemetery soul dispatcher having found a congenial mate in the *Jezy* of the French missionaries. The parallel is obvious, as André Pierre observed, "What is the message of Jesus to the Vodouists but Death which makes Life on Earth so dear?" (in conversation, 1987). That other mythic figure from Noël has also been gobbled up by the Samdi family. In the inner chamber of the Temple St. Nicholas near Port-au-Prince there is a small field of crosses, some surmounted by skulls. In a far corner of this faux-cemetery is a lifesize plastic statue of Santa Claus. Good old St. Nick in his red suit, but wearing the same embroidered black sombrero I'd seen the Gedes wear in other temples and at the cemetery, presiding over this strange altar to himself.

How to sum up this confounding god, this conflation of incommensurables? A *New Yorker* cartoon by Gahan Wilson may come as close as anything written or said to the heart of the mystery. Wilson pictures a little guy dancing on a proscenium stage. He's wearing a candy- striped coat and boater hat; heels clicking in midair while he holds his cane at a jaunty angle. Before him is a sea of grim reapers: skulls uplifted, shrouded in black, each carrying his scythe. The poor vaudevillian is dancing and clowning before this truly hopeless audience. The subscript neatly summarizes his plight, "The sudden sure knowledge that one's best efforts have come to naught." Or as Don Marquis sang of his celebrated literary cockroach Archy:

> Sing your faith in what you
> get to eat right up to the
> minute you are eaten
> for you are going
> to be eaten.

Each of those skeletons is one of the thousand miseries of Haiti, as well as our general inescapable mortality. Before them all the clown dances like Haitians dance at Carnival, in the cemetery, in their temples; like the way Gede seems to be clicking his heels and laughing in the wonderful flag André Pierre fabricated for him (figure 1). Gede is both that old heel-clicker and all the skeletons before him. They'll grab him, no matter what, and he won't stop laughing. What a metaphor! What a reality!

Figure 1. Flag by André Pierre. Photo by Dennis Nervig. From the collection of the UCLA Fowler Museum of Cultural History (FMCH X87.19).

PART FOUR

Popular Culture

10

DANCING SKELETONS
The Subversion of Death Among Deadheads[1]

Luanne K. Roth

"WHO ARE THE GRATEFUL DEAD, ANYWAY, AND WHY DO THEY KEEP FOLLOWING ME?"

> Time is like a handful of sand. The tighter you grasp it, the faster it runs through your fingers. But if you caress it, it will leave in its wake memories of its gentle flow, rather than the roughness of its stones. (anonymous Deadhead)[2]

It was early the morning of August third, commonly known to Deadheads as "the day the music died." Grabbing my bags, about to dash off to work, I heard one fragment of the morning radio news, something about Jerry Garcia—and heart failure. Immediately, my phone began to ring as panic-stricken Deadheads called their Deadhead "families" to determine if this time the rumors were "really true." "It was a long strange trip," sobbed one young Deadhead over the radio, personalizing a Grateful Dead song lyric, "but not nearly long enough."

Until Garcia died, the Grateful Dead (a.k.a. "The Dead") toured the country year round, playing wildly improvisational music, and drawing hundreds of thousands—if not millions—of followers who began calling themselves "Deadheads," or just "Heads" for short, in the 1970s (Ruhlmann 1990, 43). Deadheads followed the Grateful Dead to hear their favorite band, dance to live music, and hang out with other "cool" Deadhead-type people. What started out as a small community of fans in the mid-to-late 1960s evolved into a large, self-sustained subculture, replete with its own language, art, dance, economy, politics, and sense of spirituality. Via interviews with many Deadheads, I found that their *raison d'etre* involved one or more Deadhead traditions, including the music, the Dead community, and the dancing. Regardless of which element was more prominent for a particular Deadhead, or which served as the original attraction to the movement, there was an undeniably profound transformative experience which occurred at Dead shows that kept many followers coming back for more (Shenk and Silberman 1994; Jackson 1992; Brightman 1998). Consider Joseph Campbell's reaction published in Deadhead Blair Jackson's *Goin' Down The Road: A Grateful Dead Traveling Companion*:

> Mythologist Joseph Campbell, who'd never been to a rock concert before attending, at the age of eighty, a 1986 Dead show, "got it" immediately—he saw the rapture in the faces of Deadhead dancers and knew that he had stumbled upon a modern-day Dionysian revel. This wasn't just rock 'n' roll—it was an unselfconscious celebration of life manifested in music and dance and community. He later declared that the spirit exemplified by the Dead and their fans represented, in human terms, "an antidote to the atom bomb." (Jackson 1992, x)

Before there were Deadheads, there were "Dead Freaks," early fans of the band who were invited by Jerry Garcia—via an advertisement on the inside cover of the 1971 album *Skull and Roses*—to join a mailing list. The announcement read: "DEAD FREAKS UNITE. Who are you? Where are you? How are you? Send us your name and address and we'll keep you informed" (Shenk and Silberman 1994, 56–7). Deadhead Paul Grushkin explains that as a result of this announcement:

> The letters poured in from everywhere—all 50 states and many foreign countries. In early 1972, just prior to the band's first major tour of Europe, the Dead responded with the first official *DeadHeads Newsletter*. Bearing messages both diffuse and succinct, it provided the basis of an irregular pattern of keeping thousands of inquisitive souls up-to-date on the Grateful Dead. (Grushkin, Bassett, and Grushkin 1983, xii)

Defining what it means to be a Deadhead today is no simple feat. Deadheads are an extremely heterogeneous group of people, although ironically they generally share the same ethnicity. Deadheads Shenk and Silberman write, "Though the Grateful Dead river is fed by many streams of African music (R&B, jazz, the blues), and the Drums are energized by the spirits of Latin congeros and Japanese taiko drummers, many have noticed that the Deadhead community itself is predominantly, though not exclusively, Caucasian" (1994, 65). While the majority derive from Euro-American backgrounds, they vary widely in terms of religious orientations, educational levels, class levels, and degree of devotion to and involvement with the Grateful Dead. Although they are generally ethnically homogeneous, their behavior suggests otherwise—displaying numerous beliefs and traditions borrowed from other cultures. In fact, Deadheads mirror the band itself, primarily composed of Caucasian individuals (except Garcia, of Hispanic ethnicity) who actively value and appropriate the traditions of other cultural groups.

Of course, not every person who frequents Grateful Dead shows considers him or herself a Deadhead. Even among Deadheads, a continuum of emic classifications or degrees of Deadheadness appear, distinguishing between "professional" Heads who live on tour (e.g., who have no other homes to which they return in between tours), those who maintain homes and jobs outside of their touring schedule, and "amateurs" who attend an occasional show (Shenk and Silberman 1994, 291–2).[3] Many so-called Heads differ on the philosophical issue of whether being a Deadhead is "a lifestyle, a set of progressive social values, a religion, or strictly a musical preference" (Shenk and Silberman 1994, 60). There are many people who would be called "Deadheads" by most standards because they spend a considerable amount of time and energy with the movement, although the individuals deny such an identity. "Yeah, I see shows," many have said, "but I'm not really a Deadhead." Whether feeling inadequate for the title, resistant to any labels or classifications, or hesitant to accept the "negative" stereotypes that often accompany it, many "Deadheads" do not label themselves Deadheads, although behaviorally, they are practically the same. David Shenk comments in his 1994 introduction to *Skeleton Key: A Dictionary for Deadheads*, "If there's one thing this extraordinary American ethnic group/religion/subculture is, it is *inviting* [emphasis in original]" (xiv). Definitions of the term "Deadhead" as a voluntary identity, of course, vary greatly. This very discussion about exactly what constitutes a Deadhead could continue *ad infinitum*; in fact, Grateful Dead Merchandising has even copyrighted the term. For the purposes of this analysis, though, I use the term Deadhead as Shenk and Silberman have done, simply to refer to "Someone who loves—and draws meaning from—the music of the Grateful Dead and the experience of Dead shows, and builds community with others who feel the same way" (1994, 60).

Clearly, Deadheads are more than just fans of the Grateful Dead; they are people who have ritualized the process by which they draw meaning from the Grateful Dead's music, as well as their traditions of communal lifestyle, artistic expression, transformations reached through the music, dance, and drug use (often referred to in religious terms among

Deadheads as "sacraments"). Furthermore, Deadheads have created close-knit communities with others who feel similarly, creating a distinct subculture that embraces a unique worldview most ingeniously expressed through the art, iconography, and symbols of its members, much of which remains cleverly coded from outsiders, while functioning emically as in-group identifiers. Most outside observers, and especially insiders, agree that something spiritual and even religious occurs at Dead shows. In this vein, sociologist Rebecca Adams explores the meaning of the commonly used phrase "getting it":

> On one level . . . 'getting it' is understanding shows as spiritual experiences, though Deadheads are quick to point out that many people 'get it' in places other than at a Grateful Dead show. On another level, 'getting it' is perceiving these spiritual experiences as inseparable from the music, the scene, and a cooperative mode of everyday existence. (Quoted in Shenk and Silberman 1994, 105–6)

In fact, terms like "ritual," "church," "vision," "sacred," "sacrament," and "myth" are used emically by Deadheads to describe their behavior and the community experience.

"NOT ALL WHO WANDER ARE LOST": DEADHEAD SACRED HISTORY AND NARRATIVES

My discussion begins with some of the more influential parts of a grossly abbreviated Deadhead history—starting with the Beat Generation and early hippie culture, and leading to the Merry Pranksters and the Acid Tests. While tracing these vital historical events points to continuities in traditional behavior among current Deadheads, this discussion also demonstrates that Deadheads have not just blindly accepted traditions handed down from their hippie predecessors, but have reworked them, retaining elements of some, innovating upon elements of some, and casting aside others. By retelling the epistemological stories, Deadheads are effectively reenacting what I call a "sacred narrative." Through their current rituals of community, dance, music, material culture, and psychedelic "sacraments," Deadheads continue to recreate a mythological sacred space and time.[4]

While many observers note the Beat Generation of the 1950s as a cultural influence on 1960s counterculture, most fail to include the Harlem Renaissance (1916–1940) or the jazzy hipness of the 1940s as precursors to both the Beats and the hippies. In this neglect, observers also fail to adequately acknowledge the diversity of ethnic and cultural influences that led to the Grateful Dead, and to the development of today's Deadhead subculture. The Beat Generation, and the anti-war movement that arose simultaneously, both "influenced in great part by the African-American movement" (Baraka 1994, 4), fit into this general reaction against the conservative, pro-war period. Alternative ideas were set in motion that disrupted these conservative forces—especially those of class privilege and racial supremacy. Baraka states:

> On one hand there was the group of largely petty bourgeois white youth who were called the Beat Generation, who claimed to rebel against the complacent mediocre hypocrisy of American life. This middle-class rebellion appeared in literature heralded by Allen Ginsberg's poem *Howl*. The so-called Beats, along with other young American poets... challenged the polished ready-made academic poetry as lifeless and socially irrelevant. They also challenged the American petty bourgeois lifestyle with their varied versions of mid-twentieth-century American bohemia. (1994, 1–2)

Commonly called "The Beat Generation," or just "the Beats," the bohemian counterculture of the 1950s served as predecessors to the hippie counterculture of the 1960s, an intrinsic factor in the evolution of hippie culture. A number of continuities can be gleaned by examining some elements of the Beat poets, the counterculture that grew up around them, and other figures intrinsic in the eventual development of Deadhead culture. The story always begins with the legends of Neal Cassady and Jack Kerouac. Beat member John Holmes describes this in "The Philosophy of the Beat Generation":

> It was Kerouac's insistence that they were on a quest, and that the specific object of their quest was spiritual. Though they rushed back and forth across the country on the slightest pretext, gathering kicks along the way, their real journey was inward; and if they seemed to trespass most boundaries, legal and moral, it was only in the hope of finding a belief on the other side. (1967)

"The Beat Generation," Kerouac himself said, "is basically a religious generation" (Holmes 1967). Members of the so-called Beat Generation drew upon numerous cultural traditions that represented exotic and alternative ways of seeing and being—such as the jazzy hipness and coolness of African-American culture. The practice of drawing upon other cultural traditions, as well as the idea of experiencing everyday life as "sacred," which were vital characteristics of the Beats, continue to be visibly important today within Deadhead behavior. Deadheads view the Beats as spiritual adventurers, upon which the Merry Pranksters, and their own lifestyle, are based.

Deadhead sacred narratives recount this journey, starting in the 1940s, and evolving into the Beat Generation of the 1950s. Beat members "hung out" in a string of coffeehouses in San Francisco—the paths of which led inexorably to the Grateful Dead.[5]

> Escaping through a lily field,
> I came across an empty space
> It trembled and exploded,
> Left a bus stop in its place.
> The bus came by and I got on,
> That's when it all began.
> There was Cowboy Neal at the wheel
> Of a bus to Never Ever Land.[6]

These lyrics from the Grateful Dead song "The Other One" refer to the legend of "Cowboy Neal," a.k.a. Neal Cassady, one of the Beats and early hero of the Deadhead sacred narrative.[7] The lyrics recount the band's legendary origins, which has had profound effects on the Deadhead movement today. Like the lyrics of many Grateful Dead songs, these reference a vital part of the history of Deadheads, a history that is considered sacred and is still reenacted and reinterpreted thirty and forty years later. The story can be regarded as part of the sacred narrative because it represents Deadhead mythology, shaping Deadhead worldview and functioning etiologically, explaining how things came to be as they are in the Deadhead world. Cassady was a crucial hero in the story, his life having a domino effect on those around him. The story of the Merry Pranksters and the Electric Kool-Aid Acid Tests is also important, because it articulates the context out of which "the scene" evolved, and because, like many other Deadhead narratives, it emphasizes the dynamic of a perceived serendipitous force influencing events.

"There were the freaks, one step from the Beats," explains a Deadhead about the early hippies (Brightman 1998, 99). A number of social and political events occurring in the 1960s influenced young radicals, eliciting revolutionary reactions from the early hippies. Brightman explains:

> One cannot re-create the era out of which the Grateful Dead emerged without recalling civil rights and the Free Speech Movement, Vietnam, the Cuban Revolution, and Weathermen. But reviewing this history also reminds us that when this "Sixties band" lifted off into the 1970s, '80s, and '90s, it left a good deal behind. (1998, 8)

Deadhead narratives, however, usually do not mention these social/political issues, focusing instead on those specific events that seem to have more directly impacted the development of their subculture. Such events include the following, which appeared in a pamphlet accompanying "Dead On The Wall," an exhibit of Deadhead art:

> 1) The Beatles: The Beatles single-handedly rescued rock and roll from its doldrums and, above all, demonstrated that playing rock music could be incredibly fun. . . .
>
> 2) The Haight-Ashbury: the San Francisco neighborhood bordering Golden Gate Park . . . [was] from 1964–66 . . . a laboratory for a new humane social order based on the shared enjoyment of art, music, psychedelics, and the spirituality and sensuality of daily life.
>
> 3) The Diggers: One of the first communes in the original Haight-Ashbury, and very influential in shaping the hippie ethos that was the rootstock of Deadhead culture. . . . The Diggers kept the pre-Summer of Love Haight fed and clothed by scoring food from local supermarkets and restaurants. . . .
>
> 4) The Acid Tests: Events hosted by novelist Ken Kesey and the Merry Pranksters in the Bay Area and Los Angeles in '65 and '66, featuring improvised music, strobes and black lights, films and projections, tape loops, hidden microphones, and LSD—which was still legal—dissolved into Kool-Aid. . . .
>
> 5) The Be-In: A "gathering of tribes" held on January 14, 1967, in the Polo Field of Golden Gate Park, featuring numerous musicians, including the Grateful Dead. The Be-In was conceived by San Francisco Oracle editor Allen Cohen as an "ecstatic union of love and activism.". . .
>
> 6) Woodstock: The Aquarian Music and Art Fair, "three days of peace and music," the archetype of the outdoor rock concert as tribal gathering . . . of the postwar generation announcing their presence in the world by sheer force of numbers—an audience of 400,000—as champions of peace, community, spirituality, spontaneity, self-determination, and fun. What the Be-In was to the Haight, Woodstock was to the world.[8]

While Deadheads include the above events in their sacred narrative, they focus mainly on those involving Ken Kesey, the Merry Pranksters, and the Acid Tests. In 1965, with the proceeds made from the publication of his book *One Flew Over the Cuckoo's Nest,* Kesey and a group of free-spirited friends bought a 1939 International Harvester school bus, painted it a myriad of psychedelic designs, equipped it with interior and exterior sound systems, as well as sleeping quarters, and began to tour the country—piloted by Cowboy Neal (a.k.a. Neal Cassady). Calling themselves "The Merry Pranksters," they dressed in circuslike clothing and took great pleasure in putting on shows wherever they went, "playing tricks" on people and acting silly. They called their traveling home "Furthur," deliberately spelled to suggest traveling, and "trips" of both geographical, spiritual, and psychedelic realms. The Pranksters met the Grateful Dead (then called the Warlocks) through Kesey and Cassady. They collaborated on a series of adventurous experiments called the "Acid Tests" (Wolfe 1968).

The Acid Tests, hosted by Kesey and the Merry Pranksters in the San Francisco Bay Area and Los Angeles in 1965 and 1966, provided a way of introducing LSD, which was still legal at the time, to the rest of the world.[9] The object and purpose of these "mind-altering free-for-alls" was to push the limits of everything—including ideas about art, music, philosophy and the meaning of life. Jackson asserts they were named "'Test,' because acid [a.k.a. LSD] brought you to that . . . edge . . . psychic whitewater; to pass it was to stay in the moment, the beautiful or fierce or ecstatic or terrifying or peaceful moment that is the only golden road" (1983, 95). The purpose of the tests, according to Jackson, was to stretch the imagination. The following ethnographic excerpts from several Deadheads writing about the Acid Tests help illustrate the environment reenacted later at Grateful Dead shows. For instance, Jackson explains:

> The basic philosophy of the Acid Tests was that everything was permitted; involvement was encouraged. This meant that people would mill about freely, walk up to microphones and talk or sing into them if they felt like it. Unusual clothing was practically *de rigueur* [italics in original], with Kesey, his cohort Babbs and other Pranksters often leading the way by donning superhero costumes and other strange attire. . . . "Anything was okay" [Garcia commented]. "The Acid Tests were thousands of people, all hopelessly stoned, all finding themselves in a roomful of other thousands of people, none of whom any of them were afraid of." (1983, 55)

In a similar vein, Shenk and Silberman describe the events:

> Admission was a dollar, even for the musicians, and "everyone was involved," explains Dick Latvala, the Dead's tape archivist. "It wasn't 'audience' and 'performer'—those distinctions were deliberately blurred. *You* are *it* [emphasis in original], you are the experience you're witnessing—that was what it was all about." And "it" often lasted until dawn.
>
> The musicians—including assorted Pranksters, and the Grateful Dead [then the Warlocks]—played for hours, or just a few minutes. Neal Cassady . . . was often the "announcer," space-rapping alone or in tandem with Wavy Gravy,[10] or dancing, while Ken Kesey, dressed like Captain America, played a kazoo, or made apocalyptic noises on the Thunder Machine.[11]. . . People crawled on the floor, stirred fingers in Day-Glo paints and pressed their hands to the walls, tossed toilet paper streamers that fluttered down in the strobe lights, and glued jewels and sequins to each other's faces, while [Grateful Dead singer] Pigpen riffed down-and-dirty on "Midnight Hour," or [Prankster] Ken Babbs delivered a rap about going into orbit. . . .
>
> Flyers passed out in advance and at the door said, "Can You Pass the Acid Test??" "Passing the Acid Test," Stewart Brand says simply, "meant lasting all night." (1994, 4–5)

This notion of "passing the Acid Test" basically represents a ritual initiation into the movement, one that continues to be ritually reenacted in present Deadhead culture. "In the wildest hipster, making a mystique of bop, drugs, and the night life," Beat novelist Holmes observed in the 1950s, "there is no desire to shatter the 'square' society in which he lives, only to elude it. To get on a soapbox or write a manifesto would seem to him absurd" (1967, 22). Brightman connects this Beat philosophy to the Merry Pranksters' political style, saying:

> The wildest Prankster behaved the same way—unless he stepped forth, as Kesey had at the Berkeley teach-in, to kick over the soapbox. Why strive to change the structure of the puny environment in which you're stuck when you can see the big picture? The point is to accept it, and then rise above your environment, or alter your perception of it, by accepting the larger pattern. (1998, 36)

This philosophy helps explain why Deadheads today focus on a relatively narrow historical timeline in their sacred narratives. They pay attention, not to the social and political events into which the Acid Tests, *inter alia.*, fit, but to the direct evolutionary line of events that led to themselves. Today's Deadhead subculture represents a syncretism of historical traditions. The Beat Generation and the anti-war movement, which proved to be predecessors to the hippies, were influenced by the African-American cultural movements—all revolutionary reactions to the conservative, socially oppressive environment of this country.

Deadhead behavior has led many outside observers to hastily interpret Deadheads as "living in the past" or as "sixties gypsies surviving in the nineties" (Gans 1985, viii). While some obvious continuities are apparent, many observers fail to recognize the degree to which Deadheads actively pick and choose traditional elements to draw or discard. The Beat Generation stories about Cassady, Kerouac, and Kesey set the narrative stage for a reenactment of this Deadhead mythology. The adventures of the Merry Pranksters and the Acid Tests, also a significant part of the sacred narrative, serve as ritual initiations into the counterculture movement—rituals that persevere through Deadhead behaviors today. Evidence of such continuities are striking in the carnivalesque environment and "rituals of transcendence" of Grateful Dead shows (Brightman 1998, 51), and through Deadhead vehicles (see figure 1)—both ritual reenactments of the traveling lifestyle espoused by the Beats and Merry Pranksters. Such aspects of Deadhead culture represent continuities as well as innovations of the traditions outlined in this history.

FROM THE WARLOCKS TO THE GRATEFUL DEAD: EFFECTS OF A SERENDIPITOUS NAME CHANGE ON DEADHEAD ICONOGRAPHY AND WORLDVIEW

Another seemingly serendipitous event greatly impacted Deadhead culture. In 1969, the experimental proto-Grateful Dead rock band, originally called "The Warlocks," changed its name upon discovering that another group was already producing records under the name "Warlocks." The name change opened up new possibilities and helped direct the development of belief, narratives, behavior, and art. According to Deadhead oral tradition and several written accounts, the name "Grateful Dead" was revealed almost mystically: band member Jerry Garcia flipped open a dictionary, closed his eyes and pointed with his finger, coming up with the words "Grateful Dead." Jackson describes this incident:

> Even before The Warlocks headed for Los Angeles, Acid Tests in tow, they were actively contemplating a name change.... They threw around literally hundreds of improbable names in their search, everything from the Emergency Crew to the Mythical Ethical Icicle Tricycle, but, predictably, in this age of stoned realizations and acid flashes, the name they eventually chose was *revealed* [italics in original] to them.

Figure 1. Deadmobile named "Ellis D Tees," a material reenactment of the Merry Pranksters' bus Furthur.

> "One day we were over at Phil's [Grateful Dead bass guitarist] house smoking DMT (a hallucinogen)," Garcia told writer Michael Lydon in 1969. "He had a big dictionary. I opened it and there was 'Grateful Dead,' those words juxtaposed. It was one of those moments, you know, like everything else on the page went blank, diffuse, just sort of oozed away, and there was GRATEFUL DEAD, *big* [italics in original], black letters edged all around in gold, man, blasting out at me, such a stunning combination. So I said, 'How about Grateful Dead?' And that was it." (1983, 59)[12]

Brightman notes that in a later account of the historical moment, "Garcia didn't like the name at first but felt it was too powerful to ignore . . . [band members] Weir and Kreutzmann didn't like it, either, but people started calling us that and it just started, *Grateful Dead, Grateful Dead* [italics in original] . . ." (1998, 80). A densely encoded Deadhead bumper sticker visually recognizes this serendipitous moment (see figure 2). The words "Grateful Dead" appear as they did that fateful moment Garcia found them—in the larger context of the dictionary (from "grateful" to "gratify"). The bumper sticker contains other visual codes, including the image of young Garcia as he would have looked when the name change occurred; a single eye centered in the palm of Garcia's famous hand (with the classic missing two middle finger joints); another eye (Egyptian style) at the top of the sticker; and a Steal Your Face emblem (skull with lightning bolt) at the bottom. Taken altogether, this item of Deadhead material culture speaks to the vital importance of the serendipitous moment when the Dead's name was magically *revealed* to them.

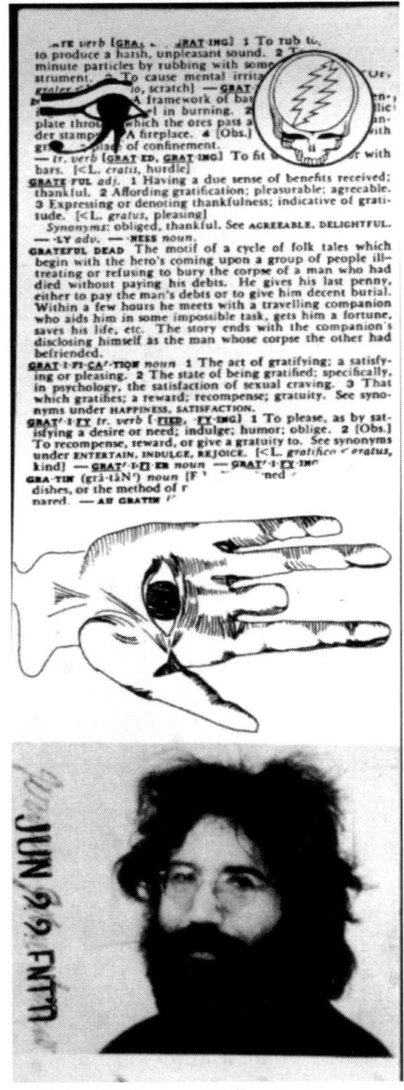

Figure 2. Bumper sticker that visually captures the serendipitous moment the words "Grateful Dead" were revealed to Jerry Garcia.

The name "Grateful Dead" refers to the motif of a cycle of folk tales in which the grateful dead man plays a leading role, described by Stith Thompson in *The Folktale*:

> In these tales we learn of a hero who finds that creditors are refusing to permit the burial of a corpse until the dead man's debts have been paid. The hero spends his last penny to ransom the dead man's body and to secure his burial. Later, in the course of his adventures, he is joined by a mysterious stranger who agrees to help him in all his endeavors. This stranger is the grateful dead man (1955, E341).

When the Warlocks changed its name to the "Grateful Dead," the doors were thrown open for widespread narrative and material folklore to develop around those two words. Jackson explains:

> "The Grateful Dead" as a new name was not exactly an instant sensation; in fact, there was even some initial resistance to it within the band. Bill Graham [the band's producer] was reluctant to bill the group under its new name for the dances he organized, but the underground acceptance of it was overwhelming, and soon "Grateful Dead" began springing up on posters and handbills all over town. "It was definitely kind of creepy to most people," Garcia commented several years ago. "They just didn't know what to make of it *at all.*"
>
> Actually, the "creepiness" is part of what made "Grateful Dead" such a perfect choice for a band name in the nascent days of psychedelia. It went beyond being bizarre for the sake of being bizarre—the more non-sensical the better seemed the rule of the day, as if groups were taking their cue from Lewis Carroll[13]—and instead offered a paradoxical concept that teased and threatened simultaneously. The name conjured up images of a joyous post-apocalyptic ascent to the heavens in some people's minds, and menacing specters like those in Northern Renaissance woodcuts, in others'. It was strangely appropriate in the psychedelic sense, too, for what the Acid Tests had been about, as much as anything, was stretching the boundaries of *everything* in pursuit of an inexplicable cosmic giggle; redefining what life could be, laughing in the face of death, or more precisely, obliterating conventional conceptions of mortality. . . .
>
> "Grateful Dead" was a fitting pie in the face of a straight universe obsessed with its own mortality, that routinely went selfishly on with its "pursuit of happiness" to make life pleasurable and cheat the Grim Reaper. "Grateful to be Dead?" (Jackson 1983, 61–2)

Brightman notes the significance of the Grateful Dead tale as well, arguing that it mirrors the altered states of an acid trip, with their "merging of visible and invisible worlds" (1998, 81).[14] Deadhead Alan Trist retold the tale in his book *The Water of Life: A Tale of the Grateful Dead,* which incorporates the traditional Grateful Dead motif:

> "You have shown me kindness," the beggar said, "and the way to the Water of Life is long and hard. You must pass through the Dark Wood then climb high into the Mountains of the North where stands the castle of a fierce ogre. The object of your quest can be found there. In order to succeed you must defend yourself against enemies and give of yourself when no one asks." (1989, 12)

The challenge "give of yourself when no one asks" has, in fact, become a code esteemed by Deadheads. A number of Deadheads I interviewed, pondering the significance of the band's name, told variations of the Grateful Dead tale. It seemed to function as a necessary key to understanding part of the Deadhead culture's philosophy. One informant, who had never read any "official" versions of the tale but, rather, learned it through oral transmission from other Deadheads, explained:

> It's the story of a hero who is going along in life and meets some poor helpless waif by the side of the road. He in some way befriends or helps the man. The hero's adventures take him into the underworld, to hell itself. And he learns that the deceased spirit of the person he helped, helps him through the adventure. And that's the grateful dead man who helps you through. (1995)

It becomes clear, in examining my informants' explanations, that the name "Grateful Dead" and the folktale to which it refers are closely tied to a self-conscious philosophy of life. The impact of this happenstance name change cannot be taken lightly; the philosophy suggested and interpreted through it influences a great deal of Deadhead behavior, including beliefs about life and death, and values placed upon traveling, living communally, sharing, and not only helping total strangers, but viewing them as "family." Deadheads embrace a sense of reciprocity, of giving when one has something to give, and receiving when one is in need. Deadhead Natalie Dollar concurs, implicitly referencing both the philosophy of the Grateful Dead tale and the nomadic history of Deadheads: "When a Deadhead, for example, offers another a place to crash for the weekend shows, the individual receiving the favor is encouraged to do the same for others in need of help 'down the road'" (1988, 27). Another Deadhead commented on this value, saying, "everybody shares whatever they have, food or wine, or drugs or whatever. As much as the music and the Dead themselves, I come for that feeling of closeness among the people. It's just like my lifeblood" (Perry 1980, 22).

Because of the value of communal living, the terms "family" and "tribe" are used by many Deadheads as more intimate synonyms for the community of Deadheads. Shenk and Silberman describe the usage of "tribe" as "one way in which Deadheads think of their community—as an extended family of people from various classes, races, sexual orientations, backgrounds, and other musical interests" (1994, 294). Although the term "tribe" conventionally refers to a group of people descended from common ancestors, within the so-called Deadhead tribe, membership is not inherited but, rather, recognized within oneself (see figure 3). Barbara Saunders writes from an emic perspective on the "tribe" of Deadheads:

> The Deadhead tribe is centered around what's missing from many ethnic, national, and religious communities: peak experience that unifies individuals into one people.
>
> Having shared with other Deadheads our most intimate moments and mind-expanding experiments, we expect from each other tolerance, understanding, and unconditional support. . . . Our dedication confuses and scares people. Even the most WASPy Deadhead knows firsthand the feelings of being discriminated against, of being closeted, and of coming out. Where the only recognized tribal links are genealogical, a brother/sisterhood among fans of a rock group makes little sense. But as a friend of mine put it, "We grew up together."
>
> Being "on the bus"[15] for any length of time includes birthing babies and mourning deaths; watching children grow up; and seeing relationships move from glances exchanged while dancing, to parenting. And through it all the music never stops; doing what moon cycles did for the ancients—providing a touchstone for the passage of time and the stages of our lives. (Qtd. in Shenk and Silberman 1994, 294–95)

Besides the gifts of food, money, gas, shelter, and alcohol/drugs, one clear example of "tribal" reciprocity among Deadheads involves the phenomenon of "miracling." A "miracle" (a term incorporated, like numerous other items of Deadhead folklore, from one of the Grateful Dead's songs entitled "I Need a Miracle") frequently occurs when someone arrives for the show without a ticket, hoping to receive one for free or for an unbelievable bargain. Douglas Hadden describes the practice of gifting concert tickets as "a ritual courtesy among Dead fans, part legend, part real." He also notes the importance of remembering and reciprocating such favors:

> The first time I heard the Dead in their own West Coast environment, I stood in line before-hand without a ticket, with friends who long before had bought

Figure 3. "Tribal" skull tattoo on a Deadhead's back.

> theirs to the "Bill Graham Presents" bash at Winterland in San Francisco. "Are you guys sure I'll get a ticket?" I asked my friends. "Ticket?" said a bearded fellow two folks in front of me. Yup. And 5 1/2 hours and the New Riders and a Grace Slick guest appearance later, the five bucks was forgotten, and the courtesy of a ticket for face value was not. (Qtd. in Grushkin, Bassett, and Grushkin 1983, 6)

At any given show, one can observe a number of people milling around with signs depicting a thematic variant of the "I need a miracle" lyric (see figure 4). Many Deadheads merely hold their index finger above their heads, signifying non-verbally that they need a ticket. I have heard many chant or sing their earnest pleas: "I need a miracle," "Please help this Deadhead see his 100th show," "Miracle me," and "I'll be your best friend for a ticket." Grateful Dead staff/crew member Harry Popick recounts a creative variant of this traditional behavior:

> You know how people are always standing by the road on the way to gigs holding up signs that say "I need a ticket" and "I need a miracle"? One time, driving to the Greek Theatre in Berkeley, I saw one guy with his hands in that position, holding up an imaginary sign! (Qtd. in Grushkin, Bassett, and Grushkin 1983, 166)

Figure 4. An elaborate "I Need a Miracle" sign variant, now retired inside a Deadhead's bedroom.

Popick's narrative reveals that the tradition of miracling is so ingrained, all the Deadhead must do to indicate his request is to hold his hands in the position of a sign. My informants indicate that the more elaborate, original, or creative the plea, the better the chances of being miracled. Examples of some more elaborate signs seem to support this belief. All of my informants emphasized the importance of giving what one has, and receiving what one needs—mirroring the hippie value of communal living.

Even the way Deadheads dance is material evidence of their communal, egalitarian ideology. When I mentioned to a Deadhead friend that I was exploring Deadhead folk dance as a genre that mirrors the Deadhead worldview, he laughed.

"Why do Deadheads dance like this?" he asked, moving his hands in graceful, swirling horizontal and vertical waves in front of his face, as if in a trance.

"Why?" I responded automatically to the formulaic structure of his joke.

"Because they're trying to keep the music from getting in their eyes!" he answered, followed by laughter from everyone present.

My friend should know, I thought; he has danced like that before. I have seen it myself a number of times. Walking around Dead shows, I noticed that sometimes people seem to be dancing together, sometimes totally apart. There seem to be a few basic dance styles, upon which Deadheads improvise with their own individual creative moves. For instance, while there might be one person off in the corner just bouncing up and down to the beat, another might be spinning continuously for entire songs, with arms straight out or reaching up in the air—without stumbling or getting dizzy. Yet another might be "noodling around," moving arms and legs as if "being played by the music" (see figure 5). Nancy Reist argues that dancing at Dead shows parallels the chanting, singing, and dancing associated with shamanism, stating that:

> Dancing draws the whole body into the rhythm of the drum, increases the possibility of hyperventilation, and induces the release of endorphins—a naturally occurring brain chemical that acts as an opiate.
>
> Altered states of consciousness are a significant and infamous part of the Grateful Dead experiences. Many Dead Heads have favorite stories about that special insight or perfect vision they had during a particularly moving show. These experiences are one of the primary attractions for many of the Dead Heads. (1997, 93)

There are often twenty or more dancers (who likely have never met each other before) dancing in exactly the same style almost in unison, often with their eyes closed—as if being controlled by a greater force than their individual selves. As the music and beat change, so does the dancing. Like a school of fish, many informal groups of dancers seem to move intuitively in a mass motion. The belief that the Grateful Dead's music moves dancers is mirrored by many of my informants; another common theme in Deadhead narratives includes the sudden and profound realization that every single person in the arena is dancing. They report it being simultaneously empowering and humbling. Zephyr describes "getting it" while at his first show:

> I started dancing and then suddenly it was like I was having a psychic orgasm, like a sense-surround psychedelic, psychic orgasm at the same time with all these people. Like the band and the people would build to a peak and then release. It was my first experience with that kind of gestalt feeling of being one with everybody, and dancing for the greater good, or whatever the hell I was doing. I remember thinking this was taking dance to the eternal fire, whatever the hell that means. (1995)

Many Deadheads attempt to define their fantastic experiences at Grateful Dead shows using argot such as "one mind," "group mind," "gestalt," "magic," "the X-factor," or "the zone." Each term refers to a state of being to which band members and the audience "travel"

Figure 5. Emic drawing of ecstatic Deadheads dancing at a Grateful Dead show.

together when the music and dance is at its most intense, exploratory, and collective (Shenk and Silberman 1994, 336). These represent the psychic or spiritual space Deadheads experience while dancing at Dead shows. Folklorist Sw. Anand Prahlad uses the term "ecospace" to describe this aspect of the Deadhead experience. He discusses spiritual symbols and iconography:

> Just as ceremonies in most religions or ritual contexts contain symbols that aid in creating a conducive atmosphere for surrender, so do these. And they are in some cases the same kinds of symbols that one finds universally. The strong scents of incense, perfumes; the ingestion of natural and synthetic substances that assist in jarring one loose from identification with the "unreal" material world and makes an encounter with the psychic world more possible. (1996)

These "common signifiers . . . are sensed and responded to by the body," Prahlad continues. "With a lessening of control by the rational mind, the body is freer to move forward into a central position as an instrument for the expressions of the spirits" (1996). The term "Dead Time" is frequently used by Deadheads to reflect this marked temporal space entered at Grateful Dead shows.Yvonne expressed this idea, stating, "It's like . . . there's no time when you're at a Dead show. It's just like Dead time. Groovy Dead Time" (1995). Prahlad's discussion about "ecospaces" applies well to such emic concepts as "The Zone," "Dead Land," and "Dead Time"—and reminds us of the sacrality of Deadhead rituals when the ordinary sense of time and space is suspended.

When Deadheads talk about dancing, they end up talking about the Grateful Dead's music. When talking about the music, they end up talking about dancing. The two are obviously integrally related. It makes sense that an eclectic dance style accompanies the eclectic musical repertoire. At times the dance is vaguely familiar to other dance idioms, such as belly-dancing, whirling dervishes, reggae dancing, rock 'n' roll dancing, and jazz dancing.

Religious studies scholar Karen McCarthy Brown writes about the significance of ritualized dance in her article, "Serving the Spirits: The Ritual Economy of Haitian Vodou." Brown introduces the concept of "the mindful body" to explain how the body absorbs experience and information, often in the form of understanding and remembering (1995). While dance can express an understanding of communal history and mythology, at the same time it can express both individual and shared spirituality. Brown argues that for practitioners of Haitian Vodou, dance is one means by which to act out and therefore comprehend personal identity, as well as power relations between characters, human and divine. The body can explore, analyze, and critique situations through dance. Like practitioners of Vodou, Deadheads dancing at Grateful Dead shows appear to be rehearsing a particular way of life and acting out egalitarian power relations. By going through this part of the ritual together, Deadheads enact a lifestyle that reflects their peaceful, anti-corporate philosophy and ethos. My exploration into Deadhead dancing supports Brown's theory that dancing acts out relationships and values. If the lack of conflict at Dead shows (and related events) is not proof enough, the iconography embraced by Deadheads, and subsequent philosophical interpretations, demonstrate how Deadhead dancing reflects a spiritual as well as a social reality.

Obviously then, the name change had a profound impact on Deadhead philosophy and worldview, expressed eloquently through the traditions of "miracling" and Deadhead dancing. It also had transformative effects on other areas of the material culture surrounding the band. The name inspired innovations by causing contemplation on the words

Figure 6. T-shirt depicting play on the words "Grateful Dead."

"grateful" and "dead". For one thing, the new name led to the popular and accepted nickname for fans/followers of the Grateful Dead band—"Deadheads"—as well as numerous items of folk speech involving plays on those words (see figures 6 and 7). The proverbial statement "If you're not a *head,* you're behind," as well as the messages "Born again Deadhead," "I'd rather be Dead," and "Long Live the Dead" appearing on bumper stickers, function well as examples of this wordplay. In essence, through its folklore, the subculture subverts conventional meanings of "death" and "dead"—transforming them into life-affirming terms, as these examples illustrate.

In addition to its effect on Deadhead philosophy and wordplay, the serendipitous name change also greatly impacted the subculture's chosen symbols. As Jackson recounts, artists looked to other cultures, particularly Tibetan and Egyptian mythology, for visual inspiration. He explains:

> Regardless of the name's origin or possible meanings, it immediately lent itself to intriguing iconography among the artists in the burgeoning San Francisco poster scene. And suddenly grinning skeletons were everywhere, as different artists interpreted the name in their own way, while announcing upcoming dances where the band would play. More than any other band on

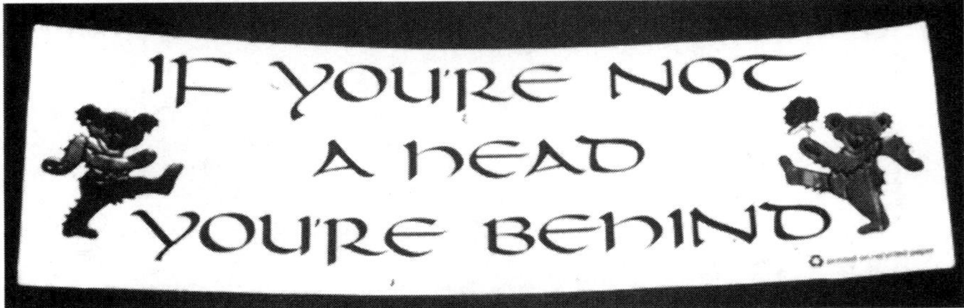

Figure 7. Bumper sticker with wordplay on term "Deadhead."

> the scene, the Dead had a name that lent itself to visual interpretation, and of course there already existed countless examples of skeletons in art over the centuries, ripe for use by the imaginative, eclectic artists. (1983, 63)

Indeed, a nineteenth century illustration of a skeleton wearing a crown of roses drawn by E. J. Sullivan to accompany the twenty-sixth quatrain of *The Rubaiyát* was adapted by San Francisco poster artists. It has since become the group's most recognized image, gracing an album cover, the band's comprehensive songbook, and even their official stationery. "I was just looking through a book one day and there it was," artist Alton Kelley recalled. "It was so perfect I couldn't believe my eyes" (Jackson 1983, 63). Shenk and Silberman cite an interview with Kelley:

> The skull-and-roses image was originally a black-and-white illustration by Edmund Sullivan that appeared in a nineteenth-century edition of *The Rubaiyátt of Omar Khayyám* [an eloquent, philosophical poem by the 12th Century Persian, Khayyám]. Artists Alton Kelley and Stanley Mouse were smoking pot in a converted firehouse, with the old horse troughs intact, on Henry Street in San Francisco when Kelley discovered the original illustration, realizing it was the perfect icon for the recently renamed Warlocks. The image, with added lettering and color, was used shortly thereafter on posters for a show at the Avalon Ballroom. "Everybody loved the image," recalls Kelley. (Shenk and Silberman 1994, 263)

Again, note the emphasis placed upon serendipity. Like Garcia, who unintentionally happened upon the words "Grateful Dead," Kelley magically stumbled upon the Persian image of the skeleton with roses (see figure 8). Brightman explains:

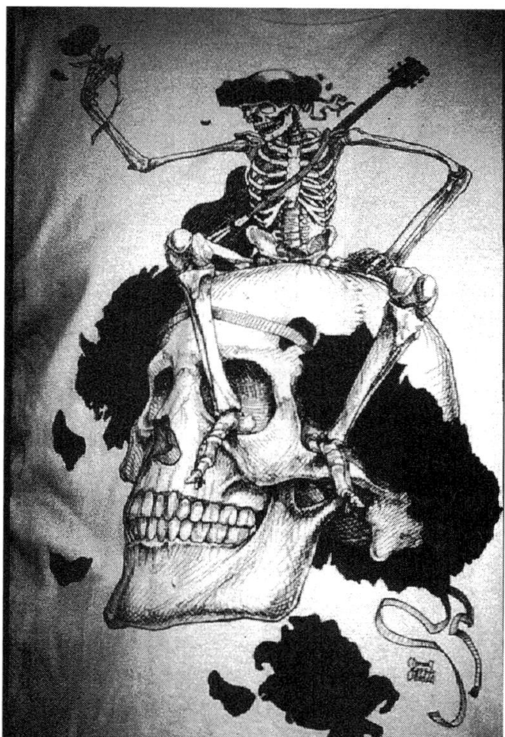

Figure 8. Celebratory skull and skeleton (holding a guitar) surrounded with roses.

> It started around 1969, when the band dispatched its first power object, the image of a skeleton walking on stilts across *The Tibetan Book of the Dead*, dragging a ball and chain. The work of a forgotten artist, it was the original Mr. Bones, a Grateful Dead icon; and Hart [Grateful Dead drummer] remembers it as a code that "let you see in the windows of people in San Francisco who were Deadheads before there were Deadheads." (1998, 3)

Owsley[16] also made innovations on the death imagery, further influencing the Grateful Dead skeleton iconographic tradition. Brightman notes that Owsley conceived the original skull and lightning bolt logo, used on the cover of the 1976 Grateful Dead album *Bear's Choice,* known in Deadhead vernacular as *steal your face* (see figure 9):

> In the early '70s, Owsley began doing fine ornamental metalwork, a craft to which he brought the same meticulous exactitude that he had brought to his chemistry. His Stealie pendants—depicting the familiar lightning-streaked skull that he designed with Bob Thomas . . . are prized by Heads. (1994, 214)

The front and back covers of Shenk and Silberman's *Skeleton Key*, which depict dancing skeletons, illustrate the Deadhead practice of borrowing from Tibetan mythology. The authors explain that "In Tibetan Buddhism these dancing skeletons or *citipati* represent the triumph of enlightenment over death. When enlightenment is achieved both earthly existence and death have no meaning" (Shenk and Silberman 1994, back cover). The skeleton iconography—dancing and smiling skeletons—that immediately sprung up around the band's name had profound effects on the community's philosophy and spirituality, drawing heavily, of course, on the ideas and images of Tibetan and Egyptian spiritual belief systems.[17] The spiritual symbolism represented by certain images of death (dancing skeletons, skull and roses, skull with lightning bolt) proliferates in the Deadhead community today, and still remains (in some instances) relatively coded from outsiders. Skeletons continue to serve as extremely positive symbols of the band and of the Deadhead community in general. The iconography consistently appears whenever and wherever the band or "the scene" is being referred to—on album covers, stage decorations, books, bumper stickers, patches, tattoos, shirts, buttons, and hats (see figures 10–12).

Religion often functions to provide a meaningful way of understanding death. Like other cross sections of society, those in Deadhead communities include a variety of religious orientations, including Christians, reincarnationists, atheists, Buddhists, and Rastafarians. This subculture seems to share, however, certain attitudes about life and death, and a recognizable group philosophy/ethos/worldview. The band's name change inspired and perpetuated a philosophy to which Deadheads adhere: most live in mortal splendor, the story goes, paying the price of a collapsed vision of the afterlife. Death is the great equalizer. Just as we live, we must also die. By coming to terms with our own inevitable death, we are able to live more fully in the present. The skeleton which dances inside us all is the core truth, a germ from the 1960s that stubbornly resists extinction.

Reist points out that symbols associated with birth and death are particularly common among shamanic cultures. "The death imagery," she explains, "often is associated with the stripping down of the ego and allows the shaman to start anew without the cultural baggage carried through life. The skeleton stands free of the flesh and its associated weakness and vices" (1997, 200) (see figure 13). Holger Kalweit argues in a similar vein that the death images associated with shamanic cultures

Figure 9. Classic Grateful Dead icon of a skull with a lightning bolt running through it, known as "Steal Your Face" or "Stealie," found in the form of a sticker.

Figure 10. Variant of the Steal Your Face icon, combined with Grateful Dead lyrics on a T-shirt.

Figure 11. Various portrayals of skeleton imagery: a postcard of a skeleton playing an instrument (left), a Steal Your Face variant with Garcia's face inside the skull (upper), and an Uncle Sam skeleton sticker (lower right).

Figure 12. Steal Your Face variant combined with a rose peace sign and Grateful Dead lyrics, embroidered on the back of a prison shirt in the early '70s.

are closely related to the death images of generation rites-of-passage and transitory rituals (1988, 90–95). Finally, Mircea Eliade suggests that the prevalence of skeleton imagery in the ritual costumes of shamanic cultures represents the spiritual death and rebirth of the shaman (1964, 158–68).

The skeleton imagery associated with the Grateful Dead and Deadheads parallels the above discussions regarding death symbols in conjunction with shamanic accoutrements. Reist makes this point more clear by discussing the symbolic significance of such iconography:

> Throughout the Grateful Dead concert experience, one encounters a number of consistent and powerful symbols. The skeleton emblem, which is also a fundamental shamanic symbol, is undoubtedly the most pervasive of these. Skeletons appear in a number of guises, including the traditional image of the skeleton and roses that comes from the *Egyptian Book of the Dead*, a skull with a yin-yang lightning bolt across the forehead, and a skeleton dressed as Uncle Sam.... (1997, 201)

Reist argues that the basic Ur-form of the skeleton evolves to reflect different circumstances, specific events, and individual idiosyncrasies (1997, 201). A skeleton with roses entails a different feeling than does a dancing skeleton, or one dressed as Uncle Sam. Hence, the basic motif is altered depending on the specific meaning of the situation.

Bruce Olds' description of the use of skeleton images during a 1979 Grateful Dead show provides a perfect example of an individual's use of skeleton imagery:

> Now you noticed some pretty strange goings on [at a Grateful Dead show]. A guy wearing an Uncle Sam outfit, another sporting a foot-long papier machier[*sic*] mask of something, still another dressed like a rat—ears, tail and all—with a bulbous, red, plastic clip-on nose. There was a group with skull decals stuck onto the middle of their foreheads.
>
> And then there was Rick Rickards. He was carrying a bamboo pole with a human skull bolted onto the end. At least, from a distance, it sure looked human. "Naw," said Rickards, eighteen, from Doylestown and a student at Central Bucks East, "it's only plastic, like the ones they have at Halloween.
>
> "See, I got it at K-Mart during a blue-lite special. You can always tell a Dead Head because if I shake it like this," he shook it up and down, "they'll start shouting and clapping and dancing around." (Qtd. Grushkin, Bassett, and Grushkin 1983, 30)

Figure 13. Emic caricatures of Deadheads as skeletons by Gary Kroman (cover of *Relix* magazine).

Reist presents another specific example of how the skeleton iconography changed to reflect a new context:

> During the year of the Egypt concerts, the skeletons were shown in the context of Egyptian symbols, such as the pyramids. Two skeletons have been shown back to back, one facing the Golden Gate bridge and one facing the Brooklyn Bridge, emphasizing the connection that the Dead Heads make between the U.S. coasts. These particular skeletons are both dressed in the Uncle Sam costumes—a particularly fascinating manifestation of the skeleton. The Uncle Sam skeleton appears in the Grateful Dead movie and on album covers, as well as in a variety of unofficial publications. He is a combination of the Grateful Dead's emblem and one of the most easily recognized symbols of the United States. The Uncle Sam symbolism represents the Dead Heads' position as members of the U.S. culture, while the skeleton suggests values that differ from those of mainstream society. (1997, 201)

Clearly, Grateful Dead iconography reflects this parody with skeletons—which are blatant symbols of mortality—laughing at death, and

Figure 14. Emic caricatures of Deadheads as skeletons, drawn by Miki Saito.

engaged in activities of daily living like dancing, playing cards, riding in Deadmobiles, and so on. (see figures 14 and 15). The iconography is utilized to subvert a strictly negative meaning of death. Recall the Deadhead response to Rick Rickards shaking the pole with skull—they danced around, clapped, and shouted in joy. Having been involved first in heavy metal culture, which also utilizes skeleton imagery, Yvonne initially had the impression that skeletons represented evil, darkness, wickedness, and violence. Following her entry into Deadhead culture, however, she began viewing the death imagery in a different light—as positive, spiritual, healthy, helpful, and as friends. To signify this change, Yvonne replaced the broken knob of her car's stick shift with a plastic skull, so that she could remind herself of the image's transformed meaning and how empowering it felt for her. She described what this alteration means to her:

> We all look like skeletons. Without our skins, muscles, hair, clothes, makeup, money, etc. We're all skeletons dancing. It's very unifying. We're all one, and no one's more beautiful or better. We're all beautiful. (Interview 1995)

Figure 15. Deadheads posing next to dancing skeleton iconography outside of Captain Ed's Heads and Highs Shoppe.

Such examples clearly illustrate the interplay between the use of death symbols and the community's worldview and values. Moreover, they demonstrate how Deadhead interpretations of the group's name, their chosen iconography, and elements of spiritual mysticism (including dance) continue to influence Deadhead philosophy and spirituality even today. The serendipitous name change from the "Warlocks" to the "Grateful Dead" profoundly impacted the development of Deadhead beliefs, narratives, behavior, and art. It led Deadheads to contemplate the meaning underlying the grateful dead folktale, which has influenced their philosophy and reinforced traditions of communality, helpfulness, and giving—evidence of which can be located in the rituals of miracling and dancing. Their reflections and play with the words "grateful" and "dead" led, as well, to many examples of Deadhead ritualized speech.

The historical event, itself serendipitous, during which the skeleton imagery was discovered and began to be used by Deadheads, caused spiritual and philosophical evolutions. The iconography began to be utilized as power objects within the community to subvert the fearsome notions of death. In effect, the name change can be held both directly and indirectly responsible for much of the sense of spirituality, worldview, aesthetics, and artistic behaviors embraced by Deadheads today. The symbolic intricacies of meaning expressed through Deadhead artistic behavior reveals how the death imagery was transformed into a celebration of life manifested in music, dance, and community. By their use of the skeleton iconography and folktale philosophy, Deadheads are essentially "laughing in the face of death or, more precisely, obliterating conventional conceptions of mortality" (Jackson 1983, 62). The dancing skeletons, which fit perfectly into the Deadhead carnivalesque environment and "rituals of transformation," represent, on a very profound level, the "triumph of enlightenment over death" (Shenk and Silberman 1994, back cover).

11

TRADITIONAL NARRATIVE, POPULAR AESTHETICS, *WEEKEND AT BERNIE'S*, AND VERNACULAR CINEMA

Mikel J. Koven

The taboo against contamination from a dead body is one of the most profound of all socio-cultural inhibitions. I often find myself quite uncomfortable at funerals, knowing that contained within that box at the front of the chapel or synagogue lies what once was a living, breathing, or possibly even joking human being. Beyond the element of grief, of having lost a loved one, there is something psychologically disturbing about the presence of a corpse: it is a reminder that we ourselves are mortal, and that we, too, one day, shall be lying in a similar box (see Freud 1950, 51–63; Harlow 1997; Small 1997).

Because of the profundity of that taboo, that almost universal fear of the dead, it is not surprising that popular films often draw upon the discomfort of being near a dead body for narrative inspiration. What is obvious to folklorists, who are used to working with traditional and often orally transmitted narratives, is that these movies, while presenting themselves as "original" texts, are sometimes based directly on, or even influenced by (whether consciously or unconsciously), traditional cultural beliefs. Many of these beliefs have been codified and narratively contextualized within traditional folktales. Stith Thompson, with Antti Aarne in *The Types of the Folktale*, as well as in his own *Motif Index of Folk Literature*, has identified enough occurrences of these beliefs within traditional narratives that he labeled them with both tale type and motif numbers.

A brief survey of the index volume of Thompson's *Motif Index* under the keyword "Corpse" reveals many motifs that would be familiar to any fan of horror cinema. For example, Thompson's motif G377, "Monster made from parts of corpse," is, of course, the Frankenstein story, although Mary Shelley's early nineteenth century novel is but one variation on that motif.[1]

Yet there are even more arcane examples that would be noticed only by those fans of "hardcore" and "splatter" movies, horror films notorious, not for explicit sexuality as implied by the term "hardcore," but by the degree of gore they contain.[2] A case in point is George Romero's zombie trilogy: *Night of the Living Dead* (1968), *Dawn of the Dead* (1978), and *Day of the Dead* (1985), wherein the dead are reanimated (although no direct cause is ever specified) with a taste for *living* human flesh; this can be found in Thompson's *Motif Index* as E422, "the living dead" (Thompson 1955–58, II: 445).[3] Even more potentially obscure for researchers who are not interested in horror cinema, particularly the kind of extreme "splatter" movies I am discussing at the moment, is the motif E121.6.1, which Thompson identifies as "Resuscitation by demon entering corpse" (1955–58, II: 415). This is a plot familiar to any fan of Sam Raimi's "Evil Dead" trilogy: *The Evil Dead* (1982), *The Evil Dead II* (1987), and *Army of Darkness: The Medieval Dead*[4] (1993). Although Romero's *Dawn of the Dead* can be read as a satirical commentary on American consumerism,[5] the film has its feet firmly planted in the horror genre. Raimi's trilogy, on the other hand, with one foot in the kind of extreme horror that Romero defined, recontextualizes the gore into the genre of slapstick comedy—imagine Romero directing the Three Stooges.

However, before I discuss the uses of corpses in comic narratives—both filmic and traditional—notice that many of the motifs which Thompson identifies as "corpocentric" fall into three main categories: there are ogre motifs (category G), motifs pertaining to "the dead" (category E), and deception motifs (category K).[6] Although I shall discuss this last category in detail, it is worth noting the distinction that Thompson makes between categories G and E, between ogres and "the dead." By "the dead," Thompson means ghosts, spirits, and demons. The Romero zombie films briefly outlined above are all category G motifs; that is, when the dead are resurrected and walking about they are within the role of the traditional ogre. The demon invasion motifs, where the dead are resurrected due to evil spirits, including the yet-to-be-mentioned E251.3.1 (Vampires eat [corpses]") motif, are category E motifs, that is, they fall within the role of the traditional ghost (Thompson 1955–58, II: 425). This distinction between ghosts and ogres, in traditional narrative and belief, is a distinction between terrestrial (ogres/zombies)[7] and aerial (ghosts/vampires/evil spirits/demons) monsters. This distinction needs further exploration, particularly as it pertains to contemporary horror cinema.

The motif category I am discussing here is Thompson's category K, "Deceptions." Within the category K motifs is one central motif pertaining to uses of dead bodies: K2151, "The corpse handed around," also known as "The Thrice-killed Corpse". Thompson summarily describes this motif as follows: "Dupes are accused of murder when the corpse is left with them. The trickster is paid to keep silent" (Thompson 1955–58, III: 480). Thompson goes on to note that this motif is primarily found in two closely related tale types: 1536C, "The Murdered Lover," and 1537, "The Corpse Killed Five Times" (Aarne 1981, 442), both of which are categorized by Aarne and Thompson as "Jokes and Anecdotes," in part explaining why these two tale types feature little more than the single motifs noted above. D. L. Ashliman expands on these tales types in *A Guide to Folktales in the English Language* (1987), and identifies further sub-tale types within this area.

Ashliman identifies tale type 1536, "Disposing of a Corpse," with the oft-cited contemporary legends "The Runaway Grandmother" and "The Dead Cat in the Package"[8] (1987, 263–264). In both of these legends, the problem of disposing of a corpse (whether pet or parent) is eliminated through the inadvertent theft of the corpse,[9] thereby alleviating the protagonists of the responsibility of disposing of the corpse themselves. Brunvand, citing Alan Dundes, identifies this legend as emerging out of the youth-centered society we inhabit, with its rejection of the aged, and its desire for inherited money and wealth (1981, 119). This links the modern legend back to "The Woman in the Chest" narrative, which I wish to focus on for a moment. Kurt Ranke's *Folktales of Germany* tells the story thus:

> A priest wanted to spy on the schoolmaster, whom he suspected of thievery. He put his mother in a chest, then took it to the teacher for safekeeping. The teacher discovered the spy and killed her, making it look like she had choked on a piece of bread. When the priest found his dead mother, he was afraid he would be accused of killing her, and he paid the teacher to help him prop her body at the top of a stairway in a tavern. A waitress accidentally knocked her down the stairs. Fearing prosecution, she paid the teacher to help her put the body in a field. A farmer, thinking it was a thief, struck the body with a stick. He too paid the teacher to remove the corpse. The teacher placed it in a sack and carried it into the woods, where he discovered some robbers. He took one of their sacks, leaving the sack containing the body with them. (Qtd. in Ashliman 1987, 263–264)

"The Woman in the Chest" narrative, although consisting of little more than the single motif (K2151), does demonstrate some wonderful complexities. For example, although the reference to the teacher's thievery disappears after the first sentence, it is still implied that he is guilty, and he most definitely *is* guilty of the murder of an old woman, the mother of a priest. The teacher is rewarded for his deceptions: he is paid three times for the same body and, although not stated directly, the robbers' sack that he absconds with probably contains some kind of booty. None of the other characters' assumptions of responsibility for the death of the old woman demand that they do anything other than hire someone else to save them from prosecution or bother. If we can extrapolate from this narrative the development of specialized services, particularly those surrounding death, like that of undertakers and funeral directors, then a fascinating portrait of socio-cultural guilt emerges. The priest (who should be responsible for taking care of his mother's corpse as both family and vocational duties demand), the waitress, and the farmer all *pay* someone else to do the work that they do not wish to do; in this case, the distasteful duties of corpse disposal. Like the contemporary legends "The Runaway Grandmother" and "The Dead Cat in the Package," these funeral responsibilities are placed on another who is paid exclusively for that kind of work, an aspect of this narrative in modern form noted by both Brunvand and Dundes (Brunvand 1981, 119).

Like "The Woman in the Chest," tale type 1537, which Aarne and Thompson titled "The Corpse Killed Five Times," tells a similar story: to relieve themselves of the potential responsibility for someone's death, and the implied prosecution that entails, various individuals repeatedly set up the corpse to shift the responsibility onto others. Richard Chase tells this American variant titled "Old Dry Frye":

> An old man choked on a bone and died. Afraid that he would be accused of murder, the host took the body to the road and propped it up. Some travellers thought the corpse was a highwayman and threw rocks at it. Seeing that the man was dead, they thought that they would be hanged for murder, so they leaned the body against a farmer's shed. The farmer thought it was a prowler and shot him. So it continued, until two rogues, also thinking they had killed the man, tied the body to a wild horse and sent him on his way. (Qtd. in Ashliman 1987, 264)

The difference between 1536 and 1537, according to the Aarne and Thompson typology, is the emphasis on the disposal of the corpse (1536), rather than the shifting of the blame (1537).

The two films under consideration here, *Weekend at Bernie's* (Ted Kotcheff, 1989) and *Weekend at Bernie's II* (Robert Klane, 1993) are film versions of 1536, The Disposal of a Corpse anecdote outlined above.

In *Weekend at Bernie's,* two young insurance adjusters, one hard-working and dedicated to moving up the corporate ladder, the other immature, slovenly, and apathetic to anything other than having a good time, discover an error in the books. While working on an excruciatingly hot Sunday afternoon, Rich (Jonathan Silverman) and Larry (Andrew McCarthy) discover that four policies had been made out to the same person, and were filed weeks after that person was dead. Discovering this oversight recoups over two million dollars for the company. Rich and Larry are anxious for Monday to arrive so they can bring this to the attention of their boss, the jet-setting Bernie Lomax (Terry Kiser), and, they hope, receive a much overdue promotion.

Bernie is thrilled with the discovery and invites the boys out to his mansion in the Hamptons for the Labor Day weekend as a reward. In reality, Bernie is less than thrilled. He has been using the company to launder money for the mob, and Rich and Larry have just discovered Bernie's dirty little secret. In desperation, Bernie consults mob boss Vito (Louis Giambalvo) for help, and requests that Vito arrange for Rich and Larry to be killed while at Bernie's. Vito agrees, and Bernie retires home to arrange an airtight alibi.

Vito, however, thinks Bernie is getting to be more trouble than he is worth. Added to that, Bernie is having an affair with Vito's girlfriend, Tina (Catherine Parks). Vito, instead of arranging for Rich and Larry to be killed, has Paulie (Don Calfa) go and murder Bernie before the boys arrive. The next day, when Larry and Rich arrive on Hampton Island, they discover that Bernie is dead, apparently the result of an accidental drug overdose. Before they can inform the authorities, a "floating party" of rich neighbors arrive, and suddenly Bernie's home has turned into "Party Central," with no one noticing that Bernie, propped up on the settee, is dead. He gets seduced, propositioned, and even ends up conducting business deals with his completely oblivious friends.

The next day, when Rich and Larry are once again going to attempt to contact the authorities, they discover Bernie's plot against them. Because they are under the impression that the killer is still coming for them, and that the killer will not hurt them while Bernie is present, they concoct a series of ruses which give the impression that Bernie is still alive: dragging the corpse around, taking it boating, playing Monopoly, sitting in the sun, and getting them into parties. Their masquerade is so successful that word gets back to Vito that Paulie did not kill Bernie as planned, and Paulie returns to the island to get the job done properly.

I have outlined the plot of *Weekend at Bernie's* in such detail because, as a modern variant of AT1536, character motivation within a "realist," or at the very least "plausible," plot is needed in order for this traditional motif to be filmically realized according to the strategies of "classical Hollywood cinema," the term given to how mainstream film constructs narrative logic. Other film narrative strategies begin with a traditional premise, and then the screenwriters develop the story to fill ninety minutes, as with *Alligator* (Teague 1980), where the contemporary legend about alligators in the sewers is the narrative catalyst for a *Jaws*-like man versus big animal film. *Weekend at Bernie's* does the opposite. It wants to end up in the traditional narrative, and in order to get there, screenwriter Robert Klane develops the plot so we end up in AT1536, rather than using it as a narrative catalyst.

Weekend at Bernie's is a modern variant of 1536A, "The Woman in the Chest": to avoid being blamed for Bernie's death, and to fool the real killer, Rich and Larry spend the weekend creating the illusion that Bernie is still alive. He is propped up on sofas during parties; he is placed on the patio with a string strategically tied both to one hand and to a pulley system so Larry can pretend that Bernie is waving to passers-by; his shoelaces are intertwined with those of both Larry and Rich for ease in walking (while Rich has his hand, ventriloquist's dummy-style, up Bernie's jacket holding his head up); and he is even propped up in a boat to allow the boys access off the island. Such are the ruses that Larry and Rich concoct in order to maintain the illusion that Bernie is still alive.

Like both AT1536 and 1537, the illusion that Bernie is still alive also confuses Paulie, who must constantly return to Hampton Island to finish his job. As in the traditional "thrice-killed corpse," Paulie kills Bernie three times: once by the overdose injection that actually kills Bernie; secondly, when Bernie accidentally slips off of a deck chair and lands on Paulie, the killer thinks Bernie is attacking him and he strangles the already dead "assailant"; and thirdly, taking no chances this time, Paulie bursts into Bernie's house and shoots the propped-up Bernie six times in the chest.

Weekend at Bernie's also features another of Thompson's motifs about corpses: Bernie's alibi for when Larry and Rich are supposed to be killed allows him the freedom to be back in New York that night, thereby enabling him to have an illicit rendezvous with Tina. When Bernie fails to show up at the appointed time, an angry Tina arrives on the island wanting to know what his excuse is. She does not believe Larry and Rich when they tell her Bernie is dead, and believes he is asleep in his room, where the boys have propped him out of the way. Tina goes up, but does not emerge for another halfhour, returning with a self-satisfied postcoital grin. When the bemused boys ask "How was he?," Tina's reply is "Never been better."[10] Thompson identifies this kind of necrophilia motif as J1769.2.1.[11] Unlike other forms of necrophilia, where the living engage in intentional sexual relations with a corpse, the essential dimension of this particular motif is the mistaken belief that the corpse is actually alive. On the one hand, in films, this can be represented by moments of horror—the unknowing person who gets into bed with a dead body discovers this, and usually screams. Here the comedy works in reverse: Tina is unaware that Bernie is dead, even after, somehow, consummating their affair. Thompson distinguishes between two kinds of necrophilia based on their placement in motif categories: the one most appropriate to *Weekend at Bernie's* is this J-category motif, classified by Thompson as motifs about "The Wise and the Foolish." More specifically, Thompson places this motif within the "absurd misunderstandings" subcategory (J1750–J1849), an apt phrase for this motif given the current filmic context (Thompson 1955–58, II: 445). Here Tina is obliviously foolish in not recognizing that Bernie is dead. The other kind of necrophilia is intentional, and is classified by Thompson under a completely different category, "Sex" (Thompson 1955–58, V: 388).[12]

This last motif also points towards some of the social criticism that *Weekend at Bernie's*, as a modern variant of AT1536 (1537), demonstrates. I noted above that some of the traditional variants of 1536 and 1537 contain a subsumed social critique regarding the lack of responsibility for the dead within a community. Frequently, these stories seem to posit, it is just too easy to either blame or pay someone else to take responsibility. Those who shirk their duty are rewarded for it. In *Weekend at Bernie's,* the satire is aimed differently: Larry and Rich are too innocent to be accused of Bernie's murder,[13] and at no time is Bernie construed as a "victim," at least not in any way that would elicit audience sympathy toward his death. Instead, the social criticism of the film is aimed at the "Hampton's Crowd," whose self-indulgences and self-obsessions make them oblivious to Bernie's dilemma. Neighbours invade Bernie's house, drink his alcohol, borrow his boat, and generally take advantage of Bernie's resources. Implied in all of this, as community standards on Hampton Island are never seen to be violated, is that Bernie is one of these people, and would, should the situation be reversed, be equally unaware if one of his neighbours likewise died. At first, Bernie is still "the life of the party," as the film's tagline reads: falling on people, coyly supplying drugs from his pocket (actually, his guests only think he is being coy), refusing to accept an offer on his car, and later, when Bernie falls off of his boat as Rich and Larry are trying to get away, he ends up doing a macabre impersonation of "body surfing/skiing," much to the delight of his neighbours.

How alienated does a community have to be for this to happen? Roger Ebert, in his 1989 review of *Weekend at Bernie's*, criticized the film, in part, because this kind of comedy requires "the other characters to be so stupid" as not to notice that Bernie is dead. But what if, in part, that is the point of the film? Ebert continues, "we can't believe they could be so unobservant" (Ebert 1989). It is unlikely that the intended audiences for *Weekend at Bernie's* are those who *do* spend their summers in the Hamptons, or write film columns for the *Chicago Sun-Times*. The intended audiences for these films are more likely to be folk more akin to Larry and Rich than Bernie. In playing to that audience, director Ted Kotcheff and screenwriter Klane seem to be implying that from the perspective of Larry and Rich, and those like them, these characters are that "stupid" and "unobservant." The film must have met with some kind of audience, for in spite of almost unanimously bad reviews at the time, it still pulled in more than thirty million dollars in domestic U.S. box offices.

In contrast to the moderate success of *Weekend at Bernie's*, the inevitable sequel did less well, in part, I believe, because it did not "speak" to its intended audience the way the first one did. *Weekend at Bernie's II* (1993) picks up almost immediately where the first one left off. Bernie is dead and in the New York City morgue; when the film opens, Rich and Larry (still played by Jonathan Silverman and Andrew McCarthy) are identifying the body (still played by Terry Kiser). As Larry signs for the release of Bernie's possessions, they discover a safety deposit box key for an offshore account in the U.S. Virgin Islands. In order to get access to that safety deposit box, they'll need to kidnap the dead Bernie and take him to St. Thomas.

Before they can do that, however, the mob, who want the laundered money Bernie had in his possession returned, takes action. They send

Charles (Tom Wright) and Henry (Steve James), two African American hustlers, to St. Thomas to consult with a voodoo priestess, the Mobu (Novella Nelson), who orders these two back to New York with a voodoo spell in order to resurrect Bernie. They hope that Bernie will then lead them to the missing two million dollars.[14] While they are trying out their spell, Charles and Henry lose their live chicken and replace it with a pigeon. This substitution is not entirely successful, and Bernie can only be reanimated when music is playing. What ensues is a race between Charles and Henry, and Rich and Larry, to determine who will hold on to the reanimated Bernie and be led to the treasure.

There *is* a folktale aspect to all of this; "reanimated corpse used to find hidden treasure" sounds like a Thompson motif, but I could not find any such reference. The living corpse motif (E422) is about as close to a traditional reference as I could ascertain in *Weekend at Bernie's II*. As I noted above, where reanimation occurs through a spiritual agency (demon, spirits, vampires, or, in this case, voodoo spells and music), it does fit within a certain aspect of folktale logic. Apparently this was insufficient to entertain an audience. Although *Weekend at Bernie's II* was given a larger budget (for exotic location shooting in St. Thomas), the film's gross domestic return was less than half of *Weekend at Bernie's* (approximately twelve million U.S. dollars).

Could Thompson's *Motif Index* determine a film's success? Using his motifs does not. However, by utilizing a strong verisimilitude to traditional narrative patternings, which includes traditional motifs, a different series of demands on the audience emerges.

The degree to which the two *Weekend at Bernie's* movies appeal to the general movie-going audience is the next aspect I wish to discuss. A crude, but useful, generalization is that when one speaks about *mass* media and the "general" audience, one is most often talking about oneself. Movie reviewers stand for the "average person," someone hired, in theory, to view all the new movies released and report on their quality in local and national newspapers, so the "average person" risks less of their increasingly expensive evening out at the movies on films they would not enjoy. Yet by definition of the job, movie reviewers are not "average people": anyone who views so many films per year is going to have a larger cache of filmgoing experiences with which to compare each new release. In their own way, and to varying degrees, movie reviewers are movie "experts"; they have a degree of knowledge that raises them ever so slightly above the everyday rank-and-file of movie audiences. As their cache of filmgoing experiences increases, so does their overall knowledge of cinema, thereby they develop a greater awareness of film *literature*; by exposure to so many different forms of cinema and filmic narratives, a greater field of comparison is open to those few individuals who see movies as our surrogates. In addition to this, journalists (movie reviewers in particular) and, even to a greater extent, film *scholars* (those with an academic background in film studies), are often older, better-educated, and more bourgeois in their filmic tastes than the "average" moviegoer.[15] Take, for example, Wally Hammond's review of *Weekend at Bernie's*, published in the British magazine *Time Out*:

> A one-joke movie which moves puerile party humour from *Animal House* to the yuppie world of work. . . . Kotcheff aims straight for the juvenile and spends most of his effort, successfully, on getting the timing right for the endless gags with Bernie's cadaver propped up on the sofa, falling downstairs, etc. But it's strictly kids' stuff and quickly palls. (1999, 1150)

Although Hammond seemingly "enjoyed" the movie, or at least recognized the successful comic timing of the gags, phrases like "kids' stuff" also demonstrate that, for him, somehow there isn't enough to keep the film going. Perhaps the movie's major flaw is identified in Hammond's first few words, as he calls *Weekend at Bernie's* "a one-joke movie," a view echoed by both film critics Roger Ebert (1989) and Hal Hinson, the latter writing for the *Washington Post* (1989). Ebert criticizes the movie for its lack of sophistication, comparing it disfavorably to Alfred Hitchcock's *The Trouble With Harry* (1955). Likewise, Hinson regrets that the gags with Bernie's corpse are "played out coarsely." Yet, as I noted above, *Weekend at Bernie's* was surprisingly successful at the box office. Therefore, in spite of the film's singular joke, its lack of sophistication, and coarse humor, somehow it found its audience.

One way toward explaining the dissonance between reviewers and audiences is based on the verisimilitude between *Weekend at Bernie's* and the AT1536/1537 tale type. It has been suggested that the most direct way for individual fiction films to be considered "folklore" is to follow some of the theoretical writings that tie folklore studies to literature. Neil Grobman, for example, proposed that one must assess "how authors use folklore in their writings". To follow this procedure requires the scholar to identify the author as being in direct contact with folklore and its scholarly debates (1979, 17–18). The problem with applying the "folklore and literature" debates to discussions about folklore and popular cinema is that individual authors whose connection with "folk culture" are more readily proveable produce literary texts. Cinema and television are much more collaborative communicative media, and, therefore, if one is required to make a connection between the text and "legitimate" folk culture, whose connection is to be considered authoritative? Bird noted a more progressive approach towards the verisimilitude between folk culture and popular cinema: we need to look at the resonance between traditional narration and popular cinema, and see how similar narrative strategies can inform both folkloristics and film studies (1996).

In highlighting the relationship between orality and literacy, Walter Ong inadvertently pointed towards a further understanding of *vernacular* cinema, i.e., films which demonstrate high resonance with an audience, but whose quality may confound movie reviewers. In *Orality and Literacy*, Ong identifies the "psychodynamics" of orality: those cognitive processes which characterize primarily oral cultures. The terms that we, in our highly literate society, use to describe the world around us—our very "literate" worldview—are often inappropriate to describe the worldview of primary oral cultures. Ong notes that orality in mass-mediated, technological societies like our own does exist in a secondary capacity (1982, 11). Yet conceiving of oral "texts," as well as other linguistic metaphors to describe primarily oral cultures, demonstrates our literacy prejudice (13). Ong notes that primary orality often lacks analytical discourse; that is, it lacks the discourse of introspection or self-reflexivity (30). Likewise, vernacular cinemas are often criticized for their lack of introspection and self-reflexivity, recalling Ebert's criticism of *Weekend at Bernie's* lack of sophistication.

Ong characterizes oral narrational strategies through a series of "psychodynamics," which I now wish to turn to in order to discuss, perhaps, what appealed to audiences about *Weekend at Bernie's*, despite the lack of verisimilitude to the critical criteria of mainstream movie reviewers. To begin with, Ong notes the importance of mnemonics and formulae for recalling oral information."In an oral culture, restriction of words to sound determines not only modes of expression but also thought processes. You know what you can recall" (33).

In *Weekend at Bernie's*, the frequent reiteration that Bernie is dead, that Rich wants to contact the authorities, or that someone is trying to kill Larry and Rich, is evidence of this phenomenon. It is not necessarily that movie audiences are slow to pick things up, or that because of MTV and the channel-surfing culture of the late twentieth and early twenty-first centuries, modern audiences have shorter and shorter attention spans. The way movie audiences receive and process information is not dependant upon literary models. Instead, this kind of reiteration moves the narrative plot forward without dependence upon literacy-like re-readings. Although we can go to see the same movie again, or rent and even purchase a videocassette of the film to watch whenever we want, these are secondary considerations for most moviegoing audiences. Films which demand rewatching, rewinding, and replaying are more "literary," in that in order to experience the narrative to its fullest, one needs to understand its overall structure.[16] From a literary perspective, this demand is more "sophisticated," more like "quality literature." "In an oral culture, to think through something in non-formulaic, non-patterned, non-mnemonic terms, even if it were possible, would be a waste of time, for such thought, once worked through, could never be recovered with any effectiveness, as it could be with the aid of writing" (35). Ong again notes:

> Thought requires some sort of continuity. Writing establishes in the text a 'line' of continuity outside the mind. If distraction confuses or obliterates from the mind the context out of which emerges the material I am now reading, the context can be retrieved by glancing back over the text selectively. . . . There is nothing to backloop into outside the mind, for the oral utterance has vanished as soon as it is uttered. Hence the mind must move ahead more slowly, keeping close to the focus of attention much of what it has already dealt with. Redundancy, repetition of the just-said, keeps both speaker and hearer [and moviegoer] surely on the track. (40)

Elsewhere, Marshall McLuhan noted that film is one of his "hot media," that is, it is high definition. "High definition is the state of being well filled with data" (1964, 36). All information required to make sense of or enjoy a film needs to be transferred to the viewer in one sitting. In which case, orality models, particularly the psychodynamics of repetition and formulae, allow that "high definition" of data transference to occur more successfully than with literary models.

The characterizations in *Weekend at Bernie's,* painted in broad strokes, also demonstrate further verisimilitude with the psychodynamics of orality. To a literary audience, the "crude" polarizations within the film seem simplistic: neat, hard-working, responsible Rich/sloppy, lazy, irresponsible Larry; Rich's virtuous girlfriend, Gwen (Catherine Mary Stewart)/Bernie's adulterous gangster's moll, Tina; live Larry and Rich/ dead Bernie; and so on. But these binary oppositions, beyond Levi-Strauss' paradigmatic structuralism (1993), are also one of the psychodynamics of orality:

> The elements of orally based thought and expression tend to be not so much simple integers as clusters of integers, such as parallel terms or phrases or clauses, antithetical terms or phrases or clauses, epithets. . . . Oral expression thus carries a load of epithets and other formulaic baggage which high literacy rejects as cumbersome and tiresomely redundant because of its aggregative weight. (Ong 1982, 38)

Although Hal Hinson's review of *Weekend at Bernie's* gives a nod to the juxtaposition between the black comedy of the film and its sunny bourgeoisie beach setting, he still finds the film "coarse," with "too many bimbos and too many drug jokes" (1989). In other words, the comedy of the film is too basic and, agreeing with Ebert, too unsophisticated. But those characterizations within the film are, I argue, the point: not in the sense of a sophisticated satirical juxtaposition of "bimbos" and "bourgeoisie"—satire being a literary phenomenon (see Bakhtin 1984)—but the film's crudeness in characterization is a further dimension in the psychodynamics of vernacular cinema.

None of this is to say or even imply that *Weekend at Bernie's* is in anyway a "progressive" film—that it somehow challenges the bourgeois notions of literary elitism. In fact, the ideology of the film is still quite conservative. Both Larry and Rich are white, American, male heterosexuals, who believe that if they work hard, they will get their reward. Even though they do not get promoted as expected for revealing the scam to the corrupt Bernie, they do end up with a suitcase full of money, and Rich gets the white, heterosexual, wealthy girl.[17] *Weekend at Bernie's II*, with its Caribbean setting, places African-American characters within its diegesis. However, these are equally crude stereotypes: Charles and Henry, street hustlers who dress stereotypically, or the Mobu, a voodoo princess. Although, in this film, it is Larry who gets a girlfriend, Claudia (Troy Beyer), an African-American native of St. Thomas, she and her father (Stack Pierce), seemingly the island's only doctor, are also students of voodoo. Larry openly ridicules Claudia's beliefs, thereby making any kind of sexual consummation between them unlikely, and avoiding the controversy of miscegenation. In case we are unsure that at some point when we were not looking, Larry and Claudia might have got up to something of which the most conservative audience member might disapprove, the final piece of voodoo magic requires the blood of a virgin (continuing the long list of stereotypes). The only one who can offer said blood is Larry. Clearly, and in no uncertain terms, neither of the *Weekend at Bernie's* movies are progressive in ideological terms. This, too, is one of Ong's psychodynamics: to challenge the social order, to call it into question, or any of the precepts which make up that order, risks forgetting the generations of work which built it (1982, 41–42). Individually, an audience member may choose to accept, challenge, or otherwise problematize the films, but as a general address to a primarily audiovisual audience, vernacular cinema cannot encourage "intellectual experimentation" (Ong 1982, 41).

Nor can vernacular cinema, or primary orality, encourage intellectual experimentation in the realm of abstract and symbolic settings (Ong 1982, 42–43). Although the worlds of the Virgin Islands or the Hamptons may seem exotic, as they are to Larry and Rich, the banal and everyday world of New York City, the office, their apartments, and their general lifestyles, are all narrative contexts to which almost any audience can relate. Even the exoticism of St. Thomas and Hampton Island, which are treated as tourist destinations, underlines the verisimilitude to our own "lifeworld" (Ong 1982, 42). To create any kind of abstraction in setting, either symbolic or fantastic, requires analytical categories that are inaccessible to primary oral cultures. Likewise, in vernacular cinema, for an audience to engage with crude polarizations and stereotypical characters, the films must be set in a world to which they can immediately relate. During the opening credits of *Weekend at Bernie's*, which sets the scene during a record-breaking heatwave, a mugger attempts to "stick up" Larry and Rich on their way to the office. Larry pushes the gun to one side and says to the mugger, "Aw, get your ass outta here, it's too hot!" The scenario is a completely fantastic response to an all-too-real situation, being mugged in New York City.

Even Ebert's criticism that the characters in *Weekend at Bernie's* are just too stupid to be believed supports another of Ong's psychodynamics: Ong notes that primary orality is characterized by an agonistic tone, that is, the scenarios are distilled into two opposing points of view:

> Many, if not all, oral or residually oral cultures strike literates as extraordinarily agonistic in their verbal performance and indeed in their lifestyle. Writing fosters abstractions that disengage knowledge from the arena where human beings struggle with one another. . . . By keeping knowledge embedded in the human lifeworld, orality situates that knowledge within a context of struggle. (1982, 43–44)

The binary oppositions noted above between Larry and Rich, and between them and Bernie, play an even larger role in vernacular cinema. The conflicts between these two camps, and the camps do shift within the diegesis, are the kinds of abstractions with which vernacular cinema, like primary orality, can operate. These oppositions encapsulate vernacular ideas that are demonstrated to the audience. In *Weekend at Bernie's*, Larry and Rich want to spend the weekend on Hampton Island/Bernie wants them dead; after Bernie dies Larry still wants to party/Rich wants to call the police; Gwen wants to know the truth about what is going on/Rich does not want to tell her. Likewise, in *Weekend at Bernie's II*, Larry and Rich want to get Bernie's money/Charles and Henry want to get Bernie's money; voodoo is used for greedy purposes by the Mobu/voodoo is used for constructive purposes to save Rich. These dichotomies encapsulate debates within the diegesis contextualized, the "lifeworld" of the intended audience, and are presented without the mediation of literary analysis.

I have tried so far to demonstrate the similarities between Ong's primary orality and what I have been calling "vernacular cinema," but is this comparison fair? Put differently, even though the two media have similar psychodynamics, they are describing very different phenomena. We experience cinema, whether elite "art cinema" or vernacular cinema, through time. As I noted above, although we can purchase a videocassette and fast-forward or rewind to specific sections (made all the more immediate through DVD technology), to experience a film requires an ordered sequence of narrative processes. Skipping ahead, or going back to what one may have missed, although possible, is not part of general filmgoing. In other words, cinema is a largely homeostatic phenomenon. It is always experienced in the present, and references to the past are not referred to or demanded unless they have direct relevance to the present, just like primary orality, according to Ong (1982, 46). In particular, the classical Hollywood mode of filmmaking, whereby narratives are situated within contexts that demonstrate a high degree of verisimilitude to the experiential "lifeworld" (49), with the direct intention of the audience's empathic participation in the diegesis (45–46), further underlines the similarities between primary orality and vernacular cinema. This is not to say that vernacular cinema is an equivalent of primary orality—once a culture has achieved literacy, I know of no way in which that can be forgotten—but it does suggest that vernacular cinema is a kind of *neo*-orality: a new form of orality, or, because of its audio-visual bias, an orality-like phenomenon.

Therefore, if movie reviewers approach films like *Weekend at Bernie's* or its sequel from a literacy perspective, they are seeing films as though they were written instead of performed. This does the films an injustice. The address to their audience is not as literacy, or even quasi-literacy, but as audiovisual or neo-orality. As such, films like these need to be discussed within the context of the vernacular cinema tradition to which they belong.

Audiovisual neo-orality explains the address to the audience for films such as *Weekend at Bernie's*; it does not explain why the first film succeeded and the sequel did not. If I am even partially correct in my connection between the psychodynamics of primary orality and the address of vernacular cinema, then the content must also be vernacular.

Folk narrative traditions, like the folktale, are one type of narrative content that has stood the test of time; these narratives would not be passed on to subsequent generations unless they had some relevance to the supporting culture. In fact, Dégh has noted that when folktales cease to reflect the culture they do indeed fall into disuse (1989). Folktales and narrative motifs regarding the problems of getting rid of a dead body, for example, can be told as jokes, be found as motifs in longer folktales, or even recontextualized on Hampton Island today in a movie.

The idea of problematic corpse disposal still has currency today (to the tune of over thirty million dollars in the case of *Weekend at Bernie's*). It does not matter whether screenwriter Robert Klane has *a priori* knowledge of this folktale or motif, or not. It has been circulating in such a way as to connect with him profoundly enough to write the story in the first place. Something about it had a resonance, and he was able to convince others of that resonance, too. *Weekend at Bernie's II,* on the other hand, only had the resonance of the first film's success. By not developing other vernacular narratives, in spite of the vernacular form of address, it did not have resonance with the audience.

But this current research is only a start. We need to further investigate not only *how* contemporary filmmakers use traditional materials, for example, tale types and folktale and legend motifs, but how those audiovisual texts are then received by their intended audiences. These motifs, with or without recourse to Ong's psychodynamics, need to be explored more fully in other comedy horror films, like Sam Raimi's *Evil Dead,* or George Romero's *Dead* trilogies. Further work needs to be done as well, on the relationship between ogre motifs and spirit motifs, and how these in turn are represented in contemporary horror cinema. This essay has merely scratched the surface of this topic.

FILMOGRAPHY

Hitchcock, Alfred, dir. 1955. *The Trouble with Harry.* Screenplay by John Michael Hayes. 95 min. Polygram Video. VHS.

Klane, Robert, dir., also screenplay. 1993. *Weekend at Bernie's II.* 85 min. Entertainment in Video. VHS.

Kotcheff, Ted, dir. 1989. *Weekend at Bernie's.* Screenplay by Robert Klane. 99 min. Cinema Club. VHS.

Raimi, Sam, dir., also screenplay. 1982. *The Evil Dead.* 79 min. 4 Front Video. VHS.

———. 1987. *The Evil Dead II.* Screenplay by Sam Raimi and Scott Spiegel. 81 min. BMG Video. VHS.

———. 1993. *Army of Darkness: The Medieval Dead.* Screenplay by Sam and Ivan Raimi. 85 min. 4 Front Video. VHS.

Ramis, Harold, dir. 1983. *National Lampoon's Vacation.* Screenplay by John Hughes. 95 min. Warner Home Video. VHS.

Romero, George, dir. 1968. *Night of the Living Dead.* Screenplay by George Romero and John Russo. 96 min. Tartan Video. VHS.

———, dir. 1978. *Dawn of the Dead (The Director's Cut).* Screenplay by George Romero and Dario Argento. 139 min. BMG Video. VHS.

———, also screenplay. 1985. *Day of the Dead.* 101 min. 4 Front Video. VHS.

Teague, Lewis, dir. 1980. *Alligator.* Screenplay by John Sayles. 87 min. Digital Gems. VHS.

NOTES

NOTES TO THE INTRODUCTION

1. For important appraisals of expressions of "bad taste" and the role of "arbiters of taste" in defining such categories, see the special issue of *Journal of Folklore Research* entitled "Arbiters of Taste: Censuring/ Censoring Discourse," edited by Moira Smith and Rachelle H. Saltzman, especially their "Introduction" (1995) and Elliott Oring's "Afterword" (1995b).
2. A parallel form of ludic provocation in an occupational setting is provided by Green 1981.
3. For another humorous death tradition of individualism associated with cemeteries, see Secretan's account of the decorative coffins of a Ghanaian fishing community (1995).

NOTES TO CHAPTER ONE (Davies)

Many people have helped me in the compilation of the jokes and other materials cited above. My thanks to Goh Abe, Anne Curry, Philip Davies, Alan Dundes, Elliott Oring, Eugene Trivizas, Roy Wolfe, and Anat Zajdman. My work in the University of California, Berkeley folklore archive was supported by a grant from the Arts and Humanities Research Board. I must also thank Peter Narváez for his advice and encouragement as editor, a continuation of his kindness to me during my visit to the Memorial University of Newfoundland.

1. Like disaster jokes, the details of the disasters are today most easily obtained from the Internet. For details of particular disasters that led to jokes see:

   www.fail.com/galley/piper-alpha.htm
   dol/eng.synysb.edu/disaster/
   www.mediasearch.org/oped/news/he19990806.html

2. Archival sources: UCBFA = University of California, Berkeley Folklore Archive. Dates of collection provided where available.
3. It is worth noting that Diana jokes existed before the crash, though they were fewer in number and only circulated locally. Like John F.

Kennedy, Diana was largely a creation of the media, a youthful picture, glamour hedged by regal divinity, a projection of sexy extroversion, though she was not as successful in concealing the underlying depression and promiscuity. They both lived by television, were killed by television, and were canonized (see O'Hear 1998) by television. The jokes told about this camera-loving Anglo princess before her untimely death reflected her strange situation, and it is easy to see how these earlier jokes were a precursor of and a springboard for the jokes that succeeded her decease:

> What's Will Carling's favourite film at the cinema?
> Poke-your-Highness (Pocahontas).
> (In oral circulation among British expatriates in Spain, and indeed Spaniards, in the mid-1990s)

> Charles: I wanted that chocolate cake.
> Diana: Give me a minute and you can have it back.
> (In oral circulation in Spain in the mid-1990s)

> Before Diana met Charles her previous partner was a full-length mirror.
> (In oral circulation in Spain in the mid-1990s)

4. Some Internet websites (as of 1999) containing Diana jokes (most of the jokes appeared on more than one site):
   www.deathsucks.com/jokes/diana.html
   www.herald.com/tropic/docs/008947.htm
   www.hjem.get2net.dk/nonline/home5/dijoke.2.htm
   www.msnbc.com/news/108086.asp
   www.ricardis.tudelft.nl/blokkendoos/misc/Diana-jokes.htm
   www.tipnet.net.av/~bpalmer/diana.htm
   Japanese readers should also consult Davies and Abe (2002).
5. Known acronymically in Australia as "wowsers," from We Only Want Social Evils Remedied, and by extension in England from We Accept No Known Ethnic Rivalry.

NOTES TO CHAPTER TWO (Ellis)

1. This article is derived from an Internet article of the same title in *New Directions In Folklore* posted on the *NewFolk* website (www.temple.edu/isllc/newfolk/index.html), where additional primary texts are exhibited.
2. Notably Regina Bendix, Simon Bronner, Christie Davies, Norine Dresser, Joseph P. Goodwin, William Hansen, Sandy Hobbs, Marilyn Jorgensen, and Alan E. Mays.

3. Such material is assumed to be in the public domain; however, out of consideration for the privacy of the persons whose virtual conversations I have observed, I have in all cases omitted e-mail addresses and signatures that would allow them to be identified. (In many cases, these are bogus or unobtainable anyhow.) I have, in all cases, identified the names of the message boards on which the jokes were posted along with the dates of the messages, so that researchers can easily revisit the original postings.
4. Also alt.*comedy.british, alt.comedy.improvisation, alt.comedy.standup, alt.humor, alt.humor.parodies,* and *no.kultur.humor.*
5. Also *alt.america, alt.firefighters, alt.politics.bush, alt.war, nyc.general, soc. culture.afghanistan,* and *talk.politics.mideast.*
6. Also *alt.autos.4x4.chevy-trucks, alt.conspiracy.jfk* [conspiracy theories surrounding the assassination of President Kennedy], *alt.dss.hack* [computer programming], *alt.fan.tom-servo* [American TV cult show *Mystery Science Theatre 3000*], *alt.music.van-halen, alt.prophecies.nostradamus, alt.strange.days* [American cult science-fiction movie], *alt.windows98, alt.writing, misc.fitness.weights, misc.survivalism, misc.transport.trucking, news.admin.net-abuse.sightings, rec.games.pinball, rec.boats, rec.motorcycles.dirt, rec.photo.equipment.35mm, rec.sport.pro-wrestling, rec.woodworking, rec.models .scale,* and *rec.games.pinball.* Boards dealing with other cultures included *alt.religion.christian.east-orthodox, soc.culture.cuba, soc.culture.czecho-slovak, soc.culture.dominican, soc.culture.indian, soc.culture.irish, soc.culture.polish,* and *soc.culture.russian.*
7. A reference to the mass murder at Columbine High School in Littleton, Colorado on April 20, 1999, in which two students wearing trenchcoats, Eric Harris and Dylan Klebold, killed thirteen people including Cassie Bernal, who allegedly expressed her faith in God just before being shot. Bernal's testimony became a staple of evangelical Christian responses to this tragedy. Interestingly, the Columbine tragedy seems not to have generated a cycle of jokes, though one item, a parody of the "MasterCard" advertisement, did circulate widely.
8. The allusion is to one of the recently deceased singer Aaliyah Haughton's most popular songs, "Try Again," from the *Romeo Must Die Soundtrack.* Aaliyah was killed in a plane crash on August 26, 2001. Among the jokes that circulated after her death was this one: Pilot: The engine won't restart. Aaliyah: "Try Again." (http://:www.deathsucks.com/jokes/aaliyahhaughton.html).
9. Pacific Standard Time is three hours earlier than Eastern Standard Time, so this item was posted at 12:59:29 PM EST, about an hour and a half after the collapse of the second Tower.

10. Another version of this list, shortened to 20 items plus the "top ten" list, was spammed (sent anonymously and without solicitation) to a large number of lists on September 23 under headings like "Heartwarming story from Ground Zero WTC." This list too had minimal impact on the tradition.
11. Cf. "Did you hear Christa McAuliffe had blue eyes. One blew right, one blew left" (Smyth 1986: 244, Oring 1987: 280, Bronner 1988: 130, Ellis 1991: 113).
12. Cf. "Where does the crew of the *Challenger* take their vacation? All over Florida" (Smyth 1986: 244, Oring 1987: 280, Bronner 1988: 130, Ellis 1991: 113-14).
13. A famous American stock car racer who died on February 18, 2001, when he accidentally crashed his car into a wall during the Daytona 500 race.
14. The first response to this item read "haha.. see..?? humour prevails" (*alt.tasteless.jokes*: September 13, 2001 01:05:01 PST). This indicates that it was indeed perceived as a joke and not simply a patriotic gesture parallel to the well-known "flag raising" photograph that was simultaneously circulating. When I showed this to a group of students on October 3, 2001, they unanimously rated it as "funny" or "very funny."
15. *dk.snak.vittighede*: September 15, 2001. The early texts are dated "September 12, 2001," which may in fact be correct.
16. "Game of whoop-ass" is a somewhat mysterious term; I've been unable to find any other use of this phrase on the Internet. I suspect it is not a reference to a game but an invented term derived from the more common slang phrase "*open a can of whoop ass*" (v): To fight; to beat someone up. See California State Polytechnic University, Pomona, College Slang Around the World. *The College Slang Research Project* (May 18, 1999). Available: http://www.csupomona.edu/~jasanders/slang/vocab-srch.html
17. For a history and sample texts, see http://www.snopes2.com/quotes/sinclair.htm.
18. See http://www.snopes2.com/rumors/binch.htm#add and Olsen 2001. Suggs (2002) remarked that the poem might have reached an even wider audience on radio, as he was aware of many stations who broadcast readings of it, often adding music and sound effects. WCBS-TV in New York, in fact, created a video version of children reading it out loud. The poem was posted on many websites (about 900 remained in place as of 6/02), and one site offered a short animated film version

that could be downloaded as a Real Media file and viewed on a computer screen. As of February 2002, the page noted, it had been downloaded 328,000 times. (See http://www.karcreat.com/Binch.html).

19. Dundes and Pagter 1996: 223. This letter too was updated and circulated in the post-9/11 days as a letter from George W. Bush to Osama bin Laden, though it did not gain nearly as much popularity as the burlesque speech. The most significant change is the following addition to the older text (given here in italics): "You rag-head son-of-a-camel-humping-bitch, *I am going to hunt your chicken-shit ass down and feed you slowly into the engine intake of one of those passenger jets your ass buggering friends like to hijack so much. As for your bootlicking sponsoring country, I'm going to* turn loose my Air Force and *bomb their* camel shit country *back to the stone-age, followed by my Army to* make *what's left into* a multi-national parking lot, and then send in my Marines to paint the *white* fucking lines on it" (*alt.tasteless.jokes*: 18 Sep 2001 00:54:53 -0400 EDT).

20. Significantly, as late as 1998 veterans' groups were selling t-shirts labeled "Weather Report for BAGHDAD / CLOUDY" decorated with an American bomber and a mushroom cloud. (*comp.sys.ibm.pc.games.flight-sim:* 18 Dec.1998).

21. Dates for these items were more difficult to determine, as it is not as easy to trace their history on the Internet as with verbal humor. In many cases, the date given is the date when the item was forwarded to me or to my source. However, earlier dates were in some cases confirmed with the help of the dated list of visual jokes at "War Gallery" Available: http://www.moviesthatsuck.com/vault/gallery.html. Other online archives of visual humor still active when this paper was written include "Current Events Humor Archive," available: http://wowpage.com/rthumor/; "Asylum Dedication to Americans Dealing with Terrorism," available: http://asylum.subnetcentral.com/davec/terror/aaterror.htm; and "Osama Bin Laden Pictures and Jokes" 2002, available: http://www.osamayomama.com/10/10_archive.htm.

22. 200 rounds of ammo: $70 / Two ski masks: $24 / Two black trench coats: $260 / Seeing the expression on your classmates' faces right before you blow their heads off—priceless. (*rec.humor.funny*: Apr. 27, 1999).

23. As rated by the appearance of "Taliban bingo," a regular inclusion in these lists and the easiest joke to search for because of its relative textual stability.

24. Available: http://cagle.slate.msn.com/politicalcartoons/PCcartoons/deering.asp.

25. Similarly, a recording circulated as an e-mail attachment later in October threatens to give the Taliban's phone number to a group of telemarketers, plaguing them with a host of nuisance phone calls.
26. Cf. the addition in the "bin Laden" version of "George W. Bush's Letter."
27. See http://www.snopes2.com/rumors/mallrisk.htm for a sample text and history.
28. Compare this typical line from the "Aboriginal musical" *Bran Nue Dae* by Jimmy Chi and Kuckles: "I bin away for 20 years now. I bin drovin' I bin drinkin' I bin Christian. I bin everything but now its time I gotta go home before I die." [Available: http://social.chass.ncsu.edu/wyrick/debclass/bran.htm.]
29. The Australian Security Intelligence Organisation, Australia's governmental national security service.
30. An identical text was also posted the same day on *rec.travel.australia+nz*: October 07, 2001 11:13:57 PST.
31. Of course, a well documented text from before October 7 would demolish this argument. I would be pleased to hear from anyone who can attest to an earlier version of this joke that circulated outside of Australia.

NOTES TO CHAPTER THREE (Harlow)

Transcription symbols:

i. The symbol ◆ indicates a speaker's laughter; ◆◆ indicates laughter of someone other than the speaker. (The use of a symbol to indicate laughter was suggested to me by Henry Glassie's use of a diamond shape to indicate "a smile in the voice, a chuckle in the throat, a laugh in the tale" (Glassie 1982, 40).

ii. The symbol [-], a subtraction sign inside brackets, indicates deletions of narrators' words, which I have made for the sake of textual clarity. Texts that are easy for the ear to follow can be confusing to the eye.

iii. Ellipses in transcriptions indicate pauses, not deletions.

iv. Words inside square brackets are my editorial clarification of speakers' references.

v. Words inside parentheses are my attempts to offer appropriate substitutes for words that I could not make out on the recordings.

1. It should be noted that "practical joke" is an etic term.
2. In other accounts, the corpse needs to be tied down because it is deformed by rheumatism or is a hunchback.

3. Wakes in the contemporary West Indies are boisterous events as well. This is documented by Roger Abrahams in his book *The Man of Words in the West Indies* (1983, 164–186).
4. Seán Ó Súilleabháin presents several synodal decrees in his book *Irish Wake Amusements* (1967b).
5. An example of such a tale can be seen in the section of W.B. Yeats' *Mythologies* entitled "Dreams that Have No Moral" (1969, 125–137). Yeats presents a tale collected by Lady Gregory in Galway, in which a man is both killed and brought back to life with a magic rod. For a discussion of resurrection in folktales, see Stith Thompson's discussion of resuscitation in *The Folktale* (1977, 255).

   An Irish example of resurrection is found in Jeremiah Curtin's *Myth and Folk-Lore of Ireland* (1890, 32). In this tale, the hero, who needs to climb a glass mountain, kills his helper and uses her bones as steps. He gathers these on the way back down, assembles the bones into a skeleton, covers it with flesh, sprinkles the bones with water from the spring of life, and the helper comes back to life.

   Lutz Röhrich discusses the motif of resurrection from bones in *Folktales and Reality* (1991, 61–64).
6. The dead are also believed to return in spirit form for reasons other than exacting vengeance. In traditional narratives, they often are benevolent spirits who are attempting to help the living or complete an unfinished task. Also, they might simply appear as an omen of something that is to come.
7. Some cultures *do* have terms for such beings. In Haiti, for example, they might be identified as zombies.
8. A relatively recent example of this can be seen in the case of a woman in Albany, New York, who was mistakenly pronounced dead. A morgue attendant discovered that she was alive when he noticed movement in the body bag and a breathing sound. The coroner who declared her dead (an elected official with no medical background), commented, "Actually when you come right down to it, this might be called a miracle of God." (Robert McFadden,"They Said She Was DOA, But Then the Body Bag Moved," *New York Times,* 18 November 1994, B7).
9. I have written about revenants elsewhere (Harlow 1993).
10. Of course, loss of autonomy can also be tragic.
11. Packie's interesting life story can be read in his book, *Recollections of a Donegal Man* (1992), edited by Steve Jones.
12. For an African example of ritual joking at funerals and other rites, see Douglas 1991, 108–111.

13. Others have documented Irish wake games, too, such as Mooney (1888).
14. The practice of integrating a dead family member into social life recalls a painting I saw at an exhibit at the Appalachian Museum at Berea College in Kentucky, in an area settled by Irish, British, and Germans. The painting, entitled "Last Picture with Grandfather," was a family portrait. The family was assembled on the porch of their house and Grandfather was among them, his head, adorned by a full white beard, visible from his casket.
15. Cross motif E235.2, Ghost returns to demand proper burial (Tom Peete Cross 1952).
16. As Firth points out in "The Plasticity of Myth in Tikopia" (1961), the same basic myth can be rendered in various forms by competing communities as support for their respective arguments.
17. An "information state," as defined by Erving Goffman, is "the knowledge an individual has of why events have happened as they have, what the current forces are, what the intents of relevant people are and what the outcome is likely to be" (1986 133–34).
18. Bauman writes that practical jokes, by their very nature, involve "differential access to and distribution of information about what is going on, with the trickster having a more 'real' sense of the situation, while the victim has a false one" (1988, 37).
19. This notion was reinforced for me when I described the prank to Davey Whelan, and he commented,"That was a ghost."
20. "Key" is a central concept in Erving Goffman's *Frame Analysis* (1986). It is the set of conventions by which a given activity, which is already meaningful in terms of a primary framework, is transformed into something patterned on this activity. A keying of these actions provides us with something that is not real or literal or actually occurring, but the staging of these actions is real and is actually occurring.
21. I myself experienced this after I played a practical joke on some County Waterford men, in collusion with a friend of theirs. The prank was so successful that, despite my amusement, I regretted my participation in what I then decided had been not funny, but unkind. The next day I was visiting with some acquaintances who had already heard of what I had pulled over on the lads, told me the story of it, expressed their appreciation and admiration, and asked me to tell them the story of it. When I confided that I actually felt badly about it, they reassured me that it had all been done in fun, and that the victims, who were somewhat self-important, had deserved to be cut down a bit.

22. The "narrated event" is the event which a story recounts (in this case the actual enactment of the practical joke); the "narrative event" is the event at which the story is told. For a discussion of the interrelationships between the narrated event and the narrative event in practical jokes, and for a look at the structures of narratives which recount practical jokes, see Bauman (1988, 33–53).
23. Cf. Roger Abrahams' article, "Black Talking in the Streets," which discusses the ways in which cursing and other verbal abuse can be either a form of play or a vicious expression of hostility. Abrahams comments that "in the most successful kinds of play, the most constant message must be the ambivalent one: this is play–this is not play. With joking activity . . . this paradoxical message is very commonly carried out by the use of the same aggressive, hostile formulaic devices found in use in real arguments, i.e., the same curses, boasts, devices of vilifications and degradation, etc." (1991, 245).
24. "Cod" is possibly related to the slang word "kid." The Oxford English Dictionary lists "cod" under "kid," and defines it as "to hoax, to take a rise out of."
25. When I mentioned to Anthony Clarke of County Down that many Irish stories have elements of trickery in them, he perked up and said almost enthusiastically, "In Irish culture we *do* play tricks on each other, slag each other."
26. I did hear one Irish instance in which the corpse's movements are not the result of a practical joke. This account, told by Ned Flynn, was presented above in the section on the humor of corpses.
27. Interspersed among Montell's (1975) accounts of the seeming revival of the dead are three accounts of the revival of the seemingly dead. In #464, #465, and #467, the "corpse" sits up because it was never really dead.
28. See Goffman's *The Presentation of Self in Everyday Life* (1959) and *Frame Analysis* (1986, 83–123 and 156–200).
29. The capacity of folklore to create situations can be seen in stories which themselves recount the enactment of folklore—the telling of a story or a riddle, the singing of a song. In an essay on the functions of Irish song, Breandan O'Madgáin observes, for example, that a story recorded by Lady Gregory (1974, 36) illustrates that, "For the Irish folk mind in the Nineteenth century, songs had esoteric powers of transforming any situation" (O'Madgáin 1975, 215). The story begins with the marriage of a poor couple that "was only a marriage and not a wedding" until the acclaimed bard Raftery happened to pass by. "There wasn't a bit but bread and herrings in the house; but he made

a great song about the grand feast they had and he put every sort of thing into the song—all the beef that was in Ireland . . ." and in this way he made the marriage into a wedding. "What matters here is not the historicity of the episode," writes O'Madgáin, " . . . but the artistic mentality revealed in the anecdote itself regarding the power of song to transform" (O'Madgàin 1975, 215–216).

30. Stories are told, songs are sung, dances are danced, and rituals are performed to create a response in cosmic forces, supernatural beings, or human beings, to create an ambiance, to create diversion, to create intimacy, to create fellowship and community, to create awareness of alternative social orders, to create a distinction between self and other, to create divisiveness, to create a contingency supportive of one's ideology. If the function of folkloric forms were primarily referential, they would not be an artistic form. Verbal art can effect change in the world both by moving people emotionally and by moving them to action; people respond to it at practical, psychological, emotional, moral, cultural, and aesthetic levels.

31. Brian applied the concept of "creating situations" in regard to genres other than practical jokes. In discussing a curse that had been uttered against a cruel landlord, decreeing that for seven generations no Lord Waterford would die a natural death, Brian commented that the members of the community "were waiting for the lord to die mysteriously. And it happened in each case. And ye know that possibly created a situation where he probably did go a bit insane. Everybody was watching and waiting to see when it was going to happen."

NOTES TO CHAPTER FOUR (Narváez)

This essay is updated from its original publication (*Western Folklore* 53 [1994]: 263–93). Earlier versions were presented as papers for meetings of the American Folklore Society and the International Society for Folk Narrative Research (Narváez, October 1991, July 1992). In addition to the friends, students, and collectors cited throughout, I would like especially to acknowledge the helpful assistance and commentary of Linda Ballard, Angela Bourke, David Buchan, Kenneth Goldstein, Robin Gwyndaf, Philip Hiscock, Martin Lovelace, Wolfgang Meider, James Moreira, Sandy Morris, Helen Peters, Gerald Pocius, Barbara Rieti, and John D.A. Widdowson. I am very appreciative of the availability of the resources of the Memorial University of Newfoundland Folklore and Language Archive, particularly the finding tools prepared by Violetta Halpert, mechanisms which greatly expedited my work.

1. All archival sources here derive from the Memorial University of Newfoundland Folklore and Language Archive (MUNFLA) and are cited by an accession number (e.g., 72-12) and a page number of a manuscript or the number of a tape recording, the latter recognizable as such by being preceded with "C" (e.g., C187).
2. Besides archival citations, many interactions are cross-referenced to Ó Súilleabháin's seminal *Irish Wake Amusements.*
3. The following list of traditional folk motifs cited in this chapter derives from Stith Thompson, *Motif-Index of Folk Literature,* 6 vols. (Bloomington: Indiana University Press, 1955) and Ernest W. Baughman, *Type and Motif-Index of the Folktale of England and North America* (The Hague: Mouton, 1966):

E200	Malevolent return from the dead
E238.1	Dance with the dead
E422	The living corpse
E431.4	Coffin carried through hole in wall to prevent return of dead
E431.15	People touch corpse before burial to avoid seeing ghost of dead person after burial
E463	Living man in dead man's shroud
E542.1.4	Ghost strikes man on face
E545	The dead speak
E545.19	Addressing the dead
E547.1	The dead groan
E554	Ghost plays musical instrument
E555	Dead man smokes pipe
E556.1	Ghost drinks liquor
E577.2.1	Playing cards with a dead man
E752.10.1	Corpse must be watched carefully before burial
J1769.2	Dead man is thought to be alive
K2320	Deception by frightening
K2321	Corpse set up to frighten people

NOTES TO CHAPTER FIVE (Meyer)

For their varying types and degrees of help in compiling the materials used in this essay, I wish to particularly thank the following individuals: Jean Carlin, Keith Cunningham, "Dawnette" in Indiana, Joe Edgette, Jim Jewell, Lise Larsen, Tom Malloy, Fred McKinley, Lotte Larsen Meyer, Terry Padrta, David Quiring, Jeanne Robinson, Vera Short, Paul Swank, and Barre Toelken. All photos are by the author.

1. Conversations in 2000 with Mr. Terry Padrta of Independence, Oregon, who claims, on the basis of family genealogical research, that his own immediate family represents "... the only Padrtas in Oregon," revealed no knowledge of the Henry Padrta commemorated on the stone, and a thoroughgoing search of the normal resources used in gravestone research (newspaper obituaries, census records, probate records, etc.) was similarly unsuccessful.
2. The examples of modern American graveyard humor I shall be discussing in this essay are all genuine: the vast majority are based upon my own fieldwork (i.e., I have actually seen and, in most instances, photographed them), while the few which are not are reported in reputable sources are duly cited.
3. Though this practice may seem odd, it is a frequently employed, almost necessary, technique in cemetery and gravemarker fieldwork. Landscapes and artifacts convey so many details that one is forced to learn to "unfocus" most material not related to his/her particular area of interest, else the distractions become overwhelming. I know one sociologist, for instance, whose successful fieldwork in nineteenth century cemeteries is quite dependent upon his ability to "see" one esoteric feature, the placement and configuration of individual markers within family plots, while at the same time effectively filtering out virtually all others.
4. Carl Lynn, who outlived his wife by a number of years, erected this doublesided marker shortly after her death.
5. Robert Mitchum, playing a broken-down ex-rodeo star in the 1952 movie *The Lusty Men,* quotes a variant of the expression in a perfectly contextualized moment of the film's action: "There never was a horse that couldn't be rode, never was a cowboy that couldn't be throwed."
6. It appears fairly likely that in choosing to provide as an inscription a favorite expression of this deceased teenager (a quite common practice on contemporary markers), those who designed the monument may not have considered all possible interpretations. But then, on the other hand ...

NOTES TO CHAPTER SIX (Kugelmass)

Research for this essay was made possible, in part, by a grant for summer support from the Graduate School of the University of Wisconsin, Madison. I would like to thank *Journal of American Folklore*'s anonymous readers for some excellent suggestions, and Marc Kaminsky and Robert Lavenda, with whom I discussed many issues within this article.

1. Curiously, Lawrence (1982, 1987) makes no link between "alternative parades" and gay culture. As I shall argue below, even a cursory reading of the Village Halloween parade's iconography suggests a significant gay presence. Indeed, many New Yorkers refer to the event as "the gay parade."
2. For a refutation of Dorson's thesis, see Peter Narváez (1997, xii–xiii).
3. See Dean MacCannell's (1976, 3) discussion of the meaning of tourism for contemporary culture.
4. The existence of the promenade may have diverted the most blatantly oppositional elements away from the parade, thereby enhancing its benign image for New Yorkers in general. At the same time, the promenade's physical proximity to their residences may explain the negative view of some Greenwich Village inhabitants. The tension between bourgeois notions of order and civility and oppositional behavior is by no means particular to the Greenwich Village Halloween celebration. Lavenda (1980), for example, discusses the transformation of Carnival in nineteenth century Caracas from a disorganized "rite of reversal" among the lower classes to a "civilized" and highly organized display.
5. The fear of possible eruption did become acute just before the 1989 parade, because of various acts of violence that had taken place in the weeks before the event. Roving gangs had been "wilding" just north of Greenwich Village, and there was considerable fear on the part of the parade's organizers that they would return on Halloween. Both the organizers and the police were relieved that year when rain kept the crowds to a fraction of what they had expected.
6. As Abner Cohen (1980, 83) argues, "Culture generally is expressed in terms of symbolic forms and performances that are by definition ambiguous. . . . Once the symbols are reduced to either politics or existential issues alone, they become unidimensional signs, lose their potency and hence their social functions." Cohen argues that both hegemony and oppositional orientations are present in every carnival in some state of balance:

   > To the extent that that balance is seriously disturbed, the nature of the festival is changed and is transformed into a different form altogether. If the festival is made to express pure and naked hegemony, it becomes a massive political rally of the type staged under totalitarian systems. On the other hand, if it is made to express pure opposition, it becomes a political demonstration against the system. In either extreme case it ceases to be carnival. (1982, 37)

7. See Stoetlje (1987) for a discussion of this issue in rodeo culture.
8. Amy Waldman, a *New York Times* reporter, described the event as follows:

> The parade was a tapestry of stories and a tableau of images. Members of one leather-clad group stopped periodically along the route for demonstrations of sadism and masochism, whipping one another. The police officers lining the route watched them stoically, as they did the women who marched topless. The sounds of the parade—a variety of music, including salsa and reggae—told another story, that of the growing number of immigrants for whom coming out is an American rite of passage.

9. Two comparable examples come to mind. Denise Lawrence's account (1982) explains the origins of the Doo Dah parade as a rebellious response to developers encroaching on an artists' enclave in Pasadena. Michael Hughey (1983) has reinterpreted W. Lloyd Warner's material on Memorial Day celebrations in Newburyport as an attempt on the part of an old elite to assert symbolically a status that, at least in economic terms, is a thing of the past.
10. See Elaine May (1988).

NOTES TO CHAPTER SEVEN (Congdon)

1. 1950 was the year of the original Spanish ed. *El Laberinto de la Soledad* (México D.F.: Cuadernos Americanos).
2. This information comes from a 1989 interview reported in Elizabeth Carmichael and Chloe Sayer's 1991 book, *The Skeleton at the Feast: The Day of the Dead in Mexico.* Sanchez de Escamilla believes her views are in keeping with general middle class belief in Puebla State. Along with her students, she participates annually in the competitive exhibition of creating a Day of the Dead *ofrenda,* or altar-like offering for the deceased.
3. Albert Camus believed that our angst comes from our strong wish to live, which is frustrated by our knowledge that we certainly must die (Garciagodoy 1998:186).
4. *Papeles picado* are cut paper banners, usually made from colorful tissue paper. Tradition says that because they are light, airy, and lacey, spirits can easily fly through them.
5. In the first few pages of her novel, *So Far from God,* Ana Castillo described an event in New Mexico where a wake for a baby was taking place. Everyone was crying, and the mother was asking God why she had to lose her daughter, when someone lets out a shriek. Everyone becomes silent and the priest goes over to the baby's coffin, which has

been pushed open, "and the little girl inside sat up, just as sweetly as if she had woken from a nap, rubbing her eyes and yawning." Father Jerome is amazed and says prayers. As the child grows up, she claimed "that all humans bore an odor akin to that which she had smelled in the places she had passed through when she was dead" (1993:22-23).

6. Chicanos are Mexican-Americans, mostly from the west coast. The term is usually associated with individuals who take a political position with their identity.
7. For Mexican-Americans, as well as any other emigrant group, the car is seen as a symbol of the American dream. Dave Hickey called it "an icon of Life, Liberty, and the Pursuit of Happiness" (1997:70).
8. Dave Hickey discusses the reversal that takes place with bad and good taste, pointing out that Liberace cultivated them both. Hickey claimed that "bad taste is real taste, of course, and good taste is the residue of someone else's privilege . . ." (1997:54).
9. Victor Turner defined ritual as "prescribed formal behavior for occasions not given over to technological routine, having reference to beliefs in invisible beings or powers regarded as the first and final causes of all effects" (1982:79). David Morgan notes that ritual engages all the senses: smells, tastes, sounds, and sights. These sensations trigger the memories which helps participants face an unpredictable world (1998:54).
10. Barbara Kirshenblatt-Gimblett pointed out that the famous art critic Clement Greenberg even went so far as to argue for wealth as a precondition for being cultured. Kitsch was to be associated with the lower classes and was the opposite of aesthetic quality promoted by the avant-garde (1998:278). Greenberg would certainly have scoffed at the use of artificial flowers on graves and altars, the eating of sugar skulls, and perhaps, even the ephemeral material of the papier-mâché *calaveras.*
11. According to Brenner, writing in the 1960s, revolution meant "loyalty to native values," and confronting messy political situations. This meaning of revolution values honesty and a strong respect for work. The native is elevated as is the peasant and the laborer (1967:185-86). These are the kinds of values that Posada embedded in the character of the *calaveras* he illustrated. They are values that are also at the heart of the Day of the Dead celebrations. Politics, good living, and death are all intricately intertwined.
12. As Masuoka notes, the Judas figure is associated with the Holy Week between Palm Sunday and Easter. Traditionally during this time, papier-mâché Judas figures were lit and burned. The Judas figures, of course,

are specifically Judas Iscariot, who betrayed Jesus. However, Judas figures can vary in form. Two common images are the devil and the skeleton. Like the *calavera*, the Judas figure can be used to mock public figures. In this manner, Judas is not only Judas Iscariot, but the figure also represents wealthy landowners and unsavory businessmen. Masuoka points out that recent examples have "included Mexico City's former police Chief Arturo 'El Negro' Durazo, who ostentatiously misused public funds, and Fidel Velazquez, Mexico's long time labor leader, who was perceived as having served the interests of the decision-makers of the ruling party over those of his constituency" (1994:3). In 1991, Miguel Linares created a Judas figure of Saddam Hussein that was burned in response to the Iran-Iraq war (1994:4).

13. Although the Linares family is now internationally well known as the most famous papier-mâché artists in Mexico, and support themselves as full-time artists, they are by no means wealthy. Masuoka explains that, in the early 1990s, as an hourly wage, they made less than the minimum wage in the United States. Until 1991 they did not own a car, and when she wrote about them in 1994, they did not have a bank account (22).
14. Pedro Linares makes molds from plaster-of-Paris for some of his pieces. Figures are often constructed piece by piece. Some larger one-of-a kind figures are made with bamboo armatures. Sometimes objects to be used as molds are purchased from markets. Plastic dolls, for example, help in constructing some of the figures. Brushes are made from cat hairs, which the Linares family claims are better than store-bought brushes (Masuoka 1994:12-15)
15. Leonardo Linares won the National Youth Prize for Folk Art in 1986. He said that it is his responsibility to not only make *cartonería*, but to teach classes throughout Mexico on how to make them. Masuoka reports that he clearly enjoys teaching (1994:24).
16. In 1984 the Museo Nacional de Arte e Industrias Populares in Mexico City held an exhibition of the work of Posada reproduced by Felipe Linares and his sons in papier-mâché form. In 1985 New York City's Museum of Contemporary Hispanic Art hosted a similar exhibition (Masuoka 1994:79).

NOTES TO CHAPTER EIGHT (Brandes)

I give special thanks to the National Endowment for the Humanities, the John Carter Brown Library at Brown University, and the Center for U.S.-Mexican Studies at the University of California, San Diego, for providing me the resources necessary to complete this project. To write this paper, I consulted libraries at Harvard University!, !the University of California, Berkeley, the University of California, San Diego, the Colegio de México, CONDUMEX, the Archivo de Indias in Seville, and the Escuela de Estudios Latinamericos in Seville. I wish to express my gratitude to staff members at all these institutions. Individuals who have provided me with bibliographic and other assistance related to this project include Liza Bakewell, Jonathan Inda, Peter Cahn, Jorge Klor de Alva, James Taggart, Waltraud Leiter, and William Taylor. I thank all these scholars for their assistance and support.

1. An obvious impossibility in medieval Ireland, since Europeans of the time had not yet discovered American tobacco.
2. In some parts of the Republic, most notably the state of Morelos in central Mexico, a third day, which falls anywhere between October 28 and October 31, depending on village, is dedicated to the "matados" (murder victims) or "accidentados" (accident victims). Th!is! custom might well reveal pre-Columbian influence. For the ancient Aztecs it was the manner of death, rather than the behavior of the deceased while alive, which determined his or her fate in the afterlife.
3. The verse refers to Francisco Madero, President of Mexico during the early stages of the Mexican Revolution (1910-1920).
4. This practice resembles other competitions recently introduced during the Day of the Dead, particularly contests that give cash prizes for the best outdoor altars (see Brandes 1998).
5. The reference is to "Don Juan Tenorio," a Spanish classical drama by José Zorilla, which is widely performed throughout the Mexican Republic during Day of the Dead season. A large part of the play takes place in a cemetery, which makes the work particularly relevant on this occasion.
6. Halloween symbols and customs have become increasingly integrated into the Day of the Dead. Many high-profile intelle!ct!uals, journalists, and other public figures vehemently oppose this trend as contrary to Mexican national interests. It is also perceived as symbolic of North American imperialism (Brandes 1998, Garciagodoy 1998). This is the meaning that the author of this calavera wishes to convey.
7. President Fox is so insistent on wearing cowboy boots, in fact, that during his inaugural ball on 1 December 2000 the normal practice of wearing tuxedos had to be suspended. It was deemed unacceptable to combine a tuxedo with riding boots. Since Fox himself would not dress in a tuxedo, male guests were instructed to wear dark colored suits instead.

NOTES TO CHAPTER NINE (Cosentino)

1. I have conducted field work in Haiti since 1986 with the generous support of the National Endowment for the Humanities, the Rockefeller Foundation, the American Council of Learned Societies, the Academic Senate of the University of California-Los Angeles, and the Fowler Museum of Cultural History. *Mesi ampil a tou*!
2. In May 2001, this British tradition of parody expanded to include an HBO "dramedy" series entitled "Six Feet Under," based on the foibles of a family run funeral parlor located somewhere in the old heart of L.A. In keeping with the theme of this essay, series' scripts skillfully wove death, sexuality, and laughter into a seamless whole.
3. In keeping with the spirit of the novel, it was later transposed to a movie starring, *inter alia*—Rod Steiger and Liberace!
4. How many Gede brothers are there? Metraux says there are at least thirty Gedes, and differentiates such bizarre manifestations as Captain Zombi; Gede Double; Gede the Spider; Gede Linto (who walks like a baby, babbles, and cries for food), Gede Caca (mercifully not further defined), and Suffering Gede (1972,115–16). In this last guise, the *lwa* is represented by chromos of Jesus Crowned with Thorns. I found such chromolithographs in several Vodou shrines, sometimes called "*Bawon*," sometimes "*Jezy*," sometimes "*Diable*." The parallels between these sacred figures seemed obvious to the serviteurs. Such proliferation is no doubt inspired by the corollated proliferation of praise names for the saints and the Virgin in Catholic litanies. But parallel manifestations of Gede are also a refraction of the confounding range of his powers: tattered and chic, sensual and brutal, mixing even life and death.
5. By way of a biblical explanation for the Bawon's finality, André Pierre had this to say, "The Bawon Samdi is Christ. Lord over the dead. Because Christ is the beginning of the dead who was resurrected on the third day. He died in the flesh, but was resurrected in the spirit. Everyone dies in the flesh, and is resurrected in the spirit." Or to put it in Old Testament terms, he used a second analogy, "[Bawon] is Adam. Guardian of the cemetery. Guardian of all the dead. Everyone's father. And Gran Brigitte is Eve" (personal conversation, Port-au-Prince, 1987).
6. According to Melville and Frances Herskovits, this connection between sex, laughter, and the god of death goes all the way back to classic masquerade traditions for Legba (Gede's progenitor) in Dahomey:

> On the last of a ten day public ceremony Legba manifested himself in the body of a young girl dressed in a purple raffia skirt and a purple straw hat. The girl came towards the drums sounding the Legba's rhythm. When she reached the drummer, she put her hand under the fringe of raffia about her waist . . . and brought out a wooden phallus. This was apparently attached in such a way that it would remain in the horizontal position of the erect male organ, and as she danced . . . toward a large tree where many women were sitting watching the ceremony . . . they ran from her, shrieking with laughter, and they were made the butt of many jokes by the spectators. (1958, 125–126)

7. Maya Deren describes a memorable instance of Gede's love and mercy. A girl near the point of death was brought to a ceremony. Agreeing to intervene, Gede possessed a female priest who placed the child on a tomb, and rubbed her body with the blood of a sacrificed goat. Then singing fervently, Gede reached between [her/his] legs and brought forth, in [her/his] cupped hand, seminal ejaculate. Although it seemed impossible, since Gede was possessing a female body, cup after cup of semen was brought forth to bathe the child, while others at the ceremony sang and wept with gratitude for this act of mercy. And though there was no reasonable way to account for it, the child lived (1953, 113–14).
8. Deren 1953, 102n. She then concludes, "Sexual obscenity and the breaking of taboos is characteristic of the death figure in many mythologies, including that of the American Indians."
9. "But Gede is a good advisor too. He tells the truth. Gede could give you a number to go to the *borlette,* but he doesn't do that. Gede can make you lose money too. When you don't follow his rules. Because in everything there is rules" (Gladys Maitre, conversation, 1987).
10. TonTon Macoute is translated as "Uncle Straw-Bag," an allusion to the bogeyman in Haitian folktales who steals away naughty children in such a sack.
11. Concerning his appetite, Gladys Maitre comments, "Even if you kill beef, goat, it's just for the people. Gede judge food otherwise. Banana. Potato. Cassav. Pepper. Things like that, that's Gede food. Gede go for fast food. Empty calories." (Conversation, 1987)
12. De-bowdlerized from Laguerre 1980, 107.
13. A popular etymology says the Chaloskas are named after a pompous nineteenth century general named Charles Oscar.
14. This description of Carnival is excerpted from Cosentino 1992, 23–29.

15. But François Duvalier was an equal opportunity dictator. He also appeared in posters next to Jesus, whose arm was drapped over the dour little man, saying, "He's my choice." To even that score, a generation later images of the Virgin Mary appeared with Aristide nestled in the middle of her Immaculate Heart. Modesty and dictatorship don't seem to go together.

NOTES FOR CHAPTER TEN (Roth)

1. A version of this chapter can be found as part of a larger essay entitled "'The Psychedelic Happy Hippie Zone': Living Museum of Deadhead Material Culture" in *Shakedown Street: The Art of Deadheads*, forthcoming from the University Press of Mississippi.
2. Poetry by an unknown Deadhead in 1981 in Grushkin, Bassett, and Gruskin 1983, 44.
3. The following definitions derive from Shenk and Silberman's *Skeleton Key: A Dictionary for Deadheads*:

   Tour - v. - To follow the band from venue to venue, seeing as many shows as possible in a series. Most band itineraries are from ten to twenty shows long. Deadheads "tour" or "do tour," as in "Did you do Spring Tour '87?"

   Tourheads - n. - The especially "deadicated" class of Deadheads who follow the band for most or all of a tour, living along the way in tour buses, inexpensive motels, friends' homes, or local student housing. Deadheads on tour watch the band's repertoire unfold, and hear songs and jams develop from city to city. Familiar faces are met at each destination, so that the shows themselves—rather than the towns they happen to be in—are "home."

   Tour Rats - Hardcore tourheads who live in the parking lot, earning road costs by vending, and waiting—or scamming—for a "miracle." The term is used with outlaw pride when describing oneself, and sarcasm when describing others.
4. Shenk and Silberman note, as do others, that "Like members of the Native American Church, some Heads prefer not to call marijuana and psychedelics 'drugs,' with that term's connotations of illness, abuse, and law enforcement. They prefer the word 'sacraments,' appropriate to the respect and gravity which they use these substances" (1994, 252).
5. For more information about the impact events during the 1940s and 1950s had on Deadhead culture, refer to Roth (*Shakedown Street*, forthcoming).

6. Lyrics from "The Other One," written by Bob Weir and Bill Kreutzmann. A live recording of this song, performed by the Grateful Dead on 13 August 1975, at The Great American Music Hall, appears on *One from the Vault,* Grateful Dead Productions, Inc., 1975/1991.
7. Neal Cassady served as the inspiration for Dean Moriarty, the hero of Jack Kerouac's novel *On The Road.*
8. Deadhead material culture was presented through the eyes of its members in a documentary exhibition entitled "Dead on the Wall: Grateful Dead and Deadhead Iconography From 30 Years on the Bus," which opened June 1996 at the Huntington Beach Art Center, Huntington Beach, California.
9. Shenk and Silberman present an excerpt from an interview with John Perry Barlow, lyricist for the Grateful Dead, which discusses the nature of the founding "acid heroes." Barlow states, "There were basically two psychedelic camps—the West Coast Ken Kesey manifestation, and the East Coast Timothy Leary manifestation" (1994, 18). Although the West Coast camp drew upon ideas from the East Coast camp (e.g., those of Leary) and vice versa, the two remained relatively distinct groups.
10. Wavy Gravy, a.k.a. Hugh Nanton Romney—clown, poet, and activist—was given his nickname from B. B. King at the Texas Pop Festival in 1969. Whenever Gravy appeared at Grateful Dead gatherings, he did so *dressed in full clown regalia.* Shenk and Silberman describe Wavy Gravy's history with the Grateful Dead:

    > Wavy earned the original passing grade at the Acid Tests by navigating through the smoldering psychedelia to assist a tripper who had begun yelling "Who cares?" into a microphone, establishing a compassionate model for talkdown still used today by the Rock Med emergency medical personnel. Wavy and the Hog Farmers [a collective household/community in Oregon founded by Wavy] have maintained a long relationship with the Dead, and act as tribal elders, helping to set up campgrounds at venues and taking care of the kids of band and crew backstage at shows, surfing the chaos on a sea of bubbles and face paint. Wavy was a founding member of SEVA [a foundation for compassionate social action], and organizes Camp Winnarainbow in Mendocino, where kids learn clowning, music, yoga, and how to be a good citizen of the planet . . . (1994, 307)

11. The "Thunder Machine" was a percussive instrument built by metal sculptor Ron Boise.

12. In some versions of the narrative, Garcia used a 1955 *Funk and Wagnall's Dictionary* (Brightman 1998, 80). Former manager Jon McIntire reports that it was the *Oxford Companion to Classical Music* that Garcia opened at random to find "grateful dead"—an "English folk song about people who are grateful to be released into death" (Greenfield 1996, 104).
13. The belief that Lewis Carroll, author of *Alice in Wonderland*, included coded references to psychedelic trips in the book is prevalent among Deadheads.
14. Jackson (1983) asserts about the name "Grateful Dead": "It is said that LSD offers a sort of transitory immortality and concomitant ego-death for the user, since the massive perceptual changes it induces frequently lead to a certain feeling of timelessness and a feeling of oneness with the tripper's surroundings. In that way, the 'best' LSD experiences seem to mirror descriptions of ecstatic religious experiences in literatures; the conventional signposts we use in day to day life to measure ourselves disappear, leaving pure experience—devoid of intellectualizations or time and space considerations—in their wake."

    For specific information regarding the role of hallucinogens in Deadhead rituals, refer to such works as: Furst (1976), Kotarba (1993), Leary, Metzner, and Alpert (1964), Reist (1997) and Sardiello (1990).
15. "The moment that you realize you are a Deadhead is sometimes called 'getting on the bus'" (Shenk and Silberman1994, 210). This phrase is taken from the Grateful Dead song "The Other One," which in turn refers to the saying used on Ken Kesey's bus (Wolfe 1968).
16. Augustus Owsley Stanley III was the chemist who helped distribute LSD to the masses in the '60s. He also served as a sound engineer for the Grateful Dead.
17. See *The Tibetan Book of the Dead, The Egyptian Book of the Dead*, and *The Psychedelic Experience: A Manual Based on the Tibetan Book of the Dead* for further information regarding these mystic traditions and accompanying iconography.

NOTES TO CHAPTER ELEVEN (Koven)

1. In fact, Thompson identifies this motif, not as the European "Frankenstein" story, but as an Inuit monster called the "Tupilac." Thompson's description of this monster is thus: "Monster made of parts of corpses of animals and vivified" (Thompson 1955–58, III: 353).
2. Freud notes, regarding the taboo against the dead (and this is particularly relevant to a discussion of horror cinema), "the most obvious

explanation would point to horror roused by dead bodies and by the changes which quickly become visible to them" (1950, 57).

3. There are subtle differences between Thompson's "living dead" motif and Romero's "living dead" zombies. Thompson defines his "living dead" thus: "Revenant is not a spectre but has the attributes of a living person. He wanders about till his 'second death,' complete disintegration in the grave" (Thompson 1955–58, II: 445). One can see by this description why Thompson chose to file this motif under "the dead" category, rather than under "ogres." However, Romero's "living dead" also continue to wander about until their "second deaths," in this case, the destruction of the monster's brain, usually in the form of a gunshot to the head.
4. Say the title aloud.
5. In Romero's *Dawn of the Dead*, the only explanation for why the dead are coming back to life, used as the film's tag line, is that when there is no more room in Hell, the dead shall wander the earth. As a satirical commentary on American consumerism, Romero is also implying that when there are no more products to consume, Americans will begin to consume each other.
6. For a consideration of tale types and motifs and how they are used in horror films, see Julia George 1982.
7. This category also includes witches (for example, G259.4—"Witch's [corpse is] heavy") and giants (G691.1—"Giants keep [corpse] on hand to eat"). It is interesting to note the similarities between the latter motif regarding giants and the above-mentioned motif regarding vampires: both monsters use the human dead as sustenance, but because one is terrestrial and the other aerial (giant and vampire, respectively), they appear under different *Motif Index* categories.
8. Aarne and Thompson, on the other hand, uses tale type 1536 as a category for the variations A–C, and identify the larger tale type number as being essentially the same as motif K2151, noted above (1981, 441–442).
9. A film representation of "The Runaway Grandmother" legend occurs in Harold Ramis' *National Lampoon's Vacation* (1983), where the Griswold's family vacation is almost disrupted by the death of the much-disliked Aunt Edna (Imogene Coca) and the inadvertent theft of her corpse (see Brunvand 1981, 103–123).
10. Rich complains that he always gets yelled at when he "just lies there."
11. Thompson defines "J1769.2.1—Dead mistaken for the living" as "Man with abhorrence for corpse sleeps with one thinking it alive" (IV: 145).

12. "T466—Necrophilia. Sexual intercourse with dead human body" (V: 388).
13. There is an implication that the more traditional message Larry's character demonstrates is that it is fine to be a slob, so long as you have hard-working friends. As for Rich's character, it is fine to be a "stick-in-the-mud" so long as you have a friend who will take you to parties.
14. Presumably, even screenwriter Robert Klane, who wrote both *Weekend at Bernie's* movies and directed the second one, forgot that Larry and Rich found and kept the money at the end of the first film.
15. In my own experience as both a writer and reader of movie reviews, the position of "film critic" (as they like to be called) goes to the editor of the "Arts Section" of various newspapers. Therefore, the local movie reviewer has established himself or herself an elite role within the newspaper work culture.
16. Linked with this formulaic psychodynamic, "oral structures often look to pragmatics (the convenience of the speaker . . .) . . . [as opposed to literary] structures [which] look more to syntactics (organization of the discourse itself)" (Ong 1982, 37–38).
17. Rich, particularly as played by Jonathan Silverman, is encoded as "Jewish." On his first date with Gwen, who is equally encoded as "Gentile," he takes her to "Hymie's Hunan," a strictly kosher Chinese restaurant in the heart of New York's Hasidic community. However, despite the inclusion of this situational joke, Rich and Gwen's ethnicity is largely ignored.

REFERENCES

Abrahams, Roger D. 1982. The Language of Festivals. In *Celebration,* ed. Victor Turner. Washington DC: Smithsonian Institution Press.

Abrahams, Roger D. 1982b. Storytelling Events. *Journal of American Folklore* 95:389–414.

Abrahams, Roger D. 1983. *The Man of Words in the West Indies.* Baltimore: Johns Hopkins University Press.

Abrahams, Roger D. 1987. An American Vocabulary of Celebrations. In *Time Out of Time,* ed. Alessandro Falassi. Albuquerque: University of NM Press: 173–183.

Abrahams, Roger D. 1991 (1974). Black Talking on the Streets. In Richard Bauman and Joel Scherzer, eds. *Explorations in the Ethnography of Speaking*: 240–262.

Abrahams, Roger D. and Richard Bauman. 1978. Ranges in Festival Behavior. In *The Reversible World,* ed. Barbara Babcock. Ithaca: Cornell University Press: 193–208.

Ades, Dawn. 1989. *Art in Latin America.* New Haven CT: Yale University Press.

Alden, Dana L., Ashesh Mukherjee, and Wayne D. Hoyer. 2000. Extending a Contrast Resolution Model of Humor in Television Advertising. *Humor* 13:193–217.

Alvin, J. 1983. *Gross Jokes.* NY: Zebra.

Alvin, J. 1983b. *Totally Gross Jokes.* NY: Zebra.

Alvin, J. 1984. *Utterly Gross Jokes.* NY: Zebra.

Ameen, Sister Ann. 14 November 1992. Tape-recorded interview, Bay Roberts, regarding a wake experience at an Anglican household during informant's childhood in Shearstown.

Apte, Mahadev. 1985. *Humor and Laughter.* Ithaca: Cornell University Press.

Ariès, Philippe. 1974. The Reversal of Death. *Death in America.* D. E. Stannard, ed. Philadelphia, University of PA Press:134–58.

Armstrong, Robert Plant. 1971. *The Affecting Presence.* Urbana: University of IL Press.

Asylum Dedication to Americans Dealing with Terrorism. 2002. *Asylum - Sick Jokes, Cartoons, Pictures and Entertainment.* (March 10). Available: http://asylum.subnetcentral.com/davec/terror/aaterror.htm.

Babcock, Barbara. 1978. Introduction. In *The Reversible World,* ed. Barbara Babcock. Ithaca: Cornell University Press: 13–36.

Baker, Ronald. 1982. *Hoosier Folk Legends.* Bloomington: IN University Press.

Bakhtin, Mikhail. 1984. *Rabelais and His World.* Bloomington: IN University Press.

Ballard, Linda. 1992. *Personal communication regarding variants of the "tied corpse" tale in Northern Ireland.*

Banks, Russell.1985. *Continental Drift.* NY: Harper and Row.

Baraka, Amiri. 1994. Cultural Revolution and the Canon. In *Disembodied Poetics,* ed. Anne Waldman and Andrew Schelling. University of NM Press.

Barnes, Sandra. 1997. *Africa's Ogun.* Bloomington: IN University Press.

Barthes, Roland. 1975. *The Pleasure of the Text.* NY: Noonday Press.

Basso, Keith .1979. *Portraits of 'The Whiteman.'* Cambridge: Cambridge University Press.

Bataille, Georges. 1986. *Erotism.* San Francisco: City Lights.

Bauman, Richard. 1972. Differential Identity and the Social Base of Folklore. In Américo Paredes and Richard Bauman, eds. *Towards New Perspectives in Folklore.* Austin: University of Texas Press: 31–41.

Bauman, Richard. 1988 (1986). *Story, Performance and Event.* Cambridge Studies in Oral and Literate Culture 10. Cambridge: Press Syndicate of the University of Cambridge.

Beardsley, John. 1987. And/Or. In *Hispanic Art in the es,* eds. John Beardsley and Jane Livingston (with an essay by Octavio Paz). NY: Abbeville Press: 43–84.

Beauvoir–Dominique, Rachel. 1995. Under Ground Realms of Being. In *The Sacred Arts of Haitian Vodou,* ed. Donald Cosentino, UCLA: Fowler Museum.

Beezley, William.1997. Home Altars. In *Home Altars of Mexico,* ed. Ramón Gutiérrez; photographer Dana Salvo. Albuquerque: University of NM Press: 91–107.

Bergson, Henri.1956. Laughter. In Wylie Sypher, ed. *Comedy.* NY: Doubleday Anchor Books: 61–190.

Blauner, Robert. 1977. Death and Social Structure. *Passing.* C. O. Jackson, ed. Westport, CT, Greenwood Press:174–209.

Block, Susan. 2001. We're All Afghans Now - Why We Should Support RAWA, Afghan Women and a Less Terrorized Global Future. *Counterpunch* (October 30). Available: http://www.counterpunch.org/block2.html.

Bogatyrev, Petr. 1977 (1926). Ritual Games in the Funerals of Sub-Carpathian Russia (trans. Egle Zygas). *Folklore Forum* 10:141–59.

Bonnemaison, Sarah. 1990. City Policy and Cyclical Events. *Design Quarterly* 147:24–32.

Bouissac, Paul. 1976. *Circus and Culture.* Bloomington, IN: University of IN Press.

Brandes, Stanley. 1977. Peaceful Protest. *Western Folklore* 36(4):331–346.

Brandes, Stanley. 1979a. Dance as Metaphor. *Journal of Latin American Lore* 5(1):25–43.

Brandes, Stanley. 1979b. *Metaphors of Masculinity.* Philadelphia: University of PA Press.

Brandes, Stanley. 1983. Humor, Agresivitat I Salut Mental a la Peninsula Iberica (Humor, Aggression and Mental Health in the Iberian Peninsula). *Quaderns de l'Obra Social* 16:9–13.

Brandes, Stanley. 1998a. The Day of the Dead, Halloween, and the Quest for Mexican National Identity. *Journal of American Folklore* 111(422):359–380.

Brandes, Stanley. 1998b. Iconography in Mexico's Day of the Dead. *Ethnohistory* 45 (2):181–218.

Bredin, Thomas F., ed. 1969. *Recollections of Labrador Life by Lambert de Boilieu.* Toronto, Ryerson Press.

Brenner, Anita. 1967. *Idols Behind Altars.* NY: Biblo and Tannen.

Bricker, Victoria R. 1973. *Ritual Humor in Highland Chiapas.* Austin: University of Texas Press.

Brightman, Carol. 1998. *Sweet Chaos.* NY: Clarkson Potter.

Bronner, Simon J. 1985. What's Grosser than Gross. *Midwestern Journal of Language and Lore* 11:72–81.

Bronner, Simon. 2002. *Folk Nation: Folklore in the Creation of American Tradition.* Wilmington, DE: SR Books.

Brown, Karen McCarthy. 1991. *Mama Lola.* Berkeley: University of CA Press.

Brown, Karen McCarthy. 1995. Serving the Spirits. In *The Sacred Arts of Haitian Vodou,* ed. Donald Cosentino, UCLA: Fowler Museum

Buckley, Anne-Kay and Christine Cartwright. 1983. The Good Wake. *Culture & Tradition* 7: 6–16.

Buckley, J. Taylor. 1996. Personalities of Dearly Departed Etched in Stone. *USA Today,* 13 February: 1A–2A.

Budgell, George. 8 July 1991. Tape-recorded interview, St. John's, with George Budgell, Northwest River, Labrador, regarding a "true" occurrence at Twillingate.

Burke, John. 1960. *Burke's Ballads, Compiled by John White.* St. John's: John White.

Butler, Gary R. 1982. "Sacred and Profane Space. " *Material History Bulletin* 15: 27–32.

Butler, Gary R. 1990. *Saying Isn't Believing.* St. John's, Institute of Social and Economic Research, Memorial University of Newfoundland.

Byrne, Moyra. 1982. Antonio Gramsci's Contribution to Italian Folklore Studies. *International Folklore Review* 2: 70–5.

Byrne, Packie Manus. 1992 (1989). *Reflections of a Donegal Man.* Edited and compiled by Steven Jones. Lampeter, Wales and Quebec, Canada: Roger Millington.

Caillois, Roger. 1961. *Man, Play, and Games.* NY: Free Press of Glencoe.

Camporesi, Piero. 1989. *Bread of Dreams.* Chicago, University of Chicago Press.

Cannadine, David. 1983. The Context, Performance and Meaning of Ritual. In *The Invention of Tradition,* eds. Eric Hobsbawm and Terrence Ranger. NY: Cambridge University Press: 101–164.

Carlin, Jean. 2001. Telephone interview with the author, 23 July.

Carmichael, Elizabeth, and Chloë Sayer. 1992. *The Skeleton at the Feast.* Austin: University of Texas Press.

Carroll, Lewis. 1916. *Alice's Adventures in Wonderland.* NY: Rand McNally and Company.

Castillo, Ana. 1993. *So Far From God.* NY: W. W. Norton & Company.

Cetola, Henry W. 1988. Toward a Cognitive-Appraisal Model of Humor Appreciation. *Humor* 1:245–58.

Chaney, David. 1983. A Symbolic Mirror of Ourselves. *Media, Culture and Society* 5:119–135.

Childs, Robert V., and Patricia B. Altman. 1982. *Vive tu Recuerdo.* Los Angeles: Museum of Cultural History, University of CA, Los Angeles.

Christiansen, Reidar Th. 1946. The Dead and the Living. *Studia Norvegica* No. 2. Oslo: H. Aschehoug,

CODCO. 18 November 1989. *CODCO.* Canadian Broadcasting Corporation TV.

Cohen, Abner. 1980. Drama and Politics in the Development of a London Carnival. *Man* 15: 65–87.

Cohen, Abner. 1982. A Polyethnic London Carnival as a Contested Cultural Performance. *Ethnic and Racial Studies* 5:22–41.

Congdon, Kristin G., Catalina Delgado-Trunk, and Marva Lopez. 1999. Teaching About the Ofrenda and Experiences on the Border. *Studies in Art Education* 40 (4):312–329.

Conrad, Joann. 1998. Stranger Danger: Defending Innocence, Denying Responsibility. *Contemporary Legend* N.S. 1: 55–96.

Conzen, Kathleen Neils. 1989. Ethnicity as Festive Culture. In *The Invention of Ethnicity,* ed. Werner Sollors. NY: Oxford University Press: 44–76.

Cosentino, Donald. 1987. Who Is That Fellow in the Many-Colored Hat? *Journal of American Folklore* (July-September).

Cosentino, Donald. 1992. Vodou Carnival. *Aperture* (February).

Cosentino, Donald. 1994. Returning the Dead. *The World and I.* (October).

Cosentino, Donald, ed. 1995. *The Sacred Arts of Haitian Vodou.* UCLA: Fowler Museum

Cross, Eric. 1964 (1942). *The Tailor and Ansty.* NY: Devin-Adair Company.

Cross, Tom Peete. 1952. *Motif Index of Early Irish Literature.* Folklore Series #7. Bloomington: IN University Publications.

Cunningham, Keith. 1996. Personal communication. 17 April.

Curtin, Jeremiah. 1890. *Myth and Folk-Lore of Ireland.* Boston: Little Brown.

DaMatta, Roberto. 1984. Carnival in Multiple Planes. In *Rite, Drama, Festival, Spectacle,* ed. John MacAloon. Philadelphia: ISHI: 208–239.

Davies, Christie. 1989. Humor for the Future and a Future for Humor. In *The Soviet Union and the Challenge of The Future,* vol. 3. *Ideology Culture and Nationality,* ed. Alexander Shtromas and Morton A Kaplan. NY: Paragon: 299–319.

Davies, Christie. 1990. Nasty Legends, Sick Humor and Ethnic Jokes about Stupidity. In *A Nest of Vipers,* ed. Gillian Bennett and Paul Smith. Sheffield: Sheffield Academic Press: 49–68.

Davies, Christie. 1996. Puritanical and Politically Correct. In *The Social Faces of Humour,* ed. Powell et al. Aldershot: Ashgate: 29–61.

Davies, Christie. 1998a. The Dog that Didn't Bark in the Night. In *The Sense of Humor,* ed. Willibald Ruch. Berlin and NY: Mouton de Gruyter: 293–306.

Davies, Christie. 1998b. *Jokes and their Relation to Society*, Berlin and NY, Mouton de Gruyter.

Davies, Christie. 1999. The Creation, Morality, the After-life and the Fission of Religious Tradition. *Journal of Contemporary Religion* 14 (3): 339–60.

Davies, Christie. 1999b. Jokes on the Death of Diana. *The Mourning for Diana*, ed. Tony Walter, 253–268. Oxford: Berg.

Davies, Christie. 2002. *The Mirth of Nations*. New Brunswick: Transaction.

Davies, Christie and Abe Goh. 2002. *Aru shu no grupu ni zoku suru hitobito ni kan suru jodan ya joku*. Kyoto: Sekai Shisosha.

Davies, Christie and Eugene Trivizas.1999. The Collapse of the Morality and National Moral Boundaries of Small Peripheral Countries. *Protosoziologie* 13(1): 210–25.

Davies, Christie and Mark Neal.1998. *The Corporation under Siege*. London: Social Affairs Unit.

Davies, Christie and Mark Neal. 2001. Particular, Statistical and Potential Persons. In *Virtue Ethics and Sociology*, ed. Kieran Flanagan and Peter Jupp. Basingstoke: Palgrave: 68–90.

Davis, Natalie Zemon. 1975. *Society and Culture in Early Modern France*. Stanford: Stanford University Press.

Davis, Natalie Zemon. 1975. *Society and Culture in Early Modern France*. Palo Alto: Stanford University Press.

Davis, Susan G. 1986. *Parades and Power*. Philadelphia: Temple University Press.

Davis, Wade. 1986. *The Serpent and the Rainbow*. NY: Simon and Schuster.

De Certeau, Michel. 1984. *The Practice of Everyday Life*. Berkeley: University of CA Press.

Dégh, Linda. 2001. *Legend and Belief: Dialectics of a Folklore Genre*. Bloomington: Indiana University.

Deren, Maya. 1953. *Divine Horsemen, The Living Gods of Haiti*. NY: Chelsea House.

Deriabin, Petr and Frank, Gibney. 1960. *The Secret World*. London: Arthur Barker

Dissanayake, Ellen. 1992. *Homo Aestheticus*. NY: The Free Press.

Dollar, Natalie J. 1988. The Development of a Strong Musical Taste Culture. Master's Thesis. Tempe: Arizona State University.

Dorson, Richard, Ed. 1967 (1956). *American Negro Folktales*. Bloomington: IN University Press.

Dorson, Richard M. 1952. *Bloodstoppers and Bearwalkers*. Cambridge: Harvard University Press.

Dorson, Richard. 1983. A Historical Theory for American Folklore. In *Handbook of American Folklore*, ed. Richard Dorson. Bloomington: IN University Press: 326–337.

Dorst, John. 1990. Tags and Burners, Cycles and Networks: Folklore in the Telectronic Age. *Journal of Folklore Research* 27:179–190.

Doss, Erika. 1999. *Elvis Culture*. Lawrence: University of Kansas Press.

Douglas, Mary. 1982. *In the Active Voice*. London: Routledge & Kegan Paul.

Douglas, Mary. 1991 (1975). Jokes. In *Implicit Meanings.* London: Routledge: 90–114.

Dundes, Alan. 1971. A Study of Ethnic Slurs. *Journal of American Folklore* 84:186–203.

Dundes, Alan.1987. *Cracking Jokes.* Berkeley: Ten Speed Press.

Dundes, Alan. 1997. Traditional Male Combat: From Game to War. *From Game to War and Other Psychoanalytic Essays on Folklore,* 25–45. Lexington: University of Kentucky Press.

Dundes, Alan, and Carl R. Pagter. 1992 [1975]. *Work Hard and You Shall Be Rewarded: Urban Folklore from the Paperwork Empire.* Detroit: Wayne State University Press.

Dundes, Alan, and Carl R. Pagter. 1996. *Sometimes the Dragon Wins: Yet More Urban Folklore from the Paperwork Empire.* Syracuse: Syracuse University Press. DuPré, Athena. 1998. *Humor and the Healing Arts.* Mahwah, NJ: Lawrence Erlbaum Associates.

Edgette, J. Joseph. 1989. The Epitaph and Personality Revelation. In *Cemeteries and Gravemarkers,* ed. Richard E. Meyer, pp. 87–102. Ann Arbor: UMI Research Press. Reprint. Logan: Utah State University Press, 1992.

Edison, Carol. 1985. Motorcycles, Guitars, and Bucking Broncs. In *Idaho Folklife,* ed. Louie W. Attebery, pp. 184–189. Salt Lake City: University of Utah Press.

Eliade, Mircea. 1964. *Shamanism.* NY: Bollingen.

Ellis, Bill. 1991. The Last Thing . . . Said: The Challenger Disaster Jokes and Closure. *International Folklore Review 8:* 110–124.

Ellis, Bill. 2001. A Model for Collecting and Interpreting World Trade Center Disaster Jokes. *New Directions in Folklore* 5 (October). Available: http://www.temple.edu/isllc/newfolk/wtchumor.html.

Ellis, Bill. 2002. Making a Big Apple Crumble: The Role of Humor in Constructing a Global Response to Disaster. *New Directions in Folklore* 6 (June). Available: www.temple.edu/isllc/newfolk/bigapple/bigapple1.html Ellis, Richard J.1996. The Sick Disaster Joke as Carnivalesque Postmodern Narrative Impulse. In *The Social Faces of Humour,* ed. Powell et al. Aldershot: Ashgate: 219–39.

Engel, Fred. 1997. Remember the Cow. *Lone Prairie Roundup* 6:73–79.

Faris, James C. 1972. *Cat Harbour.* St. John's: Institute of Social and Economic Research, Memorial University of Newfoundland.

Farries, Jane. Friday, October 19, 2001. *Not My Dog.* [Online journal] Available: http://www.notmydog.com/2001_10_01_archive.html.

Ferrante, L. P. 2002. Laughter after 9/11. *WGAw Written By* (April): 28–31.

Ferris, William R. 1980. Local Color. In *Made by Hand,* ed. Patti Carr Black. Jackson: MS Department of Archives and History: 11–22.

Fettell, Alison, and Linda Pfeiffer. 2002. Aboriginal Youth & Alcohol Related Violence Project: No More Hurt, No More Pain, No More Grog, No More Shame. No More! (Feb. 22) Available: http://www.adfq.org/fettell.html.

Fewer, Rudolph. 11 November 1991. Interview with Loretta Myles nee McCarthy from Terrenceville. St. John's: Unpublished essay.

Fine, Gary A. 1976. Obscene Joking Across Cultures. *Journal of Communication* 26:134–40.

Firestone, Melvin M. 1967. *Brothers and Rivals*. St. John's: Institute of Social and Economic Research, Memorial University of Newfoundland.

Firth, Raymond. 1961. The Plasticity of Myth in Tikopia. In *History and Tradition of Tikopia*. Wellington, New Zealand. Chapter 10.

Fiske, John. 1989. *Understanding Popular Culture*. Boston: Unwin Hyman.

Forabosco, Giovannantonio. 1992. Cognitive Aspects of the Humor Process. *Humor* 5:45–68.

Foucault, Michel. 1986. Right of Death and Power over Life. *The Foucault Reader*. P. Rabinow, ed. Harmondsworth: Penguin.

Fowke, Edith. 1984. "Notes" to *Songs of the Newfoundland Outports*. 1984. Produced by Kelly Russell. Recorded by Kenneth Peacock, 1951–1961. Pigeon Inlet Productions (St. John's, Newfoundland) LP PIP-7319. http://www.pigeoninlet.nfnet.com/history.htm

Frank Manning. Bowling Green, OH: Bowling Green University Popular Press: 330.

Franzosa, Bob, ed. 1989. *Grateful Dead Folktales*. Levant, Maine: Zosafarm Publications.

Freud, Sigmund. 1950. *Totem and Taboo*. NY: W.W. Norton & Co.

Freud, Sigmund. 1973. *Jokes and their Relation to the Unconscious*. Trans. and ed. James Strachey. NY: W.W. Norton. [Originally published 1905].

Frida Kahlo: Portrait of an Artist. 1983. A film by Elia Hershon, Roberto Guerra, and Wibke Von Bonin; edited by Caroline Emmonds, 62 minutes, An RM Arts/Hershon Guerra/WDR Production.

Friedman, Susan Stanford. 1998. *Mappings*. Princeton: Princeton University Press.

Furst, Peter T. 1976. *Hallucinogens and Culture*. Novato, CA: Chandler and Sharp Publishers, Inc.

Gailey, Alan. 1969. *Irish Folk Drama*. Cork: Mercier Press.

Galbo, Joe. 1990/91. An Interview with John Fiske. *Border/Lines* 20/21:4–7.

Gamm, Hans-Joachim. 1963. *Der Flüsterwitz im Dritten Reich*. München: List.

Gans, David. 1985. *Conversations with the Dead*. NY: St. Martin's Press.

Garciagodoy, Juanita. 1998. *Digging the Days of the Dead*. Niwot, Colorado: University Press of Colorado.

Gerould, Gordon H. 1908. *The Grateful Dead*. London: Publications of the Folk-Lore Society. No. 60.

Glass, Seymour. 2001. Beyond a Joke (18 October). Available: http://www.missblackamerica.net/coolstuff/15Beyond_a_Joke_-_Seymour_Glass.htm.

Glassie, Henry. 1982. *Passing the Time in Ballymenone*. Philadelphia: University of PA Press.

Glassie, Henry. 1983 (1975). *All Silver and No Brass*. Philadelphia: University of PA Press.

Goffman, Erving. 1959. *Presentation of Self in Every Day Life*. NY: Doubleday Press.

Goffman, Erving. 1961. *Encounters*. Indianapolis: Bobbs-Merrill.

Goffman, Erving. 1986 (1974). *Frame Analysis*. Boston: Northeastern University Press.

Goh, Abe and Sandy Ritz. 1996. *Survivor Humor in Disasters*. Research Institute for Comparative Culture, Tokushima Bunri University, Annual Report 12:20–28.

Goldstein, Kenneth S. 1985. Faith and Fate in Sea Disaster Ballads of Newfoundland Fishermen. In *By Land and By Sea*, ed. Roger D. Abrahams, et al. Hatboro, PA: Folklore Associates. 84–94.

Goodwin, Joseph P. 2001 [1989] Unprintable Reactions to All the News That's Fit to Print: Topical Humor and the Media. *New Directions in Folklore* 5 (October). Available: www.temple.edu/isllc/newfolk/reactions1.html.

Gordon, Anne. 1984. *Death is for the Living*. Edinburg: Paul Harris.

Gramsci, Antonio. 1990. Culture and Ideological Hegemony. In *Culture and Society*, ed. J. C. Alexander and S. Seidman. Cambridge: Cambridge University Press: 47–54.

Green, A.E. 1981. Only Kidding. In *Language, Culture and Tradition*, ed. A.E. Green and J.D.A. Widdowson. Leeds and Sheffield: Institute of Dialect and Folklife Studies, University of Leeds, and CECTAL, University of Sheffield. 47–76.

Greene, Graham. 1964. *The Comedians*. London: Penguin.

Greenfield, Robert. 1996. *Dark Star*. NY: William Morrow.

Grider, Sylvia. 2001. Spontaneous Shrines: A Modern Response to Tragedy and Disaster (Preliminary Observations Regarding the Spontaneous Shrines Following the Terrorist Attacks of September 11, 2001) *New Directions in Folklore* 5 (October). Available: www.temple.edu/isllc/newfolk/shrines.html.

Grushkin, Paul, Cynthia Bassett, and Jonas Grushkin. 1983. *Grateful Dead*. NY: Quill.

Guestbook. *Amanda Lang's Home Page*. Available: www.ohdear.itgo.com/fsguestbook.html

Gutiérrez, Ramón A. 1997. Conjuring the Holy. In *Home Altars in Mexico*, ed., Ramón Gutiérrez; photographer, Dano Salvo. Albuquerque: University of NM Press: 37–48.

Haas, Jack. 1977. Learning real feelings, a study of high-steel ironworkers reaction to fear and danger. *Sociology of Work and Occupation* 1 4(2): 147–70.

Handelman, Don. 1990. *Model and Mirrors*. NY: Cambridge University Press.

Hanks, Jacqueline. 1987. Pictorials. *Stone in America*. October, 28–33.

Harlow, Ilana. 1993. Unravelling Stories. *Journal of Folklore Research*. 30:177–200.

Harlow, Ilana. 1997. Creating Situations. *Journal of American Folkore* 110 (436):140–168.

Harris, Marvin. 1982. Why the Gays Came Out of the Closet. In *America Now*, ed. Marvin Harris. NY: Touchstone: 98–115.

Heath, Stephen. 1977. Translator's Note. In R. Barthes, *Image-Music-Text*. London: Fontana Press.

Herskovits, Melville. 1937. *Life in a Haitian Valley*. Garden City: Anchor.

Herskovits, Melville and Frances. 1958. *Dahomean Narrative.* Evanston: Northwestern University Press.

Hickey, Dave. 1997. *Air Guitar.* Los Angeles: Art Issues Press.

Hider, Jon. Heard on Leno's Tonight Show monologue . . . *My Thoughts* [Online journal] (October 3, 2001 10:51 PM) Available: www.jonhider.com/archives/2001_09_30_index.asp.

Hobsbawm, Eric, and Terrence Ranger, eds. 1983. *The Invention of Tradition.* NY: Cambridge University Press.

Holmes, John Clellen. 1958. *The Philosophy of the Beat Generation.*

Hughey, Michael W. 1983. Civil *Religion and Moral Order.* Westport CT: Greenwood Press.

Huizinga, Johan. 1955. *Homo Ludens.* Boston: Beacon Press.

Huxley, Francis. 1966. *The Invisibles.* NY: McGraw-Hill.

Ives, Edward D. 1962. Satirical Songs in Maine and the Maritime Provinces of Canada. *Journal of the International Folk Music Council* 14:65–9.

Jackson, Blair. 1983. *Grateful Dead.* NY: Putnam Publishing Group.

Jackson, Blair. 1992. *Goin' Down the Road.* NY: Harmony Books.

Jacobson-Widding, Anita. 1990. The Fertility of Incest. In *The Creative Communion,* eds. A. Jacobson-Widding and W. van Beek. Stockholm: Stockholm Studies in Cultural Anthropology 15:47–74.

Janoff, Bruce. 1974. Black humor, existentialism and absurdity: A generic confusion. *Arizona Quarterly* 20: 293–304.

Jameson, Frederic. 1979. Reification and Utopia in Mass Culture. *Social Text 1* (Winter): 130–148.

Jansen, Wm. Hugh. 1959. The Esoteric-Exoteric Factor in Folklore. *Fabula* 2: 205–11.

Jordan, Josephine. 1985. *Interview with Mildred Baker Jordan from Marystown.* St. John's: Unpublished essay.

Kalweit, Holger. 1988. *Dreamtime and Inner Space.* Boston: Shambhala.

Keating, Lori. 1992. *Interview with Frank Ryan from Torbay.* St. John's: Unpublished essay.

Kerouac, Jack. 1957. *On the Road.* NY: Penguin Books.

Kesey, Ken. *One Flew Over the Cuckoo's Nest.*

Kiliánová, Gabriela. July 1992. An Old Theme in the Present Time. Paper presented at the 10th Congress of the International Society for Folk Narrative Research, Innsbruck, Austria.

Kimball, Jacqueline. 1997. 'When This You See Remember Me.' *Stone in America.* August, 11–15.

Kinser, Samuel. 1990. *Carnival American Style.* Chicago: University of Chicago Press.

Kirshenblatt-Gimblett, Barbara. 1998. *Destination Culture.* Berkeley: University of CA Press.

Kirwin, William. 1977. The Influence of Ireland on the Printed Newfoundland Ballad. In *Literature and Folk Culture,* ed. A. Feder and B. Schrank. St. John's: Memorial University of Newfoundland: 130–45.

Kirwin, William, ed. 1982. *John White's Collection of the Songs of Johnny Burke.* St. John's: Harry Cuff Publications.

Klisiewicz, Bob. 2001. Outrageous Epitaphs. *AGS Quarterly* 25(3): 5–7; 24–27.

Knott, B. 1982. *Truly Tasteless Jokes.* NY: Ballantine.

Knott, B. 1983. *Truly Tasteless Jokes Two.* NY: Ballantine.

Knott, B. 1983b. *Truly Tasteless Jokes Three.* NY: Ballantine.

Knott, B. 1984. *Truly Tasteless Jokes IV.* NY: Ballantine.

Koestler, Arthur. 1964. *The Act of Creation.* NY: Macmillan.

Kolakowski, Leszek. 1962. The Priest and the Jester. In *The Modern Polish Mind,* ed. Maria Kuncewicz. Boston: Little Brown: 310–326.

Kornblum, Janet. 2001. Guarded humor returns to the Web. *USAToday.com* (26 September). Available: http://www.usatoday.com/life/cyber/tech/2001/09/26/ebrief.htm.

Kotarba, J. 1993. The Rave Scene in Houston, Texas. Texas Commission of Alcohol and Drug Abuse.

Koykka, Arthur S. 1986. *Project Remember.* Algonac, MI: Reference Publications, Inc.

Krause, David. 1982. *The Profane Book of Irish Comedy.* Ithaca: Cornell University Press.

Kuhlman, Thomas L. 1984. *Humor and Psychotherapy.* Homewood, IL: Dow Jones-Irwin Dorsey.

Kunzle, David. 1978. World Upside Down. In *The Reversible World,* ed. Barbara Babcock, Ithaca: Cornell University Press: 39–94.

Kürti, Lászlo. 1988. The Politics of Joking. *Journal of American Folklore* 101:324–334.

Ladurie, Emmanuel Le Roy. 1980. *Carnival in Romans.* NY: George Braziller.

Laguerre, Michel. 1980. *Voodoo Heritage.* Beverly Hills: Sage.

Lavenda, Robert. 1980. The Festival of Progress. *Journal of Popular Culture* 14 (Winter):465–475.

Lawrence, Denise L. 1982. Parades, Politics, and Competing Urban Images. *Urban Anthropology* 11:155–176.

Lawrence, Denise L. 1987. Rules of Misrule. In *Time Out of Time,* ed. Alessandro Falassi. Albuquerque: University of NM Press: 123–136.

Laws, G. Malcolm. 1957. *American Balladry From British Broadsides.* Philadelphia: American Folklore Society.

Leach, MacEdward. 1966. Notes. In *Songs From the Out-Ports of Newfoundland,* M. Leach collector. NY: Folkways Records and Service Corp., LP, Folkways Records Album No. FE 4075.

Leary, Timothy, Ralph Metzner, and Richard Alpert. 1964. *The Psychedelic Experience.* NY: University Books.

Legman, Gershon. 1968. *Rationale of the Dirty Joke.* NY: Grove.

Legman, Gershon. 1975. *No Laughing Matter.* NY: Breaking Point.

LeRoy Ladurie, Emmanuel. 1979. *Carnival in Romans.* (Trans. Mary Feeney) NY: G. Braziller.

Limon, Jose. 1983. Western Marxism and Folklore. *Journal of American Folklore* 96:34–52.

Lippard, Lucy. 1984. Trojan Horses. In *Art After Modernism*, ed. Brian Wallis and Marcia Tucker. NY: The New Museum of Contemporary Art: 331–339.

Lippard, Lucy. 1990. *Mixed Blessings*. NY: Pantheon.

Lippard, Lucy. 1995. *The Pink Glass Swan*. NY: The New Press.

Lipsitz, George. 1990. Mardis Gras Indians. In *Time Passages*, ed. George Lipsitz. Minneapolis: University of MN Press: 233–253.

López, Maritza. 1987. Foreword. In *The Life of the Dead in Mexican Folk Art*, ed. María Teresa Pomar. The Fort Worth Art Museum.

MacAloon, John J. 1982. Sociation and Sociability in Political Celebrations. In *Celebration*, ed. Victor Turner. Washington DC: Smithsonian Institution Press: 255–271.

MacAloon, John J. 1984. Olympic Games and the Theory of Spectacle in Modern Societies. In *Rite, Drama, Festival, Spectacle*, ed. John MacAloon, Philadelphia: ISHI: 241–280.

MacCannell, Dean. 1976. *The Tourist*. NY: Schocken Books.

Malloy, Thomas A. 2001. Personal communication to the author, 10 August.

Manning, Frank E., ed. 1983. *The Celebration of Society*. Bowling Green, OH: Popular Press.

Marcus, Adam. 2001. Laughter Shelved in Medicine Cabinet: America's sense of humor blunted by week of shock. *Healingwell.com* (Sept. 19). Available: http://healingwelldepression.subportal.com/health/Diseases_and_Conditions/Psychological/Depression/501716.html.

Marquis, Don. 1973. *Archy and Mehitabel*. NY: Doubleday.

Mason, Bruce Lionel. 1996. Moving Toward Virtual Ethnography. *American Folklore Society News* 25.2 (April): 4–6. Available: http://www.ucs.mun.ca/~bmason/phd/afsnews.html

Masuoka, Susan N. 1994. *En Calavera*. Los Angeles: UCLA Fowler Museum of Cultural History.

Matthews, Glenda. 1990. Interview with Gerald Greene from St. John's. St. John's: Unpublished essay.

May, Elaine. 1988. *Homeward Bound*. NY: Basic Books.

Mays, Alan E. 2001. Personal communication via email (Sept 24).

McCarthy Brown, Karen. 1995. Serving the Spirits. In *Sacred Arts of Haitian Vodou*, ed. Donald J. Cosentino. Los Angeles: UCLA Fowler Museum of Cultural History: 205–223.

McCarthy, Dominic. 3 September 1991. Personal communication with Dominic McCarthy, Topsail.

McEvilley, Thomas. 1992. *Art and Otherness*. Kingston, NY: McPherson and Company.

McFadden, Robert. November 18, 1994. They Said She was D.O.A., But Then the Body Bag Moved. *New York Times*: B7.

McKenna, Sonya. 1990. Interview with Anonymous from Stag Harbour, Fogo Island. St. John's: Unpublished essay.

McKinley, Fred. 1988. Telephone interview with the author, 21 February.

McLuhan, Marshall. 1964. *Understanding Media.* NY, Signet, New American Library.

Mercer, Paul. 1974. *The Ballads of Johnny Burke.* St. John's: Newfoundland Historical Society.

Mercier, Vivian. 1962. *The Irish Comic Tradition.* Oxford: Oxford University Press.

Mesa-Bains, Amalia. 1997. Afterword. In *Home Altars of Mexico,* ed., Ramón Gutiérrez; photographer, Dana Salvo. Albuquerque: University of NM Press: 123–128.

Metcalf, Peter, and Richard Huntington. 1992. *Celebrations of Death.* Second edition. Cambridge: Cambridge University Press.

Metraux, Alfred. 1972. *Voodoo in Haiti.* NY: Oxford University Press.

Meyer, Richard E. 1984a. Images of Work and Play on Contemporary American Gravemarkers. Paper presented at Pacific Northwest American Studies Association annual meeting, Pullman, Wash., 14 April.

Meyer, Richard E. 1984b. The Retrospective View on Contemporary Gravemarkers for Young Men. Paper presented at American Folklore Society annual meeting, San Diego, CA, 12 October.

Meyer, Richard E., ed. 1989a. *Cemeteries and Gravemarkers.* Ann Arbor: UMI Research Press. Reprint. Logan: Utah State University Press, 1992.

Meyer, Richard E. 1989b. Buried Not on the Lone Prairie. Paper presented at American Culture Association annual meeting, St. Louis, MO, 7 April.

Meyer, Richard E. 1990. Western Lifestyles, Western Deathstyles. Paper presented at American Folklore Society annual meeting, Oakland, CA, 19 October.

Meyer, Richard E. 1991a. Logger's Lives, Logger's Graves. *Journal of Forest and Conservation History* 35(1): 29–30.

Meyer, Richard E. 1991b. Speaking Stones and the New Epitaph. Paper presented at Modern Language Association annual meeting, San Francisco, CA, 29 December.

Meyer, Richard E. 1993. 'He Has Reached The Terminal.' Paper presented at American Culture Association annual meeting, New Orleans, LA, 10 April.

Milley, Wendy. 1991. Interview with Eileen Power from Angel's Cove. St. John's: Unpublished essay.

Millman, Larry. 1977. *Our Like Will Not Be There Again.* Toronto: Little, Brown and Company.

Milspar, Yvonne. 1981. Folklore on the Nuclear Age; The Harrisburg Disaster at Three Mile Island. *International Folklore Review* 1:57–65.

Mitford, Jessica. 1993. *The American Way of Death.* Buccaneer Press.

Montell, Lynwood. 1975. *Ghosts Along the Cumberland.* Knoxville: University of Tennessee Press.

Mooney. 1888. The Funeral Customs of Ireland. *Proceedings of the American Philosophical Society* 25:423–96.

Moran, Carmen, and Margaret Massam. 1997. An Evaluation of Humour in Emergency Work. *The Australasian Journal of Disaster and Trauma Studies* 3. Available: http://www.massey.ac.nz/~trauma/issues/1997-3/moran1.htm

Morgan, David. 1998. Domestic Devotion and Ritual. The Art Journal 57 (1) (Spring):45–54.

Morreall, John. 1989. Enjoying Incongruity. *Humor* 2:1–18.

Morrison, Monica. 1974. Wedding Night Pranks. *Southern Folklore Quarterly* 38:285–297.

Motz, Marilyn. 1998. The Practice of Belief. Journal of American Folklore 111(441) (Summer):337–335.

Murdoch, Brian. 1990. *Fighting Songs and Warring Words.* London: Routledge.

Narváez, Peter. 1991. Playing with the Dead. Paper presented at the joint meeting of the Folklore Studies Association of Canada and the American Folklore Society, St. John's, Newfoundland.

Narváez, Peter. 1992. Folkloristics, Cultural Studies and Popular Culture. *Canadian Folklore Canadien* 14.1: 15–30.

Narváez, Peter. 1994. "Tricks and Fun." *Western Folklore* 53:263–293.

Narváez, Peter. 1995. Newfoundland Vernacular Song. *Popular Music.* Will Straw, Stacey Johnson, Rebecca Sullivan and Paul Friedlander eds. Montréal: Centre for Research on Canadian Cultural Industries and Institutions. 215–19.

Narváez, Peter. 1997. *The Good People.* Lexington: University Press of Kentucky.

Norris, Grant. 7 November 1991. Personal communication, Grant Norris, Gander Bay.

Ó Crualaoich, Gearóid. 1990. Contest in the Cosmology and the Ritual of the Irish 'Merry Wake.' *Cosmos* 6: 145–60.

Ó Giolláin, Diarmuid. 1991. The Fairy Belief and Official Religion in Ireland. *The Good People.* P. Narváez, ed. NY, Garland.

Ó Súilleabháin, Seán. 1967. *Irish Folk Custom and Belief.* Dublin: Cultural Relations Committee of Ireland, Three Candles, Ltd.

Ó Súilleabháin, Seán. 1967b. *Irish Wake Amusements.* Dublin, Mercier Press.

O'Brien, Con. and Ronnie Power. 1990. Daddy Shot the Cat. In *A 'Time' in Bay Bulls,* producer Gary O'Driscoll, Side A, Item 2. St. John's: Homespun Records, cassette, HSR-003 47.

O'Flaherty, Wendy Doniger. 1984. *Dreams, Illusions and Other Realities.* Chicago: University of Chicago Press.

O'Hear, Anthony. 1998. Diana Queen of Hearts. In *Faking It,* ed. Digby Anderson and Peter Mullen. London: Social Affairs Unit: 181–190.

O'Madgáin, Breandan. 1975. Functions of Irish Song in the 19th Century." *Beauloideas* 53:215–216

Obrdlik, A. J. 1942. Gallows Humor, A Sociological Phenomenon. *American Journal of Sociology* 47:709–16.

Oh What a Lovely War. 1967 London: Eyre Methuen.

Oldford, Dana. 1990. Interview with Jean Foote from Foote's Cove. St. John's: Unpublished essay.

Olsen, Ted. 2001. The Untold Story of America's Favorite E-mail Forward. *Christianity Today* (1 October). Available: http://www.christianitytoday.com/ct/2001/140/22.0.html

Ong, Walter. 1982. *Orality and Literacy.* London: Methuen.

Oring, Elliott. 1987. Jokes and the Discourse on Disaster. *Journal of American Folklore* 100: 276–286.

Oring, Elliott. 1992. *Jokes and their Relations.* Lexington, University Press of Kentucky.

Oring, Elliott. 1995. Arbiters of Taste. *Journal of Folklore Research* 32:165–74.

Osama Bin Laden Pictures and Jokes. 2002. *Osama Yo' Mama.* (Mar. 12). Available: http://www.osamayomama.com/index.htm.

Palmer, Roy. 1990. *What a Lovely War, British Soldiers' Songs from the Boer War to the Present Day.* London: Michael Joseph.

Paris, Matthew. 1999. *The Great Unfrocked.* London: Robson.

Partridge, Eric. 1972. *The Penguin Dictionary of Historical Slang.* Harmondsworth: Penguin Books.

Paz, Octavio. 1961. *The Labyrinth of Solitude.* NY: Grove Press.

Peacock, Kenneth. 1965. *Songs of the Newfoundland Outports.* 3 vols. Ottawa: National Museums of Canada.

Peere, Isabelle Marie. 1992. Death and Worldview in a Ballad Culture. St. John's: Memorial University of Newfoundland, Ph.D. Thesis, Department of Folklore.

Perry, Charles. 1980. Dead Heads 1980. *Rolling Stone* (August): 22–23.

Peters, Helen. 1990. From Salt Cod to Cod Filets. *Canadian Theatre Review* 64 (Fall): 13–7.

Peters, Helen, ed. 1992. *The Plays of CODCO.* NY: Peter Lang.

Pocius, Gerald L. 1991. *A Place to Belong.* Montreal: McGill-Queen's UP.

Pollard, Kimberley. 1986. Interview with John M. Coleman from St. John's Regarding Aquafort. St. John's: Unpublished essay.

Pomar, María Teresa, ed. 1987. *The Life of the Dead in Mexican Folk Art.* The Fort Worth Art Museum.

Poniatowska, Elena. 1991. The Great Cemetery of Dolores. In *Dia De Los Muertos.* Chicago: Mexican Fine Arts Center Museum.

Powell, Chris, George E.C. Paton and Stephen Wagg, Eds.1996. *The Social Faces of Humour.* Aldershot: Ashgate.

Prahlad, Sw. Anand. 1996. Ecospaces and Frontiers. Presented at the CA Folklore Society conference, Berkeley.

Preston, Michael J. 1999. Never Talk to Strangers: Parental Warnings, Contemporary Legends, and Popular Fiction. *Contemporary Legend* N.S. 2: 63–72.

Quigley, Christine. 1996. *The Corpse.* Jefferson, NC: MacFarland.

Quiring, David. 2001. Personal communication. 5 August.

Radcliffe-Brown, A.R. 1965. *Structure and Function in Primitive Society.* NY: Free Press.

Ralph, Dorman. 1999. *Dorman Ralph.* Recorded by Peter Narváez. Singsong, Inc. (St. John's, Newfoundland) CD SS9908-04. http://www.singsong.nfld.com

Randolph, Vance. 1976. *Pissing in the Snow and Other Ozark Folktales.* Urbana: University of Illinois Press.

Rawson, Hugh. 1989. *Wicked Words.* NY: Crown.

Reist, Nancy. 1997. Counting Stars by Candlelight. *Journal of Popular Culture* 30:183–209.

Rogers, Nicholas. 2002. *Halloween.* NY: Oxford University Press.

Rosaldo, Renato. 1989. *Culture and Truth.* Boston: Beacon Press.

Roth, LuAnne K. Forthcoming. *Shakedown Street.* Jackson: University Press of MS.

Ruhlmann, William. 1990. *The History of the Grateful Dead.* NY: W. H. Smith Publishers, Inc.

Rührich, Lutz. 1991. (1979) *Folktales and Reality.* Bloomington: IN University Press.

Sandoval, Denise and Patrick A. Polk 2000. *Ital Arte y Estilo.* With a contribution by Dick DeLoach, photography by Estevan Oriol and Tatiana. Los Angeles: Petersen Automotive Museum.

Santino, Jack. 1983. Halloween in America. *Western Folklore* 42:1–20.

Sardiello, R. 1990. The Ritual Dimensions of Grateful Dead Concerts. Master's Thesis. Greensboro: University of NC.

Scalora, Salvatore. 1997. Flowers and Sugar Skulls for the Spirits of the Dead. *In Home Altars of Mexico,* ed. Ramón Gutiérrez; photographer, Dana Salvo. Albuquerque: University of NM Press: 63–68.

Schechner, Richard. 1981. Restoration of Behavior. *Studies in Visual Communication.* 7:2–45

Schubin, Mark. 2001. The Schubin New York WTC Letters. [Online journal] Available: <http://www.symes.tv/Schubin/schubin_0109.htm

Schwartz, Ronald D. 1974. The Crowd. In *The Compact.* E. Leyton, ed. St. John's, Institute of Social and Economic Research, Memorial University of Newfoundland. 71–92.

Secretan, Thierry. 1995. *Going Into Darkness* . London: Thames and Hudson.

Self-Composed Epitaphs. 1984. *American Cemetery,* June, 5.

Sexual Abuse, Alcoholism, Drugs: Life on Palm Island. 2002. *Australian Broadcasting Corporation: 7:30 Report.* (Jan. 7). Available: www.abc.net.au/7.30/s453800.htm.

Shenk, David, and Steve Silberman. 1994. *Skeleton Key.* NY: Bantam Doubleday Dell Publishing Group, Inc.

Short, Vera. 1996. Personal communication. 11 February.

Simons, Elizabeth Radin. 1986. The NASA Joke Cycle: The Astronauts and the Teacher. *Western Folklore* 45: 261–277.

Singer, Mark. 2002. A Year of Trouble. *The New Yorker* (20 May): 42–46.

Slater, James. 2001. Thoughts on Gravestone Humor. *AGS Quarterly* 25(1): 8–9.

Smith, Moira, and Rachelle H. Saltzman. 1995. Introduction to Tastelessness. *Journal of Folklore Research* 32:85–99.

Smyth, Willie. 1986. Challenger Jokes and the Humor of Disaster. *Western Folklore* 55:243–60.

Smyth, Willie. 1986. Challenger Jokes and the Humor of the Disaster. *Western Folklore* 45: 243–260.

Sontag, Susan. 1982. *A Susan Sontag Reader.* NY: Vintage Books.

Stein, Mary Beth. 1989. The Politics of Humor. *Western Folklore* 48:85–108.

Stevens, Catrin. 1976. The Funeral Wake in Wales. *Folk Life.* 14: 27–45.

Stoetlje, Beverley J. 1987. Riding, Roping and Reunion. In *Time Out of Time,* ed. Alessandro Falassi. Albuquerque: University of NM Press: 137–151.

Story, George M., William J. Kirwin, and John D.A. Widdowson eds. 1982. *Dictionary of Newfoundland English.* Toronto: University of TorontoPress.

Suggs, Rob. 2002. Personal e-mail communications. June 11 and June 23, 2002.

Sutton-Smith, Brian. 1960. 'Shut Up and Keep Digging.' *Midwestern Folklore* 10:11–22.

Swank, Paul Lennis. 1983. Personal communication. Canyonville, Oregon, 3 May;14 May.

Synge, John Millington. (1903–1909). *The Complete Plays of John M. Synge.* NY: Vintage Books.

Sypher, Willier. 1956. The Meaning of Comedy. In *Comedy.* NY: Doubleday Anchor Books:193–255.

Szwed, John. 1966. Gossip, Drinking and Social Control. *Ethnology* 5: 434–41.

Taft, Michael. 1990. The Bard of Prescott Street Meets Tin Pan Alley. *Newfoundland Studies* 6.1: 56–73.

Tallman, Richard. 1974. A Generic Approach to the Practical Joke. *Southern Folklore Quarterly* 38:259–274.

Terrorists. Forum: Australia & New Zealand. *Travel & Immigration Discussion & Answers.* forums @ BritishExpats.com. Available: http://britishexpats.com/archive/42/2001/10/4/49027.

Thickett, M. 1983. *Outrageously Offensive Jokes.* NY: Pocket.

Thickett, M. 1983b. *Outrageously Offensive Jokes II.* NY: Pocket.

Thompson, Stith. 1955. *Motif-Index of Folk Literature.* Bloomington: IN University Press.

Thompson, Stith. 1977 (1946). *The Folktale.* Berkeley and Los Angeles: University of CA Press.

Toelken, Barre. 1995. *Morning Dew and Roses.* Urbana: University of IL Press.

Toelken, Barre. 2000. Personal communication to the author, 11 March.

Traba, Marta. 1994. Art of Latin America, 1900–1980. Baltimore: Johns Hopkins University Press.

Trist, Alan. 1989. *The Water of Life.* Eugene, Oregon: Hulogosi Press.

Turner, Kay. 1996. Hacer Cosas. In *Recycled Re-seen.* , eds. Charlene Cerny and Suzanne Seriff. NY: Harry N. Abrams: 60–1.

Turner, Victor. 1982. *From Ritual to Theatre.* NY: Performing Arts Journal Publications.

Turner, Victor. 1986. Images and Reflections. In *The Anthropology of Performance.* NY: PAJ Publications.

Tylor, Edward Burnett. 1958. *The Origins of Culture.* NY: Harper & Row.

Underwood, Charles. 1999. Preparing Your Equine for Sale. *Rural Heritage* 24(4): 31–33.

Vallance, Jeffrey. 1996. *Blinky*. Smart Ass Press: Santa Monica, CA.

van Gennep, Arnold. 1960. *The Rites of Passage*. Chicago: University of Chicago Press.

Vanegas Arroyo, Antonio. 1905. *Gran Baile de las Calaveras*. Broadside.

Waldman, Amy. 1999. 30 Years After Stonewall, Diversity Is Shown in Gay Pride Parade. *New York Times*, 28 June: B1.

Wallis, Charles L. 1954. *Stories on Stone*. NY: Oxford University Press.

Walsh, Janet. 1984. *Interview with John Walsh from Kelligrews*. St. John's: Unpublished essay. *War Gallery*. 2001. *moviesthatsuck.com | rippin' hollywood the new ass it deserves*. (September 22) Available: http://www.moviesthatsuck.com/vault/gallery.html.

Wareham, Wilfred. 1982. Aspects of Socializing and Partying in Outport Newfoundland. *Material History Bulletin* 15: 23–36.

Warner, W. Lloyd. 1959. *The Living and the Dead*. New Haven, CT: Yale University Press.

Waugh, Evelyn. 1948. *The Loved One*. Boston: Little Brown and Co.

Westheim, Paul. 1992. *La Calavera*. Mexico City: Fondo de Cultura Económica.

Whatever-Dude. 2001. The World Trade Center Disaster - All Our Worlds. [Online journal] (September 13). Available: http://www.whatever-dude.com/posts/180.shtml

Wiggins, William H. Jr. 1982. They Closed the Town Up, Man! In *Celebration*, ed. Victor Turner. Washington DC: Smithsonian Institution Press: 284–295.

Wilde, Larry. 1979. *The Official Book of Sick Jokes*. Los Angeles: Pinnacle.

Wilson, William A. 1979. Folklore and History. In *Readings in American Folklore*, ed. Jan Harold Brunvand. NY: W. W. Norton: 444–448.

Wolfenstein, Martha. 1954. *Children's Humor*. Glendale: Free Press.

Wollen, Peter. 1989. *Posada*. London: Redstone.

Wood-Martin, W.G. 1902. *Traces of the Elder Faiths in Ireland*. London: Longman, Green and Co.

Ybarra-Frausto, Tomás. 1991a. Mexican/Chicano Customs for The Day of the Dead. In *Dia de Los Muertos*. Chicago: Mexican Fine Arts Center Museum: 24–30.

Ybarra-Frausto, Tomás. 1991b. Rasquachismo. In *Chicano Art*, eds. Richard Griswold del Castillo, Teresa McKenna, and Yvonne Yarbro-Bejarano. Wight Art Gallery, UCLA: 155–162.

Yeats, W.B. 1969 (1959). *Mythologies*. NY: Collier Books.

Zajdman, Anat. 1995. *Humor*. [In Hebrew.] Tel-Aviv: Papyrus.

Zukin, Sharon. 1982. *Loft Living*. Baltimore: Johns Hopkins University Press.

CONTRIBUTORS

STANLEY BRANDES is Professor of Anthropology at the University of California, Berkeley. For more than thirty years, he has been immersed in the study of European and Latin American ethnography with strong folklore interests in jokes, banter, and humor of all kinds. His many publications include *Metaphors of Masculinity: Sex and Status in Andalusian Folklore* (1980), *Power and Persuasion: Ritual and Social Control in Rural Mexico* (1988), and *Staying Sober in Mexico City* (2002).

KRISTIN CONGDON is Professor of Art and Philosophy at the University of Central Florida and a recent President of the Florida Folklore Society. She has published extensively, including *Uncle Monday and Other Florida Tales* (University Press of Mississippi, 2001) which won the Carolyn Washbon Award for best popular book in Florida history as well as the American Folklore Society's Dorothy Howard Prize. In 2002 she published *Artists from Latin American Cultures* (Greenwood) with co-author Kara Hallmark.

DONALD J. COSENTINO is Professor, Department of World Arts and Cultures at the University of California at Los Angeles. He has done extensive fieldwork on African and diasporic cultures in Nigeria, Sierra Leone and Haiti. He is the author of *Defiant Maids and Stubborn Farmers: Tradition and Invention in Mende Story Performance* (1982), *The Sacred Arts of Haitian Vodou* (1995), and *Vodou Things: The Art of Pierrot Barra and Marie Cassaise* (1998). He has been co-editor of *African Arts* magazine since 1988.

CHRISTIE DAVIES is a graduate (MA, PhD) of Cambridge University and a Professor at the University of Reading in England. His extensive publications on the comparative, historical and analytical study of humor include the books *Ethnic Humor around the World: A Comparative Analysis* (Indiana UP, 1990 and 1997), *Jokes and their Relation to Society* (Mouton de Gruyter, 1998) and *The Mirth of Nations* (Transaction, 2002).

BILL ELLIS is Associate Professor of English and American Studies at Penn State Hazleton. He has published widely on several genres of contemporary folklore, including topical disaster jokes, rumor-panics concerning satanic cults, and many kinds of urban legends. His books include *Raising the Devil: Satanism, New Religions and the Media* (Kentucky, 2000), *Aliens, Ghosts, and Cults: Legends We Live*

(Mississippi, 2001), and *Lucifer Ascending: The Occult in Folk and Popular Culture* (Kentucky, 2003).

ILANA HARLOW received her doctorate in Folklore from Indiana University where she wrote a dissertation on traditional narrative based on fieldwork done in Ireland. She served for six years as the Folk Arts Program Director at Queens Council on the Arts, New York City, documenting traditional life in the nation's most ethnically diverse county. Most recently, she has co-authored, with Steve Zeitlin, *Giving a Voice to Sorrow: Personal Responses to Death and Mourning* (2001).

MIKEL J. KOVEN received his PhD from Memorial University of Newfoundland, Department of Folklore, and is currently Lecturer at the University of Wales, Aberystwyth. The author of numerous articles on folklore and film, he recently published the book *Blaxploitation Films* (2001), and another book, *Jewish Cinema: From Ethnic Cinema to Cinema of Ethnicities,* is due out shortly from Indiana University Press.

JACK KUGELMASS is the Irving and Miriam Lowe Professor and Director of the Jewish Studies Program and Professor in the Interdisciplinary Humanities Program at Arizona State University. He is the author of *Masked Culture: The Greenwich Village Halloween Parade* (1994), *The Miracle of Intervale Avenue: The Story of a Jewish Congregation in the South Bronx* (1986, 1996), co-author of *Let There Be Laughter: Jewish Humor in America* (1997), and editor of *Between Two Worlds: Ethnographic Essays on American Jewry* (1988).

RICHARD E. MEYER, Emeritus Professor of English at Western Oregon University, has edited the books *Cemeteries and Gravemarkers* and *Ethnicity and the American Cemetery,* is co-author of *The Revival Styles in American Memorial Art,* and for eleven years served as editor of *Markers: Annual Journal of the Association for Gravestone Studies.* His current research includes a projected book on America's Tomb of the Unknown Soldier in Arlington National Cemetery.

PETER NARVÁEZ is Professor, Department of Folklore, Memorial University of Newfoundland. He is a past president of the Folklore Studies Association of Canada, the audio-visual reviews editor of the Association's journal, *Ethnologies,* and the sound recordings review editor for the *Journal of American Folklore.* He has published widely on a variety of folklore topics and edited *The Good People: New Fairylore Essays* (1991, 1997) and (with Martin Laba) *Media Sense: The Folklore-Popular Culture Continuum* (1986).

LUANNE K. ROTH is the Managing Editor of the *Journal of American Folklore* and an adjunct faculty member in the Department of English at the University of Missouri, Columbia. She obtained her masters degree in the Folklore and Mythology Program, University of California at Los Angeles. Her research interests include folk art, foodways, Deadhead folklore, and women in folklore.

INDEX

Aarne, Antti 294, 296, 297, 332
Abrahams, Roger 189, 192
Agatón, Enrique 227
aggression 29, 42, 46, 49, 50, 68, 100, 115, 117, 140, 221, 222–224, 319
Agwe 243
AIDS 9, 175, 194, 196, 256, 257, 259
Allen, Ken 173
Altman, Patricia 234
Arafat, Yasser 50
Ariès, Philip 11
Aristide, Jean-Bertrand 10, 253, 254, 329
Arnold, Archie A. 151, 152
Arroyo, Antonio Vanegas 212, 213, 216, 235
Arroyo, Arsacio Benegas 202
Ashliman, D. L. 296
Auden, W.H. 107
Aztecs 199, 200, 207, 214

Babcock, Barbara 181
Baker, Ronald 108
Bakhtin, Mikhail 128, 129, 133, 232
Banks, Russell 244, 258
Barthes, Roland 124
Basso, Keith 221
Bataille, Georges 247, 248
Bauman, Richard 99, 104, 109, 192, 318, 319
Bawon La Croix 243
Bawon Samdi 243, 244, 247, 252, 255–259, 327
Beauvoir-Dominique, Rachel 258
Beezley, William 234
Bergson, Henri 92
Berman, Ross 187, 188
Best, George 31
bin Laden, Osama 35, 46, 48, 50–55, 60–73, 77, 78, 315
Blanc, Mel 163
Blauner, Robert 139
Block, Susan 69
Bogatyrev, Petr 96
Borno (president of Haiti) 252, 253
Brandes, Stanley 198
Bronner, Simon 38, 66, 79, 312
Brook, Clive 143
Brown, Karen 258, 259
Brunvand, Jan 296, 297
Buckley, Anne-Kay 113, 114, 130
Burke, Johnny 127
Bush, George W. 40, 43, 50, 51, 52, 53, 55, 56, 60, 61, 67, 315, 316
Butler, Gary 113, 116
Byrne, Packie Manus 94, 97

Caillois, Roger 117
calaveras 9, 10, 198–220, 221–238, 325, 326
Campbell, Kevin 86, 88, 95, 98
Campbell, Joseph 264
carnival 114, 128, 129, 172, 175, 176, 185, 189, 193, 222, 245, 253–257, 259, 260, 272, 293, 323, 324, 328
Cartwright, Christine 114, 130
Catholic 19, 90, 113, 114, 117, 180, 202, 208, 222, 245, 253, 327
celebrities 7, 15, 16, 19, 24, 31–34, 142, 174, 178
Celtic 9, 84, 114, 122, 123, 180
Challenger (space shuttle) 23, 24, 26, 27, 29, 33, 35, 36, 45, 59, 62, 314
Chase, Richard 297
Childs, Robert 133, 234
Christiansen, Reidar Th. 115
Christmas 3646, 51, 62, 65, 194, 217
CODCO 137, 138
Colina, Angel C. 224
corpse 8, , 65, 83–86, 90, 91–101, 105–108, 110–112, 115–121, 125, 130, 131, 134–138, 223, 239, 241, 242, 246, 249, 251, 257, 275, 294–300, 303, 309, 316, 319, 321, 331, 332

Dando, Jill 31
Davidson, Harold (Rev) 17
Davies, Christie 7, 312
Day of the Dead 9, 198, 202, 203, 204–212, 214, 217–219, 221–238, 295, 310, 324, 326
de Boileu, Lambert 115, 116
de Certeau, Michel 131
deadheads 263–266, 268–272, 276, 277, 278–286, 289–293, 329, 331
Deering, John 66
Dégh, Linda 39, 309
Delgado-Trunk, Catalina 203–206, 215
democracy, democratic 10, 15, 27, 32, 69, 207, 216, 230, 253, 255
Deren, Maya 246, 249, 256, 258, 328
Disney, Walt 239, 240
Dorson, Richard M. 108, 147, 181, 323
Dorst, John 39, 40, 45
Douglas, Mary 104, 172, 317
Dundes, Alan 6, 13, 39, 46, 47, 49, 50, 68, 296, 297, 311, 315
Dunkelblau, Ed 43
Duvalier regime 10, 242, 251, 253, 254, 329

Ebert, Roger 301, 303, 304, 306, 307
Edgette, J. Joseph 154, 321
Edison, Carol 153
Edwards, Neil E. 149
egalitarianism 5, 8, 10, 234, 279, 282
Eliade, Mircea 289
Engel, Fred 147
Erwin, James 155
ethnocentrism 6, 121, 138
Ezili 243

Faris, James C. 113
Ferris, William 220
festival 65, 171, 172, 175, 181, 189, 190, 192, 193, 198, 201, 206, 257, 323, 330
Fields, W.C. 150
Finnegan, Tim (also "Finnegan's Wake" or "Finnigan's Wake") 90, 91, 110, 111, 126
Firestone, Melvin M. 113
Fiske, John 138, 191
Flambert, Rodney 248
Fleming, Jeanne 173, 185–187
Flynn, Ned 92, 93
Foley, Brian 83, 84, 92, 105, 107, 109
Foucault, Michel 134
Fox, Tony 35
Fox, Vicente 227, 228
Freud, Sigmund 1, 115, 207, 219, 221, 331

Gandhi, Mohandes 21
Gandhi, Indira 24, 33
Garcia, Jerry 263–265, 270, 272–275, 284, 288, 331
Garciagodoy 207, 208, 211, 219
gays 9, 175, 179, 186, 192, 195, 196, 323
Gedes 10, 243, 244, 245, 249, 252, 253, 256, 258, 259, 327
ghosts 86, 98, 100, 101, 108, 125, 126, 295
Glasgow, R.D.V. 8
Goffman, Erving 109, 124, 318, 319
Goldstein, Kenneth 2, 320
Gosall, Gurpal 1, 2, 174
Gramsci, Antonio 121
Gran Brigitte 243, 327
grateful dead 274–276, 292
Grateful Dead (music group) 263–293
graves, gravemarkers, graveyards 8, 11, 31, 68, 86–88, 116, 126, 128, 136, 137, 140–168, 203, 206, 216, 223, 229, 241, 243, 244–246 249, 251, 322, 325, 332
Gray, Troy David 155, 156
Grider, Sylvia 35
grief and grieving 5, 26, 28, 36, 38, 86, 97, 139, 294
Grimrac, Héctor 199
Grushkin, Paul 264

Halloween 9, 21, 35, 62, 65, 67, 70, 171–197, 225, 245, 289, 323
Hammond, Wally 303
Handelman, Don 193
Hanvey, Bobby 90, 91
Hartley, William 157
hegemony (and counter-hegemony) 7, 26–28, 32, 40, 114, 115, 121–124, 134, 323
Hemingway, Ernest 143
Herald of Free Enterprise (ferry) 15, 24
Herskovits, Melville 243, 258, 327
Hinson, Hal 303, 306
Hitchcock, Alfred 190, 303, 310

Holocaust 22
Huizinga, Johan 101
Hussein, Saddam 50, 52, 326
Huxley, Francis 245, 249

iconography 153, 172, 180, 266, 272, 281–283, 286, 289–293, 323, 330, 331
Internet 7, 16, 26, 29–34, 36, 38–42, 46, 61, 66, 70, 78, 79, 142, 311, 312, 314, 315
Irish Republican Army (IRA) 57–59, 172

Jackson, Blair 264, 270, 272, 275, 283
Jameson, Frederic 193
jokes 1–3, , 5–8, 83, 85, 86, 91, 92, 120, 128, 161, 200, 207, 221–223, 225, 240, 244, 257, 279, 296, 303, 306, 309, 311–316, 318–320, 333; disaster jokes 15–79, practical 8, 83–109, 117, 120, 121, 123, 128, 133, 138, 223, 251, 316, 318–320
Jones, Jim (Skipper) 3, 4

Kahlo, Frida 207, 223, 324
Kalweit, Holger 286,
Kennedy, John Jr. 20
Kennedy, John F. 17, 19, 20
Kennedy, Jacqueline 17, 20
Kennedy, Robert 20
Kennedy, Edward 21
Kindante, Peter 155
Klane, Robert 299, 301, 309, 333
Koestler, Arthur 221
Kolakowski, Leszek 89
Kotcheff, Ted 298, 299
Krause, David 101, 104

Lafontant, Roger 254, 255
Laguerre, Michel 243, 328
Larsen, Russell J. 147, 148
Lawrence, Denise 172, 323, 324
Leach, MacEdward 126
Lee, Ralph 182, 184–187, 189, 190, 193
Leno, Jay 43, 65
lesbians 174, 192
Letterman, David 43, 49, 50, 65
Levi-Strauss, Claude 306
Linares family (artists) 9, 199, 212, 216–219, 326
Lincoln, Abraham 17, 19
Lindbergh, Charles 17
Little, Ralph 190

MacAloon, John 181, 189
Maitre, Gladys 246, 249, 251, 328
Malone, Pat ("Pat Malone Forgot that He Was Dead") 90, 111, 112
Marcus, Adam 43
Marcuse, Herbert 191, 192
Mardi Gras 173, 184, 217, 257
Marquis, Don 260
MartÌnez, Héctor Gonz·lez 232
Mason, Bruce 39
Masuoka, Susan 218, 219, 326
Mays, Alan E. 38, 312
McAuliffe, Christa 23, 24
McCain, John 65
McCarthy, Gerry 106, 107
McCoy, L. D. "Mac" 150, 151
McEvilley, Thomas 220
McGuire, Andy 94
McKinley, Ed 145
McLuhan, Marshall 138, 139, 305
McMahan, Gary 147
Mesa-Bains, Amalia 203
Mikkelson, Barbara 70
Miller, Wiley 159
Mitford, Jessica 240
"Molly McGlocklin" 126
Monroe, Marilyn 187, 188, 239
Morrison, Monica 96
mourners, mourning 6, 26, 27, 86, 90, 91, 114, 116, 117–120, 124–126, 129, 130, 138, 139, 194, 206, 223, 236, 237, 242, 277
Murphy, Pat (also "The Night Pat Murphy Died") 127, 128

Narváez, Peter 96, 99
NASA 23, 59
necrophilia 300, 333
necropoli 164, 241
neo-orality 308, 309
Newfoundland 2, 3, 5, 8, 75, 96,113–117, 121–139, 223, 317
Nimbo 252, 253, 257

Ó Crualaoich, Gearóid 122, 124
Ó Súilleabháin, Séan 84, 94, 95, 97, 98, 99, 115, 116, 117, 122, 123, 134, 136, 317, 321

O'Flaherty, Wendy 102
Oakes, Edward 155
ofrendas 200, 203, 215, 219
Ogou 243, 245, 250
Ogun 250
Olds, Bruce 289
Ong, Walter 10, 304–309, 333
Ono, Yoko 21
orality 10, 39, 304–309
Oring, Elliott 23, 24
ounfo 245, 251, 252

"Paddy the Tay" 94, 95
Padrta, Henry J. "Pappy" 142, 143, 321
Padrta, Terry 322
Pagter, Carl A. 39, 47, 315
Palmer, Joseph 158, 159
Parker, Bonnie 156
Pascal-Trouillot, Ertha 254, 255
Paz, Octavio 114, 198
Peacock, Kenneth 3,4
Pierre, André 243, 246, 248, 250, 259, 260, 327
Piper Alpha (rig) 15, 16, 24
pleasure 1, 101, 106, 107, 113, 114, 122, 124, 126, 128, 129, 131, 133, 134, 137, 138, 139, 198, 206, 207, 211, 249, 270
Pocius, Gerald L. 114, 320
Poniatowska, Eleana 207, 225, 226
popular culture 10, 83, 121, 122, 124, 126, 137, 138, 142, 153, 190, 191, 197, 198, 212–214, 218, 233, 234, 283, 294, 303, 304, 313, 315
Portilla, Miguel León 225, 226
Posada, José Guadalupe 9, 199, 212–217, 219, 233, 234, 325, 326
pranks, pranksters 6, 90, 94, 95, 96, 97, 99, 100, 101, 103, 108, 114, 117, 119, 120, 121, 128, 129, 130, 131, 133, 138, 181; Merry Pranksters 266–272, 318
PRI (Partido Revolucionario Institucional) 227, 228, 229, 230, 231
Princess Diana 27, 29, 30, 34, 311, 312
Protestant 91, 113, 259
Puritans 148, 153, 160, 163, 250

Quigley, Christine 221
Quiring, David 149, 150

Radcliffe-Brown, A.R. 221
Raimi, Sam 295, 309
Ralph, Dorman 2, 133
Ranke, Kurt 296
Reist, Nancy 280, 286, 289, 290, 331
resistance 7, 11, 26–29, 32, 72, 136, 192, 208, 234
Richardson, Jonathan 157
Rickards, Rick 288, 291
ritual 6, 8, 11, 68, 88, 89, 96, 101, 113, 128, 129, 139, 168, 172, 181, 184, 186, 187–190, 198, 199, 202, 203, 210, 211, 219, 211, 222, 223, 243, 265, 266, 271, 272, 277, 281, 282, 289, 292, 293, 317, 320, 325, 331
Robb, Mitchell R. 51
RodrÌguez, Pedro 226
Romero, George 242, 295, 309, 332
Rossiter, Patrick 3

Salinas, Carlos 227, 229
Salinas, Raúl 229
Sandra Barnes 250
Savitch, Jessica 15
Schechner, Richard 102
"September 11" (World Trade Center disaster) 35–79, 314, 315
sex, sexuality 8, 9, 17, 28, 32, 46, 51, 67–70, 129, 133, 165, 192, 197, 221, 231, 244, 246, 247–252, 277, 295, 300, 306, 311, 327, 328, 333
Shenk, David 264, 265, 270, 277, 284, 286, 329, 330
"Shoot the Cat" 132, 133
Short, Vera 149, 322
"sick" humor 16–20, 22, 24, 41, 56, 69
Silberman, Steve 264, 265, 270, 277, 284, 286, 329, 330
Sinclair, Gordon 51
Skaggs, Julian C. 154
skeletons 9, 10, 174, 191, 198–200, 206–218, 225, 230, 233, 234, 255, 260, 283–293, 317, 324, 326, 329
skulls 9, 44, 90, 110, 136, 148, 166, 174, 198, 200, 206, 207, 208, 215, 217, 223, 227, 234, 235, 236, 258, 259, 264, 273, 278, 284–291, 325

Slater, James 142, 167
Smyth, Willie 26, 27
Sontag, Susan 192
spirituality 6, 129, 187, 196, 203, 242, 243, 263, 266–270, 281, 282, 286, 289, 291–293, 302
subversion 8, 96104, 113, 124, 128, 139, 133, 209, 263, 283, 291, 292
Suggs, Rob 51, 52, 314
Sully, James 7
Sutton-Smith, Brian 18
Swank, Paul 145, 146
syncretism 9, 116, 220, 271
Synge, J.M. 90
Sypher, Wylie 88
Szwed, John 124

taboos 125, 133, 294, 331
Tabor, Robert 188, 191
Taliban 63, 66–70, 315, 316
Tallman, Richard 10, 120
television 7, 15–27, 30–36, 57, 65, 105, 137, 138, 190218, 258, 304, 312
Thompson, Stith 274, 294, 295, 296, 297, 299, 300, 302, 317, 321, 331, 332
Tinker, Edward 233
Toelken, Barre 147, 322
Ton Ton Macoutes 251, 252, 254, 255, 257
tradition and traditions 2, 4–10, 36, 39, 45, 49, 56, 58, 65, 67, 68, 72, 73, 78, 79, 83, 85, 88, 90, 97, 103, 109, 113–117, 122–124, 126, 129, 133–139, 140, 146, 147, 165, 167, 171, 181, 182, 189, 197, 199, 206, 210–214, 216–219, 223, 225, 230, 234, 237, 250, 263, 265, 266, 267, 271, 272, 275, 278, 279, 282, 285, 289, 292, 294, 295, 299, 300, 302, 304, 309, 311, 314, 317, 321, 324, 326, 327, 331, 333
Turner, Victor 102, 180, 190, 325
Tylor, Edward 123

Valance, Jeffrey 240, 241
Van Gennep, Arnold 114
vernacular cinema 304, 307, 308
Victorians 143, 153, 157, 160, 165
vodou (voodoo) 239, 242, 243, 244, 245, 246, 250, 251, 252, 255, 256, 257, 258, 259, 282, 302, 306, 308, 327

wakes, Irish 8, 83–85, 89, 93–113; "merry" 2, 115–137
Walsh, Michael 90, 105, 111
Waugh, Evelyn 240
Whelan, Davey 93, 97, 106, 318
Widdowson, John D, A. 125, 320
Williams, Raymond 192
Wilson, Gahan 259
Wiseman, Richard 1
Wolfenstein, Martha 221
Wood-Martin, W.G. 89, 99
World Trade Center (WTC) or "September 11" 7, 35–79, 312–316

Ybarra-Frausto, Tomás 206, 209

Zedillo, Ernesto 229, 231